FATEFUL   RENDEZVOUS

Butch, 1943 *(USN)*

Steve Ewing
and
John B. Lundstrom

FATEFUL

RENDEZVOUS

The Life of Butch O'Hare

Naval Institute Press   *Annapolis, Maryland*

Library of Congress Cataloging-in-Publication Data
Ewing, Steve.
      Fateful rendezvous : the life of Butch O'Hare / Steve Ewing and
      John B. Lundstrom.
            p.   cm.
      Includes bibliographical references and index.
      ISBN 1-55750-247-1 (alk. paper)
      1. O'Hare, Edward Henry, 1914–1943. 2. World War, 1939–1945—
   Aerial operations, American. 3. World War, 1939–1945—Campaigns—
   Pacific Area. 4. World War, 1939–1945—Naval operations, American.
   5. United States. Navy—Biography. 6. Fighter pilots—United States—
   Biography. I. Lundstrom, John B. II. Title.
   D790.E95   1997
   940.54'26'092—dc21
   [B]   96-49823

Printed in the United States of America on acid-free paper ∞
04 03 02 01 00 99 98 97   9 8 7 6 5 4 3 2
First printing

Dedicated to the memory of Marilyn O'Hare Platt,
1924–1996

Contents

Maps and Diagrams

Preface

Two aspects of American history—Al Capone's downfall, and the training that has made U.S. naval aviators arguably the best pilots in the world—have in recent years each been the subject of a popular Hollywood motion picture. In these movies the two subjects were not connected, and while *The Untouchables* and *Top Gun* were both very well produced, both were fictional accounts. Many Americans would be astonished, and probably disappointed, to learn that Eliot Ness had nothing to do with Capone's actually going to prison. And *Top Gun* actor Tom Cruise is better known to contemporary Americans than any naval aviator past or present, with the exception of former president George Bush.

For those interested more in reality than fiction, the subjects of Al Capone's fall from power and naval aviation were indeed connected in American history. In the following pages the true story is presented—for the first time with O'Hare family participation—of the father who played a critical role in helping bring Capone to justice and the naval aviator son who became the original Top Gun.

Acknowledgments

Steve Ewing

No matter how exciting a research project may be, the exhilaration is greatly magnified when shared with a close friend with similar interests. Accepting my invitation to join in this first in-depth study of the life of Lt. Comdr. Edward H. "Butch" O'Hare, John Lundstrom brought considerable research experience and expertise to the presentation of Butch's Medal of Honor battle and the development of the first carrier night interception. Throughout, John—and his wife, Sandy—demonstrated an intrinsic interest in the portions of the story that were my responsibility, thereby making the book an especially meaningful collaboration.

In this same spirit of sharing, several veterans who served with Butch offered their remembrances to help me come to know and understand Butch as a pilot and as a leader. Particularly helpful were Rear Adm. Edward L. Feightner, Rear Adm. James W. Condit, Capt. Allie W. Callan, Capt. Roy M. Voris, Comdr. Sy E. Mendenhall, Comdr. Alexander Vraciu, Comdr. Claude L. Dickerson, Comdr. Richard Best, the late Comdr. Wilhelm G. Esders, Adm. Noel A. M. Gayler, Wilton Decker, Joe D. Robbins, R. L. Loesch, Donald W. Steadman, John P. Stann, Robert S. Merritt, Baynard Webster, Herman Backlund (author of *Setting the Record Straight about O'Hare the Hero*), Clyde E. Baur, ACMM, and Mark A. Hardisty, Jr., AOM 1/C. For helping me better understand the period in which Butch lived I wish to acknowledge the contributions of Rear Adm. Robert E. Riera, Vice Adm. Charles S. Minter, Capt. James Cain, Capt. John Lacouture, Comdr. Donald Lovelace, Jr., Comdr. Larry Fulton, Lt. Comdr. James Sutherland, Robert E. St. Peters, Earl K. Dillie,

David Lister, Laura Stewart, Arnold Olson, R. W. Gregory, Charles Jackson, and Mrs. G. C. Bullard.

While many already noted assisted with details helping me to understand Butch's personality, and personality development, primary acknowledgment must go to his sister, Mrs. Patricia O'Hare Palmer, and two of his Naval Academy classmates, Capt. Richard Philip Nicholson and Capt. Charles F. Putman. Throughout the project Butch's daughter, Mrs. Kathleen O'Hare Lytle Nye, provided heartfelt encouragement along with family papers. For help in researching the life and personality of Butch's father, Edgar J. (EJ) O'Hare, I am again indebted to Mrs. Palmer and especially to Butch's late sister, Mrs. Marilyn O'Hare Platt, who provided all of EJ O'Hare's surviving papers. Also, Mrs. Judy Foster served as an archival pathfinder for me both in St. Louis and in Chicago. Other contributions were rendered by Alban Weber and Tom Lowry.

Always helpful to students of naval aviation history are those friends and fellow historians who freely forward information when they learn that a special project is under way. Portions of the O'Hare story would not appear herein had it not been for the support and contributions of Dr. Clark G. Reynolds, Barrett Tillman, Robert J. Cressman, Capt. E. Earle Rogers II, Capt. Steve Millikin, and Capt. Rosario M. "Zip" Rausa. Hill Goodspeed was especially helpful with Butch's flight training records, final log book, and papers from the National Museum of Naval Aviation's collection of papers from the family of Adm. John "Jimmy" Thach.

Special encouragement and assistance were needed throughout the latter stages of this project and were provided by Mark Gatlin, senior acquisitions editor of the Naval Institute Press, and by Edward F. Lowry, Jr. Dr. Mary V. Yates proved to be the perfect editor for this study, translating my "Southern" into English and offering clear perspectives on matters I could not see for being too close to the story.

Support was generously offered by the Patriots Point Museum family, including Lt. Comdr. Charles G. Waldrop, Rear Adm. James H. Flatley III, Comdr. James Blandford, Ms. Bonnie Collins, and Ms. Eleanor Wimett. All seemed to know exactly when to offer help and when to leave me alone with my thoughts. And finally, appreciation is conveyed to all members of the O'Hare family for making me feel as one of their own, for allowing unrestricted access to their papers, and for giving me the freedom to tell this story.

John B. Lundstrom

This book could not have been written without the generous assistance of two groups of individuals. The first consists of those privileged to have known Butch O'Hare personally and who have offered precious reminiscences of him. The second includes persons knowledgeable in naval aviation history who have provided key documentary sources that cast much new light on Butch's life.

Among the veterans who flew with Butch, I would particularly like to thank Comdr. Alexander Vraciu and Comdr. Sy E. Mendenhall for their unfailing good humor and excellent responses to my many questions. Capt. O. B. Stanley and Clyde E. Baur, ACMM, provided recollections of Butch in old VF-3. In 1974 while researching my book *The First Team: Pacific Naval Air Combat from Pearl Harbor to Midway,* I had the great pleasure of staying four days with the late Adm. John S. Thach in his home in Coronado. His gracious hospitality to a neophyte aviation historian has helped me in so many ways. In researching Butch's last mission, the recollections of the surviving Black Panthers—Capt. Warren A. Skon, Hazen Rand, Dr. Alvin Kernan (author of the superb memoir *Crossing the Line*), Capt. Roy M. Voris, and Marcell F. Varner—have been absolutely essential. Others who served with Butch whom I would like to thank are Capt. Harvey G. Odenbrett, Henry T. Landry, Thomas L. Morrissey, and Capt. Herschel A. Pahl.

Family members of deceased associates of Butch have also provided crucial documents. Mrs. Mary Givens, wife of *Enterprise* fighter director George P. Givens, gave me the correspondence her husband had compiled in the late 1980s for a biography of Butch, as well as access to his personal diary. Other personal diaries of great value were made available by Randy Altemus (son of John P. Altemus), Carolyn Crews-Whitby (daughter of Capt. Howard W. Crews), Comdr. Donald Lovelace, Jr., and Dr. Clark G. Reynolds (friend of Alexander Wilding). Mrs. Catherine Jackson, wife of Rear Adm. Robert W. Jackson, kindly checked her husband's papers for me.

One of the most rewarding aspects of research is exchanging information with other students of the subject. Renowned naval historians Robert J. Cressman and Barrett Tillman and tireless researcher James C. Sawruk are valued friends who have always come through with new sources and keen insight. Dr. Izawa Yasuho, author of many fine studies in Imperial Japanese naval aviation, furnished the key reports of Butch's Japanese opponents and presented me a copy of his excellent new book *Rikkō to Ginga*. Robert John, owner of Renaissance Books of Milwaukee, graciously provided Japanese books of great importance to this project, while Bunichi Ohtsuka offered expert translation. Other researchers whom I would like to thank are Dr. Jeffrey Barlow (Naval Historical Center), Mark Maxwell (VF-6 historian), James T. Rindt (a USS *Enterprise* CV-6 historian), Phil Edwards (National Air and Space Museum), James Lansdale, Mike Weeks, Alan DeCoite (Maui Military Museum), Fred Carment, D. Y. Louie, and Col. Hattori Masanori. Naval aviation historians Benjamin Schapiro and Dr. Malcolm LeCompte are new friends whose acquaintance I made from the Internet.

Archivists and historians in several institutions provided access to the vital official documents. In particular I would like to thank Kathy Lloyd and Michael Walker of the Operational Archives Branch of the Naval Historical Center, Gibson Smith and Barry Zerby of the National Archives, Hill Goodspeed of the National Museum of Naval Aviation, Paul Stillwell of the U.S. Naval Institute, Roy Grosnick and Steve Hill of the Aviation Historical Branch of the Naval Historical Center, and Kim Robinson-Sincox of the USS *North Carolina*.

Over the years I have been extremely fortunate to have excellent editors, and Dr. Mary V. Yates is no exception. My wife Sandra drew the maps and diagrams and read the early versions of the manuscript, but that is certainly not her most important contribution to this project. Her loving support and encouragement, as well as that of my daughter Rachel, have made all the difference in my work.

FATEFUL RENDEZVOUS

Prologue

Late on the afternoon of 20 February 1942 in the Southwest Pacific, alert eyes in eight sleek Japanese medium bombers scanned the broken clouds that obscured the blue seas ahead. They eagerly sought an American carrier force discovered earlier that day lurking 460 miles northeast of their base at Rabaul on New Britain. Lt. Comdr. Itō Takuzō had left there with seventeen Type 1 land-attack planes from the Imperial Japanese Navy's Fourth Air Group to find and destroy the intruders.[1] Formed only ten days previously, the Fourth comprised mostly China veterans—tough, confident flyers whose lightning raids against Clark Field and Manila the previous December had helped crush American air power in the Philippines.

Intense storms compelled Itō to divide his strike group to search a wider area. Later the force of nine bombers that branched off to the north alerted him to the enemy's position. Now, after about fifteen minutes of flying in that direction, Itō expected contact momentarily.

Suddenly observers in the eight bombers caught sight of distant white streaks and dark slivers on the ocean—the American task force. From his perch on the Type 1's spacious flight deck, Itō leaned forward to tell his command pilot, Warrant Officer Watanabe Chūzō, to let down toward the customary horizontal bombing altitude of thirty-five hundred meters. Soon the crews discerned individual enemy ships with cruisers and destroyers deployed in a circle around an aircraft carrier. That was what one of the Japanese later described as "the traditional strategy of the Ring formation, which the United States Navy boasted to the world."

Many black flecks seemed to float in the skies above the carrier—defending fighters! However, as Itō's aviators drew closer, they discovered

1

to their immense relief the spots to be merely shell bursts, evidently anti-aircraft fire from the ships directed against the other nine bombers, from which no further word had come. Indeed, no enemy planes hove into sight. Perhaps they were pursuing the first attack wave or, better yet, still roosting on board their "aviation mother ship" (the literal translation of *kōkū bokan,* the Japanese term for aircraft carrier). If so, her "children" would be too late to contest the bombing run.

Itō maneuvered to overtake the American ships from directly astern, a favorable bombing position. Soon the eight Type 1 land-attack planes had drawn to within a dozen miles of the target and swiftly closed the distance. Less than four minutes remained before their bombardiers would toggle their payloads and pummel the carrier. Still no enemy fighters barred the way. This was going to be easier than anyone had dreamed. That *kōkū bokan* was doomed!

Without warning, red bands of machine-gun tracers skewered the bombers on Itō's right. Where had that enemy Grumman carrier fighter come from? Within a minute two Japanese aircraft had lurched out of formation—one leaking gasoline, the other streaming flames and black smoke. The Grumman resumed its slashing attacks, now against the bombers on the left. Itō's crews realized they would have to battle their way through fierce opposition to reach the target.

On board the *Lexington,* the U.S. Navy carrier marked for destruction by Itō's flyers, James Sutherland, radioman third class, stood in the aft boat pocket on the starboard side. With rapt attention he watched as a lone Grumman F4F-3 Wildcat fighter suddenly confronted the incoming formation of enemy bombers. Another bluejacket standing alongside him asked, "Which one of our boys is that?" As several Japanese bombers fell in flames, Sutherland—his eyes frozen on the aerial spectacle—softly said, "He is alone, outnumbered, and he is winning the fight. What molded him for this moment?"

1

Mother and Father March Butch to Western Military Academy

"I don't want to go!"

Edward Henry "Butch" O'Hare entered this world on 13 March 1914 in St. Louis, Missouri. Like all babies, he was more interested in the estimated time of arrival of his next bottle of milk than in the events of his new world. And, as with other babies, it would be a while before he showed any interest even in his own name. In time he would come to know that he was Eddie, Edward, and, later, Ed. It would be twenty years before he would be called Butch. His last name—O'Hare—although a proud name for him and the country that would remember it, did not fit the person, if one considers the historic meanings of surnames. Down through the ages the spelling of O'Hare has changed several times, but its meaning has remained constant: "sharp, bitter, angry." If ever a name did not fit a person, *O'Hare* did not suit Butch. From childhood until his death in 1943, Butch O'Hare would be known by all whose lives he touched to be the opposite of "sharp, bitter, angry."

When Butch got older he would learn that his father, Edgar Joseph O'Hare, so esteemed the name Edward that he himself used it throughout his adult life in preference to *Edgar*. Known to friends and family as EJ, Edgar was born on 5 September 1893, also in St. Louis, but he was only one generation removed from Ireland. His father, Patrick Joseph O'Hare, though born in Chicago around 1853, remained very Roman Catholic and very Irish. EJ's mother, Cecelia Ellen Malloy O'Hare, was born around 1873 in Ireland. Although she left the family while EJ was still a child, she imparted many of the attributes traditionally ascribed to the Irish that were often in evidence throughout his life.

The relationship between EJ and his son Butch grew to be very special. Their bond was especially strong and remained constant. While Butch loved his parents equally, EJ was the one he looked to as his model and source of direction.

Butch's mother, Selma Anna Lauth, was a native of St. Louis, born on 13 November 1890. She traced her heritage to Germany, where her father, Henry Lauth, had been born in 1844. In 1865 he joined Company K, 149th Illinois Infantry Regiment, as a private and witnessed the end of the Civil War. Selma's mother, Sophia, born in 1864 of German immigrant parents in Macoutah, Illinois, lived to see Butch graduate in 1937 from the U.S. Naval Academy. Grandmother Sophia and Butch shared a very close relationship, cemented, almost literally, by the scores of doughnuts and other kitchen delights she baked early in the mornings before he arose.

With sometimes too much affection flowing to Butch from EJ and Sophia—and certainly too many pastries from Sophia and nearby bakery owner Bill Jaudes—Selma often had to step in as principal disciplinarian. The extended absence of her entrepreneur husband left much of Butch's early training to Selma, a role she handled well; but it was not easy, given the location of their neat but crowded residence in South St. Louis and the times in which they lived.

Effervescent, Catholic EJ and reticent, Protestant Selma married on 4 June 1912. She was twenty-two and was given to understand that EJ was the same age, but in fact he was nineteen. Neither EJ nor Selma was born into money. His father, Patrick, operated a neighborhood restaurant on Morgan Street, while Selma's father, Henry, had worked as a laborer, a cooper, and finally a grocer. The newlyweds moved into the second- and third-floor apartment above her father's grocery store and remained there for over fifteen years. Henry Lauth's death, when Butch was four, left Sophia with a $30 monthly veteran's pension and the now even more welcome company of EJ, Selma, and little Butch.

Early each morning when Butch was a toddler, EJ left for his job at the Soulard Produce Market near the Mississippi River. By the time of his father-in-law's death in August 1918, however, he was putting most of his effort into his own father's restaurant. At night EJ came by the apartment for a few minutes with wife and son, then headed off to St. Louis University to earn credits in the School of Commerce and Finance. He never feared work and was fiercely determined to make a better life for himself, his wife, his mother-in-law, and Butch—the apple of his eye—and for any other children with whom he might be blessed.

In the spring of 1918 EJ learned that, indeed, another blessing was about to enter his life. His daughter, Patricia Jane ("Patsy"), was born on 14 January 1919. Now he had reason to work even harder, and he helped establish a trucking company, Dyer and O'Hare Drayage. With EJ's keen eye for business matters and his excitement at the challenge of creating and nourishing a successful enterprise, it did not take long for his company to show profit and growth.

With the arrival of baby sister Patsy, Butch's life changed. Previously not allowed to spend much time on the street adjacent to the three-story red-brick building that was home, he exploited Selma's preoccupation with Patsy's regular and vociferous demands for milk and other attentions by promising to stay off the rails when streetcars approached. Now unleashed, he eagerly explored a few blocks around Eighteenth and Sidney Streets, but his favorite path became the one into Bill Jaudes's bakery. Sometimes he played baseball in the street, but that soon lost its appeal because the other players often halted the game for lengthy discussions and impassioned appeals for rule changes. A more popular diversion was cops and robbers. Elsewhere around the country five-year-old kids played cowboys and Indians or doughboys versus "Huns." But in the neighborhoods of dusty South St. Louis, few lawns or bushes existed to offer a suitable simulation of the Old West, and the strong German ethnic feelings of the region did not favor games mimicking the Great War that had just ended in Europe. So the game became cops and robbers. It seemed that young Butch more often than not found himself the lone robber hotly pursued by a host of kiddie cops, all older and not slowed from the effects of Sophia's and Bill Jaudes's pastries. Away from his young son much more than he wished, EJ could only buy his boy a pair of boxing gloves and punching bag, then set up a small gym in the apartment and attempt to teach Butch the art of self-defense. With all due respect for his father's good intentions, Butch opted for more time inside with books, sweet rolls, and new sister Patsy. Selma joined EJ in chiding their good friend Jaudes that he was too intent upon helping Butch attain his own heroic profile of 250-plus pounds.[1]

As Butch progressed through his childhood years, it became apparent to both his parents that his disposition was, in EJ's words, more Dutch than Irish or German.[2] EJ's letters to Selma in 1926, when Butch was going on twelve, nearly always referred to him as "the little Dutchman" rather than "Eddie." It just was not Butch's nature to be vicious or spiteful. When enraged, he would hold his breath until he turned purple, giving his antagonist more reason to laugh than to feel threatened. The only exception in a personality that was developing toward reticence, even bashfulness, was his enthusiastic demonstration of physical affection in wrestling matches with EJ.

While fathers often continue to show physical affection to daughters into their school years, there seems to be an unwritten expectation that they must cease this type of behavior with sons at about the age of three or four. Love does not cease—only the manner in which it is demonstrated. Though not entirely abandoned by EJ and Butch, this feeling was sublimated into their wrestling matches. And what matches they were! At first EJ was the challenger; later, Butch. No quarter was asked or given. When the bouts began, Selma grabbed Patsy, and later baby sister Marilyn, and fled the room. Casualties were common: a chair, a table, more than one vase. When teeth finally figured among the injuries, Selma asserted her authority as commander in chief of the house and ended the matches.

While Butch's parents lamented their "Dutch" child's reticent disposition, their affection never declined, but there were times when it could not save him from being disciplined. Ever generous, four-year-old Butch once insisted that Grandmother Sophia should have a nice bright red coat instead of the black plush one she constantly wore. Showing some of the creative thinking that would serve him in later life, he took paint brush and coat in hand and forthwith produced a red garment. Upon presentation, the coat was not the only thing that turned red. On another occasion, at about age seven, Butch was sent to his room to take a nap. A cold rain prevented him from escaping outside. Bored, Butch raised his BB gun and proceeded to alter the ceiling with holes large enough to admit sun and rain. Again, another thing turned red.

At least there was school to interrupt the boredom. Beginning Fremont Public School in 1920, Butch proved to be an outstanding student in grade performance, attendance, and manners. Frequently his achievements were recognized with certificates: one Roll of Honor award certified that Butch was one of only forty-five students so recognized out of an enrollment of over a thousand.

On 9 May 1924 EJ, Selma, Butch, and Patsy welcomed Marilyn Jeanne to the family. Ten years her senior, Butch would become almost a second father to his younger sister. Throughout their lives Patsy and Marilyn would consider Butch to be the "brother of brothers," and they would have placed him just as high on the pedestal had he never gone near an airplane or entered the U.S. Navy. Patsy, separated from Butch by only five years, became more of a partner in some of his activities. Age difference and distance in miles restricted the quantity of time Butch and Marilyn shared, but the quality lacked for nothing. When Butch was with Marilyn, he fully focused on "his little queen." After leaving for private school, he nonetheless immediately began writing his sisters, even though at age three Marilyn required an elder to read his letters to her.

Especially during the summers, sometimes in company with the Jaudes family, the O'Hares escaped St. Louis to a camp on a river, either their place on the Gasconade west of the city or southwest to the Jaudes's on the Meramec. By this time Butch had substituted a .22-caliber rifle for the earlier BB gun, and the future aerial sharpshooter honed his aim by plinking cans and bottles tossed into the river. EJ taught the children survival techniques in the wild and enjoyed the process all the more because of the avidity of his three learners. Years later Butch took Marilyn to hunt white doves, but only once, for she much preferred to point a camera rather than a gun. Swimming, however, was another matter. Butch helped teach her to swim, especially under water, and patiently took the time to instruct her about anything else that captured her interest.

In looking back over their lives, many families recall a particular and special period of happiness. For the O'Hares that golden period occurred between 1912 and 1930. For all of that time the family lived above the grocery store in South St. Louis, with short trips to the river camps for back-to-nature getaways. Soon after Marilyn's birth, however, EJ established business interests in Chicago and Florida, and shortly Butch would be spending the majority of his time away from home. In the 1990s many of Butch's friends recall his ability to be at home anywhere he hung his hat, be it Bancroft Hall at the Naval Academy, a sailboat, an aircraft carrier, a barracks building, or a cabin on Maui. While none of his friends remember him ever saying so, one cannot help but wonder if, in those moments before sleep overcame him in the numerous abodes of his adult life, his thoughts drifted back to those warm, happy, fulfilled days with father, mother, sisters, and grandmother above the grocery and on the banks of the Gasconade and Meramec.

From 1924 to 1927, during Butch's last three years living full-time with his family, he continued to excel in school, was well mannered with adults and other children, and was becoming a first-class student of his father's hunting, fishing, and swimming lessons. EJ and Selma could understand his bashfulness and some of his continuing antics, such as his "parachute" jump with an umbrella off a garage roof into a snowbank, a feat witnessed with great pride by seven-year-old Patsy. Landing a good bit harder than anticipated, Butch never again took to the air with an umbrella, and only once in a parachute—and that was under duress.

Antics are a part of the life of any child, but some of Butch's raised concerns. Selma worried about his love of speed. He demonstrated very little interest in knowing how to take a vehicle apart or put it back together, but if car, cart, truck, bike, or horse was moving, he wanted to be on it. The faster something moved, the better Butch liked it, and he never hesitated to apprise EJ or anyone else that whatever conveyance they rode in or on would move faster if only they would allow it.[3] In addition to the perceived problem of speed, Selma also worried about Butch missing curfew, which was 9 P.M. Never relinquishing an opportunity to ride with anyone who would let him climb aboard, Butch usually got home before nine when riding in one of EJ's trucks. However, at age twelve Butch was invited to play a new game: spin the bottle. While the presence of others provided opportunity for only very brief kisses, Butch was interested enough to stay in the game until everyone else had to go home. And it seemed that this game, like catching lightning bugs, never took place until the last rays of sunlight had disappeared from the South St. Louis sky. Butch now began to miss curfew with some regularity. Waiting patiently behind the door was partner-in-curfew-crime Patsy, who would unlock the door upon big brother's tardy approach. Together they would tiptoe up the steps, their deeds and collaboration all the while known to their mother. Payback required Butch to tell Patsy all the details of the evening's semiromantic proceedings.

By 1927 Butch was showing some consistency in attitude and actions interpreted by his workaholic father as laziness. He also demonstrated too much affinity for chicken, sweet potatoes, and banana layer cake, along with his lifelong staples, frosted sweet rolls, tarts, and doughnuts. Too often his daily position was prone—often with a book, sometimes not. Too often he dispatched whichever sister was closest to fetch him a drink of water. It did not allay parental concerns when Butch, directed one night to get up early, go downstairs, and fix the furnace, instead chose only to light the flame in the kitchen oven and open its door.

The last straw came on a day when Butch was enjoined to go to the bakery at the end of the block where the family lived. Ordinarily he never needed to be asked twice to go to the bakery, but when the somewhat pudgy thirteen-year-old requested permission to take the car for the one-block trip, EJ and Selma decided to investigate the opportunities of military school for the overripe apple of their eye.

While the prospect of wearing a gray uniform and standing in the ranks at military school has appealed to many a teenage male, Edward Henry—later to be Butch—O'Hare most certainly was not one of them. Faced with the reality of military school, he considered running away until he came to himself and realized that leaving home was exactly what was about to happen. By this time EJ had become an attorney. To aid his preparations for court the next day, he often brought cases home and invited the children to act as judge, prosecutor, and jury. Under this procedure Butch immediately filed an appeal. His appeal summarily rejected, he then filed a stay of execution. Rejected. Resigned to his fate, he took shelter in the shadow of his ever-empathetic grandmother and drowned his sorrow in soft drinks and her much-loved sweet rolls.

Western Military Academy was the school selected to assume responsibility for administering the personal discipline that on-the-road EJ did not have time to handle. Located in Alton, Illinois, twenty-five miles distant, the school was near enough for the family to visit on a weekend day but far enough away for Butch to know he had to live by the rules of the school, and except for holidays and summer break, it would now be home.

Founded as the Wyman Institute in 1879, incorporated in 1892, and in business until 1971, Western Military Academy was very much like other private military schools across the country. Most of the students attended for one of two reasons: (1) they had a genuine interest in the military, or (2) their parents wanted them to learn discipline during their formative years. While Butch did not find himself at Western in September 1927 because he was unruly or had a bad attitude, he did need an inner discipline that would remove him from the couch and place him on his feet and help give some direction to his life.

While EJ, remembering his humble roots, did not consider himself elitist and had no desire for Butch to become such, private military schools to a high degree attracted children of the elite and gave them an opportunity to associate "with their own." Robert E. "Bob" St. Peters, who during World War II served on the famous and twice severely damaged carrier USS *Franklin* (CV-13), grew up in Alton. Close in age to Butch but younger, Bob St. Peters never met him, though both would know triumph and tribulation on board World War II aircraft carriers. In a reminiscence, Bob captured the essence of what Western Military Academy was like during Butch's years there (1927–32) and later:

> The original beautiful wrought-iron fence is still intact. I was in high school 1938–42, and we had no contact with them at Marquette High School, which was a private Catholic school. In fact, Western Military Academy, even though it was in the eastern part of the city, was somewhat isolated socially from the rest of the community. It was sorta like, "We don't mingle with the civilian rank and file." On Sundays they would be taken to various Protestant and Catholic churches, but they would be delivered by bus, file in, and file out. In other words, they were rather distant and did not fraternize with the citizens. Socially, the cadets co-sponsored dances with Monticello College girls. This too was an exclusive girls' school in nearby Godfrey. In other words, they were meant for each other on the social strata. Sometimes boys from Marquette would drive out to the Monticello campus to see if they could make contact, but for the most part they got the bum's rush. Both schools wanted their students to meet the elite. In fact, to give you a picture of how things were, a couple years ago my daughter Janice told me that she used an excuse to go to a Marquette High School basketball game only to actually meet a boy from Western Military Academy and go on a date. This was around 1970, so this gives you an idea of what my thoughts were at the time, that she felt it necessary to sneak around.
>
> They had a football team but during my time were never very good. Again, they didn't play local teams but more exclusive small schools in the St. Louis area.[4]

Most any veteran can recall his first few days in the military, just as a student remembers his first days away at school. Quite often, for both it is the first time really away from home. There is, for the first time, the realization that Mother, Dad, and other family are not there to help, regardless of the problem. For the first time, one is always "told," not "asked." For the first time, one has the option not to brush one's teeth. For the first time, one does not have the option to request a certain meal. For the first time, one realizes that the other people around really do not care whether a stranger in their midst is happy or sad. For the first time, standing in formation—as Butch would do in company with about three hundred other youths—one finds oneself in total and abject loneliness. Standing in formation with a host of strangers and knowing one is all alone can be a significant emotional event. Such an event causes one to look inside, reflect on how this day has come about, survey the options on how to escape it, and then opt for the better or best choices. A behavioral scientist would use such a moment to lecture on motivation. Someone less oriented to formal education would simply say, "This is the moment one begins walking the road toward becoming a man." Certainly not happy with this moment, thirteen-year-old Butch began to reflect, and in time he determined not only to accept the discipline and teachings of the Western faculty but also look to the life of the man he admired most: his father.

Unhappy though he was in those first days at Western, Butch nonetheless conformed from the start. He really had no choice. Rising early was not new; showering with the masses was. Dutifully he stood in front of the mirror and shaved, beard or no beard. Breakfast was no longer the treat it had been; it sustained life, but that was about all. Anyone familiar with private schools knows that the yearly budget often depends on frugality in the kitchen. During this time Butch learned to use salt and pepper on everything from beans to dessert.

The first two years at Western were difficult for Butch. While he was able to hold up his grades, being one of the younger students in any school is usually not an enjoyable experience. Last and least in physical strength and for leadership positions and places on varsity squads, lowerclassmen were always first in line for hazing and abuse. For any thirteen- or fourteen-year-old male, life is automatically difficult; it is the critical period in the transition from boyhood to manhood. While the body inches upward and strength increases dramatically in this short span, coordination does not necessarily follow. Mentally the change is somewhat easier, for the peer group defines standards of conduct, and conformity is only a purposeful thought away. For Butch, some of the physical and mental expectations were deleterious: at Western he began to smoke cigarettes, a practice forbidden at the school, with the punishment being detention on campus prior to Christmas break. This aside, good instruction and the overall favorable standards of the peer group set Butch on the path with direction, and in time he became reconciled to his military-school life and even began to like it. Never "love"; just "like."

By ages fifteen and sixteen Butch was no longer at the bottom of the Western social strata. In 1929 he was appointed cadet corporal, and while all students participated in close-order drill instruction, at least Butch now had the privilege of passing orders along instead of being the last one told what to do. In addition to the usual math, English, history, and science classes, formal instruction was offered in hygiene and first aid, scouting and patrolling, map reading and sketching. Of particular interest to Butch was training in marksmanship. Although already introduced to weaponry by EJ, Butch poured himself into this activity, not only for its intrinsic interest but also as a way of gaining prominence within the peer group. He completed his days at Western with good grades, but it was his proficiency with pistol, rifle, and shotgun that garnered the attention he treasured most.

As president of the rifle club, Butch reached the top of his own priority list at Western. Like everyone else, he was expected to participate in athletics and other activities. On 21 November 1931 Butch played the lead role in a one-act comedy, "The Prize Winner." He remembered his lines and also served as one of the scene managers, but the family recalls his greatest contribution as having been not trying to sing. His voice was effective on the stage and on the drill field, but the songs that sprang from his lips posed a threat to the stained-glass windows of the campus chapel.

While Butch's singing threatened to crack the Rock of Ages, his performance on the football field was something less than awesome. According to Col. Ralph L. Jackson, superintendent of Western Military Academy, Butch "was just an ordinary football player." The colonel acknowledged that Western's teams were sometimes ordinary, but he was quick to note that the sport "furnished the best of strenuous outdoor exercise."[5]

On the national scene college football had come into its own in the 1920s, with crowds exceeding fifty thousand pouring into new stadiums around the country. Baseball, popular since before the turn of the century, struck a benchmark in 1927 when Babe Ruth hit sixty home runs. For Butch and other teenagers in the 1920s and later, sports became in part a substitute for the combat the previous generation had experienced in the Great War, as well as a preparation for future fighting. Few at

Western Military Academy viewed football as a thing whose only function was to provide "strenuous activity." It was war! Football and war have much in common. At times during a game it becomes more important, in the mind of the participant, to separate the opponent across the line from consciousness than to win the game. A coach's main reason for being, beyond any other purpose, was to remind his charges that *their* primary purpose was to win the game. Focus on winning in football translated to winning in war.

Butch played football with mixed feelings. Among the things he did not like was the ill-fitting uniform. In his first year of varsity football he had to run two steps before his practice uniform started moving. In addition to the mud, blood, dust, heat, and cold, Butch was not favorably disposed to the end-run-type plays, because they usually meant running thirty yards across the field for little or no gain. The single wing formation popular in the 1920s was designed to put as many blockers as possible in front of the ball carrier; playing guard, Butch did a lot of running. He preferred to forget that one of his best blocks was thrown against one of his own teammates, and that he broke the huddle on occasion not having the slightest idea whom he was supposed to hit or where he was supposed to go; finally, he preferred to forget the outcome of most of the games in which he played. At least the band went undefeated.

There was, however, a more positive side to the experience of playing football. Losing only sharpened Butch's desire to win. In blocking larger and faster opponents, he learned to think under pressure and to seek weaknesses that could be exploited to even the odds. And he began to understand essentials of leadership that could not be learned on the drill field. It became apparent that teamwork was crucial to achieving the goals of the individual members of the team, and that performance under pressure was critical to earning the respect of his teammates. After surviving a number of violent blindside blocks, he deduced that the football field was no place for daydreaming, since opponents liked to approach at high speed from just behind on either side. And Butch observed that very few words from the signal caller were all that was necessary to provide direction for the team, while unnecessary discourse in the huddle or during the game more often than not had negative results. The lessons learned on the football field became part of the overall experience that would serve Butch so well in another great war only a few years away. In the cockpit of his F4F Wildcat and F6F Hellcat fighters in 1942 and 1943, Butch was ever mindful of enemy planes that might blindside him. He knew never to get into any kind of fight unless he was 100 percent focused and 100 percent committed to victory. And he grasped that in leading men, only a few words were necessary to make a point.

Toward the end of his tenure at Western Military Academy, Butch would speak of his school with pride. Enthusiastic about his activities away from campus, he nonetheless spent those first minutes with family and friends bringing them up to date on the programs at school and what was next. His pride was justifiable; Western could document the quality of its curriculum with the coveted Honor Rating, a merit gained by the cadet corps only after a rigorous military inspection by U.S. Army officers. From 1926 on, the school consistently received this rating.[6]

The program was such that Butch, upon graduation in June 1932, was deemed "fully qualified as a graduate of the Reserve Officers' Training Corps for appointment as a second lieutenant of the Infantry section, Officers' Reserve Corps, Army of the United States." The letter noted that Butch would be eligible for his commission on 13 March 1935, his twenty-first birthday, and his certification was good for five years after his graduation. Further, the letter stated, "In time of war persons under 21 years of age may be appointed in the Officers' Reserve Corps."[7]

Anyone who has ever been through an ROTC or other reserve officer program knows that some form of summer camp or other field experience is inevitable. Butch's first camp took place in the summer of 1931 at Camp Custer near Battle Creek, Michigan. He described the experience to his mother in a letter dated 25 June 1931:

I just had to stay in camp and write you. I guess you are wondering what has happened to me. I am OK except for the fact that I ought to be losing weight. We drill between seven and eight hours a day and that is really a job. For the next two days I do not have to carry a rifle as I am platoon leader.

Orders come out every three days. So far I have not been on K.P. or guard but I ought to make it soon.

There are six of us who use the Ford. We all split the gas and oil. We found a very good resort to go swimming and we have been going out there almost every night. Mayor Henderson and family are there for the summer and we saw them. They let us leave camp over Saturday and Sunday if we have a permit from our parents, so I had my tentmate make me one. We are going to the lake Saturday and stay at the hotel there all night. Three bucks for a double room.

The money just flies away. We earn 70 [cents] a day and spend about $1.50. We were given $21.35 travel money Wednesday and I have about $13 left. This is Thursday.

The meals are not so hot but we are so hungry we eat the food anyway. We get good meals in town every once in a while but we have to hold down the price a bit.

One thing about this place is that it is cool enough to sleep in the evening. We sleep on very narrow cots and filled the mattresses with straw. It took a few nights to get used to it but we can sleep on anything now.

I am growing a mustache and smoke a pipe occasionally. I am going to have some pictures taken of this place and will send them to you. Running out of paper so I will close.

Love,
Ed

At the bottom of his letter Butch included his address, and then in the great American teenage tradition, he requested stamps.

Upon completion of his program at Western, Butch marched with others before his proud parents, sisters, grandmother, and various relatives and friends. A few years later the scene would be repeated, the next occasion equally satisfying. On 7 June 1932 all was splendor, pride, and joy; an optimistic air of things to come pervaded the scene. EJ and Selma were especially pleased to learn that Butch had graduated in the upper third of his class, nineteenth out of sixty-four.[8] Grades plus other achievements earned him the designation of honor student.

On graduation day all the members of the O'Hare family and their friends rubbed shoulders with the smiling parents and friends of the other cadets. Although he was a year away from graduation, another cadet enjoying the festivities that day would be well remembered for his participation in the climactic event of World War II: on 6 August 1945 Col. Paul W. Tibbets would pilot the B-29 *Enola Gay* over Hiroshima and witness the dawn of the atomic age. While rubbing shoulders with the elite, even EJ allowed himself that day to be one of their number. In retrospect, the elite of that day proved themselves worthy of their social position. By April 1944 two dozen graduates of Western Military Academy had given their lives for their country on the seas and battlefields of World War II. With decorations and honors well beyond the number of their dead and wounded, the Western Military Academy elite served well. Indeed, very well!

2

Life off Campus, 1927–1933

"All roads lead from Western Military Academy"

Like other boys at Western Military Academy, Butch kept a calendar to mark the days when his family would visit, and he especially kept track of when they would come to take him home to St. Louis—or to Chicago, Miami, Taunton in Massachusetts, Couderay in Wisconsin, or anywhere else designated as home for holiday or summer breaks. But whether heading away from campus or just visiting for the day, the O'Hare family faithfully undertook a pilgrimage to a nearby drugstore soda fountain in Alton for vanilla ice cream. Looking up from their ice cream bowls as the Western years passed, the family noted Butch's increasing maturity. EJ observed with pride Butch's honors in the ranks and on the firing range; Selma beamed over his above-average performance in the classroom; and baby sister Marilyn noted how Butch now preferred chocolate over vanilla.

The years at Western carried Butch the vast distance from age thirteen to eighteen, from eighth grade through twelfth grade and graduation. At age fifteen—for most American students, the first year of high school—

Butch seemed barely at the threshold of his life, but in 1929 he could not know that he had already reached the halfway mark. While at Western he grew to his full height of five feet ten and a half inches and approached 180 pounds—his average weight for the rest of his life. Normally worn long from childhood, his black hair was cropped only for certain military-school or navy training. The baby fat he had carried through his first two years at Western had hardened into muscle by age fifteen. During times of more than normal exercise, his face, as is natural with many people, swiftly reflected his weight loss, revealing slimmer cheeks that drew attention to his dark blue eyes. When he carried a few more pounds, as he often did, his eyes did not seem as pronounced.

At Western Military Academy, Butch did not care at all for the uniform, especially the stiff collar. It was impressive, just like the ones worn at West Point: gray with tails, lots of brass buttons, and a black shako. Butch much preferred the loose-fitting civilian clothes that were appropriate for the woods or riverbanks. At every possible instance he headed for the wilderness with EJ. Ever the teacher, EJ instructed him in the woods or on the riverbank to the same degree as he did in the home. Butch listened at home, and when with his father in the wilderness, he hung on every word.

Butch became formally acquainted with the idea of competition at Western, but he grasped the full meaning of the concept while out in the woods, near the water, or in the water. He had an equal passion for woods and water, but his experience in the forest became more directly tied to the intense competitive spirit that was evolving within him. Deer hunting was a special joy to father and son; in this endeavor they connected as in no other. Tracking a deer required planning and teamwork. When one spotted the prey, he signaled to the other. Already they had decided who would have the privilege, and responsibility, of pulling the trigger. Skill was critical, because EJ and Butch judged their performance according to whether the deer had been killed with one shot. By his middle teens Butch consistently proved his marksmanship with one-shot kills. Within grew his love for the competition to be found in nature. There he developed the attributes that would serve him later in aerial combat. And in these hunting forays, EJ became a partner in Butch's life as well as a subject of emulation.

Butch and EJ considered fishing a competitive sport almost equal to hunting. When they fished, they did so seriously. It was not a matter of tossing a line into the water; each expected results, and each actively sought the catch. By their rules of sport, the man who caught the biggest fish of the day was considered to have done as well as the man who caught the most. When a particularly large fish was caught, whether in the Meramec River, the lake at Couderay, or the Atlantic Ocean, a camera was quickly produced to record the momentous occasion.

Success in competition breeds the confidence that allows children to overcome their natural fears. But while Butch became more self-reliant via hunting and fishing, he lagged behind in social interaction. Throughout his life he never totally overcame his shyness. EJ often had young Butch make travel arrangements with bus, rail, and air ticket clerks to instill in him more confidence in dealing with strangers. Upon meeting new people he was polite but uncomfortable, reserved, and reticent. Even in his training evaluations during his 1939 pilot training at Pensacola, instructor Hal K. Edwards noticed this trait. He wrote on 27 October 1939, "[Butch] is a little diffident and quiet on first acquaintance." Fellow instructor J. R. Dickey echoed that comment in April 1940: "He is . . . courteous and military, although a quiet type."[1]

Throughout his adult life, however, Butch demonstrated a pattern with those who would become his friends. First meeting, reserved and shy—as always; second meeting, a little more comfortable and a little more conversant; third meeting, if welcomed as friend, he became a friend for life. All things Butch's were available to his new friend. Anytime he visited the home or apartment of a friend, he never dominated conversation but for sure investigated the holdings of the icebox or refrigerator. If Butch stuck his head into your icebox, you were a friend!

Butch's closest lifelong friendships, however, did not develop at Western Military Academy. He got along well with his peers, but on campus he felt the omnipresent air of unremitting competition, whether in the classroom (where performance was ranked), on the drill field (where performance was graded), or on the athletic fields and firing ranges (where performance was the essence of the endeavor). Away from campus, however, Butch did not have to compete—except when hunting or fishing with his father, and that competition was really fun.

January 1930 was a red-letter month for the O'Hare family. The previous September, EJ had signed a contract for $11,775 to purchase a brand-new house at 4108 Holly Hills—also known as Kingshighway—and soon after the first of the year, it was ready for occupancy.[2] The second and third floors above the old grocery store on Eighteenth and Sidney Streets were the only home Butch and his sisters had ever known.

Yet there had never been adequate space to play in the old neighbor-hood, with one multistory building standing immediately adjacent to the next and the only real open space being the street. Always, however, the area was clean and neat, even as it remains in the 1990s.

The move to Holly Hills occurred on a very cold day. Settling in, EJ, Selma, Patsy, Marilyn, Grandmother Sophia, and Uncle Henry unpacked earthly treasures in the spacious house situated on a double corner lot. Nearly all of Butch's prized possessions remained in his room at Western, and several weeks elapsed before he inspected the new family residence. Although just a couple of miles from the old neighborhood, the new residence seemed much further away. This section of the city looked entirely different, with much wider streets and single-family homes in place of the row-house format characteristic of the area adja-cent to the downtown, as Eighteenth and Sidney was and is today.

The new house was brick, though not the same bright red brick of the former home. Inside on the first floor, the living room was to the right of the entrance, with the dining room and kitchen beyond. To the left of the front door was the "card room," built at EJ's insistence so that Selma could comfortably entertain her friends and engage in her most passion-ate hobby. They spent many a happy hour in this room, although Marilyn resolved never to learn the game of bridge because her mother and friends chided one another so enthusiastically for playing the wrong card. Of course, that was part of the fun; Selma cherished her own expression of competition. Sophia enjoyed a small suite of rooms at the left rear of the first floor, while behind was Henry's bedroom. Upstairs, two bedrooms, one for the parents and one for the daughters, were sep-arated by a large "middle room" that served, in more contemporary lan-guage, as the recreation room and library. When Butch came home on break, the center room became his bedroom.

While their new home happily impressed the whole family, all three children gloried in the yard. EJ was determined to make the O'Hare yard "playground central" for his children and their friends. Immediately next to the side of the house that faced the intersection of Kingshighway and Rae Street was a large swimming pool, with a concrete skating rink behind it that extended all the way to the separate garage. Both facilities still exist today. The rink shows some signs of age and evidence that its most recent use was as a basketball court, but the sixty-five-year-old swimming pool, obviously renovated, looks as though it was installed only last year.

During summers in the early 1930s, the pool and concrete skating rink did indeed become playground central for the O'Hare children and their friends. EJ and Selma were strong advocates of parents always knowing their children's whereabouts. The amenities of their magnificent yard gave the youngsters little reason to wander. Despite its advantages, however, the skating-rink area was not large enough for a game of softball. When that urge struck, the kids filtered into Rae Street, where passing cars rarely disturbed their game, but foul balls occasionally startled drivers on more heavily traveled Kingshighway. Even today, both streets remain relatively quiet.

"Quiet," however, was absent from the neighborhood after the O'Hares moved in. EJ went door to door to assure his new neighbors that everyone would be out of the pool and off the skating rink by 10 P.M., except for special occasions that would include the neighbors anyway. All the local children were welcome to use the O'Hare pool and skating rink, a generosity greatly appreciated not only by them but by their parents, too. Directly across from the O'Hare residence on Rae Street lived the family of Vourdon Fricke, an attorney who became very good friends with EJ and Selma. Fricke possessed as much wit and humor as EJ. While Selma had a sense of humor, she did not match the two men in that regard, and thus Fricke enjoyed pulling her leg with a series of letters pertaining to the O'Hare's playground central. One missive survives:

September 11, 1930

Mrs. Selma O'Hare,
Kingshighway & Rae Avenues,
St. Louis, Mo.

Dear Madam:
    This epistle has reference to the pool of buggy water you maintain adjacent to your house, which I understand you are wont to term a swimming pool. I am one of your neighbors, or rather to be more accurate, I am one of those who, although I live a block away from your playgrounds, is kept awake half of the night, if not with the sound of splashing water then with the clank of old horseshoes against iron pegs. It would not be so bad if it were not for the fact that my seven children are never invited to your Hell raising night playground, which is tenfold worse than a miniature golf course.
    Of course, if you did not play favorites, and let only some of the neighbors' children swim, I would not have so much reason to complain. I

would not mind laying awake half of the night listening to the clankety clank of the diving board and the clinkety clink of horseshoes against iron, and the unearthly yelping of the little urchins or fish, as you probably call them, who infest your aquarium, if a few of my own kids were invited. They range in age from one year to thirty-eight, and from forty-five pounds to three hundred seventy. Of course I would not think of letting them come over unless you furnished bathing suits for each one, and employed a special instructor to teach them, and feed them after they were finished fussing around the fish pool.

You must think an awful lot of your swell neighbors across the street, or next door to you, because when I pass there I see their children disporting themselves and making a lot of noise, and apparently with your entire approval, but the other night when I tried to crash the gate, two big fat guys, one who was bow-legged and the other with his eye patched up, threatened to get the shotgun and pepper us. I was told it was a community swimming pool; some lawyer across the street said that everybody would be admitted, but when I came down with my Army, the aforesaid incident took place.

If you want me to do you the honor of bringing over my gang, please insert a full page Ad in the Post Dispatch reading: "If the dissatisfied neighbor who says that although he lives a block from my manor and is kept awake all the night, will present himself at 2:00 in the morning, we will have the pool heated up for him and be glad to handsomely remunerate him and his family for honoring us with a visit." I passed the other night and noticed you are building a horse track or some kind of a shindig in the background. Do you expect to erect grandstand seats around this oval and is it a half or one mile track? What is going to happen? Are you going to have turtle races, or will it just be a place for a pack of wild hyenas to roller skate, ride bicycles and add to the terrific din that already emanates from that section[?] But, there is one good thing about the pool, and that is this, that the reflection of the lights rising up to the Heavens, enables me to take the newspaper down in my basement and read it without the aid of light in my house.

> Yours for bigger pools
> horseshoe courses, and
> more noise,

Obvious from Fricke's letter is the fact that the skating rink was not completed until the fall of 1930, but not as obvious is the point of his remark about Selma's furnishing bathing suits for his family: all those who used the pool's slide wore out the seat of their bathing suits.

The pool was never open without supervision. Though a protracted bout of tuberculosis restricted Uncle Henry's activities, he happily accepted responsibility for watching over the pool from the window of his room, which directly overlooked it. His word was law. When he said, "Out of the pool for lunch," everyone cleared the area and went home to eat. At the end of the day Uncle Henry again advised the bathers that the time was 10 P.M. and that he would see them the following day.

The O'Hare children had to observe the rules of the pool along with their guests. There were two diving boards, one only about a foot high, the other six feet high. After the high board bopped a guest one day, a rule was established that no one could stand under it while someone else was on it. The second rule was much less popular, but all—kids and parents alike, but mostly the kids—"turned to" as required every week when the pool, lacking chlorine, needed to be drained and cleaned. Butch and his new pals, who would become lifelong friends—Bob Goltermann, Emery Cramer, Lloyd Hampe, Al Willie, Frank and Billy Hillmeyer, and others—tidied up the pool with vigor because the sooner it was clean, the sooner it could be filled and they could swim again. Close friends from Butch's days at the Naval Academy and pilots with whom he served in the Pacific have commented that very few could match Butch's ease in the water. Certainly, he had a lot of practice.

There is only one story to relate regarding young women in Butch's life before 1941. From 1931 into 1937, during which time he attended Western Military Academy, Cleveland High School in St. Louis, and the U.S. Naval Academy and served his first two months as a naval officer, he seriously dated only one girl. She lived in the Holly Hills neighborhood several blocks from the O'Hare home. Very attractive and personable, she was a good family friend in addition to being Butch's romantic interest. The young lady traveled with the O'Hares when they drove up to visit Butch at Western, as well as to Couderay, Annapolis, and the several other places he would be during those years. She was part of the small group—the sisters, Bob, Lloyd, Al, Emery, Billy, Frank, and their dates—who socialized together when Butch came home. Around St. Louis in those days, if you found one, you usually found all or at least most of the others.

Butch's girlfriend would share fully half his adult life, experiencing his joys, comforting him in times of stress, and together they learned many of life's lessons. In 1937 their relationship came to an end. That Butch was required to remain single for his first two years after graduation from the Naval Academy—a policy that would change with the beginning of World War II—had nothing to do with the decision for the couple not to marry. Nor was any third party involved. Their relationship from 1931 to 1937 was their private treasure, and the details of it need not be shared. It was too significant a part of Butch's life not to mention, however, and it must be reported that the breakup created a void not only for the couple but also for both families.

In the early days of the "Holly Hills group," Butch's arrival from Western for the holidays meant a special time for celebration. By 1929 he had discovered beer and decided that he liked its bitter flavor—but then there were few things that could be taken through the mouth for which Butch did not acquire a taste. This new affinity meant that he had to teach Patsy to drive. By thirteen she needed to be able to drive her own car anyway because she had inherited her mother's spinal problems, and it was painful for her to stand on the bus en route to school.

One of the more memorable celebrations of Butch's visits happened during the 1931 Christmas holidays. Though only twelve, Patsy was summoned to accompany seventeen-year-old Butch and "the group," because they were headed for a fountain of strong waters. Patsy drove Butch's Model T Ford, a car that appeared to have fought its way through World War I—on the losing side. Upon arrival, Butch and friends quenched their thirst and, since they were already there, turned their attention to the stage show, which this particular evening featured a fan dancer. Two in Butch's party objected to the dancer; Butch and the others objected to the fan. On the way home Patsy concentrated on the road and on the task of delivering her riders safely, all the while trying not to hear the comments of the rolling anatomy symposium.

Never keenly inclined toward mechanics, Butch knew enough about things automotive to keep his Model T running. His sisters and friends wondered why he lavished so much attention and affection on the old Ford. He did not talk much about his love for motion, but it was nonetheless apparent. While other boys polished their jalopies and looked to the day they could buy the best-looking car on the road, Butch seemed content with his Model T and its two bodies, one for summer, the other for winter. Looks did not matter much; speed did. When he pulled into the alley behind the house dragging a beat-up motorcycle behind his car, his family and friends decided to advise him about his choice of toys, particularly since the friction between motorcycle and street had set the old Harley-Davidson on fire. Counseling over, Selma unilaterally told Butch to find another home for the remains of the motorcycle.

EJ better understood Butch's fascination with things that moved. While one of the first pages in Butch's flight training records at Pensacola declares that he had had "no previous training" in flying, that was not entirely correct. When Butch was fifteen, EJ arranged for his son to have a few flights, wherein he briefly handled the controls and learned a little of the basics of flight. Aviation enchanted EJ, who on at least one occasion had piled into a mail plane flown by one Charles Lindbergh to hitch a ride between St. Louis and Chicago. Later he flew commercially, when possible, instead of taking a train to his far-flung business interests. Although Butch could not take official flying lessons until he was of age, he had nonetheless become acquainted with the love of his life; the seed was planted.

Whether flying, hunting, fishing, swimming, or enjoying the company of his family, sweetheart, and other friends, Butch's visits home during his five years at Western were very happy indeed. There was, however, one occurrence that was most unfortunate, not only for him but for the entire family. In September 1932 EJ and Selma divorced, and after only a year and a half of maintaining residence at Holly Hills, EJ moved out for good. The event came as a complete surprise to all three children; Marilyn learned about it from the family maid.

A woman of exceptional beauty in her youth, at forty-one Selma was demonstrating insecurity based on concerns over aging and her problem with double curvature of the spine. Not helping was her perception that EJ was a target for other women. In this she was correct. Butch once had to physically remove a woman from a car when she would not take his father's no for an answer. At thirty-eight EJ was handsome, athletic, well read, and so interesting in conversation on a wide array of subjects that few ever left a lunch or dinner table until he had departed. EJ tried to convince Selma that she was the only woman for him, but by 1932 it was apparent to him that her jealousy and the pressure she was exerting on him to quit his remote racing business were not going to cease. In later years Selma told her daughters that she wished she could have been as supportive to EJ as she was to her live-in mother and brother. However, she could not be with her mother and brother and also travel with EJ. Too, she was uncomfortable socializing with strangers, a natural requirement of EJ's business. Love, admiration, and respect for one another continued for all their lives, but it just became too difficult for them to live together. Assigning himself as defendant in the divorce proceeding, EJ provided for Selma generously, and in 1939, when he knew his life was in danger, he made one final visit to St. Louis to share poignant thoughts with the mother of his children.

In 1927 a youthful Butch had noticed with passing interest the commissioning of two big aircraft carriers, the *Lexington* (CV-2) and *Saratoga* (CV-3)—both converted battle cruisers—but he only looked at pictures in the newspapers and did not cut out the articles. In 1933, however, he followed with considerably more fervor the occasional articles about the first American carrier to be built as such, the *Ranger* (CV-4). Ships, boats, and the water caught Butch's fancy in the months just prior to his entering the Naval Academy, but in the deeper reaches of his mind he soared in the clouds in his World War I–vintage fighter plane.

On occasion Butch discussed his love for flying, but at seventeen and eighteen it was not easy for the bashful teenager to discuss loving anything or anyone. Love means caring, and Butch hurt for a long time after his parents' divorce. Things were no longer the same in the family he had taken for granted. Butch cared about flying, but to share these thoughts with others might only set him up for more pain if that love too ended in disappointment. So the dream of flying remained for the most part just a longing. He would move in the direction of turning this dream into a reality, but the desire would be pursued quietly. He was not confident that he would succeed in achieving his dream, but he was committed to giving it his best effort. To succeed he would have to return to school, and in the summer of 1933 it was time to hit the books.

3

EJ Goes under Cover for the Treasury Department

"A dangerous principle"

It has been said that the road to success is always under construction. If this statement can be accepted as an axiom, then EJ O'Hare provides a classic example. Successful in his educational preparation and in nearly every business venture, he declined to take refuge on any plateau created by his achievements. By 1917 he had, to his own satisfaction, completed his academic studies at St. Louis University. He did not remain there to complete a degree. That alone would not open doors in his future, but the knowledge he obtained in his classes would. In the early 1920s one did not need an LL.B. to practice law, or to succeed in business. The practice of law in Missouri did require passing the bar examination, which EJ accomplished. On 21 March 1923 he received his license as attorney-at-law.

A man of high energy, as well as farsighted and success-oriented, EJ was quick to visualize potential. The trucking company he formed with Myles P. Dyer, another entrepreneur who would make a name for himself in Missouri politics, continued to grow. A good trial lawyer, EJ associated himself with a law firm whose partners over time included T. S. Rowe, T. S. Rowe, Jr., and Henry Rowe. Still, his first love remained business, and before long he was applying his legal talent almost exclusively to his business endeavors, even though he continued his relationship with his law partners in the Wainwright Building in St. Louis.

EJ, the Chicago Racing Scene, and Al Capone

EJ had barely settled into the law profession before Owen Patrick ("O. P.") Smith, high commissioner of the International Greyhound Racing Association, walked into his office. He requested EJ's assistance in drawing up an application to patent a mechanical rabbit that would entice dogs into running races at dog tracks. Already familiar with the sport, EJ immediately appreciated the rabbit's vast potential to revolutionize dog racing and eagerly helped secure the patent. Upon Smith's death on 15 January 1927, EJ successfully negotiated with his widow, Hannah, for the rights to the patent. Even before Smith died, however, EJ had begun devoting nearly all his legal energies to dog racing and the rabbit.

EJ opened the Madison Kennel Club in Illinois across the river from St. Louis, then shifted 320 miles to Chicago after the authorities closed the Madison enterprise. Just prior to his arrival in the Windy City, dog racing was illegal and operated only under court injunction. In Chicago, EJ walked softly but let it be known that he carried a big patent, and those who wished access to the mechanical rabbit would have to find a way for him to participate directly in the business. Soon after its opening, the Lawndale Kennel Club merged with a rival, the Hawthorne Kennel Club. In this connection EJ encountered another successful high-energy entrepreneur, a man primarily in the liquor business, but someone who also understood that dog tracks required little overhead, had small operating costs, and returned very substantial profits.

If Alphonse Capone had been born in another time, he might very well be remembered as an American hero rather than as the country's most infamous criminal. Had he fought in the nation's wars, his evident leadership, fearlessness, and capacity to learn would have served him well. Born in 1899 and raised in New York City, he quit school in the sixth grade and became a student of the mean streets near the Brooklyn Navy Yard. Like many teens in New York and other cities, then as now,

Al joined a youth gang only to graduate to bigger things, in his case the adult Five Points Gang. The youthful Capone looked and acted older than his years, but not unexpectedly he also made mistakes bred of inexperience combined with a volcanic temper. One ill-considered confrontation resulted in the deep knife scars that disfigured the left side of his face. Blessed with the physical strength and athletic ability that would make an opponent wish for a knife or a gun to even the odds, "Scarface" also demonstrated intelligence well beyond what would be expected of a sixth-grade dropout, and he learned well the lessons of the street and the examples set before him by his mentors, Frankie Yale in New York and Johnny Torrio in Chicago.

Before his twentieth birthday Al Capone had already killed his first man, acquired the facial scars he would carry for life, shown most of the attributes necessary for a life in crime, and started a family. In 1920, the very beginning of Prohibition, Torrio started Capone's advanced course in the rackets with the vital lesson that the use of force should be measured—that force should be employed only when necessary to maintain internal discipline and to deter or respond to outside interference. Torrio's method—sharing profits with all involved, and not seeking trouble—became Capone's method. By 1925, however, trouble had sought out the middle-aged, meek-looking Torrio. Wounded in an assassination attempt, he elected for emeritus status, consigning active control of the outfit to the twenty-six-year-old Capone.

Thoroughly trained during his five years of apprenticeship and enjoying the advantages and vigor of youth, Capone turned an already successful operation into the best-organized and best-functioning criminal organization in Chicago—arguably the most efficient anywhere in its time. While major profits accrued from supplying beer and liquor to a public overwhelmingly opposed to Prohibition's legislated drought, significant funds also rolled in from prostitution, gambling, and protection rackets. Horse racing and dog racing were not universally outlawed; whether legal, illegal, or operating under injunction, racing appealed to organized crime because big money could be made in several ways, plus there was always the possibility of these enterprises being legislated into legitimate businesses. Foreseeing the end of Prohibition, which lasted from 1920 to 1933, Capone anticipated the need to replace the loss of revenue from this closed-market endeavor, and he had a special personal affinity—if no real talent—for gambling. In the end, however, it was not his losses at the track or at other games of chance that brought about his downfall. Before he lost his freedom in late 1931, he would defend his operations against all other gangs, as well as federal, state, and local governments.

Although Capone could not have known it when they first met, EJ O'Hare would figure significantly in his eventual loss of freedom. Six years older than Capone, EJ was not intimidated by the force the mobster could bring to bear. What Capone could muster in purchased political and physical force, EJ could match in legal power with the application of patent rights to the mechanical rabbit, and later with the personal talent he demonstrated as a counselor and business manager. The full extent of the connection between the two men was known only to them, but it is possible to piece together some of the details of their complex relationship.

In the Chicago of the 1920s, any business that made money, and especially one that made good money, became a target for criminals, either organized or freelance. Each outfit carved out a territory within the city or the numerous municipalities that made up the metropolitan area. Their infiltration into businesses seemed almost absolute. Further, the gangs exerted pervasive influence, if not outright control, in the courts, in the local police forces, and especially among elected officials. The Capone outfit had need of business and financial expertise, plus managerial skill—all of which EJ possessed—and it could offer any businessman not only protection from other gangs but also political influence and plenty of money for investment. A businessman setting up shop in 1920s Chicago needed to choose a gang almost in the same sense that today one has to buy business insurance. EJ and Capone both were intensely interested in financial success, and both were fearless competitors. Pondering whether or not to go forward under existing conditions in Chicago, EJ could have decided not to remain there.[1] Perhaps he could be criticized for associating himself with dog racing and the elements that attempted to share in its wealth. At the same time, investors hoped to prove that dog racing could be fairly operated as a sport and that it deserved legal recognition from the state of Illinois.

Between 1925 and 1931, EJ operated dog tracks in Chicago, Boston, and Miami. In the summer he could be found in Chicago or Boston; in winter he headed for the much warmer environs of Miami to find thousands waiting to place their money at his betting windows. In the dog-racing business it was not unusual for twenty thousand people to show up on an evening and for over $125,000 to change hands, with admission fees and concessions adding to the take. Usually it took only a month to pay expenses; the remainder of the season offered pure profit.

Long before Butch completed his tenure at Western Military Academy in 1932, his father had entered into an arrangement with the Treasury Department that contributed significantly to the conviction of Al Capone for income tax evasion. Obvious to all observers, Capone maintained a lifestyle light-years beyond the income he acknowledged as a secondhand-furniture dealer, gambler, and part owner of a dog track.[2] Indeed, most secondhand-furniture dealers and dog-track owners did not feel compelled to surround themselves with bodyguards or to travel in bulletproof Cadillacs. And few furniture dealers had their hotel office quarters sprayed by hundreds of bullets from men in a small motorcade, as had occurred on 20 September 1926 at the Hawthorne Hotel. From controlling breweries, brothels, speakeasies, and a large interstate network for the transportation of liquor, Capone's wealth could be counted in the tens of millions of dollars.

Convicted in October 1931, his appeal rejected in May 1932, Capone remained in federal prison until November 1939. Suffering from the effects of syphilis diagnosed while he was incarcerated, his health steadily declined. The most notorious criminal in American history died on 25 January 1947.

For the most part, the story of how Capone was convicted is consistent throughout. Nearly all accounts refer to the revelations contained in court records, the papers of the U.S. attorney George E. Q. Johnson, and books by two Treasury Department officials: Elmer L. Irey, head of Special Unit Intelligence, and Frank J. Wilson, later chief of the U.S. Secret Service. In 1928 Wilson was loaned to the Criminal Investigation Division of the Internal Revenue Service to investigate Capone, and he moved his family from Baltimore to Chicago. After a difficult two-year investigation, Wilson's hard work, creative thinking, and good luck laid the foundation for Capone's indictment. The good luck involved his discovery of coded accounting ledgers after several other avenues of inquiry had led to dead ends, and his being introduced in 1930 to EJ O'Hare by John Rogers, a reporter with the *St. Louis Post Dispatch*. After Capone's death Wilson revealed in the 26 April 1947 issue of *Collier's* how he had gathered information leading to the conviction. He provided the first official confirmation of EJ's critical role. In Wilson's words, "On the inside of the gang I had one of the best undercover men I have ever known: Eddie O'Hare."[3]

EJ assisted Wilson on numerous occasions during the investigation, but the more salient contributions were the following. First, of course, was EJ's willingness to work under cover. His access to Capone's inner circle gave him knowledge only an insider could possess. A principle enunciated in sources ranging from the Bible to the writings of Machiavelli is that an insider can cause by far the most damage to anyone or to any cause. EJ's work with the Treasury Department was one more proof of this dangerous principle.

Second, EJ helped Wilson document interstate transfers of money to Capone, especially from Chicago sources to Miami. In his memoir written with Beth Day and published in 1965, Wilson said, "At the end of a year the leads and advice that Rogers passed on to me from Eddie [EJ] were of such tremendous importance that I considered them the most important single factor resulting in the conviction of Al Capone."[4]

Third, Capone and his attorney learned that the federal court would not be bound by the sentencing recommendations of the Treasury Department and the U.S. attorney—a situation that did not thrill Capone. EJ advised Wilson that Capone had imported some men from New York to assassinate him (Wilson), U.S. attorney Johnson, and special intelligence investigators Patrick Roche and Arthur Madden. Soon after hearing this information from EJ, Wilson obtained another tip via the *Chicago Tribune* that corroborated the warning; the story appeared in the newspaper the next day. While no conclusive evidence exists proving that the danger was real—and it was the practice of the Capone outfit never to use violence against federal officers, because it would only invite more pressure and quick replacements—Wilson believed the information to be accurate and immediately moved his place of residence. He also considered the tip to be further proof of EJ's value and trustworthiness. Real danger or not, EJ had acted decisively on Wilson's behalf.

EJ's fourth major contribution occurred in October 1931, when Capone's trial actually took place. EJ learned that Capone's people had obtained the jury list, and that the gang was already at work approaching prospective jurors in order to influence them by whatever means necessary. He passed the word to Wilson, who took it to U.S. attorney Johnson and Judge James H. Wilkerson. Later, when Wilkerson received the official list of jurors, it matched perfectly the names provided by EJ. To Johnson's surprise, Wilkerson advised him to go ahead with the trial. At the last moment Wilkerson traded his jury panel with that of another judge in the same building. This jury, never solicited by the gang, eventually returned the guilty verdict.

EJ's Motives

As noted earlier, the story up to this point is usually told as just related, with few variations, but what follows herein does differ with most previously published accounts as to why EJ O'Hare placed his life on the line to assist Frank Wilson and the Treasury Department in the pursuit of Al Capone. Over the years Wilson's accounts in *Collier's* and in his 1965 book have fostered the widespread belief that EJ agreed to go under cover in order to secure an appointment for Butch to the Naval Academy. In short, a deal was allegedly made in 1930.

The story that EJ negotiated with the government to help Butch get into Annapolis is appealing. It has appeared in short radio broadcasts, articles, books, and even sermons.[5] Nobody enjoys debunking a good story, but this particular one is flawed, and the constant retelling of it defames Butch, his father, and the Naval Academy. Consequently, the reasons for EJ's going under cover and the implications for Butch require careful analysis.

Frank Wilson, without challenge an outstanding public servant, never asserted that there was such a deal or that he somehow wangled Butch's way into the academy, as some accounts have stated or implied. His strongest statement on the matter was this: "Eddie's big dream was realized. His boy Butch did receive an appointment to Annapolis Naval Academy, from which he graduated with high honors." Nothing here remotely points to any deal (and, incidentally, far from attaining high honors, Butch ended up in the bottom quarter of his 1937 class).[6]

As he recorded in his book, Wilson did inquire of the reporter John Rogers why EJ would be willing to assist him as an undercover agent, to which Rogers explained that EJ had "got sucked into the Capone Syndicate," and that he had "wanted for a long time to get away from Capone, but once the syndicate sucks in a businessman they just don't let him retire." Further, Rogers is quoted as saying, "[EJ] is dead set on getting [Butch] into Annapolis and he figures he must break away. But he can't do it while Capone is on the throne." Significantly, these are Rogers's words as recalled by Wilson, and again, nowhere is it stated or implied that EJ asked for any deal. Most significant is the fact that EJ decided to go under cover *before* Wilson asked Rogers why he was doing so. If there had been any kind of deal, Wilson would have had no need to ask Rogers why EJ desired to assist in an undercover role.[7]

As with many of life's situations, motivation for an act as serious as deciding to become an undercover informant defies a single factor analysis. Several considerations influenced EJ's decision. First, EJ wanted to get Capone out of his, EJ's, business. By 1928 he had already succeeded with several businesses and did not want Capone or anyone else making decisions for him or attempting to influence him. Too, EJ thought that as long as Capone was involved in the tracks, both federal and state authorities would pursue their relentless investigations and pressure state governments to declare dog racing illegal beyond the power of local authorities to continue it via injunctions. That is exactly what occurred in 1931, when the Illinois Supreme Court finally acted. (The rationale for such legislation was that even in the absence of organized crime, dog racing was all too easy to "fix"; a particular dog could simply be overfed, underfed, or not fed at all until immediately before a race.)

Second, after the February 1929 St. Valentine's Day Massacre of seven men from the "Bugs" Moran gang (Capone's North Side rivals), local government agencies started cracking down hard on the mobs. Prior to that time they had for the most part worked at cross-purposes with the federal and state agencies that were trying to enforce Prohibition, and had maintained a somewhat live-and-let-live attitude toward organized crime. Now, however, they were not only shutting down businesses in greater numbers than ever before but were also keeping them closed longer than the usual two or three days. It appeared to EJ that local governments and the voting public who placed officials in office had at last decided to uphold the spirit and letter of the law against Capone and his ilk. The general level of violence had become intolerable, even though most of it was hoodlum against hoodlum. This, then, became the time when EJ could take direct action against Capone and have some chance for success.

Third, although Capone sufficiently recognized EJ's talent as a manager to entrust his dog-racing interests to him while he, Capone, was in prison, the two definitely did not see eye to eye on how to run the dog tracks. A letter discovered in EJ's files after his death read in part, "You know O'Hare and [Capone] had many arguments and disputes over them Tracks." The letter was signed "George," an acquaintance of EJ's who had received his information from two convicts incarcerated with Capone in Alcatraz. EJ was an attorney, not a man of violence; he needed to get Capone out of his hair, and going under cover offered him a legal way to do it.

A fourth factor was EJ's concern about his own personal standing with the Internal Revenue Service. In a front-page article on 16 November 1939, the *Chicago Tribune* asserted that EJ had offered to pay his back taxes in full and to provide inside information to avoid going to trial. Certainly in 1930 he was well aware that the IRS was already hard at work on tax cases against Capone's gang. Capone's older brother Ralph had been indicted in 1928, along with illegal-brewery owners Terry Druggan and Frankie Lake. In the early spring of 1930 Frank Nitti, Capone's second in command, was also indicted. EJ was, as he fully disclosed to his family and close friends, "associated with gangsters," and as a stockholder and operator of enterprises connected to the mob, he knew he might be investigated. He knew, for example, that the losses he had claimed in 1926 for his vinegar business might raise a flag to auditors, so he forestalled an inquiry into the matter with a January 1928 affidavit that documented his $50,000 deduction.[8] Convicted of conspiracy to violate the National Prohibition Act for declining to reveal information on the grounds of attorney-client privilege, EJ served several months in federal prison in early 1926 until an appeals court overturned the conviction. Having already suffered through this federal indictment, he had no desire to go through the process again.

Whatever his desire to get Butch into the Naval Academy, then, EJ had plenty of other, unrelated, reasons for helping the authorities convict Al Capone. But these motivations are not mentioned in Wilson's influential account. Why? With EJ and Butch both dead and Butch a national hero by the time Wilson collaborated with Beth Day on their 1965 book, Wilson no doubt wanted to honor their memory with positive reminiscences about his association with EJ. This would explain why Wilson chose to emphasize EJ's desire to get Butch into the academy instead of saying that EJ was motivated primarily by factors pertaining to personal business concerns and a distaste for organized crime. Without doubt EJ would have given his life for any of his three children, but the "deal for the academy appointment" story should be viewed with suspicion. It is certainly too simple an explanation, and it is not entirely logical. Consider the following points:

First, neither of Butch's sisters ever heard EJ speak of any deal with the government, although his desire for Butch to apply for entrance to the Naval Academy was often a hot topic. Both sisters recall that when Butch did decide to apply, obtaining an appointment was, in their words, "no big deal." Getting their brother to act, though, was a big deal, and had been from the beginning. Recall that in 1930, when Wilson and EJ first met, Butch—who was sixteen at the time, not twelve, as several authors including Wilson assert—was attending military school under protest, and had little desire to remain at Western Military Academy. Presumably he had even less interest in the U.S. Naval Academy. Patsy O'Hare Palmer states that as late as 1932 her father was still soliciting her support in persuading Butch to agree to attend the academy. In 1930, then, EJ's immediate problem was to convince his son, not to secure an appointment.

Second, the Treasury Department had no jurisdiction or authority to grant a promise that would allow Butch to enter Annapolis. Even in tax cases, Treasury could not speak for the federal courts, although it did encourage citizens to resolve tax matters voluntarily to preclude the necessity of court action. Certainly the government did not expect nor could it require anyone to become an undercover informant. But even if Treasury had had the authority to make such a deal, it would have guaranteed nothing: Butch would still have had to pass stringent physical and scholastic tests to accept any appointment (and in fact in 1932 he failed the mathematics portion of the entrance examination and therefore had to decline the appointment EJ had by that time secured for him).[9]

Finally, whatever concern EJ may have had regarding a tax audit, he did not need help from the Treasury Department to obtain a Naval Academy appointment for Butch. Well acquainted with all local politicians in St. Louis, Irish EJ was close to Irish Congressman John J. Cochran, who later appointed Butch from his Eleventh Congressional District. EJ had also lined up two other congressmen prepared to appoint Butch.

It is interesting to note that a letter dated 3 June 1930 from the War Department to Congressman Cochran read, "In accordance with the request contained in your letter of May 29th, a copy of the Department pamphlet containing full information relative to the appointment and admission of cadets to West Point has been sent to Mr. Edward [sic] J. O'Hare, 4108 Kingshighway S.W., St. Louis, Missouri." EJ was determined to keep his son in a military academy, *any* military academy, to keep him focused on his love of flying, to continue the discipline EJ did not have time to oversee, and to ensure the strict regimen that he believed Butch still needed. Of further interest is a letter sent on 29 May 1930 to EJ by Congressman Cochran stating, "I want you to know now that if I am in Congress at the time, I propose to take care of your son. You can consider that closed. Of course I will see you when I return home in July."[10] And another letter, dated 22 November 1930, from Congressman Leonidas C. Dyer of Missouri's Twelfth District to Senator Michael Kenney of Missouri read:

> My dear Senator Kenney:
>   I received your letter of Nov. 18th concerning Mr. Edw. Henry O'Hare, and of his desire to enter the United States Naval Academy in the Class of 1932.
>   I will be glad to give him an appointment, provided I have a vacancy for that Class, and provided he is a resident of the 12th Congressional District, in order to qualify for the appointment.
>   You tell him to keep in touch with me and to come to see me, personally, in St. Louis, after the adjournment of Congress next year. My office there is No. 1316 Chemical Bldg., as you, of course, know. Give him this address and tell him to see me there and that all things considered, I feel confident that I can take care of him.[11]

Obviously EJ was touching all the bases in Congress to get Butch an academy appointment. If any deal had been made with the Treasury Department, these letters either would have been worded differently or would have been rendered superfluous.

Legend versus Fact

Even though EJ went under cover to rid himself of the unwanted Capone association, he was nonetheless genuinely concerned about his son's future. Butch's sisters recall with clarity their father's worries that Butch might be tempted by the easy money to be made around racetracks. EJ emphatically did not want Butch to become associated with dog racing,[12] which became legal in Florida in 1931, or with horse racing in Chicago or anywhere else. Around the time of Capone's conviction in October 1931, the Illinois Supreme Court lifted the lower court injunction that had allowed dog racing in the state, whereupon the Hawthorne track converted to horse racing, which was legal. Right next to Hawthorne was Sportsman's Park, which also featured horse racing, and EJ became its president. Butch, now seventeen, was nearing the end of his days at Western Military Academy, and his future weighed heavily on EJ's mind—especially after the 24 October 1929 stock market crash and the onset of the Great Depression. While Butch still had not committed himself to attend any other military academy beyond Western, his interest in flying remained undiminished, and EJ attempted to exploit this angle to the maximum.

Determined to steer Butch away from the tracks, EJ believed that the best approach was to combine his son's interest in flying with the international events the boy was studying at Western and about which he read in the daily newspapers. In 1931 Japan invaded Manchuria, and war raged in northeast China. EJ could remember how when he was fourteen, President Teddy Roosevelt had bid farewell to the Great White Fleet as it departed Hampton Roads, Virginia, for its around-the-world voyage. He had followed with interest the approach of the grand fleet to Japan, where tensions were high because the Japanese believed that Roosevelt's mediation during peace negotiations in 1905 had taken some of the luster off their hard-won victory over Russia. In 1922 the Japanese reluctantly accepted a reduction of capital ships at the Washington Naval Conference. Two years later the Federal Immigration Act of 1924 totally excluded Japanese immigrants. With Japan's 1931 invasion of Manchuria, EJ became convinced of the inevitability of war between the United States and Japan. Although not anxious to place his son on the altar of war, EJ did believe that Butch would respond well to the challenge of combat. On several occasions he commented to his daughters, "If we have a war, Butch will become an admiral; if not, I fear he will become nothing."

After many heart-to-heart talks with his son, and numerous reminders to his daughters to stress the same theme, EJ was greatly relieved when, in 1932, Butch finally applied to the Naval Academy, passing his entrance tests on the second try. If nothing else, that got him away from the tracks. And considering how mortified Butch had been at having failed the tests the first time, EJ felt sure that his son would not again allow himself to be embarrassed. He was confident that Butch would graduate, fly for the Navy in a war, and eventually become an admiral. EJ would live to see Butch as a naval officer and in flight training, as well as witness the beginning of World War II. Had EJ ever known of the speculation that he had made a deal with the Treasury Department to get his son into the academy, he would have been surprised but not offended. Legend is often more interesting than fact.

4

The Naval Academy, Class of 1937

"No more 'Butching'"

Letters. . . .

By the mid-twenty-first century, writers will depend on videotapes, computer discs, and other items yet to be invented to research the lives of historical figures of the twentieth century. Christmas cards probably will never disappear, but letters are becoming less important as a means of communication.

But few sources are better than letters when one is attempting to distill the essence of another person's life. Fortunately, Butch wrote many letters to his family while a student at Western Military Academy, at the U.S. Naval Academy, on board the USS *New Mexico,* and into World War II. Well over a hundred survive, and they reveal much about Butch's life as well as his impressions of events from 1926 until shortly before his death in late 1943. Among the more interesting letters are those he wrote while a midshipman at the Naval Academy, a time when he was still a boy at heart, relatively carefree and happy. All of his classmates who had occasion to be around Butch after 7 December 1941 recall that, although he was still quiet and modest, he was otherwise a different person from the lad they had known at Annapolis. After the war began, he restricted "fun" to limited occasions, and his serious demeanor reflected the heavy responsibility of command. He once wondered, along with his closest academy friends, whether all that they endured at Annapolis was relevant or necessary. Yet when war came, he and his classmates not only understood but greatly appreciated the fullness of the 1933–37 experience.

The responsibility of command was not much in evidence during Butch's days at the academy. Rather, this was still a time to think boyish thoughts, and on occasion to act irresponsibly. It was a time to live life with an expectation of considerable longevity. And that long life, Butch believed, would be lived in a world that stretched only from the Atlantic shores of Maryland to the Pacific beaches of Washington, Oregon, and California. Problems in Europe and Asia loomed on the horizon, but Butch let EJ worry about them while he confined his interests to St. Louis and Annapolis.

In treating the years Butch attended the Naval Academy, it is perhaps more useful to present his experiences topically than to follow a strict chronology. Too, it is instructive where possible to use his own words to describe the world as he saw it. It is interesting to note that after 1927 his handwriting improved, but his ability to express himself with the written word did not change much for the remainder of his life; he could always put his thoughts on paper without difficulty. Butch was never one for flowery prose; he got straight to the point, said what was on his mind in direct fashion, and closed. Without exception, in the letters that survive he signed himself Ed during his academy years, having used Edward only while at Western—and then only sparingly. The name Butch did not appear until his pilot days. Throughout, he closed his letters "With love" or "Your loving son," except for the early days at Western Military Academy, when his displeasure at being there appeared not so much in what he wrote as in his closings, such as "Yours sincerely," "Your son," and even one unadorned "O'Hare." Before the end of 1927, however, "love" or "loving" became, and remained, his closing thought.

And before leaving the subject of Butch's letters, it must be noted that if all U.S. meteorological records for 1933 through 1938 were to disappear, the weather could be reconstructed by consulting the O'Hare letters. Fewer than 10 percent fail to mention recent, current, or expected weather, complete with temperatures and amounts of precipitation.

Surely no midshipman was ever as observant of the weather, not only for Annapolis but also for all points between Annapolis and cities north, west, and south.

Before becoming a midshipman, Butch traveled to Annapolis to attend Cochran-Bryan, the Annapolis Preparatory School, an institution that normally enrolled about fifty students who aspired to enter the Naval Academy. The grand purpose, of course, was for Butch to prepare for the academy entrance test, which he had failed on the first attempt. Even though he had passed the English part of the test, he would have to take it again along with the mathematics section, which he had failed.

Arriving in Annapolis in late September 1932, Butch reported to school, found a temporary place to live with some people who were also Christian Science in persuasion, and settled into the routine. Classes lasted from nine to noon and from one to four, with a mandatory evening study period from seven to nine. That put leisure time at a premium, but Butch eked out enough to become well acquainted with the city. He found Annapolis "certainly a quaint town" with "Main Street just wide enough for four cars if squeezed," "only electric street cars," and "two shows [movies]."[1]

Wandering through the "yard" (campus) of the Naval Academy— which was and is quiet enough at times for one to hear birds singing— Butch admired the beauty of the leaves as they neared full color and advised the many squirrels that they were lucky to live in a place where he could not take aim at them. Leaning against one of the many monuments and gazing at the sky, he made mental notes to tell his mother via letter, "You cannot describe the beauty of the clouds enough whether here or on the way here from St. Louis." Taking advantage of the academy's amenities, Butch swam in the large indoor pool and toured a submarine ("looked through the periscope and viewed the motors") and a sub chaser. He acknowledged the tour as enjoyable but concluded, "I would rather be in an aeroplane."[2]

Classes at Cochran-Bryan were interrupted on more than one occasion during Butch's tenure. On Halloween "a lot of noise" disrupted the evening study period, followed by a raid aborted because "we withstood the attack." More exciting was the "burning of our school" in mid-December 1932, when "the whole roof burned off and we were right under it for a while." None of the students were hurt; in fact, Butch and several others assisted the fire department in containing the blaze, apparently started from a chimney at the roof and second-floor level.[3]

On the weekends, with no classes to attend, Butch was off to the football games. After a 120-mile trip to Philadelphia for the annual Army-Navy game, Butch felt even worse about Navy's unfortunate loss when just outside Annapolis the police stopped the new Ford V8 Roadster in which he was a passenger. He contributed to the driver's $100 fine, money sorely missed as he made plans for the Christmas-break trip back to St. Louis ($100 by airplane, he reported, but $85 by train).[4]

Returning by train to Annapolis after Christmas, Butch wrote to his sister Patsy, "It really is strange to get back here," but he noted that the all-important entrance examination would be on 15 February rather than the twentieth. To his mother he implored, "Pray for me or hold your thumbs or something. I think that I will have a chance to pass. I am more worried about English now than math and last year I passed it." Completing the test meant that he would return sooner to St. Louis, where he would enroll at Cleveland High School to review mathematics, required by the academy because of his earlier failure and because Cochran-Bryan was not accredited. Butch could have returned to Western for this review. Inquiries were made, but it was deemed more convenient for him to attend classes in St. Louis.[5]

By March 1933 Butch knew he had passed the substantiating test and expected to attend classes at either Cleveland High or Western. Having stayed in touch with Congressman Cochran, he took an eye exam—which determined that he needed reading glasses—and completed other procedures necessary to secure the congressman's appointment. By mid-July he was back in Annapolis awaiting the final decision. Butch wrote his mother on 22 July, "I think everything is fixed up pretty nice and I believe that I will get in. At least I hope so." He added, "At the Academy this morning I was watching some of the plebes work in the gym. That is going to be good when I get there with them." There was, however, one last hurdle, the physical exam, so Butch returned to Cochran-Bryan to see his teachers one last time for advice. That apparently did not hurt, for his long-awaited appointment came through on 24 July 1933.[6]

Plebe Year, 1933–1934

Although five years at Western Military Academy had accustomed Butch to the routine of a military school, that did not make plebe year any easier. Neither he nor his classmates could relax during plebe year. One always marched at attention, squaring all corners except within one's own Bancroft Hall room. During the winter, plebes rose early to close windows and turn on the heat in the upperclass rooms. Meals were taken while sitting up straight on only one inch of chair, and were eaten "square" (lift fork straight up, direct to mouth, then lower fork back to plate in the same aggravating and tiresome path, with eyes "always in the boat"). Invariably there were more studies and chores than one could handle, or so it seemed. And a plebe was usually treated on a level somewhere between idiot and nonperson. Never intended to be enjoyable, plebe year did in its dark manner build character.

Several years later Butch revealed to Patsy that he did not believe he could stand to relive his plebe year, and no son of his would be sent to any military school. It was hard enough just to survive the rigorous academic demands and pace ("We are so busy we don't know if we are coming or going. . . . [Our] only free time is Sunday afternoon").[7] But Butch carried an extra burden not visible to others and evident to himself only when he could not push it out of his mind. That was the pain of his parents' divorce, and it clouded even the better moments of that time and added more weight to his moments of distress.

Hazing was strictly forbidden by the academy, and as Butch's roommate, Charles Putman, recalls, "There was no hazing which would have placed anyone in danger." However, Butch frequently had to perform "stoopfalls" (push-ups—usually thirty-seven, to match the graduation date of the class), crawl under a mess table and play the spoons, learn the members of the Navy football team and the school's songs and yells, and get used to the name Nero, a nickname (everybody got one) assigned to him by a first-classman. All in all, his experience with the first class (the 1934 graduates) was not that bad, even though he had to keep everything ship-shape in his first-classman's room as well as his own. As Butch related, that exalted figure, Edward M. Fagan (who would retire as a captain), told him on introduction, "We Irish ought to stick together . . . and I said certainly."[8]

With the start of classes in late September 1933, Butch wrote that he "left a really nice room (4001) to get into a cell" (room 1132); that he was in the First Battalion, Second Company; and that his room looked out onto the court. More important, "We will be presented to the regiment Friday noon and thereby become real plebes after learning how all summer."[9]

Socially, Butch could report little, for plebes were not allowed to "drag" (date). Because his longtime girlfriend kept up a steady flow of letters to him, Butch did not lose sleep over having to watch the "hops" (dances) from the balcony, even though he observed that the academy hops "have it all over Western." Although midshipmen were paid $65 a month plus 74 cents a day for ration allowance, expenses for uniforms and other items left Butch and his classmates with the princely sum of $1.75 a month. Happily, there were breaks for football games, and after Navy beat Notre Dame in Baltimore, Butch joined the horde that tore down the goalposts, determined to obtain for his nine-year-old sister a "piece of felt from the goal post." He explained, "I had a hard time getting it as everyone had the same idea."[10]

Butch's routine during plebe year changed little, being interrupted only by a visit by his dad for the Army game (Navy lost) and an eight-day Christmas break. "Friday night the 22nd we have our Christmas dinner here and we have to decorate the table for it. Everyone chips in and then we buy them all Christmas presents from the 5&10. That is going to be a lot of fun." Christmas past, exams took immediate priority, for at that time term finals were taken in late January rather than in mid-December, as is common today. Around exam time the first class did not bother the plebes much, except for requiring them to sing. Butch passed all classes, which included "Dago" (languages), "Steam" (marine engineering), "Skinny" (electrical engineering), "Bull" (English and history), and math. Some classmates flunked, but, as Butch wrote of his Army cadet counterparts, not as many as the eighty-seven plebes who failed at "the Point." To his mother he summed up his feelings about the first term: "It really will be a wonderful thing to have one stripe on my arm. You can't appreciate it though unless you go through what we are at present."[11]

Plebes along with the other classes received a welcome day and a half off after Navy beat Army in basketball, but then it was back to the rifle range, many occasions requiring full dress ("worse than Western's"), and classes. Any time a midshipman did not attain at least a 2.5 on a test, the expression was "I hit the tree." Starting a new academic term, Butch found himself "on the tree" from time to time, but he stressed in his letters that he was far from alone in hanging from those sturdy limbs.[12]

Rain was more popular with midshipmen than with students in traditional colleges, because a storm, especially one at 2:30 on a Wednesday afternoon, meant no full-dress parade. However, a little water could not cancel infantry drills or seamanship in cutters. By mid-March, warming temperatures and rain had produced the first green around the yard, and thanks to the heavily trodden fields, "it rained mud." Always an acute observer of the weather, Butch also noted that strong winds flipped over a plane during takeoff, but when patched up, plane and pilot headed out again to ride out the rest of the storm. By the spring of 1934 the end of the difficult year was within sight. "Everything is great now," Butch wrote on 1 June, because now "we are big youngsters (sophomore class) and new plebes are coming in next week." Later he judged the newcomers as "worse than we were." "It's fun to look back on it, but I'd hate to be looking forward to it."[13]

Great Friends

While Butch was pleasant to nearly all he encountered throughout his life, he set a standard for *being* a friend. And he chose his friends well; after fifty years the very mention of his name to them evokes smiles of warmth and remembrance. Bob Goltermann, Lloyd Hampe, Emery Cramer, and the Hillmeyers all remained in the St. Louis area after high school, and in one of his first letters home Butch asked his mother to check with Emery and Lloyd regarding the well-being of another friend, his Model T Ford, which he had left in their care. Friendships did not suffer over the car's demise; Butch even had his pals photograph him with the Ford's remains.

At the academy Butch came to know many, but three relationships were special and lifelong. Easy-smiling, personable Charles Francis "Pancho" "Putt" Putman from Canton, Illinois, roomed with Butch for the entire four years in Bancroft Hall. When Butch "again hit the math tree," Putt was the "Savior in this room."[14] While the two had not got to know each other well at Cochran-Bryan, they hit it off at the academy. On summer break in 1936 they vacationed together at Couderay, and they spent one Christmas together. The first two years after the academy they served together on the battleship *New Mexico*. Thereafter Putt went to submarine school in New London, Connecticut, fought in submarines with distinction during World War II, retired as a captain, and remains friends with Butch's sisters.

The second of Butch's three great pals was Morton "Mort" Haynes Lytle of Tulsa, Oklahoma. They were not roommates and did not always enjoy the same things, but a special chemistry drew the two together, enough so that Mort traveled with Butch to St. Louis during Christmas break in 1936 and visited there at other times.[15] Old O'Hare home movies quickly demonstrate how alike Butch and Mort were, not only in shyness but also as to the ease with which smiles came to their faces. After graduation Mort would go to the heavy cruiser *Tuscaloosa* (CA-37) before moving on to submarine school at New London. He too did very well in submarines in the Pacific war and also retired as a captain. In a manner to be discussed later, his life would be forever entwined with that of his academy friend.

The third of Butch's great friends was Richard Philip "Nick" Nicholson, who hailed from Valentine, Nebraska. He had spent three years in college before entering the academy and therefore did not find even plebe year much of a challenge, at least academically. The first two years at the academy were for the most part a repeat of classes "Joe Collitch" had already taken, but the last two certainly captured his interest, especially ordnance and gunnery, where he stood first in the class of 1937. Nick reported to the *Tuscaloosa* with Mort after graduation and likewise retired as a captain. Whereas Butch, Putt, and Mort drew close near the beginning of their schooling, Nick joined them only later. By their first-class year, however, the four were "inseparable."[16]

When things went well for the band of four, they were good indeed: football games, vacation trips, bull sessions on the roof of Bancroft Hall when the moon was full and the air comfortable, and sailing in the afternoons on the *PEM* (for Patsy, Edward, Marilyn), a twenty-seven-foot motor sailboat (a present from EJ) that Butch moored at the academy. "After the sail we always make a pot of java and have some crackers and jam. . . . I ought to be a java-making expert by the end of the year." The *PEM* was also a floating haven for the storage and consumption of strong waters, its passengers now admit. Tom Collins was a persistent stowaway. As if the *PEM* did not provide enough waterborne activity, Butch and Putt sought more. "I finally got permission to build a boat today," wrote Butch on 17 March 1936. "It has to be done by June and I think it ought to be by then. I am going to send it up to Wisconsin when it is done. That will give us something to do in the afternoons now that I am off the gym squad." That September, Butch, Putt, and friends sailed their handmade boat back and forth across the lake at Couderay.[17]

When things turned bad for one of the group, it became bad for all— except perhaps for Nick, who seemed always to be either one step ahead of or behind trouble when it struck. Whenever Butch was "in hack" (confined to his room or wing in Bancroft Hall), it seemed that Putt was always with him. In the spring of 1937 shortly before graduation, Butch, Mort, and Putt found enough trouble to get them sent to "the ship" (the academy's station ship *Reina Mercedes*). There midshipmen had to swab decks or do other unpleasant chores indigenous to shipboard life. The details were recorded in a letter to his mother:

> We didn't start out so very good as we were caught leaving the messhall early at Sunday breakfast. I believe we got 20 demerits and instead of being under hack I believe we will go down to the ship for the weekend, Mort, Putt and I. Then tonight we were smoking in the messhall and there was a big water fight two tables away. The OQW saw it and the heads of three tables, ours included, had to report to him. We thought we had another week on the ship for unauthorized use of tobacco but he hadn't noticed it. It really was funny.[18]

Just losing weekend liberty was enough punishment, in Butch's opinion.

Midshipman Cruises

Whereas the *Reina Mercedes* rarely inspired pleasant memories, other ships proved more rewarding for Butch, his friends, and other classmates. The first big warship Butch saw at the academy was the recently commissioned heavy cruiser *Indianapolis* (CA-35). He admired her design and fresh new paint, but little could he know that neither he nor the swift cruiser would live out their life expectancy, and that both would find their final peace and resting place deep in the Pacific Ocean.[19]

At the end of plebe year, midshipmen traditionally make a summer cruise. During most of Butch's time at the academy they rode the old battleships *Wyoming* (formerly BB-32; demilitarized in accord with the 1930 London Treaty and redesignated AG-17 on 1 July 1931) and *Arkansas* (BB-33). The *Wyoming* saw no action in World War II, serving instead as a training vessel, but despite being overage—both battlewagons were commissioned in 1912—the *Arkansas* fought at Normandy, Iwo Jima, and Okinawa, earning four battle stars before being sunk in the 1946 Bikini Island atom bomb tests.

Neither vessel impressed Butch, who disparaged the *Wyoming* as "this old tub" and the *Arkansas* as "this scow." However, the idea of a cruise to Europe did impress him: "We will be something like 'good-will ambassadors'. . . . I never thought much about those places before I came here where I might have a chance to see them." Knowing that his mother had spent much of her time hanging over the rail during a family trip from Miami to Key West, he advised her that it was just as well she could not come along. He did, however, ask her to send him a movie camera for the cruise, which she did. Although faded and altogether black in some places, the home movie Butch took in late summer 1934 on his first midshipman cruise survives. It offers clues as to what Butch thought was important: classmates straddling a spar and swatting each other with boxing gloves; midshipmen sanding a spar; a three-legged race on the main deck; main armament target practice; and finally calisthenics, which Butch no doubt magnanimously volunteered to film for the sake of history in lieu of joining in. Testing the camera before the cruise, he captured a drill session in front of Bancroft Hall, snow on the yard, and the white iron bed in his room. In Europe he took short clips of the home of Charles Dickens, some horses, a castle, Buckingham Palace, and various views of London with his friends in the foreground.[20]

On 8 March 1934 the superintendent of the Naval Academy issued Special Order Number 3-34, the itinerary for the midshipmen's practice cruise. The classes of 1935 and 1937 would go on board the two battleships according to alphabetical order—except for the football team. That put Butch on the *Wyoming*. The schedule for the practice cruise was as follows:

Arrival	Place	Departure
—	Annapolis, Md.	1 June
15 June	Plymouth, England	25 June
6 July	Villefranche, France	12 July
14 July	Naples, Italy	19 July
23 July	Gibraltar	25 July
9 August	Hampton Roads, Va.	13 August
13 August	Southern Drill Grounds	22–25 August
23–26 August	Annapolis, Md.	—

At sea Butch found himself first in the fireroom on four-hour watches with temperatures hovering around 125 degrees. "Imagine taking a bath in a half bucket of water. . . . The more you see of the Navy the better the outside seems." He also wrote that he was "so tired that sleeping on the deck feels soft." Ashore, however, things became much better. In

London he "had a good time" and observed that there were "no really big buildings and so darn many little cars." "The people treated us nice. . . . [They] would go out of their way to see that we were straightened out." "It is a great place to go if you have a lot of money." To stay warm in the cool London summer, Butch wore his blue service uniform there, but the cooler whites everywhere else.[21]

Despite Monte Carlo's proximity to Villefranche on the Mediterranean coast, Butch stayed away so as not to gamble away his money. The next stop was Naples, and he saved as much money as he could for five days in Rome. After departing Italy, the practice squadron steamed back to the United States and arrived in Annapolis on 23 August. By the twenty-fifth, Butch was on his way to St. Louis for a month's vacation. He was laden with gifts, pictures, movies from Europe, and stories of his two months and twenty-three days of sea service.[22]

Before his next European cruise in the summer of 1936, the beginning of his first-class year, Butch spent time at sea on destroyers standing watches and conducting emergency drills. The first of these cruises occurred in July 1935 during the so-called Aviation Summer, when the midshipmen received a week of aviation orientation, soon followed by another stint at sea from 22 to 27 July. Butch would have much preferred more aviation training; the destroyers, he said, "are a gripe and just something that has to be endured." He complained to his mother that he would probably "be seasick as those boats really do a lot of rolling," but he made the destroyer cruise to Philadelphia and back in good health.[23]

On board the *Arkansas* for the 1936 European cruise, the future naval officers took turns practicing to be navigator (taking star sights), serving as officer and junior officer of the deck, and standing watches, as well as attending lectures. These duties were more to Butch's liking than those of the first cruise two years earlier. The experience was practical and demanding. A gale in the Bay of Biscay kicked up a 43-knot wind, and even though the hatches and ventilators were closed, water still slopped below decks. The "way we were burying the bow I thought that I was on a submarine," Butch quipped. "We did a lot of rolling and pitching but my appetite never failed."[24]

Ashore, the trip proved somewhat of a mixed bag for Butch. He particularly did not like Paris and wrote his grandmother, Sophia, that Copenhagen was the only place he really esteemed. There, the beer was good and also cheap. Göteborg also received a passing mark. In both places, Butch wrote, "the people look decent and the cities are up to date and even modern. It would be great over here if you could only speak the language. Don't be surprised if I come home speaking broken English. That is the only way we can be understood." Before stopping at Göteborg the midshipmen had again visited England, where Butch and friends rented a car (at $21 each) and drove about five hundred miles across the center and south of the country. But just as it had been two years earlier, the best part of the cruise was its end. Annapolis meant summer vacation, and Butch and Putt raced off to Couderay to test their handmade sailboat and purge their minds of all things academic and regimented. In this, Putman later remarked, they were highly successful.[25]

Personality Development

To speak of Butch's personality development is somewhat misleading in that the personality he brought to the Naval Academy in 1933 did not significantly differ from the one he graduated with in 1937. The basic foundations of his character were set by 1933, and not until 1940, when he resolved not to drink to excess, did some changes appear. He had seen too many fellow pilots killed or injured in car wrecks while hastening back to make early-morning flights after a weekend of too much alcohol. Butch discovered that alcohol and flying did not mix, and in consideration of his fellow pilots, he placed considerably more emphasis on his responsibility to his squadron and his conduct as an officer. After the early combat in the South Pacific and his assignment to command a fighting squadron and train other pilots, his personality underwent more changes, a process to be discussed later.

While personality analysis is nearly always subjective, a strong consensus exists among those who knew Butch best. Not given to complexity and never pretentious, he matter-of-factly acknowledged his faults, sins, shortcomings, and failures, and when it was appropriate, he also acknowledged his strengths. Butch was very forthright, and the consistency between his principles and practice is borne out by his letters. Excerpts are presented here not only for the sake of the facts they relate but also to document attributes of a personality that was quite objective and straightforward; a personality comfortable with its own definition of integrity; a personality that would accept confidence only when justified; and a personality strong enough in its foundation to call forth courage when needed.

In short, if one had to reduce Butch's nature to one word, it would be *control.* Many who know of his exploits in the air might have expected that one word to be *courage,* but it may be reasoned that courage emerges from the strong personality of a man well in control of himself. Long before World War II, Butch showed his steadfastness during emergencies. A favorite family story is that Butch actually pulled Patsy and a friend out of a still-moving automobile just as it flipped over. In other crises he proved totally calm and was always first to react in a positive manner.

Butch never was free with profundities. He did say that he disliked the West Point honor system because it seemed to plant seeds of division, and that he liked the loyalty stressed at the Naval Academy. This type of loyalty integrated well with Butch's personality.

Religion often forms the basis of one's value system and principles. None of the pilots who flew with Butch remember him ever openly stating anything about religion, but he did share some religious thoughts with his mother, mostly in letters informing her of his inconsistent attendance at Christian Science lectures while in Annapolis. Occasionally he was impressed with what he heard, reporting, "I learned a lot from the lesson today." Just before graduation he wrote, "Another thing I have to tell you is that I now go to chapel. I thought I would like to see how it is—will I still have a chance—so I got myself changed the other day. It will be the first time I have gone there since plebe summer." In 1941 Butch converted to Catholicism, his father's religion, at the request of his wife-to-be. Upon his death, chaplains on the USS *Enterprise* (CV-6), his last home, and also priests in St. Louis alluded favorably to his religious convictions, but the strength of his commitment to God was known only to Butch and the Almighty. While Butch's own words may not be as fully preserved as might be desired for the purpose of recording his religious convictions, Captain Nicholson stated that "Butch was generous to a fault; he would give anything to anyone in need." According to Scripture (Matthew, chapter 25), such generosity founded upon love is most pleasing to the Heavenly Father.[26]

While one is left to ponder the religious foundations of Butch's convictions and principles, considerable evidence exists from his own hand that one could accept as "gospel" the words he spoke or wrote. In his letters Butch seems to have gone above and beyond truthfulness. He was forthright almost to the point of being offensive. His family, however, understood his directness and took it not as an insult but as an expression of his true state of mind, for they themselves spoke in the same direct manner. When Butch said to his mother in a 17 February 1936 letter, "You rather disappointed me," he was not being mean; he was only expressing a fact. Few brothers would be like Butch and announce to a loved sister that he had purchased the last remaining compact in a store to send to his girlfriend, and would forward one to his sister when the store restocked. There was nothing really wrong in having done this, but not many brothers would be so frank about it. And Butch was not given to making excuses; telling his mother that he had not written to his grandmother and uncle as often as he should have, he said only, "If I can bring myself around to it, I will write more often to them."[27]

Although Butch's honesty is amply documented, there also is evidence that he was not always faithful to rules, regulations, or the law. He picked and chose which rules to obey; he was consistent to the principles that appealed to him. About once every three months, Butch acknowledged, he had marched in a direction opposite to that indicated by the academy. Once, for example, during his plebe year when he wanted to pay a visit outside and needed "to have a permit signed to dine out," he got what he needed by declaring a woman acquaintance to be his aunt. Or again: "Sat. night we . . . drove into Washington . . . saw a good show and then came back. . . . We had some of the boys sleep in our beds so we wouldn't be missed and everything went fine." Missing a supper formation with Putt, he noted, "We got by with it too." And in a letter to Patsy he wrote, "For the last month or so we have had our pint of gin. . . . You know, you can do anything that you can get by with." Butch's objectivity and tell-it-like-it-is manner are evident in a 7 October 1935 letter to his mother: "Dago has really turned out to be something to study this year. The prof didn't put me on the tree, but I can't see how he can look himself in the face for not doing it." Although Butch sometimes told stories on himself for purely humorous effect, his readiness to admit wrongdoing was ultimately the result of his inability to be anything other than forthright and honest.[28]

In summing up Butch's character, it is fair to say that in habits and behavior he did not differ significantly from his peers. Certainly he was not the only one to find ways around academy rules. He almost never drank or left campus without Putt, Mort, Nick, or someone else, although he could no doubt have gone alone, being among the very select few to have a car hidden away for the few occasions it could be used. He met the social expectations of his group, and his conduct and attitudes were such that Putt stated, "We never expected Butch to become a war hero; he just didn't have that kind of personality: he was an easygoing guy who did what he had to do . . . but we were not surprised he became a hero as his aggressiveness was apparent in water polo . . . and Butch could always be counted on to do what he knew to be his duty." Nick's summation of Butch's personality is a little more succinct: "He was a wonderful guy!"[29]

Athletics

If, as Captain Putman stated, that water polo was a clue to Butch's aggressiveness and a hint of the hero that would emerge during World War II, a look at his interest in athletics at the academy is appropriate. On 16 August 1933 Butch wrote to his mother, "Football practice starts next week so I ought to take off a lot of weight. I am going out for it and it will take a lot to keep up with the others." However, instead of playing football, Butch and Nick immediately found themselves pressured by first-classmen to use their previous military training—Nick had just completed ROTC summer camp—for late-afternoon drills with the battalions to which they would soon be assigned. Also, the coaching staff did not encourage Butch to continue; varsity football experience at Western would have to suffice.[30]

Instead of varsity athletics, Butch joined the "Radiator Club," a group of nonvarsity athletes who returned to the warmth of the radiators in their rooms to study, read a book, listen to the radio (upperclassmen only), or just relax. Butch went to the academy as a means to an end, that of flying for the Navy, and that goal meant concentrating on staying out of the trees and passing his classes. Too, he had a car, a sailboat, and an inclination to find food and alcohol in those hours not required for study. But he did enjoy water polo.

For a time Butch played on the plebe water polo team, reporting to his mother that he played five minutes in a 19–12 victory over Penn. That certainly was more enjoyable than his initial experience during plebe summer, when he had to swim 120 yards in three minutes using three different strokes ("I made it but almost swallowed the pool in the attempt"). In his second ("youngster") year he played only with his class team, noting, "I am one of our [class's] star players." In his third year (the "second" class) Butch practiced with the varsity squad and "got to sit on the bench with the rest of the W.P. squad at the game. There wasn't much danger of me playing but you get one of the best seats in the place." By his last year (the "first" class), Butch was again playing only intramural water polo with his First Battalion team, leading them to a close second-place finish ("I still claim we were robbed"). Drowning his sorrow in his usual manner, he informed his mother that he "went out and had a ham sandwich or two."[31]

Consistent as always, Butch never failed to mention serving on the "weak" (gym) squad, or the 0530–0630 time in the swimming pool—attempts to overcome the "ham sandwich or two." Throughout his time at the academy, and for the remainder of his life, Butch gave his weight at 179½ pounds, and when he slipped above that weight he repaired to pool or gym. To eat less was never an option for Butch—few letters to anyone in the family failed to mention a request for a ham, candy, cookies, or anything else edible. ("Send some food, we're about starved.") The hams, candies, cookies, and everything else came with a regularity that was interrupted only when necessary, as when Butch had to run the 440 in seventy seconds ("and that was pretty fast for me"). To prepare for the 440, he stopped eating white bread, potatoes, milk, butter, and desserts, but when he broke the tape in sixty-nine seconds, it took him only sixty-eight seconds to cover the next 440 yards back to the table (or so the authors have surmised).[32]

Butch did not seem more involved in varsity football than any other midshipman, according to Putman and Nicholson, but in his letters he showed much more than a passing interest in the welfare of Navy's football fortunes. Ironically, the man who would play such an important role in turning around the school's program on the gridiron would also be Butch's air officer on the *Enterprise,* and one of the last men to talk with him before his final flight. Formerly one of Navy's greatest football stars, Lt. Thomas J. Hamilton had led the 1926 team to an undefeated season, drop-kicking an extra point to tie Army 21–21 in a game played in Chicago. Coach Hamilton arrived back in Annapolis for Butch's youngster year and compiled a record of 19–8 for the last three years Butch was a midshipman. The 1934 team was 8–1, with a victory over Notre Dame in Cleveland and a glorious 3–0 win over Army—Navy's first in thirteen years. Butch won an Army bathrobe with the victory and exulted, "The team returned this evening at 5:50 and the whole school and town were at the station to meet them. The Fire Department joined in the parade back to the Academy and we rode back on the hook and ladder. I always did want to ride on a firetruck." Somewhat of a prophet in commenting on Navy's only loss of the season to Pittsburgh, Butch wrote, "It was no disgrace to lose to Pitt. I have never in my life seen a better team. We were just outclassed." Pitt won the national championship in 1937.[33]

The 1935 Navy football team went 5–4, and after losing to Princeton, Butch griped to his mother, "I don't know what is the matter with our football team but there certainly is something vital missing. . . . If our team doesn't snap to soon, no one will want to go." And Butch wished he had not gone to Baltimore to be among the sixty-five thousand who saw the 14–0 loss to Notre Dame: "That stadium is also one of the dirtiest in the country. It is covered with ashes and after two minutes we were no longer blue but gray. I was so glad to get back to this place and get a shower." Things, however, got worse as Butch coordinated family plans to attend the Army game: Navy lost 28–6. Even so, it was good to see the family. EJ brought a special date: eleven-year-old daughter Marilyn. His formal invitation letter to her read:

> Dear Miss O'Hare,
>   Mr. EJ O'Hare requests the pleasure of your company for the Army and Navy football game, also the dinner dance at the Penn Athletic Club after the game. In other words, in the vernacular of the Navy, I want to "drag" with you.

The 1936 season turned out better for Coach Hamilton, Butch, and the family: the team went 6–3, with a 3–0 win over Notre Dame and a 7–0 victory over Army before eighty thousand in Philadelphia.[34]

After the 1936 season Hamilton returned to flying, and when World War II broke out he was instrumental in the development of the Navy's preflight program. Believing that athletics would add to the qualities of combat pilots, he arranged for teams to be organized and the "J-5" program created. Hamilton was also involved in recruiting over two thousand coaches into the service to assist with training. Yet by 1943 Tom Hamilton was restless and was badgering his superiors to get him into combat. On Maui in 1942 and 1943, Butch was also restless and anxious to get back in the fight. When Butch and "Coach" met on the *Enterprise* in November 1943, any desire to talk football was held in abeyance, and '34–'36 was not revisited. The new game proved too demanding!

Leisure Moments, Social Events, and a New Name

Leisure moments and social events were all but nonexistent for Butch during his plebe year, but things improved somewhat during his last three years at the academy. The highlights of every year were Christmas break and the month's vacation at the end of each summer. These occasions allowed Butch to be with his family. ("You know it was really nice to be at home. You certainly can miss the old place when you are away and know that you will be away for some time.") Too, Butch wanted to keep up with events in St. Louis; therefore, he requested that the *St. Louis Post Dispatch* be sent to him upon arrival at the academy. Few hometown newspapers received stronger testimonials than "Have been missing the old newspaper something awful" and "Thanks for the Post. . . . We got it last Sunday and it seems great to keep up with the old town once again. . . . [The] funnies are good."[35]

Of course, the *Post* was not all that Butch wanted forwarded from St. Louis. In addition to food, he also ordered cases of "white soda," for 7-Up was not then available in Annapolis. The drink now known as the Un-cola was too valuable to drink straight; Butch reserved it for special occasions off the yard for mixing with stronger waters. A favorite site was 203 Main Street, the home of Mrs. Virginia Miller, "number two Mom up here."[36]

Throughout his life Butch always gravitated to families. His own, of course, was his first choice, but when they were not near, he would seek out another family in the same way others hunted a new "favorite" bar. In Annapolis, Butch, usually accompanied by Putt, Mort, or Nick, spent as much time as possible at Mrs. Miller's, enjoying her company and that of her daughter. However, the main attraction was the kitchen, wherein "white soda," liquor, beer, ham, and cheese were stored and served chilled or warmed. More than once Butch and friends enjoyed Thanksgiving dinner at Mrs. Miller's, and for several years Butch even received mail there. For Mother's Day in 1934 Butch gave Mrs. Miller a box of candy and other gifts at Christmas. The O'Hare family became acquainted with her, corresponding and visiting even when Butch was not present. Near the end of Butch's time at the academy, Mrs. Miller moved from Main Street, so the time he spent with her declined considerably. But the quality of the many earlier visits helped sustain Butch emotionally, and no doubt his visits remained warm memories for all the Millers.[37]

During his youngster year of 1934–35, Butch got some free time on Tuesday and Thursday afternoons and on summer evenings, but only after 1 August did he have Saturday nights as well. Still, he greatly enjoyed swimming and sailing in the summer afternoons. Too, Butch had his 1933 Chevrolet. He could not drive it often, but it came in quite handy when he and his friends swam at Round Bay about nine miles from Annapolis. It felt good wearing civilian clothes and getting week-end leave that first summer after plebe year, eating and drinking at Mrs. Miller's, and gathering around the radio in the evenings. "Just now we are listening to Jack Benny and his groceries of 1936," Butch wrote soon after classes began in the fall of 1935: "I think that Benny has one of the best programs on the air and he really gets off some clever stuff."[38]

Having had some experience on the stage during his days at Western Military Academy, Butch relished providing his mother and other family members with reviews of the plays and movies he viewed in Annapolis and Washington. Given a choice between a hop and Hollywood, Butch as often as not opted for the film. Hating to miss a good movie that showed only during "the week when we can't get out," Butch let few get by him on the weekends. "Yesterday we saw the Big Broadcast of 1936. They really had some good music in it. . . . Have you seen 'Shipmates Forever' yet? That is about one of the best pictures they have put out about this place. I wasn't in it though." Referring again to pictures that featured the Naval Academy, Butch was not the least bit happy about a film being made in the Annapolis area during his youngster year because of the choice of actors: "Why didn't they get a real guy like Bing [Crosby] instead of dear old Rudy [Vallee]."[39]

Meaningful formal social events and the less formal hops held little interest for Butch; there were not many of them to begin with, his girl-friend was too far away to attend most, and according to Captain Nicholson, "neither he nor Butch were great ladies' men." It was mostly upper-middle-class girls from Washington who attended the academy hops and more formal social events, and they stayed in nearby rooming houses. Curfew was strict for the midshipmen, who usually had only forty minutes to walk their dates to the rooming houses and return. However, the Second-Class Ring Dance, held in the spring just before the midshipmen became first-classmen, held special significance. "My ring is going to have a solid head with my initials carved in it. I'll be glad to get the ring as we will be getting somewhere then." By early May 1936 Butch and the other members of his class had received their rings from Tiffany and Company: "We don't rate wearing them until the Ring Dance, but we can wear them in our room. . . . It really is some thrill."[40]

The Ring Dance rite of passage kept spirits high during the spring of 1936. "Well, it looks as if spring is here now. The place is overrun at present with taxpayers and cameras. That is always a sure sign of spring."[41] Not only would Butch's girlfriend attend the Ring Dance, but Patsy would also be present, having just graduated from high school. Mort escorted Patsy to the Ring Dance, and it was during that festive evening that Butch became Butch.

In the good-natured fun at the table where Patsy was sitting with her brother, Mort, Putt, and eight others, several people made it a point to use the generic name Butch when referring to Edward Henry O'Hare. Patsy knew her brother as Ed, and she did not like the name Butch, especially when directed at her brother. While complaining about something no one can now remember, Patsy admonished the other eleven at her table to "stop Butching!" That witty pronouncement, a polite way to say "stop bitching," was a signal moment for Edward H. O'Hare. From that evening on, he was Butch to his friends and to history.

Graduation and the Class of 1937

Anticipation of graduation ran high with Butch and his friends after their return from Christmas break in January 1937; even the usual post-Christmas depression was missing. Classes were still demanding, but Butch missed the trees, rarely even mentioning academics in the letters he sent during his last five months at the academy. Sailing in the afternoons was the primary order of the day, the many athletic events on Saturdays were attended, and the traditional class rowdiness was observed with amusement instead of trepidation. Rather than being thrown into the showers in the middle of the night, Butch sat back and saw plebes of the class of 1940 get wet. For "Hundredth Night," the plebes took charge, and Butch watched with pleasure the food thrown in the mess hall and the plebes' brief skits; he was now on the fast track heading out of town. He endured no more watches every thirteen days or so; instead he concentrated on spending $500 for a new wardrobe. He looked forward to parties in Washington with family and friends, and he was busy finding a house for June week, for even his grandmother, Sophia, would be in Annapolis for graduation. For $75 Butch rented a house on the water about five minutes from the academy. It accommodated five—ample space for Selma, Marilyn, and Sophia. EJ and close friends stayed at the Carvel Hall Inn.[42]

On 3 June 1937 the big event occurred in Dahlgren Hall. Butch marched with the midshipmen one last time, received his degree, accepted his appointment, and executed the oath of office as ensign, then spent most of the afternoon posing for pictures with members of the family and family friends. This beautiful June day the sun shone brightly on Annapolis and the class of 1937, but the O'Hare family and their friends showed enough warmth to render the day's weather inconsequential. It was a great day for all, one last memorable moment before a series of tragedies that would rapidly and relentlessly diminish the O'Hares numerically and emotionally.

A few days after graduation, Butch received a letter of congratulations from Lloyd C. Stark, governor of Missouri and three decades earlier himself a graduate of the Naval Academy. After reading this letter, Butch probably gave little thought to the question of what would befall his classmates. More likely he assumed that their experience would be predictably normal, with most in time attaining the rank of captain but fewer than 5 percent rising to flag (admiral) rank. And he probably assumed that all but three or four would live to retirement—one midshipman had died during Butch's tenure at the academy.[43]

Butch was not alone among his classmates in not foreseeing World War II. For the time being the new naval officers busied themselves with their initial assignments to the fleet and reflected on the achievements of the past four years. Nick graduated twentieth in the class of 1937. Butch ranked 255th out of 323, with Mort in the upper half and Putt right at the halfway mark. Back in the summer of 1933 the class had numbered 417; to be one of the 323 to graduate from the rigorous program was an accomplishment in itself. Relative standing, in this as in many other graduating classes, did not always mean much as an indicator of future success. Of the top twenty graduates, only one attained flag rank. Interestingly, graduates 254 and 256, those on either side of Butch, retired as rear admirals.[44]

In large part because of the war, forty members of the class of 1937 reached flag rank at or before retirement.[45] Impressive as this statistic may be, their sacrifice and wartime contributions are even more significant. Forty-one, or nearly 13 percent, lost their lives during World War II, with nearly a dozen dying in planes. The class produced two Medal of Honor recipients: Butch and Capt. George Levick Street III (in April 1945, skipper of the submarine *Tirante* [SS-420]).

Some other notables in the class of 1937 included Paul J. Riley, Patrick H. Hart, and Raymond A. Moore, all killed flying torpedo planes in the June 1942 Battle of Midway; H. S. "Sid" Bottomley and Jack B. Reid, both famed Midway flyers; Ray A. Snodgrass, lost with all hands on the destroyer *Edsall* (DD-219) off Java; Roger N. Currier, who graduated last, killed on board the *Atlanta* (CL-51) before she went down off Guadalcanal; John C. Patty, Jr., lost with the cruiser *Houston* (CA-30) in the Battle of the Java Sea; John W. King, missing off the first *Wasp* (CV-7); Stockton Birney Strong, who earned three Navy Crosses, one for bombing the carrier *Zuiho* during the Battle of Santa Cruz; and Vice Adm. Charles S. Minter, Jr., a decorated officer who returned to Annapolis in 1964 to serve as superintendent of the U.S. Naval Academy.

"Well done," class of 1937!

A REMINISCENCE OF MY FRIENDSHIP WITH ED O'HARE
Rear Adm. Carl R. "Dutch" Doerflinger, USN (Ret.)

My admission to the USNA was delayed for over a month because of some administrative paperwork. Upon arrival, the wing of Bancroft Hall, the dormitory in which plebes were billeted, was completely full, and I was assigned to a double room in an adjacent wing, which had been vacated for the summer.

So there I was, a sixteen-year-old kid, all by myself, not a friend or acquaintance within a couple of thousand miles, sitting in spartan splendor surrounded by a seabag full of oversize cotton middie blouses, drawstring pants, and high-top black shoes. I had just graduated from public high school in suburban Milwaukee and had never been away from home, except with family or friends, and my only contact with anything military was the Boy Scouts and a .22 rifle. My mood: confused, apprehensive, lonesome, overwhelmed by the Academy Yard and buildings—and scared! So I sat down on the edge of the unmade iron cot to plan my escape.

About that time, the door opened and in walked this hulking figure, loaded with "issue," who turned out to be Ed O'Hare. His admission, too, had been delayed, and [he] was the last member of our class. Assigned as my roommate, he immediately, and silently, set about folding his clothes and stowing them properly in the locker. He didn't say much, but I found myself following his example, and soon the room was ship-shape and we had a chance to get acquainted.

Ed and I, to start with, were opposites. He was big (actually pretty heavy), and I was slight. He was self-assured and exuded confidence, almost to the point of arrogance, while I was shy and uncertain. His background was military and private schools; mine, close family and public schools. He was older, relatively sophisticated, and mature.

Well, how did this oil/water mixture work out?

At first, Ed was rather stoically distant and almost unfriendly. We didn't talk much, but I sensed that he was sizing me up, and could see a little smile come out as he observed my mistakes in keeping up with a routine utterly foreign to me. On my part I watched Ed, recognizing his military experience and expertise and doing things his way, as best I could. He was soon making suggestions and volunteering a little advice—never patronizing, and often in a humorous and teasing manner because of my clumsiness. We gradually closed the gap and got into the mode of friendship and the midshipman mold.

One amusing part of this indoctrination was Ed's instructing me in the "Manual of Arms" and simple "parade" commands. Due to our late arrival, I had missed the basic plebe instruction—but Ed was a master. So after dinner, he used to drill the hell out of me in our room, with me armed with a broomstick, "presenting" and "ordering" arms, "about face," "to the rear, march!" etc. He was a stern "Drill Sergeant," but absolutely generous and unselfish with his time, and I sincerely appreciated his efforts, which saved me a lot of embarrassment and hours on the "awkward squad" (extra duty).

This relationship lasted about two months, at which time Ed and Charlie Putman became roommates, and I paired off with Hank Burfeind.

In those two months two strangers became good friends. We never had a close association as our professional paths parted—he got to flight training about a year ahead of me—and our duty stations never coincided. But I never forgot his help, freely given, to get me started.

Source: Rear Adm. Carl Doerflinger to George Givens, 4 Oct. 1987, in George Givens Papers, courtesy of Mrs. Mary Givens (spelling and punctuation have been edited).

5

To Float
and to Fly

*"I am now about to be
a military pilot"*

The Navy generally required that academy graduates, before they could take specialized training in aviation and submarines, spend at least two years at sea with the fleet, undertaking numerous different assignments and learning many tasks as an introduction to the reality of their new profession. On 1 March 1937, while still at Annapolis, Butch wrote to his mother, "We have been trying to figure out how it will be when we report aboard ship. I think it will be worse than coming in here plebe year. I put in for the NEW MEXICO but I don't know if I'll get it or not." Three weeks later he enthusiastically reported to Selma that he was indeed "going to USS NEW MEXICO." He added, "Putt is with me and Nick and Mort are on the TUSCALOOSA," and he conceded that it was "going to be a funny feeling when we report aboard for duty. Worse than even coming here as you are expected to know something now."[1]

Driving across country in the new four-door light brown Chevrolet his father had given him as a graduation present, Butch spent his time at the wheel reflecting on the four years just concluded at Annapolis. In addition to the satisfaction of having successfully completed academic work at the Naval Academy, he thought back to the early days when the plebes were sent on an Easter egg hunt even though there were no eggs. He recalled the occasions away from the yard, particularly one of the first after his plebe year, when he and three others started out on a gin party only to end up with dates at the Army-Navy Club in Washington. There was time to think of times not so pleasant, such as the scarlet fever epidemic in his youngster year when he and the other midshipmen could not leave the yard or even visit homes there. But he welcomed even the less-than-happy remembrances because they kept his mind off the new experience awaiting him as one of the most junior ensigns in the Battle Force of the United States Fleet.[2]

Battleship Sailor

The USS *New Mexico* (BB-40) was choice duty. The battleship was nearly the same age as the twenty-three-year-old Butch, having been laid down 14 October 1915, launched in April 1917, and commissioned 20 May 1918, just six months before the end of World War I. Her displacement at normal load was 28,500 tons. The main battery totaled twelve 14-inch naval rifles mounted in triple turrets placed two forward and two aft. At times she was flagship of Battleship Division Three and was designated as relief flag for the commander in chief of the U.S. Fleet (CinCUS). Like Butch, the *New Mexico* had something of a weight problem, having added about five thousand tons during her March 1931–January 1933 overhaul and modernization. In place of her old cage masts, the ship now sported a tower bridge that materially changed her entire forward superstructure. Despite new gun directors, antiaircraft guns, and communications and radar installations that were added later in an operational career that extended through World War II, she looked nearly the same at the end of that career as she did when Butch was on board. The durable battlewagon would earn six battle stars and survive several kamikaze hits off the Philippines and Okinawa before being sold for scrap in 1947.[3]

Although the anchorage off San Pedro and Long Beach in California was home port for BB-40, along with much of the rest of the U.S. Fleet, Butch caught up with the *New Mexico* in Puget Sound off Tacoma, Washington. Having reported on 30 June 1937, he made his arrival call soon afterward to the cabin of his new commanding officer, Capt. Frank Jack Fletcher—an able, jaunty sailor from the Annapolis class of 1906, who earned the Medal of Honor at Vera Cruz the year Butch was born. In 1942 Vice Admiral Fletcher led the carriers to victories during the battles of Coral Sea, Midway, and the Eastern Solomons. Butch's first assignment was in the Engineering Department's B Division and his battle station, the ammunition room of the 5-inch/25 secondary batteries. His specially assigned collateral duty—sailing—proved much to his liking. Placed in charge of the race-boat and sailing crews, he prophesied to his mother, "I'll be an old salt yet."[4]

During the brief stay at Tacoma, Butch enjoyed the cool summer evenings and the view of snow-capped Mount Rainier. However, he did not care for the city: "There really isn't a thing to do in this town. . . . They roll in the sidewalks about ten. All there is to do is go to a movie and then out to have a few drinks." In Tacoma he did discover an unforeseen function for his academy ring: it substituted for a membership card at certain clubs.[5]

Butch's worries about his new assignment ended quickly, for it soon became evident that he did know something, and that he could handle the tasks he was expected to perform. The spit-and-polish punctilio of the "Battleship Navy" proved no worse than what he had survived at Annapolis. It did not take long to learn the new routine. Of course, as he evolved into an old hand, he had to find something to complain about and give some substance to his letters home. He wrote that his "hands [were] callused already from climbing so many ladders," a complaint similar to one he had expressed in 1934, when he moved to the fourth deck (floor) of Bancroft Hall: "Pancho and I got a swell room (1413) that overlooks the bay. . . . Just think, we have five flights of stairs to climb about fourteen times a day. Not so good." Butch got used to climbing the ladders and never again mentioned them, just as he noted only at the beginning of his time on board that he had to get up twice a night to inspect engineering spaces.[6]

Before leaving Puget Sound for a cruise south to Long Beach, Butch asked one of his men to drive his car down the coast—envied duty indeed. Arriving in early August in San Francisco, Butch was quite impressed by the new Golden Gate Bridge and nearly as excited about the cool weather. The third week of August the ship returned to the San Pedro–Long Beach anchorage. Now set into a new routine, Butch had some time to relax, thanks in part to the fact that he enjoyed his engineering job. He was learning, as do all good naval officers, to give wide latitude to the chiefs and other senior petty officers to handle their duties without unwarranted interference and to let them deal with the foul balls. In his relations with enlisted men he set the proper tone and eventually earned their loyalty and trust. A fan of Glenn Miller and other big bands, Butch caught their swing music on the radio and in movie theaters. While not spending much time ashore, he did drive up to Los Angeles and Hollywood, where he found the weather warmer than in San Francisco. Not much else there captured his interest. However, he always liked fishing and spent many of his off-duty hours beside nearby mountain streams or sailing one of the battleship's boats with a line trailing over the side.[7]

Unfortunately, just as life was mellowing for Butch, the first family tragedy occurred. Back in St. Louis, his seventy-three-year-old grandmother, Sophia, was returning home one Sunday afternoon on crowded Highway 66 from a Meramec River clubhouse when the car in which she and several of her friends were riding was struck from behind. Sophia was thrown forward from the back seat and injured her head. Only a few days later, on 16 September 1937, she died at home. Everyone in the family fancied cars, but no one—not even Butch—loved to ride as much as Sophia Reichschneider Lauth. Even after a day's worth of long trips, she would suggest at dusk, "Let's take a ride." As sad as her death was for the family, they all agreed that she probably would have chosen to pass from this earth in company with her German friends in a car. Most of the family, including EJ, attended the funeral. Butch was not told immediately, because he was at sea and the family knew he could not arrive in time even if the Navy gave him leave. Informed by letter, he consoled his mother: "I really am sorry that I could not be there with you at the time but I guess that couldn't be helped." He had to agree that with EJ living in Chicago, Miami, and Boston, Sophia dead, Patsy attending finishing school in Europe, and himself away for at least a year, the once-crowded house on Holly Hills Boulevard, "so big now," was becoming less and less a home. Thirteen-year-old Marilyn would soon be gone too, and then the house would seem even bigger.[8]

As 1937 waned, Butch turned his attention away from the recent sadness and directed it toward his new duties in the Repair Division. His battle station was now in Repair IV, where he stood ready to lead crews to deal with damage control in his particular section of the vast warship. His routine revolved around engineering inspections, deck watch, movies, and more fishing. In May 1938, as part of Butch's introduction to the wider aspects of shipboard duty, he was transferred to the Communications Division and designated radio officer. His battle station became the cramped Radio I or Main Radio, again located deep inside the ship's interior and far from the blue sky he craved. His principal duty, aside from overseeing skilled radio operators deeply absorbed in sending and receiving Morse code, was deciphering classified messages.

In June the *New Mexico* entered dry dock at Bremerton, Washington. Butch had hoped for more leave than he got, but "we are so short of officers now it is pathetic." Marilyn and Patsy headed west by train to visit him in Bremerton. At the same time, Butch was attempting to clear up a couple of matters with his mother pertaining to world events. She had been fretting over a statement Butch had made with regard to the growing conflict between China and Japan. He had written, "Think I'll put in for duty in China," but he explained later that she had misconstrued his intent. Concerning Europe, Butch wrote, "What is all the talk about this war of yours? I haven't heard about any war and as long as I am not [worried] I wish that you wouldn't. That should be the least of your worries."[9]

Before his sisters departed, they had several conversations with Butch concerning the end of his long relationship with the only girlfriend he had ever had. The breakup had occurred not long after he reported to the *New Mexico*. No Naval Academy graduate could marry until two years after graduation, and thus there could have been no wedding before June 1939. Even though the breakup was now old news, the sisters had not seen Butch since it happened, and they needed to discuss the event, for they had long expected the woman from St. Louis to become their sister-in-law. In fact, Marilyn could not remember a time when "she wasn't there."

Back in San Pedro–Long Beach for the fall of 1938, Butch became a little more socially active, now that there was no longer a special girl back home. Nearly every weekend that fall, he attended football games, making it a particular point to see as many of the University of Southern California games as possible. Having caught USC's games with California, Washington State, UCLA, and Notre Dame, Butch wrote, "It isn't true football out here as you usually wind up with your coat off and sleeves rolled up and that just doesn't seem right: more like baseball weather." In addition to the games, he attended a sorority party at the Trocadero; helped get Putt a date for the Chamber of Commerce Ball, "tails and all"; joined a shipwreck party ("I have to . . . figure out what a shipwrecked sailor looks like"); and enjoyed a "hayride . . . to the beach." Ever consistent, he reported on 31 October, "We . . . had hot dogs, pie and cider," but he made no mention of his date.[10]

The time for fun grew short. Butch knew that a major cruise was in the offing after Christmas, and it would be a long time before he again saw the San Pedro–Long Beach area. On board ship he was pleased to learn that CinCUS decided not to hoist his flag on board the *New Mexico*, as previously announced, for this left the ensigns a "lot of rooms to pick from." He was able to room with Putt for the first time since academy days. And by going to sea the first two weeks in December, Butch could look forward to catching up on his sleep after social activities that had rather consistently brought him back on board in the wee hours of the morning. It appears that about this time he left the Communications Division for the Gunnery Department.[11]

In early January 1939 most of the fleet pulled out of port bound for Fleet Problem XX in the Caribbean and Atlantic. Rumor had it that the fleet would move on in late April to the New York World's Fair, something Butch and many others found appealing. On 14 January the *New Mexico* passed through the Panama Canal. Although impressed by the engineering marvel of the new century, Butch was more affected by the primitive living conditions he witnessed. In a letter to Marilyn he devoted considerable space to the subject, reminding his sister how blessed they were and telling her she would not believe how bad conditions were in Panama and other Central American locales.[12]

In March 1939, while the fleet was still operating in the Caribbean, Hitler completed his dismemberment of Czechoslovakia, a world-shaking event noted with only passing interest by Butch, who was busy with shipboard duties and with flying. He made friends with the pilots of the *New Mexico*'s detachment of Observation Squadron Three (VO-3), who flew her three Curtiss SOC-3 Seagull seaplanes. The squadron insignia, "Oswald the Lucky Rabbit" riding a 14-inch shell, reflected VO-3's principal duty of serving as gunnery spotters for the main battery. Knowing that Butch had already applied for flight training, Lt. Lance E. "Lem" Massey, the detachment CO and a fellow sailing enthusiast, let him ride several times as observer in the Seagull's rear seat and even fly the floatplane using the dual controls. A small catapult powered by a charge of gunpowder hurled the light biplane into the air, a breathtaking experience for its crew. After completing the mission, the pilot would set down astern of the battleship, taxi up the "slick" the ship created by turning her wake, and float into the plane trap. At that point the crane lowered a hoisting sling that the rear-seat man stood up to grab and hook onto the aircraft. On 12 April, Butch wrote to Marilyn, "I have been up quite a bit from the ship and it is a lot of fun. They let us fly from the back seat and we land and take off for practice. I think that I could get one up in the air and back down in one piece if necessary now."[13] Butch's friend Lem Massey died on 4 June 1942 heroically leading the *Yorktown*'s Torpedo Squadron Three against the Japanese carriers at Midway.

The deteriorating situation in Europe forced cancellation of the voyage to the New York World's Fair, and the fleet headed from Norfolk through the Panama Canal, arriving on 12 May back at San Pedro–Long Beach. Most of the sailors were disappointed at missing New York and the fair, but they were pleased to return to California. Butch too felt bad about the fair, but he was happier than most because on 4 May he had received orders to report to Naval Air Station (NAS) Pensacola, Florida, for instruction in heavier-than-air craft. Shortly thereafter the fleet passed other naval units based in San Diego, and he caught a glimpse of the Navy's newest aircraft carrier, the *Enterprise* (CV-6). She had just reached the Pacific in April after also participating in Fleet Problem XX. Someday, he mused, he would land on board her.

On 4 June 1939 Butch was detached from the *New Mexico* with one year, eleven months, and five days of sea service to add to his two shorter cruises on board the *Wyoming* and *Arkansas*. He had done well in his tour with the tough Battleship Navy. A letter of commendation signed by the *New Mexico*'s CO, Capt. Cortlandt C. Baughman, graced his personnel file. It praised Ens. Edward H. O'Hare "for assisting materially in the Main Battery Ship and Fire Control Party which won second prize for Main Battery practices for the year '38–'39."[14]

With orders to report to Pensacola on 28 June, Butch left for St. Louis and a most enjoyable visit with the family and a reunion with his high school chums. This time Putt would not join him, having opted for submarines and training in Connecticut. Shaking hands on board the *New Mexico*, the two friends who had worked their way together through the Naval Academy and their first two years as officers in the fleet, and who had shared each other's triumphs and trials, promised to stay in touch, and perhaps even to meet at Couderay for more hours on board their handmade sailboat and at the lodge. In the summer of 1939, the twilight of peace, it was a promise both were sure they would honor, but Putt's duty with the Asiatic Fleet and then World War II ensured that they never saw each other again.

NAS Pensacola

On 9 June, Butch arrived in Pensacola, a place already renowned within the Navy as the cradle of naval aviation and the heart of the flight training program.[15] Three different categories of trainees received instruction alongside each other: regular officers, aviation cadets (AvCads), and enlisted men (future naval aviation pilots, or NAPs). Butch joined Flight Class 127-0 (the 0 for officer). About the only difference between the officer program and the AvCad training was that the ensigns and lieutenants had their evenings and weekends to themselves, while the cadets had to learn to become officers as well as how to fly. The lowly enlisted flight trainees, however, often had to turn out for extra fatigue duties.

Butch used his free time to see the area and quickly became enamored of the sugar-white beaches, the blue-green Gulf of Mexico, and the beautiful sunsets, when the water turned a light aqua and the blue sky softened into pink above the white beaches. He was not fond of the high humidity, which greatly exceeded that of Southern California, but the constant breezes helped alleviate that complaint. With water surrounding the peninsula of the naval air station and with easy access to the gulf, Butch immediately planned to bring the twenty-seven-foot *PEM* to Pensacola.

Several weeks elapsed before the *PEM* could arrive at Pensacola, but Butch was on the water long before then. On 10 July he took an orientation ride for about fifty minutes in an N3N-1, a sturdy biplane trainer built by the Naval Aircraft Factory to serve both as a land plane and, when fitted with floats, a seaplane. The Navy painted its primary trainers bright yellow to render them highly visible, and with students usually at the controls, they certainly merited the nickname Yellow Peril. Flying the two-man plane—student pilot and instructor in tandem—was Lt. Cleo P. Kerschner, USNR, who became Butch's instructor in Squadron One, primary seaplanes.

Floating above the Pensacola area at a top speed of 125 miles per hour, savoring the joy of finally reaching the threshold of his ambition to fly, Butch mused on the beauty of the Gulf of Mexico and how he would explore it aboard the *PEM*. At the conclusion of the flight the N3N-1 drifted across narrow Santa Rosa Island, spotted with 6- and 8-inch coastal gun emplacements set to repel earlier threats and future enemies, and gently touched down in Pensacola Bay. After taxiing to shore, Kerschner jotted down his first daily report: "No previous training: indoctrination flight." He dated the report 6-10-39, the 6 incorrect for the month of July, and continued to use the wrong number for all daily reports through the end of the month. Although not attentive to dates, Kerschner knew how to fly airplanes, and he was a fine judge of student pilots.

Butch wrote on his information sheet, required of all student pilots, that he had not completed any previous aviation training. That was true; his experience ten years earlier at the age of fifteen had been short and informal, while the casual handling of the controls of VO-3's Seagulls was not something he shared with strangers. Three days after his indoctrination flight, Butch could not help but smile to himself when Kerschner wrote, "This student is well above average for this stage. He is able to make consistently safe landings and takeoffs." On 20 June, Kerschner's entry read, "Student handles plane more like an experienced pilot than a student. All landings and takeoffs very consistent and good. Exercises good speed control." Butch soloed on 26 July, apparently the first in his class to do so.

For Butch the initial advantage of having had some experience at the controls of an airplane did not last beyond the first few weeks. On 9 August, Kerschner noted that his student tended to skid upon entry into spirals, and on the 11 August fifteen-hour check by Lt. William W. Jones, USNR, he was still "skidding in spirals" and "flipper turns." However, Butch got an "up," naval parlance for "pass."

By 28 August, Butch had completed Squadron One. A fitness report would be completed after each squadron program, five in all. In addition to flying, Butch and the other class members were graded on intelligence, judgment, initiative, force, moral courage, cooperation, loyalty, perseverance, reactions in emergencies, endurance, and industry, as well as military bearing (neatness of person and dress). Grading was on a system very similar to that of the Naval Academy, with 2.5 being the lowest passing grade and 4.0 the top. For Squadron One, Butch received an excellent 3.6, and Kerschner wrote in the remarks section, "This officer is very courteous and tactful in his duties with others. He has a good disposition and can be relied upon to carry out additional duties. He is considered above average officer material."

For Butch, Squadron Two, primary land planes, lasted from 29 August to 27 October 1939. His instructor for this phase was Lt. H. K. "Hal" Edwards, remembered not only as an outstanding instructor but as a man whose professional bearing and personal empathy Butch found worthy of emulation. Training in Squadron Two was dual experience, and the majority of it was still in the N3N-1. Toward the end of Squadron Two, Butch switched over to the NS-1 Stearman, with basically the same horsepower, speed, and appearance as the N3N-1. Both trainers were slower than the shipboard SOCs. Despite an entry by Edwards on 9 October that read, "Student has considerable aptitude but lacks confidence," Butch completed Squadron Two with a fitness report grade of 3.57. Edwards concluded, "I consider this officer's judgment above average. He thinks clearly, is thorough in his work and very dependable. He is a little diffident and quiet on first acquaintance but is unfailingly cheerful and courteous and does not lack self confidence. He appears to be well liked by his classmates. He is fitted for promotion and should make a good naval aviator."

On 18 October, Butch wrote Marilyn that he had passed his thirty-three-hour check, completed two hours of night flying ("The first landing at night is almost as thrilling as the first time you solo. I didn't know what happened on the first one but I must have made it as I am still here"), and had begun formation flying ("That is a lot of fun also but you have to keep on the alert so you don't wind up in the other planes"). He added, "We got stunts . . . loops, cartwheels, Immelmanns, falling leafs, snap rolls and split S's. I'll take you for a good ride some day." Butch also noted that another student pilot had to parachute while attempting stunts, and that not a week went by when someone failed to stand a plane on its nose.

On 27 October 1939 Butch penned a letter to his father, poignant not only because he had successfully completed Squadron Two that day but also because it would be the last one. For these two reasons the letter is presented here in full:

Friday 27 Oct.

Dear dad

Well, I am now about to be a military pilot. I got my final check in Squad II this morning and got an up on it. Tomorrow I report to Squad III for military airplanes for the first time. All we have had so far have been primary landplanes.

Things have been going rather well here lately. The only down I received thus far was the one on the solo check. We made darn good time in going through II as it only took us eight weeks and it is listed as a 15 week course. We had a lot of good weather though and that helps a lot. In fact I have caught up with a lot of the boys that started several months ahead of us. I was the second one in the class to finish here. One of the other boys got out yesterday.

The PEM is doing fine. We had her out fishing last Sunday and we got a nice king mackerel about a yard long. We should have had about seven of them but we didn't have much luck in landing them. I had her out of the water the last few days and had the bottom painted with copper paint. The after shaft bearing was awfully loose but it's ok again now. It is rather hard to use the boat during the week now as the flying lasts until 1615 and it gets dark early.

Well dad, nothing much else to report at present. I hope you are well and that things are going alright at the track. Again I say write if you get time.

Love
Ed

Butch emerging from a
Grumman F4F-3 Wildcat,
April 1942. *(USN)*

Butch and pony, circa 1922. As a youth Butch was so shy with strangers that, to steer him toward more social interaction and help him gain confidence, his father often required him to make travel arrangements with clerks. *(O'Hare Collection)*

At the Hawthorne racetrack, circa 1928, Butch poses with his mother, Selma, sister Patricia, and baby sister, Marilyn. *(O'Hare Collection)*

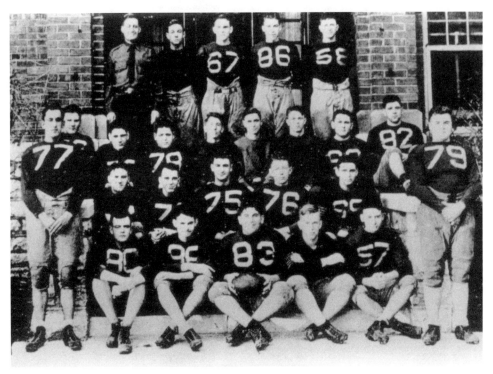

An average athlete at Western Military Academy, Butch (sitting at right in row two) was one year ahead of World War II pilot Paul Tibbets (number 79 at Butch's left), who flew the B-29 *Enola Gay* with the atomic bomb to Hiroshima. *(Courtesy of Charles B. Jackson, Jr.)*

Via his successful academic program at Western Military
Academy, Butch was eligible at age twenty-one for a reserve
commission in the U.S. Army. However, machine guns in the
sky interested Butch more than the Army's "Tommy Gun."
(O'Hare Collection)

EJ O'Hare (left) and
James A. Farley,
close adviser to then
president-elect Franklin D.
Roosevelt, Miami Beach,
1933. *(O'Hare Collection)*

Away at the Naval Academy when his Model T Ford met its end in
St. Louis, Butch returned in the summer of 1934 for a final visit with
the remains of his old friend. *(O'Hare Collection)*

Butch (center) with close academy friends Mort Lytle (left) and Charles Putman. Lytle and Putman served in submarines during World War II, and both retired as captains. After Butch's death, Mort married his widow, Rita.
(O'Hare Collection)

On graduation day, 3 June 1937, Butch stands with his
proud grandmother, Mrs. Sophia Reichschneider Lauth. Her
untimely death from injuries suffered in a traffic accident
only three months later was the first of several family
tragedies to occur between 1937 and 1943. *(O'Hare Collection)*

Butch and Jimmy Thach confer,
April 1942. *(USN)*

On 19 March 1940 Jimmy Thach tipped this F2A-1 Buffalo (Bureau Number 1393) onto its nose on the *Saratoga*'s deck. Butch flew this aircraft several times during the summer and fall of 1940.
(Courtesy of Capt. O. B. Stanley)

Fighting Three, 5 March 1942. *Top row (left to right):* Newton Mason, Howard Clark, Robert Sellstrom, Willard Eder, Howard Johnson, John Lackey, Leon Haynes, Burt Stanley, Dale Peterson, Marion Dufilho, Rolla Lemmon. *Bottom row:* Robert Morgan, Albert Vorse, Don Lovelace, Jimmy Thach, Noel Gayler, Butch, Richard Rowell. *(O'Hare Collection)*

Minus its left engine, Lt. Comdr. Itō's bomber attempts to crash into the *Lexington*, 20 February 1942. *(USN)*

Thach (in F-1) and Butch in F-13 during the aerial photography flight of 11 April 1942. *(USN)*

Hero in the hot seat: a grim-faced Butch with Thach during the ordeal of the first press conference at the Royal Hawaiian, 27 March 1942. *(USN)*

Having inadvertently hidden her face from photographers while placing the Medal of Honor around Butch's neck the first time on 21 April 1942, Rita repeated the procedure. The second enactment brought even larger smiles from President Franklin D. Roosevelt, Secretary of the Navy Frank Knox (behind FDR) and Adm. Ernest J. King. *(USN)*

Arriving in St. Louis immediately
before the 25 April 1942 parade
in his honor, Butch stands before
photographers with (from left) his
sister Marilyn, his mother, wife,
and sister Patricia.
(USN via O'Hare Collection)

The smiles on the faces of Butch and his wife convey only temporary pleasure, for Butch strongly disliked the speaking requirements of his spring 1942 war bond tour. *(USN via O'Hare Collection)*

Butch, St. Louis mayor W. D. Becker, and other dignitaries review cadets from Butch's old school, Western Military Academy. With the bombing of Pearl Harbor still fresh in the minds of Americans, the celebration of Butch's heroism was an event of national interest. *(USN via O'Hare Collection)*

6

The Sky
Turned Black

"I had nothing to do with it"

Flying over the Pensacola region in November 1939 was any pilot's dream. The first cold front had moved through the area in late September, with others following regularly, usually every four or five days. Prevailing winds moved from onshore to offshore, with the drier air welcomed by all. For pilots, the change was especially welcome, because it meant that their clothes were no longer sweat absorbers; by 1 November jackets had become desirable in the evenings and necessary while in the air. The sky shone a bright blue in the absence of oppressive humidity, and the occasional wisp of cloud was pure white.

On Wednesday, 8 November, Butch was in the air for two training flights.[1] In between he had enjoyed a short break, at which time he noticed with pleasure how the few deciduous trees around Pensacola and on the naval air station were beginning to show a little color—nothing like the turning leaves in St. Louis or Annapolis, but a welcome sight nevertheless. And the sky! Even though Butch had only a few minutes before climbing back into it, he paused to lean against his Vought 03U-1

Corsair and take in the beauty of the few white puffs of clouds between him and the brilliant azure sky.

Before the sun set that Wednesday, however, the blue and white sky would turn black for Butch.

In Chicago that day, at about 3 P.M., EJ O'Hare was preparing to depart his Thirty-third Street and Laramie Avenue office at Sportsman's Park.[2] It was a typically cool early-November afternoon, but not so cold as to require a topcoat. EJ started his new Lincoln Zephyr, warmed the engine for a few seconds, and then pulled away from the park. About ten minutes later, driving northeast on Ogden Avenue and nearing the intersection with Talman Avenue, he noticed in the rear-view mirror a black Lincoln Zephyr very much like his own. The other vehicle closed at high speed. Another glance revealed that the oncoming car carried two men; the one on the passenger side was brandishing a sticklike object.

Instantly EJ realized what was happening. Very likely he recognized this as a typical setup for assassination used by the Capone outfit: well planned, no other cars around, the right weapon, the right men. This rendezvous was not unexpected; it had been only a question of when.

EJ reacted quickly as the reality of danger struck. Left hand on the steering wheel, with his right hand he slammed the floor-mounted gear shift into second, to pick up speed. As he passed Talman Avenue heading toward Rockwell Street, he started to move his right hand from the gear shift toward the glove compartment, but quickly moved it back to the steering wheel so that he could roll down the window with his left hand.

EJ's left hand was still on its way to the door when the first blast from a sawed-off shotgun sliced through the glass, leaving a hole no more than two inches in diameter. All the pellets found their mark in the left side of EJ's head just below the ear.

No further thoughts passed through Edgar Joseph O'Hare's mind.

A second charge blew another small hole through the glass. A few pellets struck EJ's neck; others exited on the passenger side. At speeds near 45 miles per hour, the two cars traveled on side by side for a little over a second before EJ's car jumped the curb to the right, brushed a light pole hard enough to shatter its glass, rolled another sixty feet down the streetcar tracks, and then crashed into a trolley pole. The impact crumpled the Lincoln's hood and grill, forced EJ's body against the steering wheel, and pushed the steering column against the dash, demolishing the wheel.

Unknown to the two assassins, their act was observed by Peter Szent, age twenty-eight, who was painting window sills at the Garden City Plating and Manufacturing Company, 1430 South Talman Avenue, just one block ahead of the shooting scene. When interviewed by police five days later—he had delayed coming forward, out of fear—Szent stated that he had not got a good enough look at either passenger to notice anything other than that they were both middle-aged and wore black coats and hats. He had noted with interest, however, that the driver, mindful of the traffic laws, stopped at the next intersection for a red light; then on green he turned left and calmly drove away.

Szent's information, brought to the attention of the police on 13 November, indicated that some portions of the police reports written on 8–9 November were incorrect. According to the initial accounts, EJ died instantly; Szent, however, said he heard the first shot, then turned in time to see the second blast. Running to EJ's car, he found the driver unconscious but gasping for air. Earlier police reports had also registered the assassin's car as a small dark green coupe, believed to be a Ford (Fords and Lincoln Zephyrs looked very much alike). Szent identified the assassin car also as a black Lincoln Zephyr, the only difference being that EJ's car was the deluxe model with chrome and whitewall tires.

Beginning with the morning editions on Thursday, 9 November 1939, and running for nearly a month, the Chicago and St. Louis newspapers had a field day with the story. The stories began on page 1, sharing space with the latest news from the new war in Europe, where the Dutch were opening dikes to hinder the Germans should they attack; the French boasted that they had repulsed a German night raid; the Germans themselves sought the assassins who had attempted to blow up Hitler; and Britain's prime minister, Neville Chamberlain, sagaciously observed that there was little possibility for a quick termination of the war. But Europe was a long way from Chicago: Al Capone was due for release from federal prison any day, his destination not yet announced, while EJ O'Hare had been killed. In Chicago these stories of local interest commanded every bit as much attention as the distant war in Europe.

Of course, the newspapers used EJ's death to publicize Capone's imminent release and conjectured widely about a possible connection between the two events. The articles contained some information that was correct, some allegations that later events would prove untrue, and some questions that will never be answered to the total satisfaction of historians.

For weeks the local newspapers pitched in with wild, often contradictory theories regarding the shooting. Finally the police and state attorney's office offered their interpretation of the events that had led to EJ's murder. Conveniently assembled in the *Chicago Daily Tribune*—advertised as "the world's greatest newspaper" at a price of 2 cents per copy—were the various theories of the crime:

1. EJ was killed on orders from Capone for having given information to the government that led to Capone's imprisonment. First presented 9 November. Over fifty years later the best evidence supports this, the earliest theory.

2. With Capone's release imminent, the two may have disagreed as to who would control Capone's dog- and horse-racing interests, which had increased in value considerably during Capone's incarceration, in part thanks to EJ's management. First presented 9 November. In time, word of Capone's declining health militated against this theory.

3. EJ had quarreled with associates over the proceeds at Sportsman's Park. First presented 9 November; discarded 10 November.

4. EJ was to have flown to Washington on 9 November to meet with "a government man." It was not made clear whether this trip had anything to do with Clyde Nimerick, a bank robber and former bootlegger referred to in a message from FBI agent George Woltz found on EJ's body. First presented 10 November; essentially discarded 11 November.

5. The St. Louis Egan Rats mob may have been involved. First presented 10 November; essentially discarded 11 November.

6. The Capone syndicate theory appeared again because (a) "the crime was typical of Capone executions of the past," and (b) "no other mob would dare to kill a leader of the dreaded and powerful Capone organization." Presented 11 November.

7. There seemed to be some kind of relationship between municipal judge Eugene J. Holland—roundly criticized because hundreds of gambling cases were being dismissed—and EJ. The details of the relationship were unclear, but it involved a partnership in a South Side real estate enterprise. Presented 11 November, continued for weeks, and finally discarded as irrelevant.

8. EJ allegedly had been seeking a foothold in professional sports as a director of the Chicago Cardinals and was moving toward a franchise to operate roller-skating derbies in the south. First presented 11 November; soon discarded as having no connection to the shooting.

9. In October 1937 two convicts just freed from Alcatraz had written that Capone was "angry at Eddie and was making threats against him."[3] First presented 12 November; never discredited.

10. "O'Hare refused to contribute liberally to the flow of cash understood to have been sent by the gang to their leader's family." Presented 12 November; discarded.

11. Capone felt "jealousy at O'Hare's growing wealth." Presented 12 November; discarded.

12. EJ had helped the government convict Capone on income tax fraud and in return "hoped for an arrangement" that would (a) "permit him to pay up his back taxes and escape trial" and (b) ensure "preservation of the gang and its profits." Presented 16 November. The best evidence is that EJ never cared about the gang or its profits. No known documentation supports the tax matter.

13. EJ had connections with E. L. Dolan, a former Boston city treasurer who was in jail on contempt-of-court charges and awaiting trial on larceny charges. A letter from Dolan to EJ, found in one of EJ's several safe-deposit boxes, discussed activities undertaken "in Massachusetts to win public and political favor for dog racing." Presented 17 November; discarded as irrelevant.

14. EJ's slaying was linked to efforts to take over the Miami Gulfstream racetrack near Tropical Park, a business in which he was already a stockholder. Acquiring the bankrupt Gulfstream track would have threatened the financial viability of Tropical Park, purported to be a Capone business. Presented 29 November; discarded.

A month after the shooting, the authorities had discovered a great deal about EJ's business enterprises. They had interviewed Patsy; EJ's girlfriend, Sue Granata;[4] his secretary, Antoinette "Toni" Cavaretta; his supposed chauffeur-bodyguard, Henry "Kinky" Beckman; and Butch himself. Yet on 8 December 1939 the police were no closer to solving EJ's death than they had been on 8 November.

The dominant theme that emerged from those first days after the shooting still appears to be the most viable scenario: EJ died at the hands of the Capone mob. This is consistent with the strong body of evidence relating to EJ's role in Capone's tax fraud conviction. It is also supported by evidence involving Elmer "Dutch" Dowling, a top lieutenant in the St. Louis–area Wortman gang, who was shot to death in February 1962. (Killed along with Dowling was Melvin Beckman, wrongly reported in the press to be the son of Henry Beckman, but actually his nephew.) According to news reports, Dowling set up the assassination of EJ, thereby earning $10,000 for the contract and the gratitude of the Capone outfit.[5] In April 1969 the New Orleans Police Department contacted Chicago police to relay an informant's statement regarding the assassination of a "subject named O'Hara [sic]." Chicago police thanked the New Orleans police for their assistance and filled in several details, but the case is still open.

Before leaving the subject of EJ's shooting, several matters presented in the 1939 newspapers, as well as in articles and books over the years, require correction, amplification, and an attempt toward resolution. Although some are relatively minor details, in the aggregate they help piece together the puzzle that was EJ O'Hare and add to an understanding of one of Chicago's most interesting eras.

The newspapers seem never to have mentioned Henry "Kinky" Beckman without the designations *chauffeur* and *bodyguard*. At times when EJ carried large amounts of money, Kinky may well have served as a bodyguard. He was not EJ's chauffeur at the time of EJ's death; a black man whose name now escapes the sisters' memory was EJ's chauffeur, and his wife worked as a maid for EJ. To the police Beckman declared that he was a "caller" for the races and that he held the parking lot concession for Sportsman's Park. More than anything else, Beckman was a family friend. Marilyn remembers him with particular affection as her "nursemaid" and personal chauffeur. On one occasion when they were riding near the Holly Hills house, the two were teasing each other when Kinky reached over to tickle the ten-year-old Marilyn. She lurched back against the passenger door of the car and fell out into the alley, but amazingly ended up unhurt. Today she enjoys recalling this incident and other travels with her good friend.

More important were stories published in the days immediately after EJ's death that concerned his nervous demeanor and fears for his life. Somewhat of a pattern is evident in that William Johnstone, the publicity director for Sportsman's Park, Johnny Patton, secretary-treasurer of Sportsman's Park and longtime Capone associate, and EJ's confidential secretary at Sportsman's Park, Toni Cavaretta, all were quoted in newspaper accounts as saying that EJ had not been himself lately. He supposedly acted cautiously and changed his routine—for example, riding the elevated train instead of using his car. But according to quotations ascribed to Sue Granata in news reports, there were no overt signs that EJ was worried.

A LETTER FROM THE NEW ORLEANS POLICE DEPARTMENT

April 3, 1969

James B. Conmisk, Jr.
Superintendent of Police
Chicago Police Department
1121 South State Street
Chicago, Illinois 60605

ATTN: Chief of Detectives

Dear Sir:

The following information is being passed to you for your evaluation.

On April 2, 1969 this office received information from a local newspaperman that while he was in the local Press Club Bar a stranger started a conversation with him. This stranger, during an interval, stated that he had met an old friend named Jimmie Cochie (phonetic spelling) who he was raised with in Cicero, Illinois. (This Jimmie Cochie was quoted as saying that he was in New Orleans to meet one "Skinny Johnson" to "rub out" someone.) This unknown white male stated to the newspaper reporter that his old friend, Jimmie Cochie, had also told him that he and Skinny Johnson had "rubbed out" a Racing Official by the name of O'Hara in Chicago, Illinois. The unknown white male also stated that Jimmie Cochie had come from the coast, unknown whether East or West Coast.

The unknown white male who gave this information to the newspaper reporter was described as between 50 and 60 years of age, 5'8" to 5'10", greying hair, needed a shave.

We have checked all of our records on the aforementioned names with negative results and are meanwhile attempting to locate this unknown white male. If there are any further developments you will be so advised.

Meanwhile it is requested that you advise this Department if you did have such an incident involving a subject named O'Hara in Chicago, and if not, we will abandon our search for the informant.

Assuring you of our cooperation in all matters, I remain,

Yours truly,
Joseph I. Giarrusso
Superintendent of Police
BY: Major Henry M. Morris
Chief of Detectives

Toni Cavaretta provides an especially fascinating tie between EJ and the Capone outfit. EJ obviously trusted her. For example, she received and wrote out for EJ the message from the FBI later found on his body. One of her closest childhood friends, Anna, was married to Frank Nitti; the couple adopted a son, Joe. After Anna died, Toni assisted in caring for Joe. In 1942 she married Frank and was widowed when he committed suicide a year later upon learning that he would be going back to prison. When EJ was killed, Toni asked Frank directly if he was involved. "I had nothing to do with it," Nitti replied. "I think it must have been guys from Boston."[6] Years later Toni acknowledged, "What else could he say." She remained a friend of the O'Hares all her life. Marilyn and some of her children traveled on occasion to visit her. If indeed Al Capone decreed EJ's death, Frank Nitti—as head of the outfit after the boss went to prison—would not only have known about and approved the assassination but perhaps even planned it. It is clear that EJ had continued to assist governmental agencies fighting organized crime, and at least one person too many knew it. The Chicago of the 1930s had many "ears," many people who owed favors, and many who needed favors. Certainly neither Nitti nor anyone else in organized crime could tolerate an informant. The chance that Toni knew the truth, whatever it was, seems very slim; the wives and girlfriends of gangsters might be aware of what their men did for a living, but very seldom did they learn any details. That was better for the gangsters, and it certainly was better for the women.

Lurid newspaper stories immediately after EJ's murder had branded him as "Race Track Head" or "Turfman." By 11 November he had become a "front man for Capone" and a "millionaire," and newspapers continued to refer to him as such until the story itself ebbed in December 1939. In April 1942, when Butch returned stateside to receive the Congressional Medal of Honor from President Franklin D. Roosevelt, the press still proclaimed EJ a millionaire but no longer an associate of Capone. Mention was sometimes made that Butch's businessman father had been killed or was believed to have been killed by gangsters. Although it was alluded to in articles soon after the slaying, confirmation of EJ's significant role in working with the Treasury Department did not come until soon after Capone's death in January 1947 with Frank Wilson's stories in *Collier's* magazine and elsewhere. By 1949, when the new Chicago airport was named for Butch, no newspapers accused EJ of being a Capone front man—least of all the *Chicago Tribune,* whose publisher had long since learned the truth about EJ's government work and had been a prime mover in having the airport named for Butch.

Since 1976 the Treasury Department has not allowed private citizens to inspect the income tax returns on file for other individuals, even deceased individuals; insight into EJ's tax matters must come from the copies of his tax returns preserved in family files. And it is possible to get one final look at his life through the thirty-page will drawn up for his complicated estate. The will reveals that EJ did not quite make it to millionaire status. Not counting $96,000 in insurance policies for his daughters, the gross value of his estate amounted to approximately $756,000. The bulk, about $605,000, lay in his holdings in the five racetrack operating companies—Chicago, Memphis, Taunton, and the two in Miami—plus the Ocean View Corporation. Real estate in Illinois, Missouri, Wisconsin, and Florida was liquidated for about $100,000, with cash totaling $46,000—many thousands less than had been speculated in November 1939. EJ may not have been a millionaire in absolute terms, but given the dollar's purchasing power in the 1930s, he was still a wealthy man.

Claims against the estate totaled $834,000; however, EJ's executor, the Northern Trust Company, challenged many of them, so only $370,000 remained on the final debit side of the ledger. Mrs. Dorothy Hyland—widow of Martin J. Hyland (a friend of EJ's in the early days of his racing interests) and his first romantic interest after his divorce—submitted a claim for $205,000 but was awarded only $80,000 in repayment of a business loan.[7] Federal estate tax for which the government claimed $67,000 was finally settled at $45,000. And even though EJ was long gone from this world by 1946, the Internal Revenue Service claimed a $72,000 deficiency in income taxes for years prior to 1939. Northern Trust challenged the IRS claims, won several of the disputed issues, and paid $34,000, less than half what the government demanded. No issue concerned taxes for any supposed illegal income.

And finally there is the matter of the .32-caliber pistol found in EJ's car on 8 November 1939. According to police reports, the gun was discovered in the glove compartment. However, someone subsequently placed it on the seat, where the press photographed it, hence the stories that EJ had had a gun beside him during the shooting. Perhaps the weapon's real significance is its modest caliber and stopping power, not whether it rested on the seat or in the glove compartment. As one wag put it, EJ certainly was no gangster because no real mobster ever depended on a puny .32. EJ knew a .32 might deter a common thief, but even a more powerful weapon would make little difference if "the boys" had marked him for death.

Word of EJ's death quickly reached Pensacola by telegram. The Navy immediately granted Butch compassionate leave. On Thursday morning, 9 November, he and his instructor, Hal Edwards, climbed into a Vought SU-1 biplane for the four-hour fifteen-minute flight to St. Louis, with one stop for fuel.[8] Once at Lambert Field, Hal executed an unusual crosswind landing, according to Marilyn's recollection. This enabled Butch to escape several waiting news reporters and photographers. On another memorable, vastly more pleasurable, visit to St. Louis in April 1942, he would not be able to evade the press so easily.

On Friday morning the train Silent Knight arrived in St. Louis with EJ's body. Also on board were family and friends who lived in Chicago. At the flower-filled Southern Funeral Home, the casket was briefly opened for Butch and Selma prior to the wake. Gathering for a final tribute and to console their family were friends from the neighborhood, track employees, trainers, jockeys, and stablemen, plus a number of state and city elected officials, mostly from the Democratic Party.

On Saturday morning the bronze-colored casket was taken to St. Patrick's Church, where Father James Johnston conducted a simple funeral ceremony with family and over 250 friends present. Father Johnston noted that EJ "has come back now to the place [where] his father was buried" and warned, "You can't kid death, fellows. You may think this mass is for the fellow here. But it is not. It's for all of us."[9] From the church EJ was carried to Memorial Park Cemetery, where the family, led by Selma with Butch at her arm, bade farewell to husband, father, friend, and teacher. Diminished in those moments beside the grave and the high bank of flowers, all three children departed knowing that the memory of their father would sustain them in future moments of trial. Yet they walked away knowing that the sunny skies of their lives would never again be as bright.

In the more than fifty years since the deaths of EJ and Butch O'Hare, their family has endured the publication of numerous stories regarding the two. Particularly frustrating to them are the accounts based on little or no research. Even some otherwise well-researched books and articles have perpetuated undocumented—and therefore unfair—remembrances.

—In 1926 EJ O'Hare did serve several months of a year-and-a-day sentence at the federal penitentiary at Leavenworth, Kansas, after being convicted of conspiracy to violate the National Prohibition Act. Charges were filed by one George Remus, a convicted bootlegger who would later murder his wife (she was indicted along with EJ and two dozen others). Documents pertaining to the case demonstrate that EJ declined to reveal information on the grounds of attorney-client privilege. In letters sent to his wife from prison, he expressed confidence that his conviction would be overturned, and on 30 January 1926 he wrote, "Tell everyone hello for me and that this is another experience and nothing more." In fact, in September 1926 the appeals court set aside the conviction. Too often, in the family's opinion, *the successful appeal is not mentioned.* In 1939, following EJ's death, Remus sought nearly $200,000 from the estate; after losing appeal after appeal, the last in 1948 in the Illinois Supreme Court, he got nothing.

—Patsy O'Hare Palmer has stated, "I think the biggest mistake [EJ] ever made was to ask for part ownership of the dog tracks. . . . That made him a partner of Capone regardless of how he viewed it. He thought that he could run the tracks honestly and divorce himself from any association with Capone. It didn't work out that way" (Patsy O'Hare Palmer to SE, 21 Sept. 1995). EJ told his daughters, and others, that money could be made by working with gangsters, but he stressed that the association had to be strictly business. On one occasion he explained to Patsy, "I have never accepted so much as a bottle of beer from the gangsters with whom I must do business because one cannot accept anything, no matter how small, because if you do, they have you. In life you have to live with people, meet them where they are and put up with them." EJ would have been particularly upset by the claim made in one of the Capone biographies that "[EJ] enjoyed the riches [the gang] showered on him" (John Kobler, *Capone: The Life and World of Al Capone* [New York: G. P. Putnam's Sons, 1971], 236). To the contrary, EJ would have pointed to his comments to Patsy and offered the rejoinder that he brought talent, expertise, and energy to managing the tracks, thereby earning whatever money he received. His goal was not to enrich the gang. The Capone outfit ran its own betting operation and kept its own set of books. Handling the legal ticket and betting windows, EJ worked alongside the gang operation; it was the price of being in that particular business at that time.

— Chapter 3 of this work refutes the allegation that EJ entered into a deal with the Treasury Department to get Butch into the U.S. Naval Academy. When the Chicago police investigated his death, they found on his body a note from an FBI agent requesting information on a suspect. Thus, EJ had clearly continued to assist federal and local authorities in fighting crime, and by 1939 no one could say that his motives still concerned Butch at all, who after all had graduated from Annapolis in 1937. Neither did EJ, a man of means, aid law enforcement agencies with any thought of remuneration. From the available documentation it appears that EJ, by doing business with gangsters, often could not help but be well informed about their activities. As president of Sportsman's Park with longtime Capone front man Johnny Patton serving as secretary-treasurer, EJ probably learned more from Patton than any other source. According to Mrs. Palmer, EJ and Patton were close enough that EJ could converse openly with him on subjects as sensitive as Patton's marriage. The bulk of the evidence supports the argument that EJ, rather than being merely an associate of gangsters, was an entrepreneur in a high-risk business who took a stand against organized crime that cost him his life.

— Some writers have asserted that because of his father's business associations, Butch O'Hare felt a need to redeem the family honor even to the point of seeking martyrdom in battle. The O'Hare family finds this assertion ludicrous, for Butch knew his father to be a good man who lost his life fighting criminal elements. Rather than *redeem*, Butch sought to *sustain* the family honor. Like his father, Butch was a competitor and a man of courage. And like his father, Butch loved life. In his wartime letters, cited later in the text, he wrote glowingly of his excitement over being a new father and often stated how wonderful life would be when the war was over and "we will all be back together again" (Butch to Selma O'Hare, 13 Nov. 1942). These are not the words of a man who sought martyrdom.

7

Wings, Love, and War

"It doesn't matter"

Heartbroken and disconsolate, Butch returned on 25 November 1939 to Pensacola, having taken fifteen days' emergency leave for his father's funeral. On the twenty-eighth he was flying again, his daily report noting, "Refresher period after long lay-off."[1] Now in Squadron Three, Butch would spend the next three months flying the land versions of the versatile Vought 03U and SU Corsair observation/scout biplanes with top speeds of about 165 miles per hour, 40 mph faster than the trainers he had flown in Squadrons One and Two. SUs had served as first-line fleet aircraft from 1931 to 1935. Butch learned formation flying, navigation, and the rudiments of aerial gunnery.

By the end of January 1940 Butch had stepped up to the more powerful Vought SBU-1 scout bomber biplane (top speed 205 mph), a real service-type aircraft still assigned to the *Ranger* and *Wasp* air groups. He completed Squadron Three on 6 February. Ens. Cicero A. Pound, Jr., USNR, rated Butch above-average with a 3.53 on his fitness report and stated, "A highly intelligent, well balanced officer, whose flight performance has been above average. He should make an excellent pilot." Nowhere in his training records was any mention made of his recent tragedy, and nothing in his flying performance records indicates that Butch was incapable of maintaining his focus or routine. To the contrary, being busy was the best possible medicine in the cool and sometimes blustery days of the 1939–40 Florida winter.

Just as Squadron Three flying came to a close, Butch also completed Ground School, the classroom training that accounted for 40 percent of his "Final Report of Aviation Training." Subjects included aircraft engines, aircraft structure, navigation, tactics, gunnery, communications, photography, and aerology. Butch's final mark of 3.4893 gave him a standing of twenty-eighth in a class of forty-eight.

On 9 February 1940 Butch made his first flight in Squadron Four, service seaplanes, which included the lumbering "big boats." Butch was not eager to spend his aviation career with large patrol planes, and so this phase of training interested him the least of all, but there were two memorable exceptions. The first involved several catapult shots in Vought 03U-3 floatplanes, reminiscent of the *New Mexico*'s SOC Seagulls, except this time Butch was the pilot. The second occurred on 27 February, when the starboard engine of his old Martin PM-2 flying boat cut out and forced him to set down on Pensacola Bay. With only the port engine, he taxied the bulky biplane to the beach. By 9 April, Butch had completed Squadron Four. Lt. John R. Dickey, USNR, wrote, "O'Hare is pleasant, capable and very interested in his career in aviation. He appears to be unexcitable and should make a very satisfactory pilot. He is above average Aviation Pilot material, courteous and military, although a quiet type." Again Butch was rated above average, with a 3.5 on his fitness report.

On 2 April, Butch began the last training phase, Squadron Five with advanced land planes. That was why he had come to Pensacola; now he would learn the special skills of a serving naval aviator. First he completed an intensive three-week course in instrument flying in North American NJ and SNJ monoplane trainers, as well as the Link blind-flying training device. Next Butch was thrilled to take the controls of a big three-seat Douglas TBD-1 Devastator, the current fleet torpedo bomber and the fastest aircraft (207 mph) he had yet flown. Introduced in 1937 as the U.S. Navy's first carrier monoplane, the once-sleek TBD was manifestly obsolete five years later, when its brave crews would be sacrificed for victory in the Battle of Midway.

On 8 May the real fun began when Butch climbed back into an open-cockpit, fixed-landing-gear biplane, a Boeing F4B-4A fighter that had first appeared in 1932. Although about 20 mph slower than the TBD, this beautifully responsive little craft could fly circles around the larger airplane. For the next two weeks Butch used F4B-4s to practice acrobatics, advanced formation flying, and precision landings, as well as dive-bombing and aerial gunnery. In Squadron Five he recorded his best flying grades and again received an above-average mark (3.53) in his fitness report.

In his last few weeks of training at Pensacola, Butch benefited from close association with two pilots who would draw considerable acclaim for their combat leadership during World War II. Lt. (jg) William J. "Gus" Widhelm oversaw much of his instrument and night-flying training. No doubt Butch appreciated Gus even more when he learned of Widhelm's tenacity and valor at the head of the *Hornet* dive bombers in the October 1942 Battle of Santa Cruz. For his familiarization in fighters and primary combat training, Butch could not have done better than Lt. James H. Flatley, Jr., who would fight with the *Yorktown*'s VF-42 at the Battle of the Coral Sea and lead VF-10, the "Grim Reapers," from the *Enterprise* at Guadalcanal. Along with John S. Thach (whom Butch would soon meet), Jimmy Flatley and Butch O'Hare became the premier U.S. Navy fighter pilots of 1942, primarily responsible for the development of the fighter tactics that enabled the Grumman F4F Wildcat to compete successfully against the more maneuverable Japanese Zero fighter. At Pensacola, Flatley taught Butch well; as will be seen later in this narrative, Butch would repay the favor.

One who saw Butch from a perspective different from that of his instructors was fellow Pensacola trainee Lt. (jg) Willard J. Smith, who later became commandant of the U.S. Coast Guard. In his 1978 oral history Smith noted that he "got to know [Butch] pretty well and really liked and enjoyed [him] a lot." Smith described Butch's skill aloft: "We all envied him, in a sense, because an airplane was made for him or he was made for an airplane, or something or other. From the moment he stepped into an airplane, nothing went wrong. He had a touch that was unbelievable. I think he probably flew the airplanes almost as well as most of the teachers did. He was just a completely natural pilot, just tremendous."[2]

Butch completed his flight training on 27 May 1940, the date of his diploma. He had attained a final mark of 3.238 while accumulating 358.2

flight hours. On 2 May the commandant of NAS Pensacola, Capt. Albert C. Read—who commanded the NC-4 flying boat during the 1919 transatlantic flight—formally designated him as Naval Aviator (Heavier-than-Air) Number 6405, conferring on him the right to wear the coveted "wings of gold." Considering Butch's record in combat less than two years later, it is well worth noting that although he was rated above average in all his flight training, in only one category did he approach excellence. That was in fixed aerial gunnery marksmanship. All that earlier experience with BB guns, .22s, and shotguns now paid dividends in the air.

EJ would have been proud.

Meet Fighting Three

While Butch was in training at Pensacola, he was allowed to submit three choices as his preference for his next duty station. Never wavering in his fierce desire to be a naval fighter pilot, his choices were (1) Fighting Squadron Two (VF-2) on the *Lexington;* (2) VF-3 on the *Saratoga;* and (3) VF-6 on the new *Enterprise.* The Navy was not in the business of granting wishes, but in this case Butch's obvious talents earned him suitable reward. On 22 May the Bureau of Navigation cut orders assigning Ens. Edward H. O'Hare to Fighting Squadron Three, USS *Saratoga,* "for duty involving flying." He was to report by 1 July 1940 to VF-3 based at NAS San Diego.[3]

Granted twenty-six days of leave, as well as travel time, Butch set off for St. Louis with Patsy, who had stayed at Pensacola during his last six weeks of training. Arriving there the first of June, they enjoyed a good visit with their mother, Selma, before loading Butch's newest car, a 1939 Buick, for the drive to Phoenix, Arizona. (While in St. Louis the previous November for his father's funeral, Butch had noticed Marilyn coughing excessively and insisted that she see a doctor. Marilyn learned that she had respiratory problems and a weak chest; she was told to try living in a dry climate for at least six months. After EJ's death, Patsy no longer wished to remain in Chicago, and Marilyn's need for an arid climate brought both sisters west to Phoenix in January 1940.)

On the road, conversation in the Buick centered largely around the no longer "phoney war" in Europe. After months of little combat activity, Germany had overrun Denmark and Norway in April, and in May had pushed through Holland and Belgium into France. On 10 June,

Mussolini had joined in the attack on France, much to the chagrin of former Paris resident Patsy, who recounted how she had told their father that Mussolini was trouble. He had agreed with her that the war in Europe might well involve the United States. When France surrendered to Germany a few weeks later, Britain stood alone, the U.S. Congress passed the Two-Ocean Navy Act, which greatly expanded the U.S. Navy, and Butch finally awakened to the threat at hand. Patsy wondered aloud if her father's prophesy—that Butch would become an admiral if the United States ever went to war—would come true.

Rather than proceeding directly to San Diego, Butch remained in Phoenix for the last third of his leave to visit Marilyn and to attend Patsy's wedding. On 22 June, Patsy and Dr. Paul Palmer were married in St. Mary's Catholic Church. A bonus more significant than the 1939 Ford Butch gave to Patsy as a wedding present was the friendship that developed between him and Paul. Around Butch, Paul lost his shyness, and he knew shotguns and fishing rods almost as well as his new brother-in-law. To be with Patsy and Paul, Butch often arranged for cross-country flights or drove the ten hours from San Diego to Phoenix.

One of the reasons Patsy accepted Paul's proposal was that he was not in the Navy; she did not want to endure long separations. However, two years later the Navy's need for surgeons found Paul in uniform operating on wounded sailors, Marines, and soldiers in South Pacific combat zones. There he served for two long years after first having applied for duty as a flight surgeon so that he could be with Butch.

On 1 July, with bright new gold wings gleaming on his blue service coat, Butch made his way across NAS San Diego on North Island to the area allocated to the squadrons of the *Saratoga* Air Group. There he found a hangar labeled "Fighting Three." Proudly displayed above the title was one of the most famous insignias in the Navy, a mischievous black feline, the famous Felix the Cat, toting a round bomb. It showed Butch that he had reached the top level of naval aviation.

Fighting Three boasted a history as renowned as that of any U.S. naval squadron. In 1921 it was created as Combat Squadron Three, but in 1922 it became Fighting Plane Squadron Two (VF-2), intended for the *Langley* (CV-1), affectionately known as the Covered Wagon. In 1927 VF-2 was redesignated VF-6B (the *B* denoting the Battle Fleet), the first of several times it would bear that number. The next year VF-6B became VB-2B (Bombing Squadron Two) with fighter bombers that pioneered dive-bombing tactics. That was why the pilots adopted the bomb-wielding Felix insignia. In 1930 the squadron reverted to its old role and title of VF-6B, good until 1937, when a general renumbering of carrier squadrons according to their ship hull numbers produced VF-3, after the *Saratoga* (CV-3). In 1939 VF-3's expert marksmanship snared the fleet gunnery trophy, and many pilots sported the E for excellence on their aircraft. That December VF-3 took delivery of the Navy's first carrier monoplane fighter, the Brewster F2A-1, whose later overweight versions received the nickname Buffalo, seemingly as much for their declining performance as for their humpbacked appearance. However, the F2A-1 was a delight to fly, maneuverable and fast. In modern terms, VF-3 certainly was the Top Gun of its era.

Butch reported to his new commanding officer, Lt. Comdr. Warren W. Harvey. Known as Sid to his friends, Harvey had graduated from the Naval Academy in 1924 and enjoyed a wide variety of aviation duty during his long career. Well liked and respected, Harvey, according to one of his officers, "had a way of leadership that was just like a magnet." At thirty-nine he probably seemed ancient to the twenty-six-year-old ensign standing in front of him, but promotion came slow in the prewar Navy. What would now be considered rather modest rank was then far less common and more highly regarded. The rest of VF-3's experienced top brass were only slightly younger, long-suffering lieutenants: Charles H. Quinn (Annapolis class of 1926), the executive officer, and John S. Thach (Annapolis 1927), the flight officer. Little could Butch have dreamed that in less than two years he himself would be a lieutenant commander and the skipper of VF-3.[4]

Butch became the junior member of the most powerful of the social groups that made up VF-3. Accounting for nearly half the pilot complement of twenty-one, Naval Academy graduates ran the squadron administrative apparatus and led all flight formations aloft. To them Butch was another member of the club. The rest of the pilots were all ensigns in the Naval Reserve, who came from the aviation cadet program begun in 1935. They joined the Navy for three years of active duty solely in order to fly. Sometimes they felt like second-class citizens, and with justification. Until mid-1939 they were not even commissioned officers, still just aviation cadets, who ranked in limbo between ensigns and warrant officers. (The naval aviation pilots, or NAPs, all enlisted men, had it even worse than the AvCads, but none served in VF-3.) To the proud AvCads, the most senior of whom had accrued considerable flying experience, Butch was just another arrogant "ring knocker" from the Annapolis "trade school," until he showed he was different.[5]

Proving himself worthy of the first team was Butch's initial task in VF-3. The only way to do that was to fly and fly even more. Production difficulties prevented VF-3 from receiving enough Brewster F2A-1s to go around—they got only ten instead of the required eighteen—so he was assigned one of the nine Grumman F3F-1 biplane fighters that VF-3 had retained. Beginning on 2 July, Butch undertook an arduous schedule of training flights that included gunnery, tactics, field carrier landing practice, the actual carrier landing qualification, and night-flying hops.[6]

On 24 July, Butch enjoyed the excitement and pride of his first carrier landing ("the most thrilling action sight there is in peacetime") on the huge *Saratoga* at sea off San Diego. She was one of the ships he had dreamed about as a youth. At nearly nine hundred feet the world's longest warship, the *Sara*, along with her sister the *Lexington* (CV-2), was a hybrid originally designed as a battle cruiser. On both sides of her island and massive stack—which bore a wide black vertical line to distinguish her from the *Lex*—were pairs of 8-inch gun turrets that seemed incongruous adjacent to a flight deck full of aircraft.[7]

Two days later Butch graduated to the F2A-1, whose top speed of 301 mph made it by far the fastest aircraft he had flown to date. For Butch, July 1940 brought the most monthly flight hours in what would become three-plus years in the squadron, but the hard work paid off with his gradual acceptance as a full-fledged member of VF-3.

Soon after joining the squadron, Butch fell under the watchful eye of the tall flight officer with the soft southern drawl. In turn, Lt. John Thach would himself be surprised by the quiet, affable new ensign. In an obscure joke, Thach's Annapolis classmates had dubbed him Jimmy, after his older brother James, who graduated in 1923, the year John became a plebe. The incongruous nickname stuck, to the bane of careless historians, who definitely need to take notice of Jimmy Thach. He became one of the Navy's outstanding pilots, a leader with the rare gift of being a true innovator.

In a fighter pilot Thach especially admired two attributes: flying ability and a strong "competitive spirit." To see how his newcomers stacked up in those areas, Thach developed the concept of the "bitching team," or, more politely, the "humiliation team." Thach found that a freshly minted naval aviator often was "rather full of himself and sometimes a little cocky." Self-confidence in fighter pilots was a good thing, but not to the extent that they thought they had nothing new to learn. Thach liked to take a rookie out for a dogfight just between the two of them. Long experience had shown that all things being equal, namely ability and seasoning, the pilot with altitude advantage almost always slipped onto his opponent's tail and could not be shaken. Thach would give the greenie plenty of height and wait for him to come on down. Then Thach would calmly read a newspaper or munch on an apple and use his opponent's blunders to win the twisting duel.

Thach got around to playing his game with Butch, only with unexpected results. This day up over North Island it was the rookie who "didn't make any mistakes," Thach related. "I did everything I could to fool him and shake him, and he came right in on me and stuck there, and he could have shot me right out of the air." No novice had ever beat him before. Highly impressed, Thach spoke to Ens. Rolla S. Lemmon, one of the best of the AvCads, and bet him the rookie would triumph over him, too. "Oh, they never do," Lemmon replied and took the wager. After Thach collected his money, he added Butch to the bitching team.

Of all the naval officers who served with Butch, Jimmy Thach best knew his ability in the air. He noted that when Butch began flying, he learned how to do it properly: "He got the most out of his airplane. He didn't try to horse it around. He learned a thing that a lot of youngsters don't learn[:] that when you're in a dogfight with somebody, it isn't how hard you pull back on the stick to make a tight turn to get inside of him, it's how smoothly you fly the plane." In the complex gunnery runs that only U.S. naval aviators were trained to do, Butch especially profited from the acute "sense of timing and relative motion that he may have been born with." In Thach's opinion, not only did Butch have the tools to excel as a fighter pilot, he also possessed the spirit to prevail at all cost: "He really had a dedication to winning, and he probably had worked a lot of this out in his mind." Thach remembered how during the first month Butch flew with VF-3, he devoured everything available on aerial combat doctrine. Even more important, he understood what he read and translated it into action. According to Thach, Butch "just picked it up faster than anyone else I've ever seen." Flying with pilots the caliber of a Jimmy Thach only sharpened Butch's impressive skills.[8]

Settling In

During the summer of 1940, while the German Luftwaffe challenged the Royal Air Force over the skies of Britain, Butch took his place in the normal VF-3 flight schedule at North Island. He started as a wingman, one of a pair who flew on either wing of their section leader. Three three-plane sections made up a division, and the two nine-plane divisions made up the flight echelon of the squadron. Butch looked forward to the day when he would have the seniority and experience to lead his own section. His ground job was assistant engineering officer.

In Butch's first days with VF-3, he bunked in the Bachelor Officers' Quarters (BOQ), but soon after, he moved in with academy friend Nick Nicholson and his wife, Dorothy. Never much of a loner, Butch was highly pleased with the arrangement. For the next several months deployments at sea on the *Saratoga* were infrequent and of short duration. Therefore Butch enjoyed free time ashore away from base. His routine became flying, fishing, hunting, and just enjoying life. Paul, Patsy, and Marilyn were only about a ten-hour drive away in Phoenix. One high point of that grand summer occurred on 28 August, when Butch learned of his promotion to lieutenant (junior grade) to date from 3 June 1940.

That September VF-3 took delivery of its first Brewster F2A-2s, which allowed the squadron to relinquish the last F3F-1 biplanes. An improved version of the F2A-1 with a more powerful 1,200-hp engine, the F2A-2 had a top speed of 323 mph at 16,500 feet, 90 mph faster than the F3F-1. The heavier weight on essentially the same airframe, however, caused a rash of landing-gear failures. In November, Butch got to fly an F2A-1 cross-country to Newark and brought back a freshly minted F2A-2 to San Diego.

In December 1940 Lieutenant Commander Harvey departed VF-3 for a coveted temporary assignment as aviation observer with the Royal Air Force in Britain. He left Lieutenant Thach, who had become executive officer in October, in command. Some months later Harvey was to return to VF-3, while Thach himself went to England. After that Thach would presumably go to another squadron either as XO or CO to help spread the word. But tragically, on 12 December during a stopover in Washington, Warren Harvey died from a heart attack. Thach considered him "one of the finest naval officers I had ever known."[9]

To Thach's surprise, he retained command of VF-3 despite his lack of seniority. He was one of the first members of the class of 1927 to have his own squadron. Flamboyant but cordial, resolute but fair, Jimmy Thach was a spectacular fighter skipper, well liked and respected by his men. He recognized and encouraged the talent in Butch, but he never played favorites. One of Butch's squadron mates, Lt. (jg) Noel A. M.

Gayler (Annapolis class of 1935, later an admiral and commander in chief, Pacific), described Thach as "almost a father figure" who rewarded his pilots by carefully giving them increased responsibility. The continued presence of Thach as Butch's senior officer would have a profound influence on Butch's career.[10]

In January 1941 a new XO reported to VF-3, Lt. Donald A. Lovelace (Annapolis class of 1928). He and Thach worked extremely well together. Although Lovelace operated somewhat in the shadow of his more colorful skipper, his quiet professionalism and evident skill contributed strongly to the excellence of VF-3. He and Butch got along particularly well. In the morning Butch would drive by the Lovelace residence to pick up Don on the way to North Island. Occasionally Don's elementary-school-age son, Don junior, would pile into the back for a ride to school. Fifty years later Don Lovelace, Jr., recalls those days fondly, remembering Butch as a family friend, and how he enjoyed riding in the rumble seat of the Model A roadster "jalopy" that served as backup for the Buick often used by Nick and Dorothy Nicholson. Fortunately Don junior was not riding in the Model A the time the brakes failed while Nick was at the wheel. As Nick sped involuntarily through lighted intersections, he wondered aloud how VF-3's engineering officer could pay so little attention to the brakes of his own car.[11]

Butch's "best friend" and constant traveling companion in San Diego was his dog, Penny. Butch obtained an official identification card for Penny, photograph and all, that allowed "Master O'Hare, Jr., ID #00, to pass to All Telephone Poles and Fire Hydrants for Nature Calls." The pass to U.S. Naval Air Station San Diego, California, carried an expiration date of 31 February 1910 and was dutifully signed by the assistant executive officer, "I. P. Freely," whose name, strangely enough, fails to appear in the Naval Register.

Butch was popular within the squadron but developed no especially close friendships, even among fellow Naval Academy graduates. Gayler noted that he was "not aloof but liked his own company." Butch was equally welcome in all of the social groups that made up VF-3. O. B. "Burt" Stanley, Jr., one of the senior VF-3 AvCads, described him as a "prince of a guy" who was "liked and admired" within VF-3, particularly for his calm and levelheaded flying, superb marksmanship, and unaffected modesty. His friends knew something about the circumstances of EJ's murder, but in deference to Butch the subject was never discussed.[12]

On occasion Butch brought a friend with him on his regular visits to his sisters in Phoenix. He kept close tabs on Patsy because she was expecting her first child. A daughter, also named Patsy, was born in March 1941. In the meantime, on 20 February, while Butch was flying from the *Saratoga* during a short deployment off the West Coast, Marilyn eloped with Philip Edward Tovrea, Jr. Although Phil Tovrea was a rancher at the time of his marriage to Marilyn, he joined the Army after Pearl Harbor, trained as a pilot, and ended the war an ace with eight confirmed kills, all German fighters. Unfortunately Butch had little time to get to know him before the war separated them even more. One of their best moments together, however, occurred on 11 April 1943 when Butch flew from San Diego to Phil's training base near Los Angeles to give him an "orientation" ride. In fact, he picked Phil up to carry him back to San Diego for a family reunion.

To Hawaii on the "*Big E*"

Since spring 1940 the majority of the U.S. Battle Fleet had operated from Pearl Harbor on Oahu in the Territory of Hawaii. President Franklin Roosevelt believed that keeping the fleet there rather than in its customary West Coast anchorages served as a greater deterrent to Imperial Japan's ambitions in East Asia. A disagreement over whether the fleet would be secure in Hawaii cost the commander, Adm. James O. Richardson, his job. On 1 February 1941 Adm. Husband E. Kimmel took over the newly created Pacific Fleet and inherited all the problems of maintaining fleet readiness at Pearl.

So far in his naval career Butch had not made it to exotic Hawaii. The *New Mexico* never sailed there while he was on board, then VF-3 was too busy working up the new Brewster fighters to go to sea, and by early 1941 the *Saratoga* was scheduled for modernization at the Bremerton Navy Yard in Puget Sound. Finally in April 1941 the opportunity came, when VF-3 received orders to deploy to the *Enterprise*. VF-6 from the *Enterprise*'s own air group was to go ashore to exchange their Grumman F3F-2 biplanes for the latest Grumman F4F-3A Wildcat fighters. On 9 April the *Saratoga* Air Group flew out from North Island for a short shakedown on the *Enterprise*, and Butch made his first landing on the "*Big E*." Without doubt he recalled how in the spring of 1939 he had thought of someday flying from this beautiful new flattop.

By coincidence, a Warner Brothers crew was on board the *Enterprise* filming landings and takeoffs for a motion picture entitled *Dive Bomber*. It starred Errol Flynn, Ralph Bellamy, and Fred MacMurray. For the past several weeks the movie company had been filming extensively at North Island and on the *Enterprise*. Butch had been around the filming of Hollywood movies at the academy, so this was nothing new. What he could not know at the time was that this picture, despite its melodramatic plot, would become a cult classic among naval aviation buffs because it captured in vivid Technicolor a now far-distant era. Not only does the *Enterprise* display her prewar white hull and maroon deck, but TBD Devastators, SB2U Vindicators, and other carrier aircraft from both the *Saratoga* and *Enterprise* air groups strut in their elaborate multicolored 1940 paint schemes. Even while the movie was being made, their brilliant plumage was painted over with a coat of light gray to provide some protective camouflage in anticipation of wartime conditions. Although it would be a strain to find which F2A-2 belonged to Butch on 9 April, he no doubt made faces into the camera from his cockpit as he awaited the signal to lift off CV-6's flight deck and fly back to San Diego.[13]

On 21 April, Butch went back on board the *Enterprise* for the voyage to Hawaii. She was the flagship of Vice Adm. William F. Halsey, Jr., commander, Aircraft, Battle Force, the Navy's senior carrier admiral. On 27 April the *Enterprise* Air Group flew to Ford Island in the center of Pearl Harbor. Soon after she left for a quick round-trip to San Diego and back.

For VF-3 the stay on beautiful Oahu proved extremely frustrating because of problems with the temperamental F2A-2s. In addition to the always troublesome landing gear, there was an unexpected glitch in the Wright R-1820-40 Cyclone radial engines that often caused crippling damage to the master rod bearings, particularly on high-altitude flights. Now as engineering officer, Butch sweated over the extensive disassembly required for each ailing powerplant. Determined to learn where the trouble came from, Noel Gayler, Butch, and an engineering chief, Clarence J. Williams, aviation chief machinist's mate, fitted various oil temperature and pressure gauges onto the engine of an F2A-2. On one occasion Butch took the Brewster aloft only to have the engine freeze. One of the striker mechanics, Clyde E. Baur, seaman second class (and later also a chief in VF-3), related what happened: "O'Hare nosed the plane straight down. He made two complete circles of the airfield in his dive and made a perfect dead-stick landing. All in a day's work." The

VF-3 brain trust traced the engine failures to improper oil seals supplied by the Bureau of Aeronautics. Butch thought highly of "Willie" Williams, later leading chief with VF-3.[14]

Scheduled to return to the *Enterprise* on 20 May, Thach could bring out only half his fifteen F2As, and that portion was hardly ready for more tactical exercises. On the twenty-fourth he raised his concerns directly with a sympathetic Halsey. Both the VF-3 rookies and the pros desperately needed to practice gunnery and other basic skills. Thach confessed, "I'm not even sure I could hit anything." That same day Halsey canceled VF-3's deployment and sent the squadron back to Ford Island for independent training.[15]

Thach spent the rest of May and most of June restoring combat-readiness to VF-3. Everyone in the squadron worked twelve-hour days. To bring back their shooting eye and hone their teamwork, the pilots flew numerous gunnery and tactical flights, including night operations that made a special impression on Butch. Acute shortages of .50-caliber machine-gun ammunition were alleviated only by the pilfering of bullets from neighboring VF-2. Even so, on their gunnery runs the pilots qualified by firing only one round from one gun instead of a burst of twelve. That certainly taught them to conserve ammunition, an ability that paid great dividends for Butch. Even more important, more than half the pilots, including Butch, earned the E for gunnery excellence proudly displayed on their assigned aircraft.

Tired but proud of its efforts, the squadron left Pearl on 25 June on the *Saratoga* bound for San Diego. Almost as a farewell present, Halsey finally acceded to the wishes of his fighting squadrons and decreed a new basic flight formation of two-plane sections, leader and wingman, in place of the much more cumbersome three-plane sections.[16]

Rita

In July 1941 Butch experienced one of the most interesting two-week periods of his life. For the second time he took a welcome break from his squadron to ferry aircraft to and from the East Coast. Leaving San Diego on 15 July, he and a passenger, Lt. Comdr. Elliott W. Shanklin from the cruiser *Portland* (CA-33), flew across the Southwest in the land version of the Curtiss SOC-3 Seagull. After dropping Shanklin off at Dallas, Butch continued to Norfolk. There on the eighteenth he delivered the plane and evidently rode a train to New York. On Saturday the nineteenth he reached Floyd Bennett Field, where he expected to pick up a new Grumman F4F-3 Wildcat fighter to bring back to San Diego, but he was told that the aircraft would not be available until Monday.

On Sunday, with nothing else to do but wait, Butch introduced himself to another Navy pilot in the same predicament, Lt. (jg) James W. Condit from Torpedo Squadron Five (VT-5) on the carrier *Yorktown* (CV-5). Butch suggested that the two travel over to Coney Island to pass the day, and they were off to enjoy the rides and attractions. One of the first they saw was the parachute jump from a high tower. Deciding that this activity looked "too dangerous," they continued on. Later they happened to pass the parachute jump again just as an elderly couple were completing their descent. Seeing the two naval aviators in uniform, they proudly announced to Butch and Jim that "they were through and the 'sailors' could have it now." So shamed, the two pilots made the jump and afterward decided that it was more fun than perilous. Two years later "Pop" Condit and Butch would fly into combat over Marcus Island. Butch would return to his carrier, but Pop would be shot down and spend the rest of the war as a prisoner of war.[17]

On Monday morning, 21 July, Butch climbed into the cockpit of a Wildcat for the first time. After a familiarization flight, he was back in the air bound for San Diego. Following stops in Washington and Dayton, Ohio, he landed in St. Louis late Tuesday afternoon to spend the night with his mother. Reaching home, he learned that Christine Goltermann, Bob's wife, had just given birth. Off to the hospital to pay his respects to the new parents, Butch got much more than he expected.

During his first few seconds in the hospital room, Butch's attention was directed to Christine, but he then noticed another woman, petite and beautiful, in the room. Sitting quietly was Rita Wooster, formerly of Muscatine, Iowa. Christine and Rita were good friends, both of them nurses at the hospital. Butch conversed with Christine, but he was having trouble focusing on her instead of the other nurse in the room. Even Rita noticed that Butch could not seem to keep his eyes on Christine as he continued to talk to her. After he asked Christine for the fifth time how she was, it became apparent that his best wishes might be with her, but his mind was not.

Having already offered a brief smile upon being introduced, Rita now began to feel a little uncomfortable, glancing sideways at Butch without moving her head. Somewhat nervously, she gently played fingers through the ends of her hair. Finally she moved ever so slightly, to tug her skirt down even though it was already as far down as it would go. Excusing herself, she left the room for a minute.

Easily reading Butch's face and actions, Christine told him, "Butch, I have good news and bad news for you." He told her to tell him the bad news; he had already seen what was good. "She is single, but she has just recently broken up with someone, and she may not be ready to start another relationship."

"It doesn't matter," replied Butch.

There was no question in his mind how he felt; all his circuits were alive; he felt great; he felt so good it hurt. It had to be love.

Returning to the room, Rita announced that it had been a long day and she needed to leave. Butch asked if he could drive her home. Christine agreed that this was a good idea. Arriving at their destination after a short drive, Butch apologized to Rita for what he was about to say, prefacing it with the statement that he had to fly out of St. Louis the following morning and did not want to say goodbye without letting her know exactly what he was thinking and what his intentions were.

He then asked Rita to marry him.

Rita reminded Butch that they had just met. Butch replied, "It doesn't matter."

Rita responded that she was several years younger.

"It doesn't matter."

Rita observed that certainly he could not expect her to say she loved him on the basis of knowing him for only a few minutes.

"It doesn't matter."

Rita noted that Butch was not Catholic and stated that she could only marry a Catholic.

"It doesn't matter, and I'll take instruction to convert."

Rita then told Butch he was making a lifetime decision off the cuff. Butch, gently but directly and with obvious sincerity, informed her that he did not have the time to pursue her in a more conventional manner. His schedule and responsibilities, along with the worsening international situation, left him no other course of action. He knew how he felt, he understood commitment, he did want to marry her—and that's all that *did* matter!

The next morning Butch was back in his Wildcat, setting down in Tulsa, Dallas, Midland, and El Paso for fuel. Leaving El Paso on the morning of the twenty-fourth bound for Phoenix, he happened to fly with an enlisted pilot (one of the NAPs) ferrying another Wildcat to San Diego. He was Joseph E. A. Wedder, aviation machinist's mate first class, from VF-2. Over the New Mexico–Arizona border, Butch lost contact with Wedder and could not find him. After landing at Phoenix he learned that an aircraft had crashed at Sacaton, about thirty miles south of there, and got a ride out to the crash site. There he found that Wedder had died instantly. He informed the authorities in San Diego and was told to remain in the area to assist both Navy and civilian interests. Investigators learned that Wedder had evidently got lost and landed far to the south at Nogales, where he was unable to find 100-octane gasoline. Even so, he tried to make Phoenix with the fuel that remained, unaware that the fuel gauge was defective. The F4F ran out of gas, and Wedder stalled while trying to reach level ground. After five days in Phoenix handling Navy business, Butch was ordered on to San Diego, arriving on 29 July.[18]

For the next six weeks Butch drove from San Diego to Arizona on weekends to take instruction in Roman Catholicism. On Saturday, 6 September 1941, only six weeks after their first meeting, Butch and Rita were married in St. Mary's Catholic Church in Phoenix. The event was also a high moment for Paul and Patsy Palmer, Paul standing in as best man for Butch, and Patsy hosting the postwedding meal at the Palmer residence. Patsy was also pleased that Rita had elected to wear the same wedding dress Patsy had worn for her own wedding only fifteen months earlier.

The newlyweds had very little time for a honeymoon. Butch had flown on the fourth, and on the eighth he was back in the air. The newspaper photograph of Butch and Rita, he in his white uniform and she in her wedding dress, was captioned "Off to Hawaii Today on Honeymoon." Some honeymoon! Butch sailed on board the *Saratoga,* and Rita booked passage on the Matson liner *Lurline.* Placed in a stateroom with three other women, all quite attractive, Rita learned that the three were "ladies of the night." Admiring her beauty, the trio invited her to join the profession. With more grace than required for such an invitation, Rita declined. Fortunately there was an opportunity for another honeymoon, this one at Big Bear Lake, California. There Butch and Rita succeeded in getting farther away from the world than had been possible on the Hawaiian trip. At Big Bear Lake they could forget the war that seemed to be coming, a conflict that would, as it did for so many, change their lives forever.

"It Really Works"

In July 1941, when Butch and Rita first met in St. Louis, key events were set in motion that ultimately brought war to the Pacific. The Japanese ousted the Vichy French from southern Indochina, from where they could directly threaten Singapore and the Dutch East Indies. President Roosevelt immediately declared an oil embargo and froze Japanese assets in the United States. Japan's secret response was to begin serious planning for war against the United States and Britain.

During August, between Butch's weekend trips to Arizona, VF-3 completed an extensive regime of instrument training in North American SNJ-3 advanced trainers. Afterward the squadron happily divested itself of the troublesome F2A-2s and on the twenty-second took delivery of its first F4F-3 Wildcats. The rugged Grumman had a respectable top speed (331 mph) as well as decent climb and maneuverability. Unfortunately Thach again could not get enough fighters for the whole squadron. In the meantime he prepared for another deployment back to Hawaii, this time on the *Saratoga,* which had completed her modifications at Bremerton.

On Monday, 8 September, two days after being married, Butch flew out to the *Sara* along with the rest of the air group. VF-3 spent the next six weeks in tactical exercises either from the *Saratoga* or over Hawaii before starting back on 22 October for the West Coast. Almost inevitably, the "*Sister Sara*" was due for another stint in dry dock at Bremerton. As usual, critical shortages in aircraft and matériel greatly hindered VF-3's combat-readiness. On 30 October, Admiral Halsey complained to Washington that VF-3 possessed only six F4F-3s, although its authorized strength was twenty-three (eighteen plus five spares). Should the necessary seventeen F4F-3s not be forthcoming, Halsey threatened, he would replace them with the latest (and worst) version of the Brewster Buffalo, the F2A-3. The war rendered the whole question academic.[19]

When they reassembled in early November 1941 at San Diego, VF-3's situation was, to use Thach's word, "deplorable." On only one occasion in the last year had he been able to put up as many as eighteen planes. Now reinforcements only trickled in from the East Coast, evidently because of a labor strike against the makers of the propellers. Even the handful of Wildcats he had were lacking their gun sights, not to mention

pilot armor and self-sealing fuel tanks. Thach understood the real reason for this neglect: the Navy high command did not consider the Pacific
Fleet to be, in his words, the "first team." Following the basic strategy
of supporting Great Britain, top priority in everything favored the
Atlantic Fleet, battling German U-boats in an undeclared war.[20]

Although neither the president nor the Navy brass took the
Japanese threat very seriously, Thach certainly did. He happened to see
a report published in the 22 September 1941 Fleet Air Tactical Unit
Intelligence Bulletin that thoroughly shocked him. It described a new
Japanese carrier fighter called the Zero, reputed to have remarkable
performance: top speed between 345 and 380 mph and an armament
of two 20-mm cannons and two 7.7-mm machine guns. Other reports
that Thach may have seen warned of the Zero's incredible maneuverability and high climb rate. He thought the reports might be exagger-
ated, but he could not afford to ignore the possibility that he might
have to face an opponent that could outperform the Grumman F4F-3
Wildcats just received.

Working at night with matchsticks on the table of his home in
Coronado, Thach evolved a lookout doctrine in which two pairs of
fighters flew abreast and watched each other's tails. The configuration
permitted them to evade and counterattack enemy fighters no matter
how they came in. Thach called on Butch, who led the second section in
his division, to test the idea. He took the role of defender and wired the
throttles of four Wildcats so that they could not attain full power. Butch,
meanwhile, led four attackers with performance unhindered. Trying a
series of simulated attacks, Butch found that in every instance Thach's
slower fighters had either ruined his attack or actually maneuvered into
position to shoot back.

After landing, Butch excitedly congratulated Thach:

"Skipper, it really worked. It really works. I couldn't make any attack
without seeing the nose of one of your half-throttle airplanes pointed at
me." He found the exact timing of Thach's countermoves to be uncanny.
With Butch's help, Thach had created a totally new mutual defensive
tactic for fighters that offset the advantage of a superior opponent. He
called it the beam defense position, but it soon would become famous as
the Thach weave.[21]

Despite all the frustrations of balky fighters or insufficient numbers
of good ones, Thach knew that his strength lay in superb pilots: "I was
fortunate in having had with me, more or less intact, the same fighting

team for a year or more. We had developed teamwork tactics to a point where every pilot knew what the other pilots were going to do, and very few signals were needed in the air. We had a fighting machine." Sooner than Thach realized, his "fighting machine" would be tested in battle.[22]

The Day of Infamy

At 0800 on 7 December 1941, all *Saratoga* Air Group personnel turned out for a rare Sunday work session in the hangars at North Island. The entire base bustled with activity as squadrons completed packing their baggage and loaded their gear onto trucks. The *Sara* was expected that afternoon after her recent refit at Bremerton, and the air group would embark in less than twenty-four hours for a swift voyage to Hawaii. One hundred planes waited to "waddle down" to the dockside and be hoisted on board. Included among their numbers was Maj. Verne J. McCaul's Marine Fighting Squadron 221 (VMF-221) with fourteen F2A-3 Buffaloes. Unfortunately VF-3 could count only nine F4F Wildcats, half-strength for a naval fighting squadron.

Thach released several VF-3 pilots to eat lunch off the base. In the meantime, the *Saratoga* slid into her berth at North Island. Butch was driving home to be with Rita in their apartment in Coronado when the car radio announced shocking news. As he came through the door, he turned to Rita and said, "The Japanese have attacked Pearl Harbor: we are to board *Saratoga* as soon as possible. It's war!"

That afternoon, with the *Saratoga* now on a war footing, the order of loading was changed, with VF-3 now scheduled last. After ground crews loaded the nine flyable Wildcats with fuel and ammunition, the pilots dispersed them around the field. As VF-3 engineering officer, Butch helped evaluate four other F4Fs undergoing major overhaul on the base and decided that his mechanics could finish two of them on board the carrier. That gave Thach eleven Wildcats: eight F4F-3s, two F4F-3As (an export version of the F4F-3 with slightly less performance), and the XF4F-4 (an F4F-3 rebuilt to test folding wings). Two Army pursuit squadrons went on alert to cover North Island. Later the VF-3 pilots and their wives gathered in their ready room on the base, as the squadron belted more ammunition; Rita and Butch were not the only couple that had married in the past few months. The disbelief had worn off, and now the pilots felt a burning desire to get at the enemy. Around midnight

Butch went home. The *Sara* loaded the last of the 103 planes at 0300 and made ready to sail.

By 0700 the VF-3 pilots had reassembled on North Island. "There were smiles, tears, cheers of encouragement as officers and men left their wives and children on the dock" to board the *Saratoga*. At 0910 she got under way and eased through the channel past Point Loma and out into the Pacific bound for Pearl. Butch was on his way to war.[23]

8

Four Minutes over the *Lady Lex*

"Opportunity, technique, and guts"

Not until Sunday, 14 December 1941, when Butch O'Hare and nine other VF-3 pilots set down at NAS Kaneohe Bay on the northeastern shore of Oahu, did he experience a true sense of being at war.[1] The previous week had seen the *Saratoga* rush from San Diego on a strange, jittery voyage marked by wild rumors, such as a Japanese carrier lurking off Monterey, and dashed hopes for retaliatory combat. Prior to entering Pearl Harbor the *Saratoga* dispatched most of her planes to cover her approach and be ready to fly from land bases should the enemy return while she was in port.

When Butch last stopped there that fall, Kaneohe had been an efficient, bustling base for patrol squadrons flying Consolidated PBY Catalina flying boats, as well as a comfortable haven for carrier air groups roosting away from their flattops. Now the most prominent landmark was a stack of "burned and bombed" PBYs, courtesy of a shellacking by enemy carrier bombers and fighters. Once Butch landed, closer inspection revealed burned-out hangars, shattered glass, and bullet-scarred walls. If the scene was bleak, the welcome for the *Saratoga* flyers proved warm. Friends and strangers crowded around to tell their stories of the infamous seventh of December. Butch ate a hasty lunch, then unexpectedly received orders to fly back out to the *Sara*, because her entrance into Pearl was delayed.[2]

The Weeks of Futility

The next morning Butch rode the *Saratoga* past devastated Battleship Row to her berth off Ford Island. It was a sobering experience to see where two thousand shipmates had fought and died. As Burt Stanley wrote, "The wreckage about Pearl Harbor was all that we had feared." Wounded battlewagons rested in the mud, the capsized *Oklahoma* (BB-37) and *Utah* (AG-16) showed their bottoms, and the forsaken *Arizona* (BB-39) still smoldered. Jimmy Thach recalled his surprise at the expressions on the faces of onlookers on the dock: "Every one of them looked like they were frightened. They'd been through a pretty harrowing experience and were pretty well shaken. We didn't really feel this way at all. Of course, we [hadn't been] there and we were just mad because we wanted to get out and catch those people that did that to Pearl Harbor." Noel Gayler later remembered that in addition to the eagerness to fight, VF-3 felt "absolute confidence that we were going to win."[3]

Thach and Butch left the ship to round up some more fighters and necessary spare parts. The bad news was that the fleet pool could provide only two Wildcats, giving VF-3 a total of thirteen (ten F4F-3s, two F4F-3As, and one XF4F-4). The good news was that for once, parsimonious supply officers opened their storerooms to fill every request they could. Even so, it took some "midnight requisitioning" by Chief Willie Williams and his mechs to get the last of the parts Butch needed.[4]

All throughout 15 December and well into the next day the *Saratoga* frantically off-loaded her cargo and took on supplies. After flying ashore, VMF-221's Buffaloes got hoisted right back on board. VF-3 slept on the *Sara*, then reported back to Ford Island before dawn on the sixteenth. Aside from final preparations prior to sailing, Thach needed to carrier-qualify three pilots and wanted to give them some field carrier landing practice before they tried the real thing later on the *Saratoga*. To the dismay of their elders, two of the three rookies ground-looped their mounts and scraped their wing tips—easy to do in the tricky Wildcats. After hurried consultation with Gayler, Butch, and the senior chiefs,

Thach decided to fix one F4F right on the field and hoist the other on board the *Sara*. They only just made it before Butch and his crew had to report on board. The *Saratoga* and her escorts got under way just after 1200. Don Lovelace brought the other F4Fs out to the ship and landed without incident. The *Saratoga* Air Group comprised sixty-seven aircraft—thirteen VF-3 Wildcats, forty-three Douglas SBD-3 Dauntless dive bombers (flown by the group commander, Bombing Squadron Three, and Scouting Squadron Three), and Torpedo Squadron Three's eleven TBD-1 Devastators—plus the fourteen Marine F2A-3 Buffaloes of VMF-221.

Once clear of Pearl, Task Force Fourteen steamed west with the *Saratoga*, three heavy cruisers, a seaplane tender crammed with Marines, a fleet oiler—one of the oldest and slowest in the fleet—and nine destroyers. Butch and his fellow pilots were quite curious as to where they were going. On the seventeenth a large map of the Pacific appeared in the *Sara*'s wardroom, with Wake Island, two thousand miles to the west, marked in red crayon. Butch would not have desired any other destination. The whole nation took great pride in the spirited defense of Wake Island, almost the only bright spot in the gloom of the past ten days. Now the *Saratoga* would break through the ring of besiegers and on Christmas Eve deliver vital reinforcements. Once within range, the Marine fighters and possibly some of the Navy dive bombers were to fly to Wake while VF-3 protected the task force.[5]

Seemingly not worried that VF-3 numbered only thirteen fighters, one of them a prototype ostensibly on board only for tests, Butch and his fellow pilots felt quite satisfied with the plan as they knew it. They were eager to use all the fighter tactics so carefully practiced during peacetime, and they joshed about "light bulbs" (tracer bullets) while counting the number of "bombing days" left before Christmas.[6]

The actual situation facing the task force commander, Rear Adm. Frank Jack Fletcher, Butch's former CO in the *New Mexico*, proved far more complicated than Butch and others realized. He could advance no faster than 12 knots, the speed of his slowest vessel, the oiler *Neches* (AO-5). The morning of 21 December, as TF-14 plodded westward across the date line, the Japanese introduced a new factor into the equation. Up to this point only their land-based bombers, operating from distant bases in the Marshalls, had attacked Wake. Now their carrier planes struck the island, demonstrating that at least one enemy flattop was lurking nearby. Fletcher's superiors in Washington and at Pearl considered whether he might possibly have to fight a major battle just to get to Wake.

On the morning of 22 December, when the ships had closed to about 520 miles northeast of Wake, Butch got his first chance to fly since reaching Pearl. Rough seas washed over the *Sara*'s plunging bow and greatly hindered the oiler's efforts to refuel the destroyers. Lovelace's six VF-3 F4Fs handled the early-morning combat air patrol (CAP), with Thach's half-dozen fighters set to relieve them. Around 1015 the squawk box summoned the First Division onto the flight deck to man planes. Butch led the second section. Taking off into a stiff wind, Thach's division climbed toward patrol altitude, but suddenly Lt. (jg) Victor M. Gadrow, the skipper's wingman, experienced engine trouble. To maintain radio silence, Thach turned the lead over to Butch and raced back to the *Sara* to warn her that one of his planes needed to land back on board immediately. Gadrow followed in his failing Wildcat but barely got within a mile of the carrier before he stalled and went down. The F4F sank immediately in the turbulent seas. Vic Gadrow was VF-3's first wartime loss. Although he graduated from Annapolis two years ahead of Butch, he was a latecomer to aviation, having earned his wings in the spring of 1941. Like Butch, he had married only a few months before the war broke out.

The dawn of 23 December found the task force within 450 miles of Wake, still too far away to support the island. Despite fueling delays, Fletcher expected to effect the relief as scheduled the next day. However, the Japanese invasion force had already landed troops on Wake. Warning of that dire development reached the task force at 0753, followed two minutes later by a recall order from Pearl Harbor. Reaction on the *Saratoga*'s bridge was immediate and acrid. Thach, among others, believed that the Japanese had only "one small carrier," which the *Sara* could easily destroy. (Actually, two carriers, the *Sōryū* and *Hiryū*, whose seasoned air groups outmatched the *Sara*'s, were prowling west of Wake.) He was not the only officer to approach Rear Adm. Aubrey W. Fitch, the air task group commander, and recommend that the advance continue. Fitch later recorded that he had to leave the flag bridge because of "mutinous" talk. He knew that Fletcher, whose flagship was the heavy cruiser *Astoria* (CA-34), had no choice but to obey the order and withdraw. No doubt a bitterly disappointed Butch joined in the general cussing. Because of the failure to relieve or avenge Wake, one disgusted *Enterprise* pilot dubbed the proceedings the "war between the two yellow races."[7]

Before the *Saratoga* could even conduct a memorial service for Gadrow, Butch witnessed another tragedy that for him helped to personalize the war. During the forenoon of the twenty-third Lt. (jg) Harold D. Shrider of Scouting Squadron Three (VS-3), one of his Annapolis classmates, died when his SBD failed to gain flying speed and splashed just ahead of the carrier, whose bow brushed its outstretched wing.

On the voyage back to Pearl, the *Saratoga* flew the VMF-221 Buffalo fighters off to Midway Island, where they would meet their tragic end in June. The irrepressible Noel Gayler, eager to keep the VF-3 pilots combat-ready, intensely lobbied both Thach and Capt. Archibald H. Douglas, the *Saratoga*'s CO, for permission to fly a gunnery training mission and drop the sleeve on board so that individual scores could be assessed. The actual exercises went well on 27 December, but when Gayler tried to deliver the sleeve he was towing, he dragged it over six aircraft parked on the flight deck. The next day Butch joined the merriment when the squadron summoned Gayler to a ceremony on deck where they presented him with a large cardboard rising-sun medal for becoming a Japanese ace.[8]

Along with the rest of VF-3, Butch ended up on 29 December at Kaneohe, where a welcome bag of mail waited. Thach doled out short liberties to Honolulu, but Butch and the others found the city much changed, with the sale of beer and liquor suspended by martial law. In the meantime, after wheeling and dealing with the shore establishment, Thach could still assemble only a mixed bag of a dozen assorted F4Fs and two Brewster F2A-3 Buffaloes.

Fearing a Japanese return engagement, the admirals preferred to keep the carriers out of Pearl, so on the thirty-first they hustled the *Saratoga* back out to sea. Butch flew one of the Wildcats out to the ship. The new task force commander was Rear Adm. Herbert F. Leary, a nonaviator like Fletcher. His name probably engendered as little interest for Butch and the other young tigers of naval aviation as that of Adm. Chester W. Nimitz, the former chief of the Bureau of Navigation who took over the Pacific Fleet that very day. They would all learn that Nimitz was the ideal commander to restore American superiority in the Pacific.

New Year's Eve came and went "sans celebration, sans hangover," in the words of Burt Stanley. Adding to the general lack of merriment was a submarine scare at about 0200 on the first. General quarters was sounded, rousing the pilots from their bunks and to their ready rooms. It was an omen. The fleet staff chose to call the *Saratoga*'s make-work cruise west of the Hawaiian Islands an "offensive patrol," but Thach and Butch could not see what was so "very offensive" about it. Leary's ships just chugged along at low speed through unfriendly seas. The only bright spot occurred on 3 January, when an All-Navy (AlNav) dispatch announced numerous promotions to temporary rank. Both Thach and Lovelace jumped up to lieutenant commander, and Butch scrambled to find his own double-bar collar insignia for his new rank of lieutenant.[9]

The next day a painful attack of kidney stones forced Thach to relinquish command of VF-3 to Lovelace. The skipper's misfortune set the tone for the rest of the ill-starred cruise. On the fifth Butch managed to get aloft for gunnery exercises, a real chore because the huge *Saratoga* waddled through the waves. Rather ominously, scouting flights spotted submarines all over the area, hardly comforting as TF-14 zigzagged at a leisurely 7–12 knots in order to conserve fuel. Leary steamed southeast to rendezvous with the *Enterprise*, whereupon VF-3 was to exchange all its F4F-3s for VF-6's F4F-3A Wildcats. Doubtless that prospect failed to thrill Butch, for he knew that the F4F-3As could not match the regular dash-3 in performance, particularly at higher altitudes. On 8 and 9 January seawater actually ran across the bow and down into the *Sara*'s forward elevator well, and the next two days proved little better.

On Sunday evening, 11 January, as Butch and the other VF-3 officers ate dinner in the wardroom, a massive explosion shook the *Saratoga* like a rag doll in a dog's mouth. Thach recalled that "it sounded like the bottom of the ship [had blown] out," as the *Sara* rolled violently to port and started back again. Dishes bounced into the air, and a surprised Lovelace snared a roll before it dropped to the deck. They all burst out of their chairs and ran for their duty stations—in VF-3's case, its ready room. Compliments of the Imperial Japanese submarine *I-6*, the *Saratoga* had swallowed one torpedo on the port side amidships that flooded three firerooms and killed six sailors.[10]

While the engineering gang corrected the list to port and, quite remarkably, cranked up 16 knots, the VF-3 pilots sat in their ready room cracking jokes until they were told to go to bed. Turning out early the next morning, Butch found the flight deck aft and the aircraft parked there covered with fuel oil and sprinkled with metal fragments. The *Saratoga* limped northeast toward Pearl. It was obvious that she would be under repair for many months, and her flyers needed to find another flattop.

At dawn on 13 January, Lovelace led most of the *Saratoga* Air Group to Ford Island. Butch drew one of the two F2A-3 Buffaloes. Shortly thereafter VF-3 shifted to the Marine field at Ewa west of Pearl Harbor and assembled their gear transferred off the *Saratoga*. After temporary repairs, she was to sail to Bremerton, her customary port, for a complete refit. At Ewa, Butch gratefully unloaded the unwanted F2A onto VF-2, the *Lexington*'s fighting squadron, which still reluctantly flew the Brewster product. Thach returned from the hospital on 17 January, and VF-3 settled in, flying dawn alerts for the Army's Seventh Interceptor Command while working in some flight training during the day. Butch got to tool around running errands from Ford Island to Ewa in the land version of the Vought OS2U-1 Kingfisher, the aircraft that replaced the old SOC Seagulls on the battleships.

By 20 January VF-3 had acquired five more Grumman Wildcats, for a total of seventeen, enabling the pilots to fly more regularly in their own planes. Butch took his first flight in F4F-3 Wildcat Bureau Number 4031, an aircraft that he would soon immortalize. Originally assigned to VMF-211, 4031's engine failed to start on 28 November 1941, the day the Marines flew out to the *Enterprise* for the voyage to Wake. It was as if 4031 desired better than the fate that would befall its compatriots there. Left behind at Ewa, 4031 survived 7 December and was transferred on 15 December to VF-3, which assigned it the plane number F-15. Like most VF-3 F4Fs, it lacked self-sealing fuel tanks or pilot armor, keeping it on a par with Japanese aircraft. Since joining VF-3, 4031 had received the elaborate new paint scheme with the rudder bravely sporting thirteen alternating red and white stripes. Butch's flight log shows that he flew 4031 whenever circumstances permitted.

On the evening of 24 January the VF-3 pilots, wearing their pistols, piled into a school bus for an outing at the Royal Hawaiian Hotel on Waikiki Beach. It was one of the first times the elite resort was open for servicemen to relax. This time, though, they shared only one bottle of liquor, so the hilarity was a bit subdued. Late the next afternoon VF-3 reported back to Ewa, and Butch flew a night patrol.

On the twenty-sixth, when Thach was alerted to prepare for sea duty at short notice, VF-3 found out why the Navy had been so nice to them. Soon after, VF-3 was attached to the *Lexington* Air Group in place of VF-2, the famous "Flying Chiefs," whose pilots were mostly enlisted men. When the *Lexington* sailed on her next cruise, VF-2 remained ashore to replace its F2A-3 Buffaloes with Grumman F4F Wildcats. Thach divested himself of the XF4F-4 prototype and obtained two more F4Fs. That gave him the regulation eighteen fighters for the first time in many months and stabilized the VF-3 flight schedule of three six-plane divisions, each consisting of three two-plane sections. Butch led the second section in Thach's First Division, and his assigned wingman was Lt. (jg) Marion W. Dufilho, a personable Louisianan who had graduated from Annapolis in 1938.

On 28 January VF-3 shifted over to Kaneohe to get better acquainted with the *Lexington* flyers. Their new group leader was Comdr. William B. Ault, a grizzled, highly experienced forty-three-year-old pilot who had once taught aviation theory at the Naval Academy. The other three squadron commanders were Lt. Comdr. Weldon L. Hamilton (Bombing Two), Lt. Comdr. Robert E. Dixon (Scouting Two), and Lt. Comdr. James H. Brett (Torpedo Two).

The *Lady Lex*

On the last day of January VF-3 joined the general exodus of the *Lexington* Air Group (eighteen fighters, thirty-seven dive bombers, and thirteen torpedo planes) flying from Kaneohe out to the *Lex*. Butch brought 4031 (F-15) and landed without incident, but one of the young pilots cracked up his Wildcat, necessitating a major overhaul by Butch's engineers. After settling in, Butch and the other pilots speculated as to where they might be going, but nobody who knew was telling. They now belonged to Task Force Eleven under Vice Adm. Wilson Brown. TF-11 had twice experienced deep frustration from having to turn back before launching raids against the Japanese. The first occurred in late December when Brown was recalled short of the Marshall Islands in order to support the *Saratoga* off Wake. Scheduled to attack Wake in late January, TF-11 had to retire when a submarine picked off its fleet oiler, the old *Neches*.

On this trip Brown expected to be out only a couple of weeks before returning to Pearl. His first task was to escort an oiler to meet Vice Adm. Bill Halsey's Task Force Eight near Johnston Island. Indeed, the very day the *Lex* sailed, Halsey with the *Enterprise* and, separately, Frank Jack Fletcher's Task Force Seventeen with the *Yorktown* executed the long-awaited first Pacific Fleet counterattack. They pounded the Marshalls and Gilberts with air attacks and ship bombardments. Halsey did not require the oil, so on 2 February, Nimitz sent Brown directly south toward remote Canton Island in the Central Pacific.[11]

Settling in for his first cruise on the *Lady Lex*, Butch quickly discovered a great contrast in efficiency and morale between her and her sister, the *Saratoga*. The *Lex* seemed an especially taut and happy ship. Thach attributed the difference to her leadership, particularly Capt. Frederick C. Sherman, the tough CO, and Comdr. Herbert S. Duckworth, a former VF-2 skipper who was now air officer. Thach described the *Lexington* as "administered in every way to enhance the value of the air group. The training of the air group at sea in gunnery and bombing was given high priority." Stanley also noticed the "better spirit aboard the *Lex*." In contrast to the mood on the snake-bit *Sara*, here the "life jackets were put away—available but not omnipresent." He prophesied a "happy cruise," which for Butch would be a gross underestimation.[12]

On 5 February as the task force dipped further south into much warmer weather, Brown advised his captains that they would soon cross the equator. The *Lexington* was notorious for the exuberance of her line-crossing shenanigans. That day her Shellbacks, those old salts already initiated into the realm of King Neptune, met secretly to plan the mayhem they would inflict on the lowly Pollywogs. In VF-3 only Lovelace and Gayler held exalted Shellback status, but they suffered for it when the rest of the pilots laughingly tied them to a bulkhead. Soon Don and Noel took their revenge. Along with the other Pollywogs, Butch had to put on a heavy flight suit and wander uncomfortably around deck in the tropical heat, looking for "icebergs" using two Coke bottles tied together as makeshift binoculars. After dinner the Shellbacks held court in the wardroom and meted out appropriate punishments. The next morning the Pollywogs had to submit to King Neptune's pleasure and run the gauntlet on the long flight deck. The line-crossing ceremonies were reminiscent of the high jinx Butch endured (and sometimes enjoyed) at Western Military Academy and Annapolis. Except for the return voyage to Pearl, however, he never crossed the equator again.

At noon on 6 February, Brown received orders to continue southward into the South Pacific, where he passed from Nimitz's control to directly under Adm. Ernest J. King, the commander in chief of the U.S. Fleet in distant Washington. King certainly had work for TF-11 and the recently created ANZAC naval command under now Vice Admiral Leary. Ever since 23 January, when they stormed ashore at Rabaul on New Britain in the Bismarck Archipelago, the Japanese had directly threatened both eastern New Guinea and the Solomon Islands—the gateway to the Coral Sea and Australia beyond.

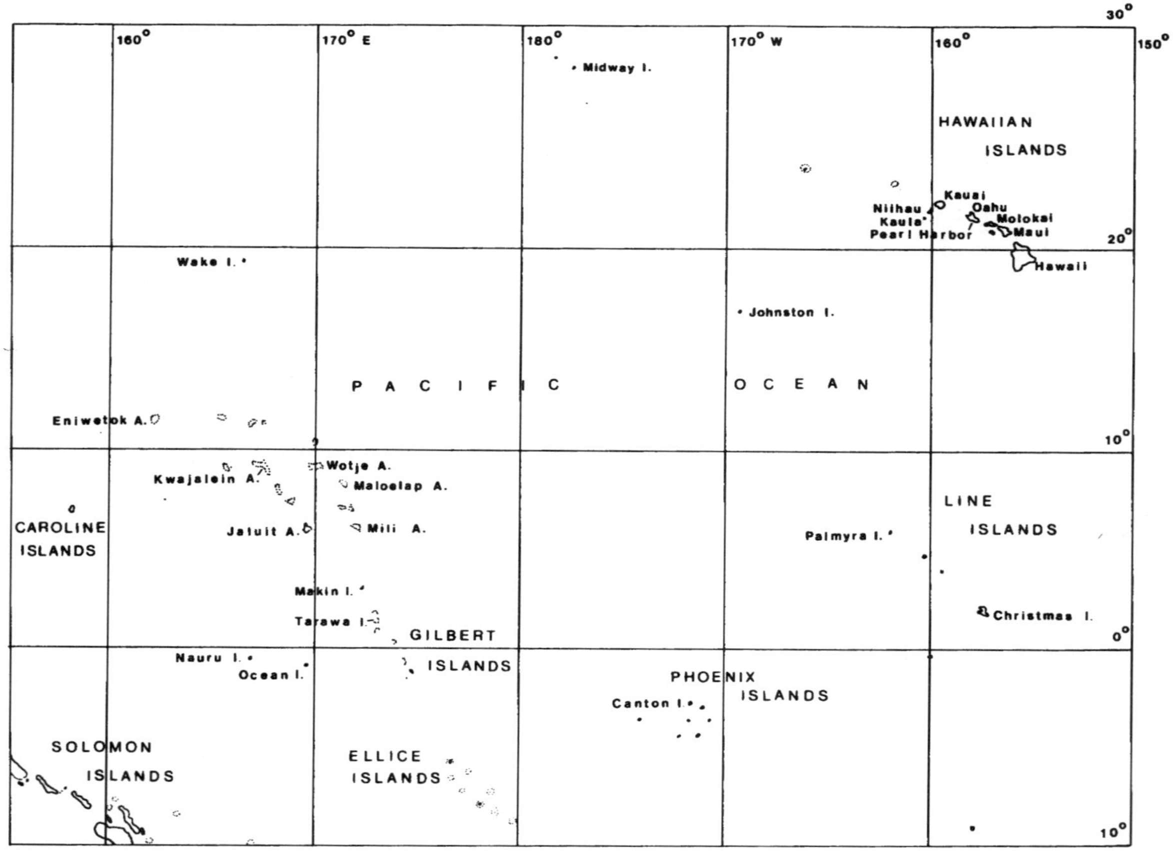

The Central Pacific

His new destination gave Brown many reasons for worry. First, no one had anticipated a voyage longer than a few weeks. The ships of the task force, other than the *Lexington,* had not taken on full provisions, and even her vast larder could not hold sufficient fresh food. Butch's stomach soon rebelled at the measures necessary to overcome this deficiency. Far worse than the lack of food was the plunge into the remote Southwest Pacific, where no American carrier had yet operated. Searching the available charts of island groups, mostly based on Royal Navy surveys conducted one hundred years or more earlier, Brown could find no secure refuge for his leviathan of a flattop short of Sydney, Australia. In his memoirs he described his concern: "In moving to the southwest Pacific with no friendly harbors we could enter, we were jumping off into space and had to take future necessities on faith."[13]

On 8 February, while the task force steamed eastward of the Phoenix Islands, VF-3 suffered a fatality. Through an oversight the ship did not have enough starter cartridges, a sort of shotgun shell used to crank the engines. In order to preserve those they had, Butch's men started the Wildcats by means of bungee cords, an elastic line rigged on a block and tackle. That afternoon a block broke loose from where the line was tied to the deck and crushed the chest of one of the VF-3 engineers, Edward Frank Ambrose, aviation machinist's mate third class. He died four hours later. The next evening a somber Butch attended the memorial service conducted by the ship's chaplain.

The day of the funeral VF-3 started flying regular combat air patrols. The pilots looked forward to the duty, for the cool air at altitude offered temporary relief from the torrid temperatures on the poorly ventilated *Lex,* where, as Lovelace wrote, "it takes only a few minutes out of the breeze to liquefy you." Butch's turn to fly came on 10 February, and while aloft, he watched another heavy cruiser and two destroyers join Brown's force. On the fourteenth while on CAP, Lovelace's division encountered a Royal New Zealand Air Force Hudson bomber searching out of Suva in the Fiji Islands. That really emphasized how far the ships had come from Pearl Harbor. In the night sky the Southern Cross and other strange constellations beckoned Butch's curiosity.[14]

On 13 February TF-11 had received orders from King to conduct offensive operations in the Solomons area. King wanted both to retard further Japanese advances in the South Pacific and to draw their attention away from the Dutch East Indies, more vulnerable now that the defense of Singapore was collapsing. Brown decided to raid Rabaul. On the sixteenth, off Fiji, he made contact with the ANZAC Naval Squadron of four cruisers and two destroyers under Rear Adm. John G. Crace, Royal Navy. Fuel considerations forced Brown to leave Crace as a rear guard to protect his oiler. In the meantime, he would move northwest from Fiji and east of the New Hebrides and the Solomons to approach Rabaul from the northeast. At dawn on 21 February from within 150 miles, the maximum attack range of his torpedo bombers, he would launch air strikes against Rabaul. If circumstances permitted, he hoped to follow up by bombarding Rabaul's Simpson Harbor with a heavy cruiser and two destroyers.

The *Lexington* Air Group plan envisioned launching well before sunrise, sending the strike southwest over narrow New Ireland to hit Rabaul at sunrise. One division of fighters would go in first to strafe the Vunakanau airfield west of Rabaul, in hopes of knocking out the enemy Zero fighters before they could take off, while the SBD dive bombers and TBD torpedo bombers dealt with the ships in the harbor. On the seventeenth Thach laid out the battle plan to VF-3. To his great joy, Butch learned that the skipper's First Division of six Wildcats, in which he had the second section, would lead the attack. He certainly believed that a real fight was in the offing. On the eighteenth Australian intelligence placed eight vessels in the harbor as well as a dozen fighters and perhaps thirty-six bombers at Vunakanau Field.[15]

On 19 February, Thach turned out the entire squadron in clean dungarees for a prebattle inspection. To Butch's amusement, he instructed all hands to shave off any beards they had grown, "so they won't be a fire hazard." VF-3 was raring to go. Now it was just necessary to sneak in and surprise the Japanese.[16]

Battle off Bougainville: A Surprise No More

In the early hours of 20 February, one day before the scheduled raid on Rabaul, TF-11 moved warily northwestward past Bougainville at the top of the Solomons chain. Vice Admiral Brown and his staff customarily assembled well before dawn on the flag bridge high on the *Lexington*'s island, where they enjoyed a "grand view of the activity of the carrier." As Brown recalled, "Night was over, dawn would soon break, the air was fresh, cool and stimulating, in marked contrast to the oppressive heat of the night before." To Butch and the other young aviators, Wilson Brown was a remote figure. Because the elderly nonaviator admiral—at fifty-nine, the oldest flag officer afloat—exhibited a slight tremor, they rather callously dubbed him "Shaky." Little did they realize how much the genial Brown, superintendent of the Naval Academy from 1938 to 1941, cared for his flyers: "I used to wonder what the thoughts of our young pilots may have been, and those of the aircrews standing by to be launched, most of them [actually, all] for their first air combat. They were tense, serious, on edge—but at the same time seeking to make light of what was in store. Indeed, they all acted as if they were tuning up for a major baseball or football game."[17]

That morning the admiral informed Captain Sherman that he wished a precautionary search ahead, and Sherman assigned six VS-2 SBDs to the mission. Brown's unpublished memoir describes a typical dawn launch as seen from his perch:

> The entire Force was coming to life, and the operation of a carrier flight deck is the finest example of team work and skill to be found. To watch the preparations for the first morning flight about an hour before dawn is an experience never to be forgotten. Planes are tuning up all over the deck. Planes from below are coming up on the elevators, others going down. Men in red jerseys, men in yellow jerseys, men in no jerseys, all the colors indicating their respective duties, swarm about the machines, gassing, arming, shifting about the deck in orderly disorder. Pilots and crews stand by in their flying suits. The pilots are briefed. Everyone grabs a cup of hot coffee when the chance offers, rubbing their eyes, sweaty with tropical heat. . . . About five minutes before launching, the LEXINGTON picks up speed and heads into the wind. Quiet and order settle on the flight deck. On a signal from the flight officer on the bridge below us, the first plane takes off gracefully over the bow, dipping so near the water one held one's breath for fear that he may dip too far. Others follow in rapid succession until all are away. Then the whole task force turns back to its base course. The sun's rim comes over the horizon. Day is upon us.[18]

Butch likewise rose early on 20 February to fly the first CAP whenever Sherman chose to deploy it. Trusting to the ability of his CXAM air-search radar and fighter director officer, Lt. Frank F. Gill, to ferret out intruders, Sherman preferred to keep the six Wildcats on board for the time being. After breakfast Butch waited on alert in the VF-3 ready room along with Thach, Stanley, and their three wingmen from the First Division. The plane captains saw to it that the engines of the F4Fs parked aft on the flight deck were kept warmed up and ready to go.[19]

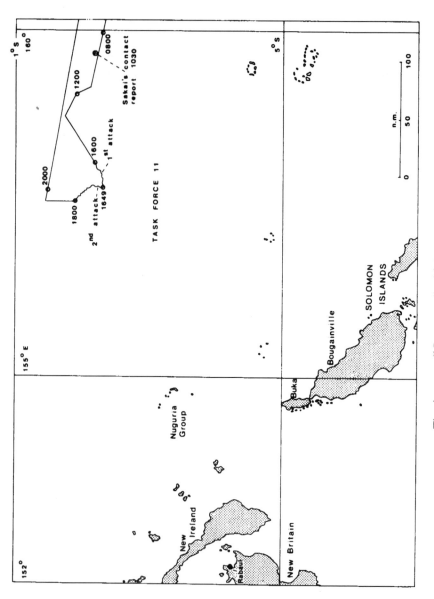

The Action off Bougainville, 20 February 1942

At 1015 the CXAM radar discovered a suspicious contact skulking thirty-five miles south, so Sherman abruptly gave orders for Thach's pilots to man planes. At 1030 Brown turned the task force northwest into the wind, and all six Wildcats were aloft five minutes later. Butch gathered his wingman, "Duff" Dufilho, and took his place in formation. As the F4F pilots joined up, they were surprised and excited to hear "Red" Gill break radio silence and give a steer south-southwest after the bogey. For Butch the thrill quickly changed to frustration when the skipper gestured for him to turn his own and Stanley's sections around toward the ship. Thach later remarked with considerable understatement of Butch, "He didn't want to go back." With Rabaul over 450 miles away, Thach expected to find only a lone snooper, a flying boat or medium bomber—something his two F4Fs could handle. He wanted to have his other two sections in reserve should more search planes show up. Butch watched his leader and wingman, Ens. E. Robert Sellstrom, Jr., disappear southward toward a large thunderstorm.[20]

At 1100, after Gill sent him about forty miles from the ships, Thach nearly collided in a rain cloud with an enemy four-engine Kawanishi H6K4 Type 97 flying boat (of a type later code-named Mavis by the Allies). After pursuing the huge aircraft through the squall, Thach and "Doc" Sellstrom hammered their opponent into the sea. At 1112 thick black smoke from gasoline burning on the water became visible even to Butch thirty miles away. Unfortunately the Kawanishi, commanded by Lt. (jg) Sakai Noboru of the Yokohama Air Group, had already done its job, having warned Rabaul at 1030 of enemy ships discovered 460 miles northeast.

No sooner had Thach and Sellstrom returned than Gill piped up with word of another intruder. That was Warrant Officer Hayashi Kiyoshi's Type 97 flying boat, which covered the search sector immediately to the south of Sakai. He had come over to amplify Sakai's contact. To Butch's intense displeasure, Gill chose Stanley's third section to make the intercept and again kept him in reserve. Stanley and wingman Ens. Leon W. Haynes likewise made short work of their flying boat, which never had the chance to radio its encounter to base. At 1218 Butch saw another pall of smoke marking the grave of a second Yokohama Air Group crew.

At 1240 the *Lex*'s radar picked up a third bogey eighty miles west, but the third time was not the charm for Butch. That contact only closed to seventy miles, and by the time it disappeared at 1317 from the radar screen, the First Division was low on fuel. At 1326 the *Lexington* commenced launching Don Lovelace's Second Division of six F4Fs as relief CAP, followed by a dozen SBDs from VB-2 for the afternoon search. After the two flights had departed, plane handlers respotted the flight deck forward to clear space to bring Thach's fighters on board.

Once back on deck, Thach and Stanley rendered brief reports to the captain and joined Butch and the others in the wardroom for lunch. Having missed the squadron's first air battle, Butch was, in Thach's words, "fit to be tied." The four smiling victors recounted the details of the Lex's and VF-3's first two aerial kills to an eager audience. Thach stressed that his combat "was just like another gunnery run—the same sort of thing we had been practicing for months."[21]

Also distressed like Butch, but for different reasons, was Wilson Brown. In discovering TF-11, Sakai had put Brown's plans for attacking Rabaul in serious jeopardy. Brown had good reason to believe that the Japanese knew he was coming, and he lacked the fuel for an extended battle against an aroused enemy. He called off the raid, a decision that did not sit well with Ted Sherman and some of the admiral's staff who had urged him to fight his way in, if need be, to Rabaul. Instead of withdrawing immediately, Brown decided to feint an attack. He turned southwest directly toward Rabaul, thus exposing the task force to a possible long-range strike that afternoon in return for a more convincing effort to divert Japanese forces away from the Dutch East Indies.

The Japanese Respond

Prodded by what was actually a false alarm the previous day, Vice Adm. Gotō Eiji, commander of the Twenty-fourth Air Flotilla at Rabaul, nervously awaited the results of the morning search on the twentieth. Sakai's report at 1030 of strong enemy forces 460 miles northeast only confirmed his worst fears. Gotō had immediately available at Rabaul a total of twenty-six fighters and eighteen "land-attack planes" (medium bombers) from the Fourth Air Group, and, once they returned from the morning search, seven flying boats of the Yokohama Air Group. Now he had to determine whether to hit the Americans immediately with his land-attack planes while their carrier (or carriers) could not retaliate or wait until the next dawn and risk an air strike on Rabaul. The key problem was that on the twentieth he could provide no fighter escorts. Fifteen of his fighters were the old open-cockpit, fixed-landing-gear Mitsubishi

A5M4 Type 96 carrier fighters (later known to the Allies as Claudes), which simply lacked the range. The rest were the superlative new Mitsubishi A6M2 Type 0 carrier fighters (Zekes), which could fly such a long mission with belly tanks, but no such tanks had yet been delivered to Rabaul.[22]

At 1310 Gotō issued orders for the eighteen land-attack planes, waiting on alert at Vunakanau Field, to attack the enemy task force that afternoon. The Japanese much preferred to deal with ships by using aerial torpedoes, but they too were not yet available at Rabaul. Thus, the land-attack planes each carried two 250-kilogram bombs for a horizontal bombing run. That, along with the dearth of fighter escorts, placed a heavy burden on the bomber crews of Capt. Moritama Yoshiyotsu's Fourth Air Group, but they felt equal to the task. Formed only ten days previous at Truk, the group was still working up, but all of the land-attack crews were veterans. They and their aircraft came from the Takao Air Group that on 8 December 1941 had helped pulverize Gen. Douglas MacArthur's Far East Air Force on the ground at Clark Field in the Philippines.[23]

The medium bomber the Fourth Air Group flew was Japan's most modern, the Mitsubishi G4M1 Type 1 land-based attack airplane (in Japanese, *rikujō kōgekitai*, abbreviated *rikkō*). Its fat, cigar-shaped fuselage with large glassed-in machine-gun blisters combined with the wide, sharply pointed wings to create a distinctive appearance. In the fall of 1942, air intelligence analysts with MacArthur's Fifth Air Force formulated a simple system of code names for Japanese aircraft, using male names for fighters and female names for bombers. They christened the Type 1 *rikkō* Betty, because the "real Betty was an attractive American nurse . . . described as being *well endowed*." The Japanese *rikkō* crews gave the Type 1 the less romantic nickname of *hamaki* ("cigar") and later, when its defensive drawbacks became better known, the "Type 1 lighter." Butch's combat career would be profoundly linked with Bettys.[24]

A pair of 1,530-hp Kasei ("Mars") radial engines gave the Type 1 good speed for a bomber, 266 mph at 13,780 feet, while large fuel tanks provided phenomenal range, a strike radius up to 800 miles. The payload, however, weighed a rather modest 800 kilograms, either bombs or one aerial torpedo. Defensive armament comprised four 7.7-mm Type 92 machine guns set in the nose, the dorsal blister, and both beam blisters, as well as a powerful 20-mm Type 99 cannon in the tail. The Type 1's principal drawback was its lack of self-sealing fuel tanks and protective armor, although up to this point in the war few had fallen to fighter attack.

At Vunakanau, Lt. Comdr. Itō Takuzō, the Fourth Air Group's senior flight leader (*hikōtaichō*), took personal command of the mission. A graduate of the fifty-sixth class (1928) of the Naval Academy at Eta Jima, Itō had specialized in seaplanes before joining the Fourth Air Group, where his overwater navigational experience was especially valued. He rode in the command aircraft of the first *chūtai* (nine-plane division) along with the *chūtai* leader, Lt. Seto Yogorō (Eta Jima sixty-first class, 1933). On 11 August 1941 Seto had led the Type 1's very first combat mission, a strike by twenty-seven *rikkōs* against Chengtu in China. As was common in the Imperial Japanese Navy, neither Itō nor Seto had actually trained as a pilot; both were observers. Lt. Nakagawa Masayoshi, a highly regarded young pilot (Eta Jima sixty-fifth class, 1938), led the second *chūtai* of nine aircraft.

The Fourth Air Group departed Vunakanau Field at 1400. One of the first-*chūtai* aircraft suffered mechanical difficulty and remained on the ground, leaving Itō with seventeen bombers. Shortly after takeoff the group encountered increasingly bad weather, compelling Itō to detour around a number of squalls. Finally he divided his force into two elements to spread out and try to find the enemy. Nakagawa's nine land-attack planes branched off to the north, while Itō's eight held course.

The Annihilation of the First Wave

After lunch on the *Lexington,* Thach's division went off duty. While Stanley and Haynes rested in their quarters, the skipper and Butch joined Gayler's Third Division waiting on alert in the ready room. There the two leafed through air intelligence reports trying to determine the model of enemy aircraft shot down that morning. Lovelace's six pilots uneventfully circled ten thousand feet over the ships, while Commander Duckworth's Air Department prepared six more F4Fs (including two borrowed from the First Division) for Gayler's Third Division to take their place. Since only sixteen of the eighteen VF-3 Wildcats could fly that day, just four remained for the First Division should Thach need them.

At 1542 a jagged vee on the CXAM's A-scope drew the attention of the *Lex*'s radar operator. Within the limitations of his primitive equipment, he placed the contact seventy-six miles due west of the task force and approaching at perhaps eight thousand feet and 150 knots. The contact soon disappeared from the radar screen, an annoying attribute of that particular type of radar wave, whose pattern of electromagnetic lobes created a number of null areas according to the range and altitude of the contact.

With Lovelace's division getting low on fuel and an attack now at least a possibility, Sherman ordered Gayler's pilots to depart slightly ahead of schedule. From overhead, Lovelace saw the *Lexington* turn starboard into the wind at 1606 preparatory to conducting flight operations, so he started down in anticipation of landing. Gayler's division took off at 1615, and the flight deck crew began the arduous task of clearing the deck for recovery by pushing forward the approximately twenty-seven aircraft (four F4Fs, eleven SBDs, and about a dozen TBDs) parked astern.

Even while the respot got under way, trouble was brewing. At 1614 the *Lex*'s radar had picked up a large bogey seventy-two miles west. Tracked for eleven minutes before it too faded, this contact likewise seemed to approach. Gill loosed Gayler's six F4Fs after the enemy. At 1621 Brown turned the task force to port out of the wind and resumed the base course to the southwest. A searchlight flashing from the *Lexington* warned Lovelace's division to back off, and Gill soon gave them the steer as they frantically regained altitude.

In the meantime, the contact reappeared at 1625 only forty-seven miles west and closing fast. Simultaneously Sherman ordered Duckworth to suspend the respot, get all aircraft pushed aft, and make every effort to launch the fifteen fueled F4Fs and SBDs before bombs detonating on the flight deck caused a conflagration. The call for "torpedo defense stations" resounded throughout the massive warship as she worked up to 30 knots. Checking the list of available fighters and pilots, Duckworth announced over the bullhorn, "Thach in 13, Sellstrom take 2, O'Hare in 15, Dufilho, 4," soon followed by, "Pilots, man your planes." Butch lost no time clambering back into faithful 4031, adjusted his flight gear, and waited for word to start the engine. Stanley and Haynes ran to the VF-3 ready room, then out onto the flight deck, but they were out of luck. All the fighters were taken. Along with Thach's Wildcats, crews from VS-2, some minus flight helmets and other gear, jumped into the eleven SBDs to get them aloft once the deck was clear forward.[25]

The approaching enemy were the nine land-attack planes of the second *chūtai,* which had just climbed to 3,500 meters (11,685 feet). After alerting Itō at 1635, Nakagawa initiated his level bombing attack from north and upwind of the target. With their throttles pushed to the maximum, Noel Gayler's Third Division watched the oncoming enemy bombers grow in their windshields. To Gayler they appeared to be a new type, camouflaged in a mottled green and brown pattern. At 1639 with the enemy only ten miles from the ships, he and his wingman Ens. Dale W. Peterson rolled into an overhead run from about two thousand feet above the tight enemy vee-of-vees. Following Gayler closely were the second section of Lt. (jg) Robert J. Morgan and Ens. Richard M. Rowell and the third of Lt. (jg) Rolla Lemmon and Ens. John H. Lackey. Between 1639 and 1641 the superb marksmanship of these six Wildcat pilots slashed three land-attack planes out of Nakagawa's formation.

Lookouts on the ships spotted nine bombers beset by fighters. Observing that the flight deck forward was very nearly clear, Brown started turning TF-11 starboard into the wind so that the *Lex* could launch planes. Proud of his flight deck crew, Duckworth boasted, "The respot was the fastest respot ever made in carrier history. It was as if some great hand moved all the planes aft simultaneously." Sitting in their fighters as she came around to the north, Thach and Butch could see "some smoke and airplanes falling."[26]

At 1643 with their second attacks, Gayler and Peterson sent bombers four and five spinning in flames. One of them was evidently Nakagawa's own, carrying the master bombardier. That seemed to confuse the remaining Japanese crews, who flew on past the ships. Finally they regrouped and swung around to overtake the *Lex* from astern. Some of the cruisers cut loose with their 5-inch antiaircraft guns, whose "big, black shell bursts" threatened Gayler's fighters more than the Japanese below them.[27]

Simultaneous with the last two kills, the Fly I officer, Lt. Easton B. Noble—one of Butch's flight instructors in 1940—coached Thach's F4F up to the line, listened to him rev his engine, and dropped the flag. The Wildcat hurtled up the deck and into the air. Well back in the pack of SBDs and F4Fs, Butch awaited his turn, anxiously watching as the bombers, although steadily decreasing in number, drew nearer. That certainly led to speculation about what would happen if their bombs caught him still on deck in a fueled aircraft. Finally Butch got away, and at 1646, as the last aircraft took to the air, the *Lex* herself opened fire as the Japanese reached their bomb release point.

Brown later noted, "Our fighters electrified all of us by making their kills mostly within sight of our ships." The surviving bombers stoically closed up as the F4Fs carved up the formation. Their discipline impressed Brown: "Despite the heavy antiaircraft fire from all our ships, they steamed calmly and deliberately, with shells bursting all about them, to their point of release. The only thing I had ever seen like it was a drill exercise with our Army Air Force off the Virginia Capes when I had towed a target, and had been amazed at the accuracy of their bombing." This time the bombing proved not accurate at all, because of the loss of the lead plane and Sherman's adroit maneuvering. The nearest bombs struck the sea fully three thousand yards from the *Lexington*.[28]

More exciting to the *Lex*'s crew than the actual bombing was an attempt a few minutes later by Nakagawa to crash the carrier. From low off her starboard bow the crippled lead bomber lurched in her direction trying to stay aloft long enough to reach the flight deck. Brown later recalled that "time seemed to drag endlessly" as Sherman tried to swing the *Lex* out of the way. At twenty-five hundred yards her starboard 1.1-inch cannons and .50-caliber machine guns opened fire. One of Brown's staff, "a famous duck hunter," yelled at the closest gunner, "Lead him . . . damn you, lead him." According to Brown the automatic fire commenced to "fairly tearing the pilot and plane to pieces. And as the plane swung by, only a few yards from where we stood, we saw that the pilot was dead, slumped at the controls, as he plunged into the sea." Stanley, an unwilling spectator, remarked, "He would have really made a mess of our flight deck if he had reached it."[29]

Shortly after the four remaining *rikkōs* had toggled their payloads, Lemmon and Rowell from the Third Division, as well as Lt. Albert O. "Scoop" Vorse and Lt. (jg) Howard F. Clark from the Second Division, cut one of their number out of formation. The other three Japanese split up, desperately running downhill as fast as they could trying to escape. Don Lovelace and Lt. (jg) Howard L. Johnson from the Second Division tangled with one, but after sustaining hits in his engine, Johnson incautiously approached the bomber from astern. Explosive rounds from the 20-mm tail gun peppered his Wildcat, wounded him in the legs, and forced him to bail out. The bomber kept on going. Seeing Johnson's parachute blossom, Brown directed the destroyer *Patterson* (DD-392) southeast to make the rescue.

Pushing his overloaded Wildcat for all it was worth, Thach managed to draw ahead of one of the fleeing bombers. To his horror he saw another F4F roaring in from directly astern of the same aircraft. That was Ens. John W. Wilson from the Second Division. Before Thach could warn him to break off, a 20-mm cannon shell from the *rikkō*'s tail stinger struck Wilson's windshield and probably killed him instantly. The F4F dropped into the sea about five miles from the *Lex.* Thach followed through and flamed the bomber. Another appeared below. He and Ens. Willard E. Eder from the Second Division knocked that *rikkō* into the sea. Lt. Edward H. Allen, the VS-2 XO flying one of the SBDs just launched from the *Lexington,* used his twin .50-caliber nose guns to flame a maimed bomber trying to limp away. Soon after, he and his radioman, Bruce Rountree, aviation radioman first class, finished off another cripple.

Only one *rikkō* from the hapless second *chūtai* managed to withdraw southwest, but a pack of Wildcats—Thach, his wingman Sellstrom, and five from the Third Division—clawed its tail. Ultimately Thach managed to rein in his boys and thought that the lone Japanese plane had escaped. That was not the case, however, for it had the misfortune to meet another pugnacious Dauntless. That was the SBD-2 flown by Lt. Walter F. Henry, XO of VB-2, who was returning from the afternoon search. Skillfully using his favorable initial position, Henry overtook the speedy *rikkō* and splashed it eighty miles from the ships.

"Careful Timing:" Butch versus the Second Wave

TF-11's air defense did a magnificent job breaking up Nakagawa's attack and destroying the assailants. All Butch could do was watch. While gaining height after the mad scramble from the *Lexington,* he saw bombs tumbling down from the first wave and wondered whether "the ship would be there to land on when I came down." By the time he reached combat altitude, "there were so many of our fighters, I couldn't get in on the brawl." He gathered Duff Dufilho, who also never had a chance to fight, and continued climbing over the ships as the only effective CAP. The skipper and six other VF-3 pilots pursued the sole survivor of the first wave far away from the task force. Down to fumes in their fuel tanks, Lovelace and three other Second Division pilots, plus one from the Third Division, awaited the first opportunity to land back on board after the *Lex*'s weary flight deck crew again manhandled the TBDs forward.[30]

While the second *chūtai* fought and died, Lieutenant Commander Itō with the eight *rikkōs* of the first *chūtai* neared the battle area from the northeast. En route they had climbed to 4,500 meters (14,765 feet) and searched the horizon dotted with clouds lower down toward the ocean. Far off in the distance many black spots seemed suspended in the air. Beneath them telltale marks on the sea disclosed a task force: cruisers and destroyers surrounding at least one aircraft carrier. Worried that the specks were enemy fighters, the Japanese were relieved to discover them actually to be bursting antiaircraft shells obviously directed against the second *chūtai*. Instead of going straight in from the flank with a difficult cross-wind angle, Itō decided to make his bomb run from directly astern of the enemy carrier as she held course northward into the wind. He led the formation around in a left turn for a wide detour to the south to take the proper heading astern of the ships. The first *chūtai* let down toward 3,500 meters (11,485 feet) for the actual bomb release.

The first inkling of more danger for TF-11 occurred at 1649 during Nakagawa's dramatic suicide attempt against the *Lexington*. Her radar detected bogeys thirty miles north-northeast, but things were still too chaotic aloft for Gill to wring out some F4Fs to check out this possible new threat. Seven minutes later the *Patterson,* busy rescuing Howard Johnson, noticed a formation of aircraft circling about ten miles northeast of the ships and flashed a warning to the flagship. Gill confirmed the observation at 1700, when his radar placed bogeys nine miles east. He loosed Butch's section against this new enemy and tried recalling Thach and Gayler to protect the force.

Rather surprised to discover themselves the only available fighters, Butch and Dufilho raced eastward. Seeing the enemy bombers wheel around to the south, Butch cut inside their turn to get between them and the ships. Following standard procedure, he and Duff charged their guns, turned on the light bulbs in the temperamental N2AN illuminated gun sights, and triggered brief test bursts. Butch's four .50-caliber M2 Brownings worked fine, but to Duff's consternation, none of his would shoot. Butch gestured his wingman back to the ship, but Dufilho would not leave even after Butch "shook his fist at him."[31]

By 1706 Butch and Dufilho had caught up with Itō less than a dozen miles astern of the task force. Reaching twelve thousand feet, they enjoyed an altitude advantage of a thousand feet or so over the descending bombers. The first *chūtai* flew in a wide, flat vee-of-vees, with following planes stepped up slightly above the leaders. Butch—and everyone else on the American side—thought that nine planes constituted the second wave, but actually there were eight. No defending fighters materialized out ahead over the target, so the Japanese thought they might get a free shot at the carrier. They did not see the two Grummans poised high over their starboard side. Butch knew that he alone must deal with these bombers just two or three minutes from dropping their steel eggs against the *Lex:* "There wasn't time to sit and wait for help. Those babies were coming on fast and had to be stopped."[32]

His instincts honed by countless hours of gunnery practice, Butch maneuvered for a high-side pass against the trailing bomber on the extreme right. Lining up his shot as the lead bombers passed by, he swooped into range, smoothly placed the pipper of his gun sight ahead of the target for the proper deflection, and squeezed the trigger for short bursts as he roared into point-blank range. His quarry was the *rikkō* flown by Flight Petty Officer Second Class Kogiku Ryōsuke, the sole wingman in the third *shōtai* (section). The fiery spurts of Butch's tracers caught the entire formation by surprise. His bullets ripped through Kogiku's fuselage and tore open one of the fuel tanks fitted inside the wing, causing avgas to gush forth. The stricken Mitsubishi abruptly lurched to starboard.[33]

Scoring so quickly enabled Butch to shift to the next target up the echelon. He had to pull up slightly to let the first bomber drop out of the way, then set his sights on the Type 1 flown by Flight Petty Officer First Class Maeda Kōji, the third-*shōtai* leader. Again he stormed to within one hundred yards, aimed for the pilots, and likewise enjoyed rapid results when his incendiaries ignited gasoline leaking from one of the holed fuel tanks. Streaming black smoke, Maeda's *rikkō* also fell behind the others, but not before his frantic gunners fancifully chalked up two Grummans. Maeda later described how his burning aircraft avoided destruction: "Miraculously, however, the flames were put out by one single spurt of liquid [actually, CO_2 gas] from the fire-extinguisher."[34]

Butch recalled, "I attacked, and two of 'em dropped out of formation. Naturally I was very pleased, and I guess a little surprised, too. That was my first pass at 'em. One was smoking and the other was trailing gasoline. . . . So I pulled up and recovered. Then I noticed my wingman was gone. I didn't know what happened to him." Actually, Dufilho had followed Butch into the fray, hoping to divert defensive fire away from his leader, with some success. One of the Japanese aviators (believed to be Maeda) told the *Japan Times and Advertiser* "of the terrific dogfight that ensued," never realizing that he was fighting only one opponent capable of shooting back.[35]

Although Butch understandably notched the first two bombers as kills, neither Maeda nor Kogiku was through. Despite being shot out of formation, both *rikkōs* later caught up in time to drop their bombs. As Butch explained, "When one would start burning, I'd haul out and wait for it to get out of the way. Then I'd go in and get another one. I didn't have time to watch [them fall]. When they drop out of formation, you don't bother with 'em any more. You go after the next."[36]

Recovering from his first pass, Butch crossed over to the left side of the formation. Swiftly rolling into his second high-side run, he targeted the rearmost bomber on that flank, the *rikkō* flown by Flight Petty Officer First Class Mori Bin, no. 1 wingman in the second *shōtai*. Not realizing that one or at most only two fighters were even present, Mori dramatically recounted how "enemy planes swirled around us, zooming, banking, diving, attacking us from all directions." Drawing near, Butch targeted the engine on the opposite (starboard) side of the bomber, so that if his aim was short, the big .50-caliber slugs would tear through the cockpit and the near engine. However, Butch's aim was perfect; in Mori's words, "The left tank and the right engine had been damaged. The speed of the plane dropped alarmingly, and we knew that we could not follow the squadron." As Mori sought to retain control, he fell further behind the others. However, his gunners tallied Butch's F4F no fewer than three times as he pressed his attacks against other targets on the left side. Mori dumped his bombs and withdrew immediately, never having had the chance to bomb the *Lexington,* and "flew low over the sea, almost skimming the surface of the water."[37]

Seeing Mori's bomber fall away, Butch swung his aiming point ahead to the left trailing aircraft in the center vee and barreled in for another of his patented close-in side attacks. That *rikkō*, Itō's no. 1 wingman, was commanded by Flight Petty Officer First Class Uchiyama Susumu, the senior observer. At such short range, Butch simply targeted the pilots and scored. Uchiyama's left wing and engine erupted in flames, and this time there would be no pulling out short of the sea.

Butch kept hammering against the left side of what remained of the formation. The puffs of black smoke that bloomed a thousand feet short of the bombers warned him that the ships were firing their 5-inch antiair-

Butch O'Hare versus the First *Chūtai,* 20 February 1942

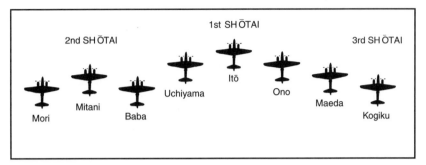

First-*chūtai* formation

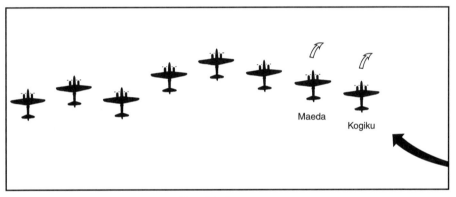

Butch's first pass

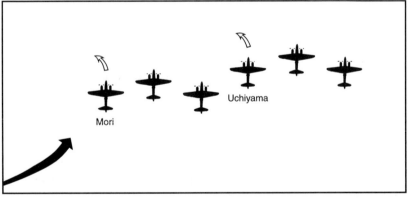

Butch's second pass

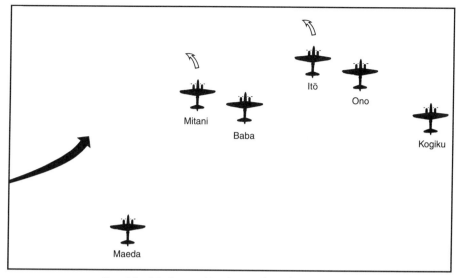

Butch's third pass (in the midst of cruiser AA)

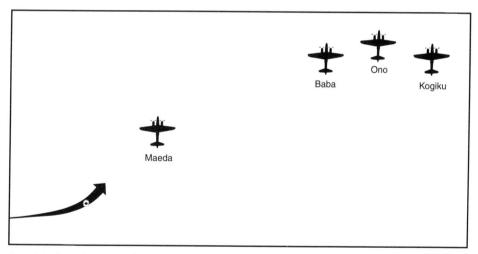

Butch's fourth pass—bombing. Subsequently: Baba shot down eight miles south by Ens. E. R. Sellstrom; Ono badly damaged, crashed at Nugava Island; Mori chased by VS-2 SBD, ditched at Rabaul; Maeda and Kogiku returned to Rabaul.

craft guns. That meant that the enemy planes were fast approaching the bomb release point. Ignoring the AA, Butch came around again for a third high-side pass and bored in against what had become the left trailing *rikkō*, flown by young Lt. (jg) Mitani Akira (Eta Jima sixty-sixth class, 1938), the second-*shōtai* leader. Mitani's Mitsubishi swiftly sustained fatal hits and dropped away, exposing Itō's lead bomber to Butch's earnest attentions. From close on its port quarter, he pored slugs into its left wing with amazing results. To Butch's surprise—and no doubt to Itō's as well—the nacelle exploded, and the heavy Kasei double-bank radial engine tumbled free, leaving a charred, gaping hole in the left wing.

Catching up to the other bombers—and, incidentally, again claiming Butch's Grumman as it assaulted Mitani and Itō from the side—Maeda wrongly thought that an AA shell had struck the commander's aircraft, so violent was the blast that severed the engine. Just after Itō's mutilated bomber spun out of formation, Butch drew down against Maeda's *rikkō* but had to relent when his guns quit after firing only about ten rounds each, the last of his eighteen hundred bullets. Although he had done his best, he still fretted over what the surviving Japanese might do to the *Lex*. Reduced now to the role of spectator, he pulled away from the bursting 5-inch shells to see what befell the task force.

Butch later related what went through his mind during his first air battle. "It was just careful timing," he explained. "You don't have time to consider the odds against you. You are too busy weighing all the factors, time, speed, holding your fire till the right moment, shooting sparingly. You don't feel you are throwing bullets to keep alive. You just want to keep shooting." Always a careful practitioner of deflection shooting, Butch was fully aware that every gunner in the enemy formation had targeted his Wildcat. Yet he never gave them the opportunity to score but broke off his runs cleanly before being drawn astern of his targets. "You've got to keep moving. When you're sitting (and you do have to sit to fire) you've got to get your shots off and then move again. The longer you sit the better chance you've got to get hit."[38]

In the past several minutes things had been pretty exciting for the ships as well. At 1702 lookouts discovered six to eight enemy bombers approaching from the starboard quarter. That put Ted Sherman in an "impossible situation." Five Wildcats were waiting to come on board, and four would surely ditch from lack of fuel if they were not recovered immediately. Given the impossibility of acquiring replacement fighters in the remote South Pacific, that alone could cripple the *Lexington*'s offensive capability. Yet steaming straight into the wind to land planes rendered her extremely vulnerable to the imminent horizontal bombing attack. Beginning about 1706 Sherman commenced zigzagging at 30 knots while continuing to head north. Perched on the *Lex*'s stern, Lt. Aquilla G. Dibrell, the landing signal officer, waited for the brief intervals when the carrier was pointed into the wind and coolly brought in one F4F after another. At 1709, as Lovelace, in the last or the next to last Wildcat, breasted the ramp, the *Lex* blasted away with her 5-inch AA battery. Taxiing forward after catching a wire, Don noticed that "all hands were running for cover," and for good reason: bombs were falling. Intent on his maneuvering, Sherman turned to "Ducky" Duckworth, the air officer, and said, "You can land those fighters now." He smiled: "The last one just came aboard, sir." Relieved, Sherman immediately ordered the rudder put hard to port.[39]

As the Japanese bombers stormed the ships from astern, the suspense became terrific for those onlookers not absorbed in their tasks. Along with many others, Wilson Brown gaped as Butch "with incredible courage . . . took on the nine bombers [*sic*] single handed. Every moment I expected to see his small craft shot down by Japanese gunners." The admiral added, "All of us on the flight deck and the bridges became so intent watching the aerial battles that it was hard to concentrate on our duties. At times the entire ship's company burst into cheers as our fighters shot the bombers down into the sea. It was not as though we were in the midst of a life and death struggle, but as if we were at a baseball game." On one of the cruisers a correspondent broadcast to her crew a blow-by-blow description of the action. The drama and exhilaration as Butch sliced through the first *chūtai* were never forgotten by those privileged to witness it. Three flaming bombers could be seen falling at one time while the formation continued to shrink.[40]

About the time Butch finally ran out of ammunition, bombardiers in the three *rikkōs* commanded by Flight Petty Officer First Class Ono Kosuke (Itō's no. 2 wingman), Flight Petty Officer Second Class Baba Tokiharu (Mitani's no. 2 wingman), and Kogiku (Maeda's sole wingman already roughed up by Butch) loosed their payloads against the carrier. Crowded together in tight formation, the remnants of the first *chūtai* delivered a bomb pattern far more accurate than the first wave's effort. Of the six 250-kilogram bombs aimed at the *Lexington,* the nearest raised a large splash only one hundred feet astern in her wake and sprinkled fragments on the flight deck aft. Having sustained further damage and at any rate well out of position, Maeda went after the cruiser maneuvering off the carrier's port bow. His two bombs struck the sea between 100 and 150 yards from the port quarter of the heavy cruiser *Minneapolis* (CA-36).

Even after the bombing, the Japanese would not give up against the *Lexington*. As Maeda withdrew, he kept an eye on Itō's maimed *rikkō* below: "As it was diving toward the sea leaving a streak of black smoke, I noticed the pilot was trying desperately to change the course of his death-descent so that the plane would head directly for the enemy aircraft carrier." He later reported that in true samurai fashion, Itō's aircraft—faithfully followed by that of the "sub-commander" (Mitani)—crashed, "bombs, crew and all, into the shining deck of the enemy plane carrier." Maeda's wishful thinking notwithstanding, Itō missed the *Lex*—no one noticed where Mitani splashed—but certainly gave her a scare. Its engineless left wing clearly visible, Itō's bomber lunged for her port side. Sherman adroitly kept the carrier's stern pointed toward the new intruder, and Itō just could not match his maneuvers. Nose dipping ever more steeply, the *rikkō* staggered past the *Lex*'s port side and at 1712 finally splashed fifteen hundred yards off her port bow. Sherman swerved to avoid steaming over the wreckage burning on the water.[41]

After the bombing, five *rikkōs* from the first *chūtai* remained aloft. Four—Maeda, Ono, Baba, and Kogiku—withdrew relatively close together around ten thousand feet, while Mori limped out alone at low level. Maeda and Kogiku evidently got clean away, and at 1950 they landed back at Rabaul, the only two from either *chūtai* to reach base. Mostly courtesy of Butch, both *rikkōs* required extensive repairs before they could fly again.

Doc Sellstrom, Jimmy Thach's wingman, downed Baba about eight miles south of the task force. Led by Thach and Gayler, the other F4Fs swarmed over Ono's *rikkō* after AA perforated the right engine. "The enemy planes flocked around us," Ono later told a war correspondent, "thinking they had an easy prey to kill." Thach soon discovered that once a Type 1 land-attack plane put its nose down and ran full out, it became difficult to catch. Although the VF-3 pilots shot Ono's bomber full of holes and killed several of the crew, they could not bring it down. One of Ono's gunners startled Gayler with a direct hit on the windshield—fortunately a 7.7-mm bullet that only pocked the heavy Plexiglas, instead of a 20-mm shell that might have blasted through. Despite the long chase, Thach had to let Ono go. Rapidly running out of fuel after so much had drained out of the tanks, Ono headed for Nugava Island, a coral atoll in the Nuguria group east of New Ireland. At 1925 he crashed on the beach, where he and his surviving crew members sought help from the natives.[42]

Proceeding out on his own at low level, Mori encountered three VS-2 SBD Dauntless dive bombers on anti-torpedo-plane patrol, but only the intrepid team of Allen and his radioman Rountree jumped on his tail. Like Thach, Allen found a wounded enemy bomber to be surprisingly fast, only a few knots less than his SBD, so it took him considerable time to ease into range. Several times he and Mori's gunners exchanged shots until they had expended all of their ammunition. Still Allen would not relent. Mori wondered, "What is the matter with that plane? Why didn't it fly back to its aircraft carrier?" Finally, after 150 miles, Allen tried one more gambit before both the sunlight and his fuel ran out. He managed to get underneath the bomber so that Rountree could fire his free gun. When that failed, Allen had to let his doughty opponent go. Later Mori lost his way in a storm, groped through the darkness, and finally at 2010 ditched in Simpson Harbor at Rabaul.[43]

Picking up the Pieces

Now that combat had ended, Butch gave in to the tension he had so tightly held in check. "Time seems to stand still while you're at it. . . . Naturally you're pretty keyed up. Your mouth and throat get so dry it's hard to talk. Mine was so dry I thought I'd lost my voice." After getting no answer over the radio, he reported, "I screamed in the cockpit to see if my voice was OK. It was. Only the transmitter was sour." Descending into the landing circle around the *Lexington,* he had to wait until the maintenance crews could refuel and arm Lovelace's five F4Fs for relief CAP. They took off at about 1745, and the deck was rapidly cleared to bring Butch and the others on board.[44]

Swinging around on final, Butch anticipated receiving the cut from the landing signal officer and dropping onto the deck. Suddenly, a nervous gunner, manning one of the .50-caliber water-cooled machine guns on the *Lex*'s port quarter, briefly blasted away at the slow-moving Wildcat. Butch nevertheless came on in and landed. After F-15 was chocked into place, members of the flight deck crew jumped onto the wings and leaned over to ask how he was. "I'm okay," Butch replied. "Just load those ammo belts, and I'll get back up. But first I want a drink of water. My throat feels swelled shut." His flight suit and helmet were sopping with sweat. No one on the *Lex* yet knew that he was the one who had chopped up the second wave.[45]

Told that he would not be launched, Butch extricated himself from the cockpit. Clyde Baur, aviation machinist's mate third class, one of his mechs, stepped onto the wing and eased him out of the chute harness. To Baur's query, Butch replied that he had shot down seven and asked what was wrong with the airspeed indicator; he had had to land without it—a rather thrilling proposition. Baur found the single bullet hole in F-15's port wing that had disabled the system.[46]

Butch strolled aft along the port side to where he could look down into the gun platform. According to Thach, Butch calmly said to the now deeply embarrassed youngster who had fired at him, "Son, if you don't stop shooting at me when I've got my wheels down, I'm going to have to report you to the gunnery officer." That was sufficient punishment. Butch later explained, "I don't mind him shooting at me when I don't have my wheels down, but it might make me have to take a wave-off, and I don't like to take wave-offs."[47]

The *Lexington* recovered all but two Wildcats. Lt. (jg) Howard Johnson was wounded, but safe, on the *Patterson,* but the other pilot, Ens. John Wilson, was dead. No ship sustained any real damage, something Brown considered extremely fortunate, given the savage nature of the assault. His first impression was that thirty heavy bombers had attacked, and between twelve and twenty went down. At 1915 he reversed course to the southeast and began his intended withdrawal to refuel and decide how he might tackle Rabaul again—with, he hoped, more carrier strength.

Rabaul, Truk, and Tokyo were appalled at the annihilation of the land-attack squadron of the Fourth Air Group, fifteen of seventeen *rikkōs,* including every one of the flying officers. All that the surviving crews could claim in return was one enemy cruiser or destroyer sunk and one carrier set afire, as well as eight defending Grumman fighters shot down. In addition to the land-attack planes, two big flying boats from the Yokohama Air Group fell in battle and another went missing, along with a reconnaissance seaplane (both were noncombat losses). A tremendous hole now existed in the air defense of the region. Worried that the American carrier force might still be coming, Combined Fleet headquarters immediately ordered the First Air Group to fly to Truk from the Dutch East Indies while Rabaul hunkered down for a possible raid. A more important effect of the air battle was postponement for five days (to 8 March) of the planned invasion of Lae and Salamaua in eastern New Guinea. As will be shown, this delay proved significant for the next U.S. carrier operation in the region.

Unaware of the strategic implications of their successful defense of TF-11, the VF-3 pilots assembled late that evening in their ready room, where Thach listened to their individual reports. He had them speak into a wire recorder, "just as we came in, dirty, wounded, oil-soaked, before we could do any second thinking." (Unfortunately these precious recordings evidently went down on 8 May with the *Lexington* during the Battle of the Coral Sea.) Thach found that the accounts "fitted into place like a jigsaw puzzle."[48]

Puzzled over the type of bomber VF-3 had fought—one that resembled the U.S. Army Air Force's Martin B-26 Marauder medium bomber more than anything the Japanese were thought to have—Thach instructed each pilot to sketch the particular attribute of the aircraft he best remembered. The composite featured the "nose of a moose," a fuselage like a "big cigar," sharply tapered wings, and a single vertical tail—a fairly accurate rendition of the Mitsubishi Type 1 land-attack plane. Thach was impressed by the aircraft: "It had speed and it had guns and it was manned by a very experienced crew that wasn't going to quit." The U.S. Navy would rarely see again in the South Pacific the brown and green mottled camouflage scheme (in Japanese, *kumogata,* or "cloud formation") used in the Takao Air Group. These land-attack planes had also retained the original Takao unit markings: two horizontal white tail stripes evidently outlined in red above the individual aircraft letter-number combination, also in white. That denoted the second *daitai,* one of the two major divisions within the Takao Air Group. American observers thought that the combination of red-outlined stripes and white letters resembled their own red-and-white-striped rudders.[49]

After that eventful day Butch just could not sleep. Hunting a midnight sandwich in the wardroom, he discovered his CO similarly bothered. According to Thach, "We talked over the battle again and I guess we finally got to sleep an hour or two later—still right on the crest of the wave." Later that morning Thach called his pilots together and analyzed the battle. There had been mistakes, he admitted, especially in the attacks from dead astern that had cost two F4Fs and one life. "The main thing, however, was the fact that the Japs had shown us that our tactics, expert marksmanship and teamwork were right." Despite their considerable defensive firepower, enemy land-based bombers were vulnerable if tackled in the right way. Butch's superb performance personified this right way.[50]

The *Lexington*'s senior officers estimated that on 20 February the Japanese lost eighteen or nineteen of the twenty planes (eighteen bombers and two flying boats) sent against TF-11. They discovered that in four minutes (1706 through 1709) Butch completed no fewer than four passes against the second wave and shot at seven bombers. He felt certain that he had polished off six—that many rising-sun flags grace the entry in his log book. Thach agreed with his tally, as did Brown, in congratulatory messages on 21 and 22 February 1942. However, Sherman's report of the twenty-third ultimately credited him with five bombers destroyed, because four of the supposed nine bombers had been seen overhead after Butch pulled off. Thach, Gayler, Lemmon, Peterson, Sellstrom, and Lieutenant Henry (VB-2) each received credit for one aircraft destroyed, plus many shared kills along with other pilots, while Lieutenant Allen (VS-2) might have got another. On 25 February VF-3 stenciled rising-sun flags beside the cockpit of every F4F that had scored. None matched F-15's proud victory tally of five.

In retrospect, using all available records, it appears that three *rikkōs* (Uchiyama, Mitani, and Itō) fell to Butch's fire immediately, one (Mori) later ditched, and two (Maeda and Kogiku) sustained heavy damage. In return, F-15 suffered two hits from "friendly" AA shell fragments, but only the one enemy 7.7-mm bullet in the port wing.

The Reluctant Hero

Once Butch was identified as the hero who had singlehandedly demolished most of the second wave, he became the center of attention. The day after the battle, Stanley went down to the metal shop and fabricated a trophy that the squadron presented to him. Soon Butch caught wind of the recommendations for decorations being compiled. On 23 February, Sherman put him in for a Navy Cross, then the Navy's third highest award behind the Medal of Honor and the Distinguished Service Medal. The proposed citation praised Butch's "courage, skill and good thinking" in destroying five bombers, conduct that proved to be "of greatest value in preventing the ship from sustaining serious damage or possible loss."[51]

Butch leaned on Jimmy Thach as hard as anyone could lean on his CO. They had become friends as well as professional colleagues, which made the conversation about the recommendation much easier; but it was nonetheless difficult. "I don't want a medal," Butch pleaded. "The other officers in the squadron could have done the same thing and we all know it." Thach reminded him that indeed several, including himself, were being considered for decorations. "Butch, can you imagine me going to the Task Force Commander and asking him not to put me in for a medal? As it stands for the moment, you, Lt. [Edward] Allen and I are being recommended for the Navy Cross; Gayler, Lemmon, Stanley and Sellstrom for the Distinguished Flying Cross. Maybe the people on up the line will decline to make the award, but the recommendation is going forward." Subsequently Thach described how Butch begged him "for one whole evening not to recommend him."[52]

In his endorsement of Sherman's report, Brown seconded all of the recommendations, added Sherman's own name to those for the Navy Cross, and urged that the decorations be awarded. However, it was the action message Brown sent on 24 February to admirals Nimitz and Leary that sealed Butch's fate. After correcting previous descriptions of the battle, Brown added a rare mention, for such a high-level dispatch, of one specific individual's achievement: "Lieut. Edward H. O'Hare chiefly responsible for the destruction of 6 planes." That brought Butch to the attention of the Washington brass, specifically Secretary of the Navy Frank Knox and Admiral King, who really got the ball rolling.[53]

On 23 February, Butch and the rest of VF-3 enjoyed a laugh over Radio Tokyo's proclamation that an American carrier of the *Lexington* type had been "left in flames." Stanley commented that the Japanese radio announcer—a man, in those pre–Tokyo Rose days—"had forgotten to put a comma between left and in." The broadcast stated that "one bomber failed to return." Stanley felt that "a comma would have helped that sentence too." Butch would have been even more amused had he seen Japanese newspapers sporting one of Maeda's photographs of TF-11 retouched so that it looked as if the American carrier in the center had blown up.[54]

In the last week of February TF-11 reached quieter waters and refueled. Not available were provisions, however, and the *Lex* had to transfer stores to the cruisers and especially the tin cans. On 27 February, Brown advised Nimitz, "Absolutely necessary reprovision, repeat, reprovision this force not later than 15 March." Butch's stomach had already deemed that alarm long overdue. By early March the *Lex*'s larder had run short of almost everything except canned spinach and beans, eventually reducing their meals to spinach in the morning and beans and spinach in the afternoon. Thach thought "those pale, tan-colored beans were the most tasteless things" he had ever eaten. He even dreamed that saboteurs were stuffing the beans with clay and putting them back in their containers. A gourmet like Butch must have suffered agony at such insipid fare. Thach reckoned at twelve pounds the average weight loss the pilots of VF-3 suffered during the cruise.[55]

On 4 March while TF-11 again fueled in the New Hebrides, Butch discovered that newspapers throughout the United States had carried front-page stories crediting him with shooting down six bombers somewhere "west of the Gilbert Islands." He was being compared with the U.S. Navy's first—and to that point only other—ace, Lt. David S. Ingalls, who had destroyed six German aircraft during World War I while flying with the Royal Air Force. Butch came in for some good-natured teasing from his fellow pilots. "We all asked him for his autograph," Stanley wrote at the time: "He took it well and I feel deserves the publicity he got." Lovelace agreed, noting in his diary, "Butch O'Hare is very modest in a natural sort of way."[56]

Over the Mountains

On 6 March, Rear Admiral Fletcher's Task Force Seventeen with the *Yorktown* hove into sight north of New Caledonia. Brown now wielded two carriers (with about 135 aircraft), eight heavy cruisers, and fourteen destroyers—the greatest concentration of Allied naval strength yet achieved during the Pacific War—and his superiors expected dramatic results. Hoping to forestall the next Japanese advance expected to occur momentarily, Brown determined upon another try at Rabaul, this time from the southeast. At dawn on 10 March fifty-three strike planes from the *Lexington* were to attack Rabaul while a like number of *Yorktown*-ers plastered a small airstrip at Gasmata on the south coast of New Britain. As before, Thach and Butch were slated to fly with the VF-3 fighter escorts and strafe the Rabaul airfields just prior to sunrise.

On 8 March while the task forces crossed the Coral Sea, the Japanese gained a foothold in eastern New Guinea by capturing Lae—famous as Amelia Earhart's last stop in her ill-fated 1937 flight—and Salamaua in northern Papua. Yet the invasion force was vulnerable. According to Brown, "This was the very break we had been hoping and praying for— an opportunity to catch Japanese navy and transports away from the concentrated defense of their shore-based planes." He hoped to redirect his planned attack to Papua but faced formidable difficulties. It seemed too risky to penetrate far into the narrow waters between New Britain and New Guinea to strike from north of Papua. Forewarned, the Japanese would simply scatter. A carrier raid against Lae and Salamaua from directly south in the Gulf of Papua seemed possible, but that entailed flying over the steep Owen Stanley Mountains, in places as high as ten thousand feet—too lofty for TBD Devastators lugging torpedoes to surmount, and always a threat to aircraft because of chronic poor weather. On 9 March, Brown learned of the existence of a single suitable mountain pass at seventy-five hundred feet located forty-five miles south of Lae and Salamaua. He decided to attack the next morning with his full air striking force, including one squadron (VT-2) carrying torpedoes. That would afford Butch another memorable combat mission.[57]

The morning of 10 March found Brown and Fletcher far up the Gulf of Papua and only forty-five miles off the rugged south shore of New Guinea. Ted Sherman and the other *Lexington* air planners had carefully assessed the effective range of their aircraft. Given that the distance to Lae and Salamaua was 125 miles, Sherman opted for a staggered departure by squadrons rather than concentrating the whole group. Thach's eight VF-3 escort F4Fs (including Butch in F-15) took off first at 0749 to clear the deck, followed by the rest of the strike group of thirty-one SBD Dauntlesses and thirteen TBD Devastators. The dive bombers and torpedo planes left immediately, while the *Lex* recovered Thach's Wildcats at 0822 to top off their fuel tanks. They got away the second time at 0839 and raced after the rest of the group. Lacking drop tanks (which no F4Fs had as yet), Thach figured he could remain over the target only ten minutes or so. The *Yorktown* strike group (ten F4Fs, thirty SBDs, and twelve TBDs) departed a few minutes after the *Lex*'s contingent.

Cruising faster than Jimmy Brett's VT-2 TBDs, Bill Ault with the *Lexington* SBDs bounded ahead as they climbed to sixteen thousand feet. Relieved to find the crucial pass largely free of clouds, Ault peeled off to remain there as a beacon should the weather close in. Thach caught up with Brett's lumbering torpedo planes as they neared the pass. No doubt quite glad that he was flying a Wildcat instead of a Devastator, Butch watched a small drama unfold. It became obvious that the heavily laden Devastators might not clear the mountains, for the ground was rising faster than they were. According to Thach, the TBDs "were still below looking up at the ridge, and I was sitting right on top of them."

Brett radioed Thach, "You'd better go ahead. I don't think we're going to make it." He replied, "No, I'll wait here a little bit. I've got enough gas. I can wait a bit."

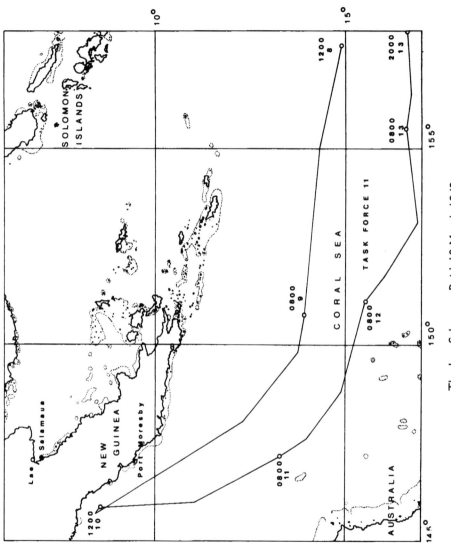

The Lae-Salamaua Raid, 10 March 1942

"All right, hold it. I've got an idea," Brett responded. A gliding enthusiast, he noticed bright sunlight illuminating a particular patch of green below. That cloudless space meant a current of warmer air that would be rising above the rest. Increased lift from the fortuitous updraft "washed" the Devastators over the pass. To inform Sherman that he had surmounted the feared obstacle, Brett radioed the code word "Halfway House." That brought smiles to Butch and the other naval aviators, who remembered it as the name of a small roadside diner located halfway between the city of Pensacola and the naval air station where most of them had trained.[58]

Thach led the eight F4Fs out ahead of the TBDs and soon passed the SBDs while swiftly descending toward the target area visible at the edge of the distant sea. Each Wildcat lugged a pair of 30-pound fragmentation bombs that Sherman insisted they drop onto the airfields. By 0920 VF-3 had reached Huon Gulf. No Zeros were in evidence, but plenty of ships could be seen between Lae at the northwest corner of Huon Gulf and Salamaua on a little peninsula about sixteen miles south. The attackers surprised sixteen Japanese transports, destroyers, and auxiliaries, a light cruiser, and farther east even a seaplane tender—all caught without air support.

Worried about Zeros possibly lurking above, Thach detached Butch and Duff Dufilho to fly top cover. He knew that Butch did not particularly care for that duty, but "if I was going to have anybody up there, I wanted . . . Butch. . . . I figured that no matter how many enemy planes there were coming in, he could give them a busy time before they got down to us."[59]

Noel Gayler's four F4Fs swung north toward Lae to support VS-2's attack. They shot up AA guns, dropped their "dinky little bombs" around the airstrip, then strafed warships in the harbor. Gayler quickly dealt with the only aerial opposition, a brave Mitsubishi F1M2 Type 0 observation seaplane (Pete) from the *Kiyokawa Maru* Air Group. AA at Salamaua destroyed one VS-2 SBD flown by Ens. Joseph P. Johnson, the only loss suffered by both carrier air groups for the whole raid.

Thach and Doc Sellstrom enthusiastically worked over Salamaua, sprinkling their bombs on buildings around the airfield, while VB-2 and VT-2 attacked ships between Lae and Salamaua. Soon Butch and Dufilho came on down for their own turn against Salamaua, then rejoined Thach patrolling over the harbor. They played tag with AA bursts, saw heavy bombs explode on and adjacent to the ships, and watched Brett's TBDs torpedo the transport *Yokohama Maru* in Salamaua Harbor. For lack of a better target, Thach, Butch, and their wingmen ganged up on a small auxiliary minesweeper and, like Gayler, were impressed by the obvious power of the heavy .50-caliber slugs against unarmored or lightly armored targets.

With an eye on the clock, Thach rounded up the eight VF-3 F4Fs, none the worse for wear, and covered the withdrawal of the *Lex*'s strike planes. As they left, the *Yorktown*ers took their romp around the harbor. The mountain pass remained clear, and the rest of the flight, over rough but beautiful scenery, proved uneventful. Butch landed back on board the *Lexington* around 1110, little imagining that nearly eighteen months would elapse before he next fired his guns in anger.

Brown turned the task forces southeast and withdrew without Japanese interference. The Lae-Salamaua strike was very successful, constituting the worst defeat suffered by the Imperial Navy to this point in the war. Three transports sank and six other ships sustained damage. The surprise attack delayed the Japanese advance against Port Moresby and the Solomons for a month or more and directly led to the confrontation in May in the Coral Sea.

On 14 March, the day after Butch's twenty-eighth birthday, VF-3 swapped the six F4Fs fitted with armor and self-sealing fuel tanks—which did not include Butch's 4031—to VF-42 on the *Yorktown*, in return for two "of their oldest crates." Two days later the task forces parted, with TF-11 and the *Lexington* headed for Pearl and Fletcher's *Yorktown* bound for the Coral Sea. Long, lazy days ensued as the *Lex* recrossed the equator and drew closer to Hawaii. Returning to civilization, Butch surely wondered what had happened in his absence.[60]

On the morning of 26 March the *Lexington* Air Group flew from the ship to Ford Island in the center of Pearl Harbor. Butch brought faithful 4031. The aviators all had a surprise coming. Lovelace wrote, "As soon as we were parked pilots from other squadrons began to congratulate us right away, and made much to do about our battle. It made us feel pretty good." Butch with F-15's five flags attracted a good deal of attention—many handshakes and slaps on the back. Later he witnessed another heartwarming sight. As the gallant *Lex* entered Pearl to tie up at Ford Island, cheers resounded throughout the harbor. It was a fitting way to end a tremendous cruise.[61]

Butch in working clothes on Maui.
(O'Hare Collection)

Butch, Howard Crews (left), and Foster Blair pose in front of one of VF-3's four Corsairs, Maui, February 1943.
(Courtesy of Capt. Howard Crews)

Butch with his daughter Kathleen, or "Buttons," as
he affectionately called her, June 1943.
(Courtesy of Kathleen O'Hare Lytle Nye)

Butch's Boys: VF-3 on Maui, July 1943. *Top row (left to right):* John Stanizewski, John Johnston, Robert Hobbs, Ashton Roberts, George Rodgers, Harvey Odenbrett, James Nichols, Robert Locker, Charles Palmer, Edward Philippe, Sy Mendenhall, Charles McCord. *Third row:* Bayard Webster, Thomas Hall, Robert Merritt, Bascom Gates, Clifford Seaver, William Davis, Donald Kent, John Benton, Herschel Pahl, Robert Klingler, Lindley Godson. *Second row:* John Ogg, Thomas Willman, Wilton Hutt, Thaddeus Coleman, Allie Callan, Alex Vraciu, Richard Trimble, Albert Nyquist, Malcolm Loesch, William Rose,

Howard Crews. *Front row:* Richards Loesch, John Altemus, Foster Blair, Henry Fairbanks, George Bullard, Butch, Paul Rooney, Joe Robbins, Alfred Kerr, Robert Neel, Cyrus Chambers. *(O'Hare Collection)*

Crews, Bullard (center), and Butch with friends at the great luau on Maui, July 1943. *(O'Hare Collection)*

The CO's division on the *Independence*, 6 September 1943.
From left: Alex Vraciu, Butch, Sy Mendenhall, and Willie Callan.
(O'Hare Collection)

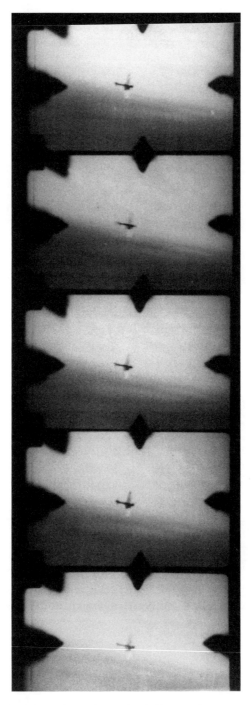

Gun camera footage of Butch's Zeke kill at Wake, 5 October 1943.
(Courtesy of Comdr. Alex Vraciu)

Butch gives a thumbs-up to Rear Admiral Ragsdale at Wake, 5 October 1943. *(USN via O'Hare Collection)*

Ens. Andy Skon, fall 1943. *(Courtesy of Capt. W. A. Skon)*

Butch and Chief Willie Williams talk things over at
Wake, 5 October 1943. *(USN via O'Hare Collection)*

Lt. Comdr. Bill Dean (first row, second from the right) and the rest of
Fighting Two in their ready room on the *Enterprise*, November 1943.
(Courtesy of Thomas Morrissey)

Rear Adm. Arthur Radford shows the strain of the past few days in a photograph taken in late November 1943 on the *Saratoga* shortly after he transferred from the *Enterprise*. *(USN)*

Lt. Comdr. John Phillips (right) and his TBF crew on 25 November 1943. Hazen Rand, the radar operator (wearing helmet and goggles) is in the center, and Alvin Kernan is on the left. Perched on the wing is radio operator Ray Sullivan, who did not fly on the Black Panther missions. *(Courtesy of Dr. Alvin Kernan)*

Adm. John Towers greets Butch's mother and sister Marilyn on 18 February 1951 during the dedication of the O'Hare Room at the Naval Academy.
(USN via O'Hare Collection)

Chicago mayor Richard Daley (far left) was host to the O'Hare clan on 20 February 1992 for a special ceremony commemorating the fiftieth anniversary of Butch's Medal of Honor flight. Seated from left are Mrs. Marilyn O'Hare Platt, Mrs. Kathleen O'Hare Lytle Nye, and Mrs. Patricia O'Hare Palmer. *(Courtesy of Mayor Richard Daley)*

CHAPTER 9

The Uncomfortable Hero

"I don't want a medal!"

On the campus of Western Military Academy, Col. Ralph L. Jackson stopped to button his topcoat before venturing into the cold early evening of Tuesday, 3 March 1942. Walking near the dormitory, he could not help but agree with the cadets that spring could not be too far away. There might be some more snow, one final blast of winter's fury, but by the end of the month the earliest-blooming plants would appear. That was something to look forward to.

A loud yell from the dormitory interrupted his reverie—then two more shouts, followed by pandemonium.

Jackson hurried to the dorm, threatening, "Somebody is going to get demerits for this!"

"What is all this screaming about?" he demanded of the first cadets he encountered.

"Our Lt. Edward O'Hare just shot down six Japanese planes. It's on the radio."

Within ten minutes every cadet in the dormitory knew of Butch's feat.

They screamed and yelled as though Western had just won the state championship in football. They showed absolutely no decorum whatsoever, and for once Colonel Jackson could not have cared less. He exulted as loudly as any of his cadets.[1]

In Keokuk, Iowa, Rita O'Hare was helping her sister, Mrs. Mary Humble, put Mary's six-month-old daughter, Chrissee, to bed when the phone rang. A reporter from the *Chicago Herald-American* inquired, did Rita know her husband was a hero?

"No, what did he do?"

Relieved that the news about Butch was not bad, Mary resumed putting Chrissee to bed. From the next room she could hear Rita telling someone that she was very proud, that she did not know where Butch was, and that he had said in his last letter that he was very lonesome for her. Hearing the conversation end, Mary asked, "What's going on about Butch?" Before Rita could answer, the phone rang again. Smiling at each other, both sisters knew this call too would be for Rita, as were the dozens of others that came all through the night from across the country. The next day Mary quipped in one interview, "I may be Mrs. Humble, but I'm not humble today."

In St. Louis the phone also rang at 3711 Bates Street, Selma O'Hare's new residence since the sale of the "big empty house" on Holly Hills only a few blocks away. Across the hall in the brick apartment building lived Selma's brother, Henry, and his wife, Nellie. After the first call, Selma hastened to Henry's apartment to share the news when the phone sounded again. By the time she was able to reach her brother's apartment, reporters and photographers from the St. Louis newspapers had already arrived. Quickly retrieving a photo of Butch taken early in his Naval Academy days, Selma—comfortable with strangers for perhaps the first time in her life—smiled into her son's portrait as photographers snapped her picture. The next day that photo of Selma appeared in hundreds of newspapers, along with the story of Butch's feat, a short sketch of his life, and Selma's synopsis of her emotions: "I'm the proudest mother in the land. He always was crazy about airplanes."[2]

Nearly all the first articles appearing in newspapers around the country identified the late E. J. O'Hare as Butch's father and described him as having been a manager of racing interests in Chicago, Boston, and Miami. Many mentioned that he had been killed in gangland fashion, but most refrained from making any statement about EJ's association with Al Capone. Only one, the 4 May 1942 issue of *Time*, reverted to the sensationalism of the Chicago and St. Louis newspapers in the first days after EJ's death.

For Selma the interviews in the first week of March were just the beginning. Like it or not, she too had become a celebrity much in demand not only for newspaper interviews but also for radio broadcasts, speeches, and innumerable special guest appearances. Ironically, Selma was describing her own personality when she told an Associated Press interviewer that her son was "reticent" and that Butch "would not want any publicity, even as a national hero." She added knowingly, "I don't think he'll like it."

Newspapers in St. Louis and Chicago were already battling over the new hero. The *Chicago Sun* ended an article with the comment, "Eddie O'Hare is just 'an average American.' Before they are through with us, the Axis and the Japs will find out that there are several million more where he came from." Taking umbrage, the editor of the *St. Louis Star-Times* wrote, "Where he came from is St. Louis." This was the opening salvo of claims for the hero born and raised in St. Louis but who had often visited his father in Chicago. Phoenix, where Butch and Rita had married and where both his sisters lived, also put in its claim.

Thus, seemingly everybody wanted Butch, but for the moment he was unavailable to all except the *Lexington* and her air group. On 8 March the public frenzy for Butch was satisfied by Selma's participation in a national radio broadcast from New York. Obviously nervous and openly stating that she dreaded the appearance, Selma nonetheless received an ovation equal to those that greeted the other guests— actresses Bette Davis and Merle Oberon—as the patriotic program "Keep 'Em Rolling" opened at the Mutual Broadcasting Company studio in the Amsterdam Theater, Times Square. Even in the early days of the war the media recognized the role of women, this program being dedicated to the "unsung women who are the strength and staff of America-at-home." Reading from a script, Selma related how she first heard the news of Butch's feat. She explained that her son would not like his newfound publicity; that she would feed him fried chicken, candied sweet potatoes, cranberry sauce, and banana layer cake when he came home; and that everyone needed to get behind the president and do all they could to help the war effort. Leaving the stage to another warm ovation, she acknowledged that she was very proud to have participated, but that the occasion had been one of the greatest ordeals of her life. However, "if I have been able to help at all, it was worthwhile."[3]

Returning home, Selma addressed the St. Louis unit of the American Newspaper Guild and found some comfort in humor, jesting that she was disappointed that Butch had not shot down the other planes flying with those he did get. But the attempt at humor revealed her nervousness, and the audience knew, as she did, that her son was still close to the enemy. She was right. On 10 March, as previously related, Butch flew on the Lae-Salamaua raid.

On 12 March 1942, Task Force Eleven was ordered to Pearl Harbor. While the *Lady Lex* and Butch were still nearly two weeks away from Pearl, Chicago newspapers shifted gears slightly to report on 13 March how the new air hero would receive $15,000 from the sale of a building on Sherwin Avenue as part of the settlement from EJ's will. Butch would not hear of this until after 26 March, when the *Lexington* docked at Pearl.

The day after arriving on Oahu, Butch endured the same ordeal as his mother. VF-3 received one week's leave at the Royal Hawaiian Hotel, but Butch was greeted there by a horde of reporters and radio announcers instead of the traditional pretty Hawaiian girl carrying a lei. Sitting uncomfortably on a piano bench beside Jimmy Thach, he frequently deferred to his squadron commander during the barrage of questions fired in his direction. For the first of many such times, Butch responded that it was easier to face Japanese fighter planes than reporters.

And shortly after, Butch learned that he would be going back to the States, for he had greatly impressed no less a personage than Admiral King, the imperious commander in chief of the U.S. Fleet and a proud former captain of the *Lexington*. On 31 March paperwork crossed the desk of Capt. Donald B. Duncan on King's staff, instructing him to "initiate temporary orders by dispatch in order that above [Butch] may be returned at earliest opportunity to report to BuAer [the Bureau of Aeronautics] for temporary duty to be instructed and then sent to various training centers for student aviators to lecture regarding carrier operations." The actual dispatch reached Pearl Harbor on 6 April, whereupon Admiral Nimitz asked the advice of Butch's nominal superior, Rear Admiral Aubrey W. Fitch, commander of Carrier Division One. Fitch completely misunderstood the reason why King wanted Butch back in the States. If someone was needed for the training program, then Thach should go back to lecture the troops. Fitch recommended that Butch not be detached from the squadron at this time. Nimitz knew better. His response to King on 8 April was simply "Lieutenant O'Hare available now."[4]

While reporters at Pearl Harbor, and others later in Washington, St. Louis, and other localities, described Butch as modest, bashful, and even

embarrassed by all the attention, they overlooked the key to his personality: he was modest because he was honest. He truly did not believe that
he had done anything unique, certainly not anything other members of
his squadron could not do or would not have done had they been in the
same situation. At times during the ten weeks when Butch was the center of attention, he became sufficiently annoyed to respond sharply, not
only to the press, but also to family. However, even those few outbursts
failed to taint his image in the press. Here was a good-looking, modest
aviator who had waded alone into a large flight of enemy planes, shot
down several, and effectively broken up their attack on his floating
home. He was a hero to the press, to America, and to the U.S. Navy.
Whether he liked it or not, that was the way it was. To this point nearly
all the news coming out of the Pacific had been bad. Now here was
something, someone, genuinely to cheer. The adoration and respect
poured upon Butch came from a society greatly in need of a hero and a
positive event to celebrate.

Of course, Butch did not find things all bad. During a broadcast on
Monday, 30 March, by radio station KGU in Honolulu, he enjoyed the
opportunity to say hello to Rita ("Here's a great big radio hug, the best I
can do under the circumstances") and to his mother ("Love from me to
you").[5] And on 8 April he thanked the Grumman Aircraft Corporation
for 1,150 cartons of cigarettes, a grand total of 230,000 smokes. Employees at the Bethpage, New York, plant had passed the hat and collected
$583.11 to buy the cigarettes in appreciation of his combat victories in
one of their F4F Wildcats. A loyal Camel smoker, Butch opened a carton
of Lucky Strikes, deciding that it was the least he could do for the good
people back in Bethpage. In his letter to the Grumman employees he wrote,
"You build them, we'll fly them and between us, we can't be beaten." It
was a sentiment he would voice often in the following two months.

On 3 April, Washington had directed that photos be taken of Butch
seated in and standing by the type of plane he had flown. A week later
he and Thach took aloft from Kaneohe two of the VF-3 F4Fs, accompanied by a photo plane. The resulting motion and still pictures of Thach
flying F-1 (Bureau Number 3976) and Butch in F-13 (BuNo 3986, an
F4F he actually never flew during the last cruise) would become famous.

On 11 April, Butch went up in faithful F-15 (BuNo 4031) for the last
time. The next day he said farewell to Noel Gayler and eleven other VF-
3 pilots, who with all the squadron Wildcats were transferred to Lt.
Comdr. Paul H. Ramsey's VF-2, preparing to go on board the *Lexington*. She sailed on the fifteenth from Pearl Harbor for what would be her

final cruise. That same day Butch left on a large flying boat bound for San Francisco. Despite his joy at getting to see Rita, Selma, and the rest of the family, he felt sorry not to be going back out with his teammates on the *Lady Lex*. A little over three weeks later she became the first U.S. aircraft carrier lost in World War II.

Early on Thursday, 16 April, Butch was met at San Francisco by reporters and photographers. He did not have much time for interviews, but one of the Associated Press pictures was picked up around the country. Interestingly, the sleeve of Butch's aviation-green winter working uniform coat displayed the stripe and a half of a lieutenant (junior grade), the rank he had achieved in 1940, while his shirt collar featured the "railroad tracks" of a full lieutenant, his temporary rank since January 1942. Although he did not know it, both ranks would soon be incorrect.

Quickly boarding a commercial airliner, Butch flew to Phoenix, via Los Angeles, and landed just after dark. Running down the ramp from the plane, he greeted Rita with an embrace that turned her face nearly as red as her auburn hair. Next came hugs for Patsy and Marilyn. Everybody talked; nobody listened; the women cried. Butch asked about Patsy's newborn daughter and also Marilyn's first child, also a daughter, whom he would later refer to as "the Judy one." Paul's father, Dr. E. Payne Palmer, had earlier told reporters that Butch, before the war, used to fly over the Palmer residence at low altitude to announce his return to Phoenix from San Diego. "Probably would have had the airline pilot do the same tonight except he knew we would all be here," he added. In an exuberant mood, Butch answered reporters' questions cheerfully but let it be known that he was in Phoenix for a vacation. Few reporters, their readers, or autograph seekers took the hint, however, and the Palmer phone remained off the hook from late Thursday night until Saturday afternoon, when Butch and Rita departed for Washington. That day the news that U.S. aircraft had bombed Tokyo and three other major Japanese cities electrified the entire country. That was, of course, the celebrated Doolittle Raid of sixteen Army B-25 medium bombers led by Lt. Col. James H. Doolittle departing from the deck of the USS *Hornet* (CV-8).

At 0735 on Sunday, 19 April, Butch and Rita—looking much better than they felt—emerged from a commercial airliner at Washington National Airport. Waiting were several reporters and Lt. Comdr. Harold B. "Min" Miller, a well-known public relations specialist familiar with naval aviation. The Navy had assigned him to oversee Butch's temporary PR duties, but he also made the ordeal bearable. Congenial and smooth, he always knew where to go next, what to say and what not to say, and he had a great knack of making all around him feel comfortable. A solid professional, he did not have to give up his affability to meet the demands of his post. And, especially vital, Miller also knew how to terminate an interview and how to whisk Butch and Rita through a crowd.

Miller announced to the press on Sunday morning and all through Monday that Lieutenant O'Hare did not know why he had been summoned to Washington, but he did not deny speculations that the purpose of the trip might be for Butch to receive a decoration and/or a promotion. The hot rumor now was that there would be a Congressional Medal of Honor for Butch. In fact, the final approval for the medal occurred on 16 April.

Sunday passed quickly for the O'Hares, with Miller holding their obligations to as few as possible so that the couple could rest. Monday, however, proved a busy day, and more than one observer speculated that Butch had apparently had no time for the haircut and shoeshine he clearly needed. As he was shuttled from one group of VIPs to another, Washington's "take" on Butch was that he was modest, somewhat embarrassed by all the flap, handsome, and very nice, and although not overly articulate, he nonetheless conveyed humor. His favorite comment was that he hoped his next aerial combat would not take place in front of an audience, such as the one on the *Lexington,* so that he would not again become "cannon fodder for the press."

To the White House

On Monday evening Miller again reminded the O'Hares that they must be at the White House the next day for a 10:45 meeting with President Roosevelt. Although excited about the prospect of meeting the president, Butch and Rita both were emotionally exhausted. The stress on Butch was manifested not only in an occasional sharp comment but also in a cold sore that had erupted just above his left upper lip. Some photographers airbrushed the blister out of their pictures; others did not.

On Tuesday morning, 21 April, Rita was sufficiently rested to look her best. Butch was excited but still a bit tired, and the cold sore remained. Ready or not, it was time to go to the White House. After a short, uncomfortable wait, Butch and Rita were ushered into the president's office. With the president were Secretary of the Navy Frank Knox;

Admiral King; Congressman John Cochran of Missouri, who had appointed Butch to the Naval Academy; two Navy bureau chiefs, Rear Adm. John H. Towers (Aeronautics) and Rear Adm. Randall Jacobs (Navigation); and Capt. Frank E. Beatty, aide to Secretary Knox. Immediately afterward, members of the press were invited in.

Enjoying his first real opportunity to decorate an American hero during World War II, FDR was in a particularly jovial mood. Perhaps the most renowned American wartime flyer up to this point had been the late Capt. Colin Kelly (West Point 1937) of the Army Air Corps. He had been the pilot of a B-17 bomber whose spectacular solo attack on 10 December 1941 in the Philippines supposedly sank the Japanese battleship *Haruna*. Roosevelt and other Washington insiders knew that the *Haruna* was still afloat. However, Kelly had courageously remained at the controls of his crippled bomber under heavy fighter attack to give his crew the chance to bail out. He earned a posthumous Distinguished Service Cross, the Army's second highest award for gallantry. America needed heroes, and for Colin Kelly the press was allowed to embellish the hero's true story. For Butch O'Hare, this would not be necessary.[6]

The president cheerfully invited Butch, who was blinking incessantly, to stand at ease, but he was too rigid with trepidation to appear relaxed. Rita, wearing a blue dress to match Butch's dark blue service uniform, was asked by the seated president to step up for an introduction and a short chat. Now Roosevelt, noticing the lieutenant (jg) stripes on Butch's sleeve, drew him closer and joked that he "had not had enough time to get the usual fixin's" in regard to his rank insignia. The president went on to tell Butch and the others that there would actually be two ceremonies. The first was to hand Butch papers notifying him that he had been promoted to the temporary rank of lieutenant commander, to date from 8 April 1942. Even though Secretary Knox had signed the order, Roosevelt called Butch's attention to the fact that his own signature of approval was at the bottom.[7]

With his throat as dry as it had ever been on 20 February over the *Lexington*, Butch replied softly, "That is very nice, thank you very much." He had good reason to be surprised. Just a few months before, he had been a lowly lieutenant (jg), then a temporary lieutenant. In fact, Butch's promotion to temporary lieutenant commander was almost unheard of, for the Navy did not distribute middle-level rank as readily as the Army. In the Naval Register, Butch now jumped nearly twenty-three hundred numbers. Although from the Naval Academy class of 1937, he now held rank equivalent to a senior member of the class of 1930. Not until 1 July 1943 did the next 1937 graduate reach the rank of lieutenant commander. On 23 May 1942 Butch was advanced thirty numbers in his permanent grade of lieutenant (jg) "for eminent and conspicuous conduct in battle."

Turning slightly away from Butch to face the press more directly, the president stated that the next portion of the ceremony was more important than the promotion just announced. Reading the Medal of Honor citation, FDR employed his renowned skills as an orator to emphasize the more poignant words and phrases:

> For conspicuous gallantry and intrepidity in aerial combat, at grave risk of his life above and beyond the call of duty, as Section Leader and Pilot of Fighting Squadron Three, on 20 February 1942. Having lost the assistance of his teammates, Lieutenant O'Hare interposed his plane between his ship and an advancing enemy formation of nine attacking twin-engined heavy bombers. Without hesitation, alone and unaided, he repeatedly attacked this enemy formation, at close range in the face of intense combined machine-gun and cannon fire. Despite this concentrated opposition, Lieutenant O'Hare, by his gallant and courageous action, his extremely skillful marksmanship in making the most of every shot of his limited ammunition, shot down five enemy bombers and severely damaged a sixth before they reached the bomb release point. As a result of his gallant action—one of the most daring, if not the most daring single action in the history of combat aviation—he undoubtedly saved his carrier from serious damage.[8]

The reading completed, President Roosevelt handed the citation to Butch, and the two men shook hands. FDR took the Medal of Honor from its small blue case and asked Rita to assist him in unclasping the long baby-blue ribbon. This done, Roosevelt directed her to place the ribbon and medal around her husband's neck while he and Butch again shook hands. Intent on getting the ribbon over Butch's head, Rita inadvertently blocked her own face from the photographers' cameras. The press pleaded: Would they do it again? With broader smiles than for the first act, the ribbon passed over Butch's head again with him bowing considerably lower this time so that Rita would not have to reach so high.

The main events completed, Roosevelt asked Butch what he would like to have incorporated into a new Navy fighter plane. "Something that would go upstairs faster," he replied, referring to the F4F Wildcat's disadvantage relative to the Japanese Zero fighter in climbing ability. For several years Butch would be credited with having given the president a tip that supposedly led to the development of the Grumman F6F Hellcat. Actually, the first experimental XF6F-1 was already under construction and would fly on 26 June 1942. Butch's suggestion, however, was one of several from combat-experienced pilots that did influence Grumman's decision to place a more powerful engine in the second version of the Hellcat. That powerplant, a 2,000-hp Pratt & Whitney R-2800-10, would enable the Hellcat to more than hold its own with the Zero in climb and in other respects after its first combat in August 1943. By the end of the war the Hellcat had recorded a 19–1 kill ratio and was one of the key factors in the destruction of Japanese air power.

Turning from the discussion of a new fighter plane, the president asked Butch how long he would be in Washington. Amid laughter from the press and Navy officials, Butch could only give the same answer he had told reporters: "I don't know." Roosevelt glanced at Admiral King, who replied, "Until the Navy is through with him." And that was it; the audience had lasted about fifteen minutes.

With the morning ceremony over, Lieutenant Commander Miller escorted Butch to several meetings. Perhaps the most significant was his appearance before a congressional committee to help lobby for naval funding. On Wednesday, Butch was flown up to Bethpage to visit Grumman Aircraft, where he again thanked employees for the cigarettes, watched production of the F4F Wildcat, and talked with plant officials. Publicity surrounding the event featured the Wildcat; privately, Butch discussed the new Hellcat with Grumman engineers.

On Thursday, 23 April, Butch was back in Washington to participate in the first of the two main facets of his temporary duty with the Bureau of Aeronautics: promoting the sale of war bonds. In a radio broadcast that evening Secretary of the Treasury Henry Morgenthau, Jr., announced that the voluntary war bond sales campaign offered American wage earners the opportunity to declare war on the enemy. As part of that same broadcast Butch said, "Just give us enough trained men, enough ships and planes to approach even terms and we'll come out on top."[9] To meet the goal of raising $1 billion a month would require a concerted effort by the president, government officials, employers, labor, entertainers, and war heroes. More specifically, each of the country's fifty million wage earners was being asked to designate 10 percent of his or her income for the war effort. As much as anyone, Butch could appreciate the need for funds, for he knew all too well how lacking the Navy was. In 1942 the Navy possessed only seven aircraft carriers; the vast new construction was a full year away; and the effect of losing even one F4F Wildcat fighter was tangible. Butch believed strongly in his message, but despite speech-writing help and coaching from Harold Miller, he felt inadequate to the task. His delivery was never smooth, whether the words were Miller's or his own.

That Friday, as Butch and Rita looked forward to flying to St. Louis, they accepted an invitation from Comdr. Austin K. Doyle and his wife for lunch. The meal and visit went well despite constant interruptions by the Doyle children to ask for Butch's autograph. After the request had been repeated several times, Mrs. Doyle's suspicions prompted her to follow her children to the street, where she found them selling the autographs to friends and passing strangers alike. She quickly quashed the prosperous enterprise.[10]

The St. Louis Parade

On Friday evening Butch and Rita flew by commercial airline from Washington to Chicago, en route to St. Louis. Again they became the object of long stares from several passengers who thought they looked familiar. After staying overnight in Chicago to call on Butch's aunt, Catherine Burris, and several friends, the O'Hares boarded another airliner bound for St. Louis. This time Butch made sure no one would know him: he kept his name off the passenger list. Only when the plane arrived in St. Louis shortly after 10 A.M. on Saturday, 25 April, did fellow passengers know that they had shared a flight with America's new war hero.

Preparations for the visit to St. Louis had begun even before the Medal of Honor presentation. On 18 April, the day before Butch and Rita arrived in Washington, an editorial appeared in the *St. Louis Post-Dispatch* proposing an invitation to Butch to return to his home city for a "rousing old-time hero's reception." Mayor William Dee Becker and Thomas N. Dysart, president of the Chamber of Commerce, adopted the idea that same day. Becker's letter to Secretary Knox stated in part, "St. Louis is the home of Butch O'Hare. No finer inspiration could come to this great service training and war supplies production area than that which would attend his presence here in a civic celebration designed to honor his glorious achievement."[11]

On Sunday, 19 April, the St. Louis newspapers had carried optimistic comments from the Navy Department with regard to a patriotic celebration for Butch, but on Monday the Navy's Public Relations Office stated that permission would not be granted for him to attend any such program. On Tuesday, however, Knox informed the press attending the Medal of Honor ceremony that "he was sending Commander O'Hare out to St. Louis to present to the city the Naval 'E' for excellence as the first big city which went over the top in a campaign for funds for the Naval Relief Society."[12] Wednesday's St. Louis newspapers joyously announced the celebration and reported that the mayor was asking people of the area to attend a Saturday noon-hour parade downtown and a presentation ceremony at Soldier's Memorial.

On Thursday morning the newspapers carried stories focusing on Butch's concerns. Through the Navy Department, Butch informed the planning committee in St. Louis that he did not favor the idea of a big parade and special luncheon. He would, however, agree to a smaller procession and a brief ceremony at Soldier's Memorial so that he could present St. Louis with the Navy E pennant for exceeding by 20 percent its goal of raising $89,000 for the Navy Relief Society.

As the Chicago and Southern airliner taxied up to the Naval Reserve hangar at Lambert Field, the passengers on board realized that something was different. Planes did not usually stop there, and certainly reception committees typically did not meet scheduled flights. After allowing the other passengers to leave the plane, Rita—again wearing a dark blue suit to complement her husband's uniform—stepped outside, followed by Butch. Present to greet the couple were Mayor Becker's wife, the official reception committee, reporters, and photographers, as well as Selma, Patsy, and Marilyn. After Butch embraced his mother and sisters, Mrs. Becker presented Selma and Rita with large bouquets of American Beauty roses, and all endured the inevitable photo session. Waiting impatiently on the airport apron, Butch and his family stood still for the photographers, with only Selma managing to keep a smile on her face all the way through. Although Butch, now wearing proper lieutenant commander stripes on his uniform, was the center of attraction, a hat worn by Marilyn also made a lasting impression. Some weeks later a cartoonist satirized the brown high-pointed "witch" hat in a political cartoon. It would have played well in the 1939 *Wizard of Oz* movie, and even Marilyn now wonders why she picked that day to wear it.

Ushered into the Naval Reserve building, Butch and Rita were separated. She was escorted into a room full of female reporters for the ordeal of her first formal press conference. There she related that her biggest thrill of the entire whirlwind week had been her reunion with Butch at the Phoenix airport. Uncomfortable with the proceedings, with the probing and sometimes trite queries, Rita smiled when she did not want to respond to a question or to repeat herself. Still, she admitted to worrying when she did not know where her husband was in the Pacific and explained that she liked airplanes but had never been in one piloted by Butch.

Selma, Patsy, and Marilyn likewise were interviewed while waiting for Butch and Rita to complete their own press conferences. Their focus was the same as Rita's: center all the attention on Butch. They corrected one "fact" that had appeared in local newspapers during the week. The name Butch did not originate in childhood; he got it during his last year at the Naval Academy. And though he was Butch to Rita, Patsy, and Marilyn, he remained Edward to Selma.

Meanwhile, Butch—in company with Harold Miller—was again asked to recount his story of the big fight on 20 February. Ill at ease with the constantly popping flashbulbs, reporters asking questions all at the same time, and radio commentators talking as fast as machine guns, Butch tried unsuccessfully to relax. He did say that only five planes had flamed and dropped out of formation, and that one other may not have made it back to base; that his own plane had been hit by enemy fire only once; that he hoped to get a little sleep and visit with the family while in St. Louis; and that anyone in his squadron could have done the same thing. "It's like a football team—you train all week and play on Saturday." But tension, discomfort, and the lack of sleep finally caught up with him: when one reporter asked whether he had shot down high-level or dive bombers, he replied sharply, "Don't you guys read the papers?" Not taking offense, the reporters backed off; obviously Butch was out of his element. But he calmed down just as quickly as he had flared up, and his boyish smile warmed any heart offended by his brief show of frustration. And to assure the horde before him that there were no bad feelings, he repeated his by-now standard remark, punctuated with a grin, "It's a lot easier out there than it is right here."[13]

Press conference over, Butch and Rita were ushered to a waiting car to head for the parade route. Other cars immediately behind carried the family, the reception committee, and members of the press. Temperatures were in the low fifties, a stiff wind blew, and rain fell intermittently. At the starting point at Sixteenth Street and Washington Avenue, Butch, Selma, and Rita stepped into the back seat of a big black open phaeton. Now wearing the impressive blue-ribboned Medal of Honor around his neck, Butch took his place in the middle, alternately sitting on the seat and perching high on the convertible boot. Selma sat on his right and Rita on his left. The noon-hour parade began on time with the police motorcycle escort moving first. Next came an eighty-five-piece band from Jefferson Barracks and a forty-member drum corps. Following the brown-uniformed band came the massed colors of veterans' organizations from the St. Louis area, the sight of so many American flags exerting considerable emotional impact. Several hundred bluejackets from the Naval Training School and cadets from the Naval Reserve Air Training Station preceded a truck packed with newsreel and newspaper photographers. The centerpiece consisted of Butch's car (with a six-man Marine honor guard alongside), two other convertibles, and three enclosed cars that conveyed Mayor Becker, Charles Belknap, Butch's sisters, Lieutenant Commander Miller, and the reception committee.

Bringing up the rear of the parade, which took only eight minutes to pass a given point, was the band and entire 350-member student body of Western Military Academy. Smartly clad in their gray jackets, white trousers, and white hats, the youngsters marched as impressively as the adult units ahead of them. No one was out of step—a feat for all who marched down the parade route, because in places the bricks were slick from the rain, and the gaps between the streetcar rails and bricks were wide enough to lose a shoe in. Colorful bunting festooned the storefronts and office buildings along the parade route; "Remember Pearl Harbor" pennants fluttered; confetti poured out of windows down to Washington Avenue; cheers rose above the music of the bands; police strained to keep the estimated sixty thousand observers on or near the sidewalks; and Butch, Selma, and Rita smiled and returned the waves of enthusiastic well-wishers. Most, of course, were strangers, but some familiar faces appeared along the route: boyhood friends from the old neighborhood at Eighteenth and Sidney, chums from Holly Hills, Selma's card-game friends and other mothers whose sons were in uniform, and Rita's friends and other nurses from DePaul Hospital. Butch ordered his car to stop so that he could shake hands with his old friend, police captain George Dineen.

Butch's vehicle left the parade route to head directly to the reviewing stand in front of Soldier's Memorial. The other parade participants continued east on Washington, turned south onto Broadway, and headed west on Chestnut toward the reviewing stand. There Butch reviewed the parade, saluted the flag each time it passed, and returned the salutes of the passing units.

At the end of the eight-minute processional, the Western Military cadets proudly marched past their most famous graduate. Expected by the O'Hare clan to be a moment of happiness, even one good for a laugh, the appearance of Colonel Jackson and the student body actually produced much the opposite effect. Returning the colonel's salute, Butch forced several quick smiles. Rita smiled, but Selma, Patsy, and Marilyn found mirth as difficult as Butch did. It hit them all at once. The boys were so young, those toward the end of the ranks becoming progressively smaller. As impressive as they were and as glorious a moment as it was for the Western cadets, all the joys, triumphs, happy moments, and tragic moments since Butch's Western days seemed for the O'Hares to well up into intensely bittersweet emotion. So many of the joys of youth had passed; family alive during Butch's Western Academy days had gone; perhaps the best days of life were over; and perhaps these smartly dressed children in their neat ranks and precise stepping formation would be thrown into the same furnace of war from which Butch had just emerged. The war itself might still be lost. And what about their own babies, and those yet to be born?

A blessing for all the O'Hares, these thoughts were interrupted when someone announced the next event. Seated beside Mayor Becker and Charles Belknap, a manufacturing executive who headed the Navy Relief Fund campaign in St. Louis, Butch chatted amiably with the two between coughs. The sporadic rain started again just as the program began, and nine training planes flew over. In need of a cigarette and a shave, his five o'clock shadow evident during this noon hour, Butch waited for his turn at the podium. After an invocation by Lt. Comdr. J. G. Armstrong III, a chaplain from the Great Lakes Naval Training Center, Belknap offered opening remarks before introducing Selma, Rita, and then Butch. Stepping to the podium, Butch hesitated to lay out his speech, three handwritten paragraphs on lined notebook paper, offering to reporters—who earlier in the day had asked for an advance copy of his speech—convincing evidence that he was a man of action rather than words. Looking up from his notes out onto parade participants standing at attention and civilians peering from underneath umbrellas, Butch spoke to them and into more than a dozen microphones representing national and local broadcasting companies:

> It is good to get back but it will be a relief to get back to my real job, which is flying and fighting. Looking into machine guns is not nearly as hard as facing cameras.
>
> St. Louis is to be congratulated upon the success of its splendid Navy relief drive. Those of us in the fleet appreciate the fighting spirit which the Middle West has shown and, I know, will show in the future. If you give us the guns, the ships and the planes, I assure you we will fight [with] them and will win with them.
>
> It is my great privilege to read a letter to the honorable Mr. Becker by the Secretary of the Navy, Honorable Frank Knox: My Dear Mayor Becker: The Navy Department is both happy and proud to award the Navy "E" to the City of St. Louis as a mark of its enduring gratitude for the generosity shown by its citizens in far exceeding the quota set by the Citizens Committee for Navy Relief. Because of my inability to attend the ceremonies of award of the Navy "E," I have delegated Lt. Commander Edward H. O'Hare to represent me and to express on my behalf and on behalf of the thousands of officers and men of the Navy the boundless appreciation we all feel at this moment.
>
> If you could but know how materially the families and dependents of the Navy's fighting men will benefit by reason of this remarkable generosity, your citizens would feel most heartened indeed. It means so very much to them to know that should the tricks of fate and the tide of battle overtake them the Navy Relief Society—thanks to the spirit and magnanimity of all those who have so freely contributed—will step in and relieve distress wherever and whenever it may occur.
>
> Therefore, speaking for our splendid fighting forces on the seas, under the seas and in the skies, we ask you to accept this award of the Navy "E" as a token of our great appreciation, not only for the acts of contributing citizens, but as a mark of gratitude toward the St. Louis Citizens Committee for Navy Relief, so ably directed by Mr. Charles Belknap, all of whom worked untiringly toward the success of the campaign.

Braving wind and rain without a hat or overcoat for most of the ceremony, Mayor Becker relieved Butch at the podium to make an acceptance speech, his prepared remarks frequently referring to Butch's exploits. Although the mayor spoke at considerably greater length than Butch, the essence of his speech was conveyed in two sentences: "It is peculiarly fitting that you, of all men, should be the one chosen to come here today bearing the Navy 'E' as our Greater St. Louis community's symbol of excellence for a job well done. For, if ever there existed the living, breathing embodiment of all that the Navy 'E' stands for, you are that living, breathing embodiment."[14]

Turning to Butch, the mayor said, "We are carrying our hearts on our sleeves for you Eddie O'Hare, and you might as well carry them away with you on your wrist as well." Then he presented Butch with a gold navigator's four-dial watch engraved with the words "To Lt. Commander Edward H. O'Hare, USN, from a proud and grateful City of St. Louis, April 25, 1942." As Butch accepted the watch, Mayor Becker said, "May it give you useful and faithful service—but know that long years hence, after it has ticked its last tick, still time will go on through which the name Edward H. O'Hare will stand with Perry, Hobson and our other deathless Navy heroes as one of America's greatest of the great."

Butch received other gifts. The mayor handed over a large brass key to the city; Michael J. Hart, president of the Board of Aldermen, offered a resolution-of-honor scroll; and Luther M. Slinkard, representing the St. Louis Industrial Union Council of the Congress of Industrial Organizations, proclaimed another resolution of honor at the conclusion of the official ceremony. Butch watched as the band played "Anchors Aweigh," and another St. Louisan, Charles J. Decker III—who had survived the 27 February sinking of the *Langley* (the Navy's first carrier, converted to a seaplane tender)—raised the blue pennant with a white E. Then the band played the "Star-Spangled Banner," and the formal thirty-minute ceremony—and Butch's ordeal—concluded. It was a day to remember for St. Louis and for the O'Hare family. But in the wet, cold early afternoon of Saturday, 25 April 1942, Butch was just glad it was over. Or so he thought.

No sooner had Butch, Rita, and Selma climbed into a sedan to leave Soldier's Memorial than the crowd broke through the police lines to rush the car. The human swarm meant well, of course, but a mob is a mob, and on this occasion Butch missed the evasive attributes of his fighter plane. It took police several minutes to disperse the crowd, and a few minutes later they had to start all over again. It was pouring hard by now, but the police literally had to pull people off the car.

Arriving finally at Selma's apartment on Bates Street, Butch enjoyed a quick nap before heading to the Club Continental at the Jefferson Hotel for a party with family and a few friends. Other guests in the large dining room immediately recognized the hero and rose and applauded as Butch approached his table. Quickly the orchestra broke into "Anchors Aweigh," and all laughed when Butch commented, "That's a tough tune to dance to."

On Sunday morning Selma, Patsy, and Marilyn poured over the newspapers to cut out the front-page stories and pictures. Only now did the reality of Butch's place in history dawn on the family. One could not see large headlines reading "60,000 GIVE O'HARE HERO'S WELCOME HERE" or phrases like "the nation's outstanding individual combat hero of the war" without realizing that Butch now belonged to the city and the nation as well as to his family.[15] Remembering the mob scene after the ceremony, someone commented that Butch might be safer back in the Pacific.

Butch's parade was compared with those honoring the St. Louis Cardinals' 1926 National League championship and Charles Lindbergh's 1927 homecoming after his New York–Paris flight. The local police were fully aware from those two occasions that they would need everyone on duty for crowd control. Meanwhile, the Streets Department employed nearly forty men and several machines to pick up confetti. One man leaning from a tall building dumped a large quantity of packing paper without first shredding it sufficiently. Had it struck the Japanese with the same force expended on the people below watching Butch, the city might well have honored him with a parade of his own.

Many cities had requested Navy permission for Butch to attend a variety of ceremonies and honors, but the war had first call on his services. Even as Butch rolled through downtown St. Louis, the Navy announced that he would return to Washington on 28 April to resume his regular duties. He was to speak to aviation cadets at the naval air stations at Norfolk, Miami, Corpus Christi, and Jacksonville, among others, and then return to the fleet. Such stops as these were sometimes referred to as the Dancing Bear Circuit. The idea was to be seen, make a patriotic speech, mention war bonds, perhaps attend a reception, and then move on to the next stop. With Rita and Lieutenant Commander Miller in tow, Butch addressed servicemen as well as industrial, business, and community rallies. Although he enjoyed the people, he hated nearly every minute of it. However, this was the best way, for the moment, that he could serve his country. It was his duty, and he would do what was asked of him, although much of it made plebe year at Annapolis look good by comparison. It did not last forever, though, and what followed was much more to his liking. On 11 May orders were cut transferring him from his temporary duty with the Bureau of Aeronautics and assigning him as commanding officer of his old squadron, Fighting Three. He was to complete his public relations duties and report back to the squadron in Hawaii no later than 19 June.

Before he left St. Louis on Monday evening, 27 April, Butch discussed with the family the many requests he was receiving to visit cities and give interviews, business endorsements, and autographs, and even to become an author. A proposal from the publisher Farrar and Rinehart to the Navy Department Bureau of Public Relations was Marilyn's favorite. She wondered aloud, "How in the world do they think Butch would be willing to write a book when his major literary inclination is to send me to the store to buy him comic books?" Laughing with the rest of the family, Butch agreed with his baby sister that he was not up to literary endeavors. Without consulting him, the Navy responded on 23 April to the publisher, "Do not anticipate the Lt. Commander will write a book."[16]

A less happy moment was shared with Patsy. While discussing her husband Paul, she mentioned to Butch that she had a premonition of Paul being on a sinking ship in the Pacific, something that actually did occur later. Patsy and the other family in the room were surprised not only at Butch's sharp reaction but at the tone in which it was offered: "Don't talk about such things! You don't know what it is like to see men die in combat or to drown off a sinking ship. It's horrible!"

The subject was quickly changed, but the outburst offered one more piece of evidence that Butch was no longer the person they had known. The war, with its pains, demands, and responsibilities, had taken its toll on Butch just as on countless others. While proud that her son was developing into a man who took his responsibilities seriously, Selma could not help but be concerned that his serious nature and newfound responsibilities would erode the gentle spirit she knew him to be.

The family also discussed the numerous proposals in and around St. Louis to honor Butch. Most concerned recommendations to name things after him, such as a twenty-thousand-seat public-school stadium or any one of several streets, roads, avenues, and highways. Butch and Selma decided that while these suggestions were well intended, they were not fair to all the other St. Louis–area men serving their country. Patsy and Marilyn did not necessarily agree with their mother and brother, but they did not argue the issue. After Butch left town and the two sisters headed back to Phoenix, it fell to Selma to continue representing him at innumerable patriotic functions and to be the one to say no to the continuing offers to christen things after him. So shy, reticent, and openly averse to being with strangers in the past, Selma O'Hare tapped an inner strength that had always been there and dutifully marched off to every

---

SCENARIO

ACT 1: Japs? Where?
       Page O'Hare!
ACT 2: Six! There!
       Up, O'Hare!
ACT 3: None in air—
       Thanks, O'Hare.

Source: New York Sun, 6 Mar. 1942.

---

patriotic function to which she was invited. Never totally comfortable on these occasions, she nonetheless enjoyed most of them and presented honest smiles. Only once would she shed tears, during the invocation on 25 April 1942 on the reviewing stand in front of Soldier's Memorial when a special blessing was invoked for "This Thy son Edward."

From all the letters, phone calls, and telegrams Selma received from the mothers of other servicemen, she perceived that she had an important role to play in acknowledging the concerns of women. She also knew that there were times when they just needed to communicate private thoughts that only another mother would understand and appreciate. And she could share one overriding apprehension with so many other mothers: her son had come home, but not to stay. The war still raged, and some sons would never return.

By mid-June 1942 Butch was headed back to Pearl Harbor to take command of VF-3. Passing through San Diego, he decided to stop by the Nicholson household to say hello to Dorothy. He thought he would have little chance of seeing Nick, who no doubt would be out on patrol in his submarine. But on that day Nick, having not been home for several days, managed to get leave for only twelve hours to see his wife before sailing to the Aleutians. At 2100 he had politely but firmly kicked his brother-in-law out, leaving only four hours before he had to report back to his sub and the war. Two hours later a knock summoned him to the door, and there stood Butch, most pleasantly surprised. They had a joyous reunion. Nick fondly remembers that evening quite well. It had been a long time since the two great academy friends had been together, and never again would Nick see his friend, the uncomfortable hero.

10

The King of Maui

"Fame hath its privileges"

Beginning in the early 1980s, many veterans retired from the careers they took on after the great Pacific war. With no rigid schedule to keep for the first time since their summer vacations in high school five decades earlier, they relished the opportunity to travel, both geographically and back in time. Some were drawn to Hawaii, where they had served or trained before moving westward with powerful forces toward Japan. At Pearl Harbor, on the island of Oahu, they pause within the beautiful memorial built directly above the sunken USS *Arizona* and recall with clarity why the blossom of their youth was expended in such a horrifying manner. Looking up from the hulk of the ship that holds the remains of over one thousand of her 7 December 1941 crew, a veteran of the Pacific war can still see the moorings of Battleship Row, U.S. Navy warships in the harbor, and familiar landmarks on Ford Island. Across the harbor, however, things have changed considerably since 1945, with new houses approaching the tops of surrounding hills, and with many new high-rise buildings casting long shadows over the once singularly prominent Royal Hawaiian Hotel. Even so, at Pearl Harbor a World War II veteran can get his bearings and find enough familiar in his field of vision to recapture bittersweet memories of long ago.

After a short thirty-minute flight to the island of Maui, second largest of the Hawaiian Islands, some veterans look for Puunene (pronounced poo-neh-nay), site of a large World War II naval air station. In nearby towns, residents of any age can show the way to contemporary airports, the elaborate resort hotels, or exotic Polynesian cultural and natural attractions. However, only locals contemporary in age with World War II veterans can point to where the large base once sprawled on a six-mile isthmus connecting two mountainous areas.

After a lengthy search, obtaining permission to enter private property, and by driving down a track that only the magnanimous would term a "service road," a veteran can again stand upon the ground where so many planes once took off, practiced the art of war, landed, and were serviced for the next flight. The control tower provided the best view of the airfield, but all that remains now is its concrete base. Memory re-creates long runways and parking areas, but today only a small part of the tarmac survives, and even that is nearly overgrown with grass. Closer inspection reveals a few badly rusted aircraft tie-downs. Rumor has it that some concrete bunkers still exist on the property, but few guides now know where they are. Even when the dugouts can be located, the foliage is so thick that approach is difficult. Gone too along with all the wood and metal buildings is the din of piston aircraft engines, a sound pervasive day and night in the 1940s. Standing in the silence broken only by the whoosh of the wind brushing through acres of sugarcane, the veteran is disquieted to realize that a place once so familiar is now so strange. Land that produced sugar before the war has reverted to its original use; that brief period when its function was to train young men to kill is past. Yet in memory this piece of ground remains a place where life, even though unpredictable in the 1940s, was embraced with full, noisy, enthusiastic vigor.

Butch O'Hare spent nearly all of the last year and a half of his life on Maui. That stay was broken only in the spring of 1943 by a welcome three-month sojourn in San Diego, and by brief periods at sea on carriers for training and combat. Torn from his family by war, Butch made the most of his time on Maui, directing his energy to training his new command, making new friends, and even adopting another family (with, of course, their refrigerator). No period of his life, even plebe year at the Naval Academy, proved as intense as his last eighteen months. Whether flying, training, fishing, hunting, eating, or visiting, he was totally focused on the moment. Nearly all who remember him from those days fondly recall how "Butch just loved life."

Around 18 June 1942 Butch returned to Pearl Harbor to find the Pacific Fleet celebrating its tremendous victory two weeks before over the Japanese carriers off Midway Island. At NAS Kaneohe Bay, Lt. Comdr. Jimmy Thach greeted him warmly. They had much to talk about. In April after Butch left for Washington to receive the Medal of Honor, Thach had turned over a dozen VF-3 pilots and all his Wildcats to Lt. Comdr. Paul Ramsey's VF-2 to fight on the *Lexington*. On 7–8 May she helped win the Battle of the Coral Sea but succumbed to torpedo damage with a fiery end. Lost too in the battle were four of Butch's old VF-3 teammates.[1] Thach also related how in late May he reformed VF-3 with a few old hands, rookies, and a most welcome batch of VF-42 combat veterans and rushed them on board the *Yorktown* in time for Midway. Despite stateside orders to command his own fighting squadron, Lt. Comdr. Don Lovelace volunteered to help his close friend Thach mold VF-3 into a team. Tragically, on 30 May, Don was killed when another Wildcat crashed into his fighter while landing on the *Yorktown*. On 4 June VF-3 earned great renown at Midway, both in the great strike that sank three enemy carriers and in defense of the gallant but ill-fated *Yorktown*. Thach used the tactic that he invented and Butch helped develop, his beam defense position (later called the Thach weave) to defeat fierce attacks by upward of a dozen Zeros.

On 19 June in a ceremony at Kaneohe, Butch formally assumed command of VF-3, relieving Thach, who had received much-deserved orders home. Later in 1942 Thach wrote, "I know of no one I'd rather see take my old command into new battles." For Butch it was one of the proudest moments of his life. Now he had become the CO of his first and only squadron. Among the many young and eager but inexperienced fighter pilots were a few familiar faces from old VF-3, including classmate and friend Scoop Vorse (who became Butch's XO), Bob Morgan, Duff Dufilho, Bill Eder, John Lackey, and Lee Haynes.[2]

The next day Butch took the controls of a fighter for the first time since 11 April. He now flew the F4F-4, the latest version of the Wildcat, which featured folding wings and six machine guns instead of four, but because of the additional weight it proved less responsive than its predecessor. Little did he know that he would never again fly the F4F in battle. This day, however, he led his twenty-five Wildcats from Kaneohe about ninety miles southeast across the sea to join VF-72 and VF-8 at NAS Maui at Puunene, a base commissioned that January (NAS Maui was renamed NAS Puunene in November 1942). Originally a small strip run by the Territory of Hawaii, Puunene's dirt runways and parking areas were expanded in 1942 to accommodate one carrier air group, with two 50,000-gallon aviation gasoline tanks, revetments, aircraft utility shops, and wooden housing for personnel. The station CO was Capt. John L. Murphy, an irascible pioneer naval aviator (wings 1918) who would have many dealings with Butch in the next sixteen months. VF-3 found itself at Puunene so that the pilots could fly without interfering with the crowded air traffic over Oahu. Too, the weather was perfect for both day and night training nearly every day of the year.[3]

Butch viewed with some concern the lack of accommodations for both aircraft and personnel at Puunene. However, construction to handle the growing number of planes and men was proceeding—never as fast as anyone desired, but good things were happening. Spartan quarters and equipment were only part of Butch's problem. Before he could fret about the heat and dust, or the insufficiency of men, planes, supplies and time, he had to worry about his new role. It was a far cry better than the Dancing Bear Circuit, but his discomfort with the speech-making and other requirements of that role had involved only himself. So much of Butch's increased seriousness stemmed from his awareness of the great responsibility he now assumed for training these fine men of VF-3, veterans and rookies alike, and leading them into battle.

One drawback, in Butch's mind, was his meteoric rise in rank without more seasoning as a junior officer. He worried that his relative lack of experience might cause him to overlook something important, especially administratively. He also faced the prospect of leading men senior to him in age and length of service, but not in stripes. The first of these was highly regarded Lt. Alberto C. "Ace" Emerson, who had earned his wings in 1932 as a reserve ensign and most recently had been the Yorktown's hangar deck officer. Emerson left to become VF-72's XO on 11 July. Three days later Lt. Stanley E. Ruehlow (Annapolis class of 1935) reported as VF-3's XO. He had flown with VF-5 and VF-8 before joining Butch. A fine officer, Ruehlow doubtless felt relief (Butch likely also) when on 24 September he was posted to VF-10 with a CO and XO considerably senior to him.

On the credit side of the ledger, Butch would no doubt be older than most of his charges, he had combat experience, and he remembered his father's example of self-confidence. Also important, he enjoyed virtual autonomy because VF-3 came directly under Commander, Carriers, Pacific Fleet (ComCarPac), in distant Oahu, with no air group commander in between. Butch became de facto "King of Maui," and if he did make a mistake, who would challenge him? That happy thought aside, he would move carefully, even feel his way, as he organized his squadron, trained his men, and saw to their overall welfare.

Immediately after Butch took command, ComCarPac relegated VF-3 to a role reflected in its reclusive existence at Maui. The loss of carriers at Coral Sea and Midway meant that there were not enough flattops to go around for all of the available fighting squadrons. Someone had to stay ashore, and it was Butch's turn. Newly arrived VF-5 took VF-3's accustomed slot in the *Saratoga* Air Group. In early July, ComCarPac increased the fighting squadrons from twenty-seven to thirty-six fighters, so Butch had to help make up the difference. Offered imminent prospects for action, Scoop Vorse volunteered to join VF-6 on the *Enterprise;* other pilots left for VF-5 and also VF-72 on the *Hornet.* Soon all of the old VF-3 hands were gone.

Thus, to Butch's dismay VF-3 became a reserve pool of pilots and aircraft for other squadrons headed for combat in the South Pacific. By mid-July VF-3 was down to eighteen F4Fs, and that was only the beginning. The Guadalcanal campaign that kicked off on 7 August 1942 would eventually siphon most of VF-3's resources. To Butch ComCarPac assigned pilots mostly fresh out of training, and just about the time he got to know them, they joined squadrons bound for the South Pacific. Casualty lists filtering back to Maui occasionally listed some who had been assigned to Butch. Lt. Marion Dufilho, his wingman in the 20 February fight, was killed on 24 August 1942 while with VF-5 in the Battle of the Eastern Solomons. Nearly as great as Butch's hurt at seeing a familiar name on a casualty list was the pain of knowing that even a little more time training with him might have made a difference.

Despite being isolated at Maui, Butch accomplished a number of important tasks. Following Thach's lead, he continued a unique exchange program with the U.S. Army Air Force fighter squadrons stationed on Oahu. Bored with standing watches and now less likely to see further combat in Hawaii, the Army pilots welcomed the opportunity for a short familiarization tour with VF-3 at Maui. They checked out in Wildcats, received an introduction to the Navy's fighter doctrine, and practiced simulated carrier landings ashore. (One of Thach's protégés, Capt. John C. Wilkins, actually served for a time as a fully carrier-qualified F4F pilot with VF-72 on the *Hornet* in the South Pacific.) Among those USAAF pilots on temporary duty with VF-3 in July and August 1942 were first lieutenants Kenneth M. Taylor, who shot down two Japanese planes at Pearl Harbor, and Francis S. Gabreski, later one of the top-ranking fighter aces in Europe.

On 20 August Lt. Comdr. Jimmy Flatley's VF-10 transferred to Maui after coming out from the mainland to Pearl Harbor. In the next month the two squadrons would become well acquainted through training flights and the exchange of some pilots. Perhaps the most important legacy of VF-3's association with VF-10 was the latter's adoption of Thach's beam defense position built around four-plane divisions. Although Flatley knew of Thach's defensive tactic, for the time being he preferred to fly six-plane "flights" and use tactics employed in the European air war. There a flight that came under attack would "break"—that is, split up, evade the enemy, and climb to gain altitude advantage. Butch knew that the weave was superior, especially for the slow-climbing Wildcats. He patiently and persistently worked on his old Pensacola flight instructor, who finally saw the light and became the next of Thach's disciples after Butch. By 12 October, just prior to deploying on board the *Enterprise,* Flatley had converted VF-10 from six- to four-plane flights and taught his men the weave. Indeed, on 26 October in the Battle of Santa Cruz, VF-10 used the tactic to perfection. Soon after, Flatley came up with the name Thach weave for the maneuver that was, in his words, "undoubtedly the greatest contribution to air combat tactics that has been made to date."[4]

On 17 September, Butch turned over all of his F4Fs to VF-10. For the next three months, and with very few exceptions, VF-3 would have to be content with SNJ trainers and Grumman J2F-4 utility amphibian biplanes. For distinct intervals during this time, no planes at all were available. This became VF-3's low point as a fighting squadron. Butch and his pilots were particularly frustrated about sitting on Maui while the battle raged for distant Guadalcanal, but the Navy and the Marines often did not have enough planes in the South Pacific even for all the pilots already down there.

In October Vice Adm. John Towers (Naval Aviator Number 3) took over the top naval aviation administrative command in the theater, ComAirPac (Commander, Air Forces, Pacific Fleet). One way he tried to make up to Butch for putting VF-3 temporarily on the shelf was to give him first crack at the first Vought F4U-1 Corsair (BuNo 02166) in the islands. For two years naval fighter pilots had been itching to get at the controls of the sleek, long-nosed, inverted-gull-wing carrier fighter. Teething problems had long delayed its arrival in the fleet. The Corsair, as well as the XF6F-3 Hellcat being developed by Grumman, offered hope for gaining air superiority over the Japanese Zero. One Marine fighting squadron (VMF-124) was slated to take the Corsair into combat in early 1943, while two naval fighting squadrons (VF-12 and VF-17) were to receive F4Us in January 1943 to work up for carrier operations. Powered by a 2,000-hp Pratt & Whitney R-2800-10 Double Wasp radial engine, the F4U was 70 mph faster than the F4F-4 Wildcat and also over 5,500 pounds heavier—an eagle as opposed to a bumblebee. The Corsair's principal drawbacks were poor visibility over its long nose and inferior landing characteristics, especially, as the Navy soon discovered, when coming on board a carrier. On 28 October, Butch signed out the impressive bird at Ford Island and eagerly took it aloft. The next day he nonchalantly set down on Maui, where the Corsair created a sensation. He spent the next several weeks testing the F4U, rebuffing jealous pilots attempting to wheedle rides of their own, and returned it on 18 November to Pearl. Fame hath its privileges.[5]

"Butch's Boys"

On 21 October, Butch detached some pilots to VF-6, which was preparing to sail on the *Saratoga* for the South Pacific. Among those taking their places in VF-3 were Lt. (jg) Sy E. Mendenhall and Lt. (jg) John P. Altemus. Altemus, for one, was not too pleased at being transferred to the backwater at Maui, but he had already heard about Butch: "They say he is a peachy guy, personally." Mendenhall and Altemus were the first newcomers who would manage to stay with Butch through the first Maui sojourn, the reorganization of the squadron in March 1943 at San Diego, and the return to Maui that summer. They were really the first of "Butch's Boys," an exclusive band who drew so close to their leader that fifty years later the mention of his name is sufficient to cause them to drop everything, grab a chair, sit down, and reminisce, with nearly all the recollections punctuated with smiles, grins, and laughter. Many cannot separate Butch from Maui, because that was where they got to know him, and their stories quickly bounce from tales of combat to training to socializing to leadership to inspiration and then back to combat, because that was what it was all about, and all were interrelated. In short, Butch's Boys were Butch's Boys in all things, then and now.[6]

As a leader, Butch was unparalleled in the eyes of his squadron mates because of his unique personality. On the subject of war, he was serious—very serious. No aspect of combat was taken or spoken of in a light vein. Butch let no error escape his attention, nor did he allow any of his pilots to ignore it. One example (of many) will suffice.

In early 1943 Ens. Allie W. "Willie" Callan had pounded on desktops to get into VF-3, for he knew that Butch wore the Medal of Honor and that his squadron would be one of the first, if not the first, to receive the new Grumman F6F-3 Hellcat. Expecting Butch to be a mean, lean fighting machine, Willie was "almost disappointed to see he was down-to-earth and almost a slob." Yet he discovered that Butch had his own ways of making his wishes known. On 30 August 1943 while on combat air patrol the day before the raid on Marcus Island, Willie was worried about his dwindling fuel and did not maintain his assigned position. Upon landing, Butch inquired about the problem and then calmly told him, "Forget the gas; if you can't stay in formation, I'll find someone who can." In his usual succinct manner, Butch had forthrightly conveyed what needed to be said. In combat, a lone pilot is very often a dead pilot. On reflection, Callan saw the seriousness of his mistake and how it could have jeopardized others in the squadron as well as himself. Considerably "down in the mouth" for having drawn the ire of his hero-leader, he had been sitting by himself for about twenty minutes when Butch reappeared.

"Let's have a game of acey-deucy," Butch cheerfully announced. Declining the "captain's" invitation was not an option, so Willie played. More about the game later, but significant here is Butch's unique brand of leadership. He first determined the facts; made a short, direct statement of lifesaving implications; let the point and the lesson sink in; and then returned to lift the spirits, and confidence, of his charge.[7]

Other leadership attributes that endeared Butch to his men were his manifest courage and his ability in the air. These two qualities were not unique; other pilots were brave and fine aviators. Yet Butch displayed singular personality traits beyond courage and competence in the air. First, as he demonstrated when he originally joined VF-3, he was not the stereotype of the Naval Academy graduate. Sy Mendenhall remembers Butch showing nowhere near the formality that many other academy graduates, including at least one temporarily in VF-3, demanded or practiced. "Butch was very relaxed, even casual; he didn't do everything by the numbers, and he certainly wasn't 'Mickey Mouse.'"

Second, Butch was noted for brevity and for his ability to convey a message in just a few words. When Butch assigned Sy to lead his second division, he looked him in the eye and said, "I want you to know you are responsible for those people." Mendenhall added, "That was it; when Butch spoke seriously, you listened because you knew he wasn't going to repeat it." On a lighter note, Sy recalls another incident when he and three other pilots spent a Sunday afternoon drinking beer in their quarters—one of the four wooden buildings at Puunene, each of which housed about eight officers. Thinking Butch was miles away, the pilots threw empty bottles across the hall into another pilot's vacant room and then began shooting at the bottles with their .38 revolvers. This went on for nearly two hours, their aim not improving during the exercise. During a lull to reload, they recoiled in horror when Butch, clad only in shorts, slowly peered around the doorjamb and said, after shaking his head, "You guys are supposed to be the leaders." That was the last they heard of the incident, but they knew they had incurred Butch's displeasure and never did it again.[8]

Third, Butch was a competitor. All the pilots under his command were competitors, but he raised that quality to a higher plateau. Recall the game of acey-deucy to which Butch challenged Willie Callan after having rebuked him for not staying in formation: Butch lost that game. He also lost to Sy on more than one occasion. And every time Butch lost, he would stalk off for fifteen to twenty minutes, then return to insist on one more. And if he lost that game, he would demand yet another try. While much is made in these pages of Butch's inclination to approach the lunch or dinner table with enthusiasm, he would pass up meals, if necessary, until he finally triumphed in these impromptu matches. Butch simply "had to win."[9]

Fourth, even though he was a leader, and their leader, the men of Butch's command simply liked him. That was nothing new; as considerable written documentation throughout his life attests, people had always enjoyed his company. Part of this attraction centered on his ability to lead men, but much of it is attributable to his obvious and genuine concern for those around him. He liked people; he cared for people; it would have been difficult not to reciprocate. Sy Mendenhall recalled, "I just felt like he was a friend I had known forever." Ens. Edward L. "Whitey" Feightner, whose stay with VF-3 in the fall of 1942 was brief but highly memorable, noted that "Butch would have been as popular on Maui as he was even if he did not have the Medal of Honor: he was interested in other people." Too, it did not hurt that Butch had a keen sense of humor. Recalling gunnery practice, Sy had to laugh about how when Butch counted the holes in targets, he would note his own red-dye hits and with an impish grin and a glint in his eye credit himself with Sy's pink hits and all others, regardless of color.[10]

Butch concerned himself not only with his pilots, but also with the squadron's enlisted men, headed by Willie Williams, his superb leading chief. If anything, their regard for and loyalty to Butch exceeded that of the aviators. He expected a great deal from his mechanics, ordnancemen, yeomen, and other specialists, but they discovered that once they made Butch's team, there was nothing he would not do for them. This feeling intensified in late 1942, when Butch had to turn over most of his enlisted men to other commands as part of a general streamlining of the fighting squadrons. He and Williams handpicked those few who remained.

Clyde "Buzzy" Baur, who rose from seaman second class to chief aviation machinist's mate while serving thirty-one months with Butch, related a characteristic story. In January 1943, newly promoted to first-class petty officer, Baur happened to be towing a Wildcat past the Puunene headquarters building when a station officer decided he was going too fast and put him on report. A few days later the executive officer of VF-3, Lieut. Lester S. Wall, Jr., brought the matter to Butch's attention at a disciplinary "captain's mast." Butch cautioned Baur to slow down and be more careful around the station officers, then dismissed him—end of incident.

To Baur's shock, Wall sharply interjected, "Hold on, Baur." He told Butch that he personally was putting Baur on report for using foul language to a fellow officer. Butch asked Wall if he was serious, to which the XO replied yes. Butch turned to Baur and said, "Get back to the line." From the squadron yeoman Baur later learned that after he left, the fireworks began: "You had barely cleared the door when O'Hare came from behind his desk and faced right up to the Exec and said, 'You go pack your bags, I'm going to Pearl to get your new orders. You don't put any of my men on report!'" Baur felt that Butch had become dissatisfied with his exec, and that the incident in his office was only the tip of the iceberg. Yet as Baur wrote, Butch "was right there for me. I was no angel, but I was one of the team."[11]

Fresh out of operational training, Les Wall had joined VF-3 in early September 1942 and jumped to XO that month after Ruehlow's departure. He deemed it necessary to assert himself and impart more spit and polish to the squadron. On 24 October, just after coming on board VF-3, Johnny Altemus recorded in his diary, "This guy Wall is a typical 'EAGER' Annapolis boy—Class of '39. He got his wings last summer & is now busy telling all the boys how it's done." It was inevitable that somewhere along the line Butch and Wall would not see eye to eye. Wall was too junior to remain XO for long, and Butch gave him the opportunity for a clean start in VF-11.[12]

Good Times on Maui

Training did not take up all of Butch's time on Maui—far from it. Tension needed release, and even in leisure, Butch led the way. A local couple, Frank and Ethel Hoogs, took to Butch and offered him exclusive use of a small cottage on the beach and a station wagon during off-duty hours. In turn Butch invited Lt. Charles W. McCord, one of his three ground administrative officers, to share the cottage. He and McCord hit it off from the beginning, mainly because they enjoyed many of the same activities, but perhaps also because Charlie was a nonaviator; Butch may have felt particularly comfortable sharing social time with Charlie precisely because he was someone whose life did not depend so directly upon him.

The cottage served as a social center not only for Butch and Charlie but also for the officers and men of the squadron. One of Chief Radioman Wilton Decker's favorite remembrances was the occasion when Butch and Charlie came by the enlisted barracks to invite him, Chief Williams, and the other VF-3 enlisted crew for a Sunday-afternoon picnic. Butch arranged for their transportation, and instead of Spam he served what the Navy considered gourmet fare: thick steaks and coveted liquid refreshments. The men enjoyed a great afternoon of food and games. "Butch did not have to do this," recalled Decker, "but that was Butch, always trying to look after us with that personal touch."[13]

When not eating or playing volleyball on the beach, Butch would wend his way "through the wire" to the sea. Ever resourceful when left to his own devices, he often borrowed a boat and outboard motor from a neighbor and set out on the ocean. Whitey Feightner had heard of Butch's love for the water before he had occasion to socialize with him, but even advance word did little to convey the extent of Butch's comfort in the water. While the fair-complected Whitey "turned red" under the sun's rays, Butch assumed alternate shades of red and brown, rolling over from time to time while floating, sometimes four hours at a stretch, to even out his coloration. Although Feightner and other squadron members greeted the CO's love for the water with varying degrees of enthusiasm, Butch insisted that all join him in the sport of fishing. Diving deep into the transparent water, Butch would surface with various varieties of fish, some caught with his bare hands, others with more conventional instruments. Then he would lecture his captive audience on how to prepare the catch. "Always bite an octopus behind the ear," Butch would tell his guests, and some like Feightner nodded affirmatively while their stomachs did loops and spirals.[14]

Lesson over, Butch was back into the water, floating like a cork, munching on raw fish—which tasted like an old rubber tire, according to Feightner—and moving only when necessary to adjust his Japanese goggles or switch his tanning surface. Returning to the beach, he would expound upon spear-fishing techniques and then offer lessons in body surfing. He eased off that activity after he caught one wave wrong in November 1942 and hurt his neck, then compounded the injury by falling off the wing of his plane. While the clumsy J2F Grumman Duck was not his favorite airplane, it could float, so Butch frequently set down when the ocean was calm, turned off the engine, and tossed a line into the water to catch lunch.

When not seeking fish, Butch loaded his shotgun, mounted a horse, and trooped off into the hills to shoot game birds, mostly pheasant. He always ate what he killed. Just as he could hold his own in the sea with the natives of Hawaii, he resembled an old cowhand when it came to riding. "Though Butch was apparently born in the saddle," Feightner recalled, "the rest of us were having more than a little trouble." Butch amazed his squadron mates with his marksmanship from horseback.

Surprised at Feightner's continuing equine difficulties during a mounted camping trip up a 10,025-foot extinct volcano into Haleakala crater, he sent the ensign back to fetch supplies in the Duck. Three days later Whitey located the small party in the crater—the so-called House of the Sun, twenty miles around and twenty-seven hundred feet deep—and dropped the goods, but he could not climb back out. Winds streaming into the huge crater counteracted the lift under the underpowered J2F's wings. In no mood to demonstrate to the watching CO that he handled a plane no better than he did a horse, Whitey finally realized that he could escape on the opposite side. Butch's concerns regarding the ensign's abilities evaporated when he later heard that Whitey scored four kills while with VF-10 at Guadalcanal. He took no credit for teaching Whitey about aerial combat, but Whitey still acknowledged the debt.[15]

Butch's hunting forays on Maui were not necessarily for his own stomach or pleasure, though he always loved to eat and hunt. At times he provided fresh game for particular friends who lived a good distance from the naval air station. In fact, he often let them know that he and others from VF-3 were coming to dinner by air-mailing a note while flying slowly over their homes. On 21 June, the day after Butch reached Maui, he received an invitation to dine with the Von Tempsky family, renowned for their gracious hospitality. Gordon Robert "Boy" Von Tempsky and his wife, Mamie, lived about thirty-five hundred feet up the slopes of Haleakala on an estate blessed with beautiful verdant grounds and a grand view of the valley and ocean. It was Erehwon Ranch (*nowhere* spelled backwards) stocked with horses available for pleasure riding or to serve as mounts for hunting game birds. Robert and Mamie felt a special closeness to the pilots because their son Gordon flew fighters with the Army Air Forces.

Robert's sister, Countess Alexandra Von Tempsky Zabriskie ("Alexa," or "Lex," as her many friends fondly called her), dwelled nearby. Whether one arrived at her house for dinner, a picnic, a party, or just a game of cards, Lex was the consummate hostess. Divorced and childless, she was forty-nine when Butch first met her. A skilled artist and portrait painter, she was equally accomplished as a conversationalist and, perhaps more significantly, a listener. Butch quickly came to think of her as a surrogate mother, and she in turn adopted him and a multitude of other servicemen who trekked to her door. After fifty years she is still "a very emotional subject" for retired U.S. Navy captain John Lacouture, a plebe at the

Naval Academy during Butch's first-class year: "She was a superb lady and thousands of World War II men, mostly naval aviators, loved her like a mother." Lacouture recalls that Fleet Admiral Chester Nimitz and Alexa were on a first-name basis, and that Nimitz presented her with a signed photograph of the Japanese surrender, averring that she "as much as anyone present at this ceremony [was] responsible for making possible this picture." Jimmy Flatley declared her "a one-woman USO." Patsy O'Hare Palmer recalls that "Butch . . . and all the men just adored her. . . . [She] was so fabulous to everybody."[16]

The hospitality and homelike atmosphere Butch found at Lex's and at Erehwon Ranch were offered to him by another family as well. Frank Hoogs, an administrator at the Wailuku Sugar Plantation, and Ethel, his California-born wife, opened their fine home to naval aviators, but their relationship with Butch was unique. So warmly received by Lex and the Von Tempskys, he assumed that the welcome would be the same with the Hoogses. It was, and in time their friendship grew very close. However, on first introduction Frank and Ethel were a little startled when Butch strode past them, their two maids, and their two young daughters straight to the refrigerator and opened the door to see what there was to eat. He rarely made himself right at home on first meeting, but this time he did. Confiding in 1976 to Patsy, Ethel recalled many happy memories of Butch, but she still had to chuckle when remembering his first visit. Shortly afterward, Butch acquired his own shelf in Ethel's refrigerator. Navy ace Alexander Vraciu, Butch's wingman in 1943, remembers with a smile Butch "ordering" him into the station wagon so they could "run over to Frank and Ethel's and get a snack." Sy Mendenhall also traveled with Butch to their home, where he was royally entertained before, during, and after the great meals. The Hoogses, according to Sy, were "the greatest host and hostess to ever invite me into their home; they couldn't do enough for us."[17]

It is apparent that people such as Alexa Von Tempsky Zabriskie, her brother and his wife, and the Hoogs family were patriotic. When they and others, like the women who visited Puunene for the Sunday dances at the Officers' Club, went to such great lengths to show the servicemen their appreciation, it was not only an expression of kindness to the men in times of duress but also an acknowledgment that these servicemen were the very people to whom the people of Maui owed their lives. The Japanese had already attacked Oahu on 7 December 1941, and twice that month subs shelled Kahului on Maui. There was genuine concern that the enemy would return. They might well have done so, had the June 1942 Battle of Midway gone in favor of the Japanese.

The stress experienced by the inhabitants of Hawaii was no greater than that felt by the naval aviators on Maui. Throughout most of his time there, Butch suffered trouble falling and staying asleep. Even though Whitey Feightner knew Butch for only a month, he recalls how deeply and personally he took things. The great strain grew more pronounced while out at sea, but even at Puunene, Butch tossed and turned, unable to switch off his attention to the burdens and details of command. The worries of every man in the squadron were his worries. When things went right, that was the way it was supposed to be. When things went wrong, no matter how or with whom, that became his problem. Now unable to restrain the myriad problems stealing into his mind, Butch wrote to Patsy requesting sleeping pills. They helped. Just as in his football days at Western Military Academy, when the first block or tackle ended the "butterflies," now the first turn of a propeller removed worries of everything but the mission at hand.

Many of Butch's family did not know of his sleeping problems, nor did they fully understand the tensions he battled. For the most part he made it a practice not to pass his burdens on to the family. In his letters he was matter-of-fact to upbeat. Military complaints did not find their way into his epistles; the censor would have deleted them anyway.

To some degree writing letters proved as good a medicine as medicine itself. While writing, at least his mind was back home. For all his time on Maui, Butch addressed the vast majority of his letters to Rita. They communicated feelings strictly the domain of husband and wife. To Selma, his sisters, and his uncle he occasionally wrote "community" letters, one typed dispatch addressed to all. Nearly every one included news of food, and even a contingency plan for fishing trips: "Even if we don't get any fish we carry a case or two of beer along and that makes up for it." Butch and his squadron were well supplied with meat, coffee, sugar, and liquor—everything except eggs. For Thanksgiving 1942 he reported to Marilyn that he had been "eating turkey for several days and in several places on Maui. . . . I've put on 20 pounds . . . just living too good I guess." On 9 October 1943 he wrote to Marilyn saying that he had started to send some pictures of steaks they had eaten at the Hoogses', "but that would be too cruel."[18]

While not one to complain much, Butch did express some consternation about the home front in a letter to his mother dated 3 September
1942. After inquiring about the tires on her car and the availability of
gas, he stated, "Maybe it will do some of them good to get out of their
cars for awhile so they will know a war is going on somewhere." When
reporting on the war, he seemed to find no middle ground. In November
1942 he joked to Marilyn, "If we get out to sea I'll try to get a Jap to
send to you; the only trouble is what would you do with him?" Turning
serious, he wrote to his mother on her birthday, "I hope before many
more birthdays we will all be back together again and this war will be
ended." Writing to Marilyn in October 1943, six weeks before his death,
his perspective on the progress of the war was on target: "It is going to
be wonderful when this war is over and things get back to normal. I
think it still has a while to go however."[19]

"We're Going Home to Reform—Hurrah!"

Finally in mid-December 1942 Butch acquired enough Wildcats to
resume systematic gunnery training to sharpen skills that for the veterans had grown rusty and for the rookies needed yet to be mastered. In
January 1943 he received two especially fine officers to help him run VF-
3. His new XO, Lt. George C. Bullard, was a red-haired 1938 Naval
Academy graduate who had earned his wings in January 1941. As a
member of Cruising Scouting Squadron Five, Bullard had flown SOC
floatplanes from the heavy cruiser *Pensacola* (CA-24) and witnessed
Butch's Medal of Honor fight on 20 February 1942. That fall he happily
made the transition to fighters. In his strong professionalism, "the Bull"
proved as earnest and serious as Butch, and he was a meticulous administrator. Lt. Howard W. "Sandy" Crews, a former AvCad who had
earned the Silver Star with VF-5 at Guadalcanal, became the operations
officer. Surprised to learn the identity of his famous new commander and
most pleased to meet him, Sandy exclaimed in his diary, "'Butch'
O'Hare Skipper b'gawd." Other VF-5 vets reporting to the squadron
were Lt. (jg) Francis R. "Cash" Register, an ace credited with six kills—
one more than Butch; Lt. (jg) Foster J. "Crud" Blair; and Lt. (jg)
Richards L. "Dix" Loesch, Jr., recovered from wounds inflicted at
Guadalcanal. Dix had briefly served in VF-3 in June and July 1942

before being posted to VF-6. Butch welcomed all the newcomers with a party at his beach house.[20]

In January an old friend returned to VF-3 in the form of F4U-1 Bureau Number 02166, the Corsair that Butch had flown the previous October and November. This time the CO let the other pilots take the bent-winged bird aloft for familiarization and gunnery exercises. In early February two more Corsairs were delivered to the squadron, and a fourth arrived on the fifteenth. The pilots speculated that the squadron would reequip with F4Us, particularly when they turned in all their F4F Wildcats. However, VF-3 also relinquished nine of its most junior pilots to VF-11, which was preparing to leave for the South Pacific. Butch came back from headquarters unusually grim-faced and told Mendenhall, "Sy, I almost lost you today." Butch's Boys seemed destined to remain in limbo in a placid backwater of the Pacific war.[21]

At least in VF-3 legend, one of the F4Us played a role in getting VF-3 orders home. Clyde Baur related how Butch supposedly gave in to the entreaties of a senior officer who wanted to fly his Corsair. The officer promised that if anything happened to the aircraft, he would grant any request Butch made. This worthy evidently blew a tire while landing and honored his promise when Butch asked for VF-3 to be sent to the States. Baur recalled that the CO and Chief Williams visited the enlisted barracks one night: "O'Hare had a grin a mile wide. He said, 'How long does it take you to pack? We're leaving for the States tomorrow.'"[22]

Of course, things are never that simple. VF-3 went home in order to become part of a new carrier air group destined for one of the newly commissioned carriers expected to reach the Pacific that summer. The old era of breaking up teams and shifting squadrons around as needed was supposed to be over. Butch did not care why he was going home, just that it was happening, for awaiting him in St. Louis were his wife, Rita, and a baby daughter he had never seen. Crews noted in his diary that on the evening of 16 February, Butch called his senior officers out of a movie to inform them that the squadron was to return the four Corsairs to Pearl Harbor by the next evening. The old seaplane tender *Swan* (AVP-7) would transport the rest of the pilots, the enlisted personnel, and the squadron gear from Kahului to Pearl.[23]

On the morning of the seventeenth Butch, Bullard, Crews, and Register roared down the Puunene runway in their majestic Corsairs and joyously accorded Maui "a real farewell demonstration." At Ford Island,

Butch turned in his aircraft and transferred the last half-dozen pilots he had received over to VF-11. Again reunited, the rump of VF-3 sailed on 24 February on board the large seaplane tender *Chandeleur* (AV-10) bound for San Diego. Butch and the others relaxed and "played acey-deucy, gin rummy, dominoes & Hollywood." Each hour brought him fifteen miles closer to the reunion he so desired.[24]

11

Home and Back

"Things are looking up"

After a week at sea, the seaplane tender *Chandeleur* docked on 2 March 1943 at San Diego. As soon as Butch could get away, he eagerly departed on leave for a fast trip to St. Louis, where Rita was living with the Golter-manns. For the first time he would behold his one-month-old daughter, Kathleen, whom he would lovingly call "Buttons." On 3 September 1942 the expectant father had written his mother, Selma, "Just can't wait until February," when the baby was due. In his 22 December "community" letter Butch praised the pictures of Patsy's daughter and newborn Paul junior ("looking the part of a wrestler") before again alluding to the "big day" next February. He described the good things on Maui and added, "Only thing missing is the wife. If only I would have brought her along with me in June it would have been wonderful." Now, it *was* wonderful. With Kathleen's birth, on 6 February, it was doubly wonderful. Butch knew that the next few months would be a great time in his life. In early April the O'Hare threesome would find a house in Coronado and make it a home.

Butch hastened back to San Diego to preside over a pivotal event, the reorganization of VF-3 and its incorporation into its own air group. Pending the arrival of Comdr. James R. Lee from the South Pacific, Butch stepped in as acting group commander. A 1928 Annapolis graduate, "Bucky" Lee had greatly distinguished himself as CO of the *Enterprise*'s Scouting Squadron Ten (VS-10) during the Guadalcanal campaign. On the morning of 15 March, Carrier Air Group Six was commissioned, along with its new components: Fighting Squadron Three, Bombing Squadrons One and Two, and Torpedo Squadron Seven. Butch sent the customary announcement to Commander in Chief, U.S. Fleet. As yet none of the squadrons possessed many pilots or aircraft—indeed, other than VF-3, only acting COs were present.[1]

Writing on 22 March to the family in St. Louis, Butch summed up the past week: "Things are looking up. We have quite a few pilots and about a third of our planes and they are really good ones this time." He had set up shop in a hangar at South Field, one of the three subdivisions of NAS San Diego on North Island, and undertook the expansion of VF-3 while training for an operational assignment that he knew could not be too long in coming. Budding fighter pilots began arriving, and also a dozen factory-fresh Grumman F6F-3 Hellcat fighters. Eventually Butch would have over fifty pilots and three dozen Hellcats. On 19 March he took his first flight in the Hellcat, something he had anticipated for nearly a year since his visit to Grumman in Bethpage, New York. He flew Bureau Number 04827, the fifty-second F6F-3 accepted by the U.S. Navy.

Back on 30 June 1941 the Navy had placed an order for Grumman's proposed XF6F-1 to hedge its bets should the long-awaited Vought XF4U-1 Corsair not work out as a suitable carrier fighter. With input from Lt. Comdr. Andrew McBurney Jackson and others from the Bureau of Aeronautics, Grumman designed into the nascent Hellcat superior visibility over the nose, so vital both for gunnery and for carrier landings. The XF6F-1 first flew on 26 June 1942, three weeks after the Battle of Midway (and a month *before* a downed Zero fighter was recovered in the Aleutians). Its performance proved disappointing, largely because of its 1,600-hp Wright Cyclone engine.

Following the suggestion of Butch and many others, Grumman switched the XF6F-3's powerplant in July, adopting the 2,000-hp Pratt & Whitney R-2800-10 Double Wasp—the same engine as in the Corsair. The resulting XF6F-3 was a marriage made in heaven. It seemed to embody all of the F4F-4's good traits, such as ruggedness and excellent high-speed control, and more. Weighing nearly twice as much as the Wildcat, the massive Hellcat featured the largest wing fitted on an American single-seat fighter during the war. The wide-track landing gear gracefully folded into the wing—no more hand-cranking, as with the knock-knee F4F. Much faster than the F4F-4 (376 mph versus 320 mph for the F4F-4), it also enjoyed a greatly increased climb rate (above ten thousand feet, nearly as swift as a Zero) and, with a 150-gallon drop tank, far superior range. Ammunition for the six .50-caliber Browning M2 machine guns was increased from 240 to 400 rounds per gun. All in all, the XF6F-3 was a great horse of a fighter, a much better carrier aircraft than the long-nosed, bounce-prone F4U.[2]

Production of the F6F-3 by Grumman quickly went into high gear, and the Navy accepted the first one in September 1942. By January 1943 there were enough at Norfolk to begin equipping Lt. Comdr. John Raby's VF-9, a part of Air Group Nine training for the new *Essex* (CV-9). Butch's VF-3 was the first West Coast squadron to receive the new Hellcats.

A second fighting squadron in training at NAS San Diego was VF-12, commanded by another well-known Navy character, Lt. Comdr. Joseph C. "Jumping Joe" Clifton. VF-12 had received F4U-1 Corsairs in January 1943—only the second squadron after the Marines of VMF-124—and labored mightily both to get acquainted with their fractious mounts and to qualify them on carriers. Ultimately VF-12 would lose fourteen pilots while working up with the Corsairs, only to relinquish the F4U-1s for F6F-3s before going into combat. However, in late March 1943 they boasted to their compatriots in VF-3 that the Corsair was far superior to the Hellcat, at least 50 knots faster, although official performance statistics put the F4U's advantage at only 16 knots.

Butch's Boys naturally took umbrage, and with the blessings of both COs, VF-3 and VF-12 determined on a race to see which of the aircraft could first attain ten thousand feet from a standing start. With all the pilots in attendance, two VF-12 Corsairs lined up on the tarmac abreast of two VF-3 Hellcats flown by Cash Register and Dix Loesch. Using full blower with engines at a deafening roar, the four "horsed" their aircraft off the ground and climbed as steeply as they could. The Corsair proved a slight winner, but neither Butch nor the rest of VF-3 cared. In the Hellcat they now wielded a weapon that could most definitely take the fight right to the enemy and win.

At the end of March, Fleet Air, West Coast, appropriated two of Butch's four lieutenant pilots and all seven jg's to fly Grumman F4F-4 Wildcats with Composite Squadron Twenty-one. Lt. Comdr. Lloyd K. Greenamyer's VC-21 was working up for duty on the escort carrier *Nassau* (CVE-16) commanded by Butch's old luncheon companion, Capt. "Artie" Doyle. For Butch the untimely loss of most of his experienced pilots was a heavy blow. As events transpired, neither Sy Mendenhall (who had tonsillitis) nor Johnny Altemus (broken ankle) could go, which was fortunate for them. On 23 April the *Nassau* sailed from San Francisco bound for the 11 May invasion of Attu in the Aleutians. While providing ground support and CAP missions, VC-21 suffered a terrible time from tumultuous seas, thick fog, and strong winds. On 14 May, Lt. Douglas Henderson, who had joined VF-3 in November 1942 as one of the first of Butch's Boys, perished while strafing in the aptly named Massacre Valley. Powerful "williwaw" wind gusts shoved his Wildcat into a mountainside. Greenamyer's Wildcat simply went missing. On the sixteenth Cash Register sank with his plane after a strafing run against enemy positions near Holtz Bay. No one on the *Nassau* regretted leaving Attu on 20 May. In late May she returned to San Diego, where Butch happily welcomed back to the fold Lt. Paul C. Rooney and jg's Dix Loesch, Crud Blair, and Richard B. Trimble.[3]

Meanwhile, Butch had his hands full training and evaluating his growing brood of young pilots who had joined in March and April. One of the new ensigns, Herschel A. Pahl, later summarized Butch's approach: "Right away he started working out with us getting to know us in the air and teaching us his ideas on tactics and how to get the most out of the new plane." Pahl added, "We tried to live every day to the fullest and scrambled for every minute in the air we could get." Butch tolerated the antics of his fledgling fighter pilots as they tore up the skies over Southern California, dogfighting each other and the twin-engine Army Air Force Lockheed P-38 Lightnings based nearby. Butch's stalwarts, XO George Bullard and Howard Crews, his operations officer, and Sy Mendenhall proved invaluable in the long process of getting a green squadron ready to fight. Also helpful were two old *Hornet* hands: lieutenants (jg) Henry A. "Al" Fairbanks and Robert S. "Moose" Merritt, who fought at Midway with VF-8 and in VF-72 at Guadalcanal.[4]

One day it was Ens. Willie Callan's turn to fly with the skipper. Anxious to show how well he could fly formation, he latched onto Butch's Hellcat, moving in as close as he dared. Butch gestured for his wingman to loosen out as he began maneuvering, but as soon as he could, Willie closed in tight again. Butch shook his head and waved him out and back to where he wanted him to stay. After the next series of violent maneuvers, there was Willie tucked in tight again. Butch glanced at him, looked away, then rolled the big Hellcat toward Willie as hard as he could. The only response Willie could make to avoid a collision was to push the stick forward and duck straight down. Rather surprised, he rejoined the CO a few minutes later. Butch positioned him correctly, and he stayed there. Lesson taught and learned.[5]

Ens. Alexander Vraciu, another rookie reporting to VF-3 at the end of March, was destined, with nineteen victories, to become the Navy's fourth highest ace. The year before, Butch had spoken to the aviation cadets at NAS Corpus Christi, where Alex was in flight training. Thrilled now to hear of the formation of Butch's new squadron at San Diego, he won a coin flip to get orders to VF-3. Once there, he was highly impressed by both the flying and the down-to-earth personality of his new commander. During his first flight with Butch, Alex, like Callan and perhaps half the squadron, flew tight formation to show Butch he could do it. As with the others, Butch motioned him out to where he wanted him to be.

Once Butch firmed up the squadron flight organization, he chose Alex as his wingman. He recognized a kindred spirit and enjoyed teaching him about air combat in a no-nonsense, give-and-take manner, imparting invaluable lessons that Alex later acknowledged helped save his life on more than one occasion. Once while practicing dogfighting with the skipper one on one, Alex found himself losing the turning edge, for Butch knew far better how to get the most out of his Hellcat. To evade, Alex pulled up into sun. As he put it, he "caught hell" when they got down. Butch told him that killing both of them in practice was not a good way to go. Alex credited Butch's constant emphasis on lookout doctrine for saving his life on 16 February 1944 during a fierce melee over Truk lagoon. About to dive against the airfield, he remembered Butch's oft-repeated admonition to check high over the left shoulder before going into a fight. Sure enough, a Zeke had him in its sights, its guns already blinking fire. Alex evaded the attack and downed three Zekes and a Rufe float-fighter on that memorable mission. As proud as he was to fly with Butch, he came especially to value the opportunity to get to know him more closely, particularly after the squadron returned to Maui in June.[6]

Taking a break on 11 April 1943 in the midst of working up VF-3, Butch took a North American SNJ-4 trainer over to Santa Ana Field to fetch brother-in-law Phil Tovrea for a grand get-together in Coronado. There they and three other pilots drank beer while Kathleen slept and Rita and Marilyn cooked dinner. Butch insisted that all the fellows enjoy some of his mother's homemade grape jelly. The boys continued to drink and devour the jelly. Forgetting to turn on the heat, the women kept pouring flour into the gravy to get it "right," and Kathleen kept sleeping. The boys had too much to drink, Butch demanded that the fellows stop eating up all his mother's grape jelly, the gravy looked and tasted like glue, and Kathleen slept on. Any other time, this might have been considered a bad day. But as they headed for bed, all agreed it had been a great time. Then Kathleen awoke.

On another occasion that spring when Butch planned to make the short hop to Phoenix to see his sisters, he learned that one of his young ensigns, Joe D. Robbins, also had a sister living there. Having spoken to Butch only once and worried when he was called to the CO's office, Robbins was surprised when Butch invited him to accompany him to Phoenix in another F6F. For part of the flight Butch turned the lead over to Robbins. After a most welcome visit, they flew back to San Diego that afternoon. Robbins remembered Butch as "one of the nicest persons on this trip. You would never know he was my CO or the 'hero' that he was. He was always that way."[7]

One of Butch's major tasks was to get the squadron carrier-qualified. On 27 April he made his first carrier landing in a Hellcat on board the escort carrier *Altamaha* (CVE-18). Some of his rookies had already acquired valuable experience in touch-and-go landings on the *Wolverine* (IX-64), a side-wheel steamer converted into a flattop on Lake Michigan. Others had flown off the escort carrier *Charger* (CVE-30) in the Atlantic. In May the VF-3 pilots completed field carrier landing practice, responding to the gestures of a landing signal officer while setting down on a specific spot on the tarmac at North Island. On the eleventh Ens. Richard H. Stone was killed when his F6F crashed during carrier landing practice. At the end of May and in early June the squadron conducted carrier qualification and catapult launches during a couple of short cruises on board the *Altamaha*. George Bullard worked with the neophytes to acquaint them with shipboard life. That was vital because Air Group Six was under orders to proceed to Hawaii. On 6 June VB-1 and VB-2 left on the escort carrier *Barnes* (CVE-20) and on the twelfth flew to Puunene.

On the evening of 14 June, Butch said his fond goodbyes to Rita and Kathleen before going on board the escort carrier *Prince William* (CVE-31). Loaded with the full complement of forty-eight VF-3 pilots and twenty-eight F6F-3s, the *"Pee Willie"* sailed early the next morning for Pearl Harbor. Eight more Hellcats rode as cargo on the freighter *HMS Athene.* Commander Lee and VT-7 departed San Diego at the same time. During the evenings Butch enjoyed playing a game called Michigan with Sandy Crews, Paul Rooney, Sy Mendenhall, Bob Merritt, and Johnny Altemus.

In his memoir Herschel Pahl related one of Butch's subtle "object lessons" during a meeting in the ready room:

> "Butch" carefully and with a serious attitude went around the ready room handing one small piece of dark brown paper to each officer. After he finished, he told us to take a good long look at the paper and memorize the color well. Then he simply told us to put it away in our billfolds or in a safe place where we could look at it from time to time. Then he told us that if we ever discovered that the brown paper had suddenly turned "blond," we should let him know at once. At first the incident seemed like a pointless joke, but as the weeks and months went by, there was never any doubt about its real meaning.

Before they risked their own lives and those of their teammates, Butch wanted to know if any of his men no longer desired to fly fighters in combat.[8]

On the morning of 22 June the *Pee Willie* steamed into Pearl Harbor past Battleship Row to a berth at the north end of Ford Island. There the Hellcats were lowered to the ground and towed to the airfield. In port besides the venerable *Enterprise* was the *Essex,* the first of a new class of large, fast flattops that would transform carrier warfare in the Pacific.

At 1300 Butch led eighteen F6Fs back to his old stomping grounds at NAS Puunene on Maui. Altemus, one of the old hands, noticed that things had changed: Puunene "is much larger, the field itself is much improved & the taxi-ways have been paved." However, he added, "there is still the perpetual red dust & wind & mosquitoes & heat." The VF-3 billet was in something called Area A, more than a mile from their ready room. Altemus found that the bar in the Officers' Club had been moved farther away—"probably a good thing!" he joked.[9]

That evening Butch happily gathered the old hands and some of the new boys to visit the Hoogs family at their home, where they all enjoyed a "reunion dinner," as Howard Crews dubbed it. According to Pahl, one of the newcomers, "The Hoogs were very kind and gracious and soon conveyed to us the feeling of glowing warm friendship that is unmistakably Hawaiian."[10]

Settling in at Puunene, Butch worked out a three-day operating cycle divided according to the twelve-plane flights led by himself, Bullard, and Crews. On the first day a flight would work from 0800 to 1600, plus a night mission if weather permitted. The second day was similar, minus the night flying. The third morning the flight turned out early for a predawn CAP directed by "Pineapple Control," often a practice intercept of the flying boat inbound from San Francisco. Landing back at Puunene, the pilots got the rest of the day off, a welcome chance to relax or blow off steam.[11]

Butch worked the squadron hard to get the pilots ready for battle. Capt. George F. Rodgers, USN (Ret.), remembered his CO during these days as "undemonstrative" and someone who "seldom smiled." Repeatedly in talks in the ready room Butch urged his boys to "anticipate": "This is no drill. We aren't playing funsies. You have to anticipate every move your opponent may make. If you sit there fat, dumb and happy— you're dead." A correspondent from *Yank* magazine dropped in at Puunene to answer the question "What's Butch O'Hare doing these days?" He found the pilots of the duty flight loitering in the ready room playing checkers using Coke-bottle caps: "Then Butch comes in and reads the flight orders, and they rush to their lockers and get on their coveralls, parachutes, helmets and goggles. When they're ready for take off, O'Hare gives them a few final pointers on new tactics." While Butch was aloft, the correspondent had the temerity to ask someone in the squadron where the CO kept his Medal of Honor. The answer he received perfectly reflected Butch's philosophy. The medals were in storage "for the duration," because "you can't wear medals on work clothes."[12]

On 30 June, Bucky Lee led Air Group Six (twenty-six F6Fs from VF-3, twenty-nine SBDs from VB-1 and VB-2, and thirteen TBFs from VT-7) on board the *Enterprise* for four days of exercises south of Oahu. Aware that the number of their air group—six—was the same as the *Enterprise*'s own hull number, the pilots had hoped they might be assigned to that battle-proven warship. Once on board they marveled at the damage that remained from the bomb hits she had suffered the previous October in the Battle of Santa Cruz. Officers' country on the second deck was still "tent city." To Butch and VF-3 it seemed unlikely that the *Enterprise* would long remain in the islands before returning home for a full refit. If so, Air Group Six would have no ship—"all dressed up & no place to go," as Altemus put it. On 1 July VB-2 was decommissioned and its personnel transferred to VB-1. Henceforth each carrier air group would have one bombing squadron of thirty-six aircraft. On 3 July Air Group Six returned to Puunene "and the dust," as Crews complained.[13]

The sixth of July proved a rough day for VF-3. Ensigns Ashton A. Roberts and Thomas D. Willman collided twenty-five miles north of Maui. Willman parachuted into the water immediately, stayed afloat, and was later rescued, while Roberts limped back to Puunene with his mutilated F6F. Meanwhile, back at Puunene, Lt. (jg) John O. Benton stood his Hellcat down on its nose.

On 9 July, Butch took VF-3 over to NAS Barbers Point just to the west of Pearl Harbor and joined the rest of Air Group Six for another hop out to the *Enterprise*. More exercises were in the offing, this time in concert with the *Essex,* flagship of Rear Adm. Ted Sherman, Butch's CO on the old *Lexington.* Altemus, for one, found the *Big E* to be "hot & stuffy below decks—but a relief to be away from the dirt & dust & wind on Maui."[14]

The high point of the training cruise was a simulated strike at dawn on 12 July against Pearl Harbor by the *Essex* and *Enterprise.* The idea was to reprise the huge Japanese raid of 7 December 1941 with mock attacks on the Oahu airfields as well as the harbor itself. At 0612 the *Big E* dispatched Lee with twelve F6Fs, twenty-nine SBDs, and a dozen TBFs from 125 miles southwest of Barbers Point. Most of the aircraft stayed low under the radar to avoid detection, but Butch's four-plane division drew a special assignment as decoys. West of Oahu he climbed to twenty thousand feet to get on the Army Air Force radar while monitoring the Interceptor Command radio frequency. With adroit maneuvers, Butch drew defending fighters away from Oahu and helped open the way for the "attacks," which were very successful. Two divisions of VF-3 buzzed the airfields. Tragically, Lt. (jg) William Rose in Al Fairbanks's division was killed over Ford Island when he collided with a Curtiss P-40 Warhawk flown by 1st Lt. Gordon M. Lewis of the Army Air Force's Forty-fifth Fighter Squadron. Meanwhile, the two dozen VF-3 and VF-9 CAP fighters defending the two carriers were ruled to have defeated all the land-based air counterattacks. That afternoon Lee took Air Group Six back to Maui. Two days later the gallant *Enterprise* sailed from Pearl bound for Bremerton and the long-needed refit.[15]

On 15 July all three squadrons constituting Air Group Six were renumbered with the numeral six. Thus, Butch's VF-3 was redesignated VF-6, while VB-1 changed to VB-6 and VT-7 to VT-6. The move ensured that each squadron bore the same number as its parent carrier air group. Down in the South Pacific, Lt. Comdr. Louis H. Bauer's VF-6—"Bauer's Flowers," the Shooting Star squadron that had fought on the *Enterprise* from December 1941 through August 1942—became a component of Air Group Three on the *Saratoga*. Its new designation was VF-3. There was an amusing follow-up to the exchange of squadron numbers. Without official sanction, Bauer quickly discarded the shooting-star emblem of old VF-6 for the more famous Felix the Cat, long associated with VF-3. Of course, Butch continued displaying Felix, since 1928 an important part of his squadron's tradition through all of the past number changes. Until late 1944 the two naval fighting squadrons unwittingly used the same insignia on their aircraft and flight jackets, until the interlopers (the ex–Shooting Stars) were told to drop the feline. They got their revenge in the end, however, when Butch's old squadron was decommissioned in 1945. VF-3 adopted Felix, which to this day remains an honored insignia with its successor, VF-31, the Tomcatters.[16]

On the afternoon of 26 July the Hoogses organized a fabulous luau at the Allen beach house north of Wailuku on Maui. The entire squadron was present, along with many of the Hoogses' friends and numerous Hawaiians attired in native costume, playing music and dancing. Butch circulated in his Hawaiian shirt, obviously enjoying himself tremendously. The Hawaiians put on a marvelous show, joined by individual dancers of whom the enthusiastic Al Fairbanks seemed especially noteworthy. The main course was supplied by a giant pig roast. Hot rocks were placed in the pigs' stomachs prior to the pigs themselves being wrapped in banana and tea leaves and positioned above hot coals. The whole assembly was then covered with "burlap bags & then dirt," as Altemus described, and left to cook for three hours in a "sort of steaming & boiling process."

When done, the pigs were lifted out of the pit and put into large tubs, ready to be devoured by the guests who sat at long tables. Altemus listed the different foods offered: "roast pig, poi, opihi (snails & shrimp), loco (intestines), squid boiled in coconut milk, luau chicken, taro root, pineapple, coconut, cake, salmon, and beer." That day Butch's gustatory expectations were more than fulfilled. After dinner, Hawaiian girls placed leis on and delivered the customary kisses to Butch, George

Bullard, Howard Crews, and Fairbanks. The Hoogses had thrown a "great party," one never forgotten by those who attended, and a tremendous boost to squadron morale.[17]

The magnificent luau was actually a sort of graduation dinner for the VF-6 rookies. It also signaled the end of a peaceful interlude for Butch, for now he was preparing in earnest to go to sea and into combat. Twice in the last days of July he was summoned over to Pearl for conferences with the staff of ComAirPac. To the rest of VF-6 the usually laconic Butch did not explain what he was doing. Altemus wrote in his diary, "As usual he has nothing to say about anything," but it became obvious that a major change was in the offing.[18]

12

Marcus and Wake

"On the Evil I"

On 20 July 1943, while Butch and the rest of VF-6 trained hard and played hard on Maui, a new type of small carrier made her debut at Pearl Harbor. In contrast to the boxlike, rather dumpy escort carriers (CVEs), this flattop looked leaner and meaner, with her flight deck and small island perched atop a narrow cruiser hull. Four small smokestacks on the starboard deck edge enhanced the rakish appearance.

The newcomer was the *Independence* (CVL-22), commanded by Capt. George R. Fairlamb, Jr., formerly CO of the *Wolverine*. Commissioned on 14 January 1943, she was the first of nine light carriers (CVLs) originally laid down as *Cleveland*-class light cruisers. Their conversion took place at the urging of President Roosevelt himself in order to fill the gap until more of the massive *Essex*-class flattops could be built. The new CVLs were fast—effectively about 29 knots, as opposed to 18 for most of the CVEs—and quite able to keep up with their bigger sisters. Speed, however, came at the price of only modest protection. Standard displacement for the *Independence* was 11,500 tons. She measured 622 feet overall and 190 feet in width, but her flight deck, only 552 feet by 73 feet, was actually a little narrower than those of the escort carriers. After landing his big Hellcat on the *Independence,* one former Wildcat pilot described the experience as "hitting a splinter with a bolt of lightning."[1]

Originally CVL air groups were smaller duplicates of those carried on the big carriers: a fighting (VF) squadron with a dozen fighters (at first F4Fs and later F6Fs), and a composite (VC) squadron with nine SBD dive bombers and nine TBF torpedo bombers. Thus, the *Independence* left for war with Air Group Twenty-two (VF-22 and VC-22) under Comdr. James M. Peters. By the time she reached Hawaii, though, experience showed that this particular mix of aircraft was inappropriate for the diminutive flattops. Lacking folding wings, the SBDs proved cumbersome on deck, and Air Group Twenty-two swiftly dispensed with them. Vice Adm. John Towers's AirPac headquarters at Pearl Harbor experimented to see what might be the optimum number and types of aircraft for the CVLs, whether only fighters or a combination of fighters and torpedo planes.

Casting around for more fighters to put on the CVLs, AirPac gazed hungrily at VF-6's three dozen Hellcats. On 1 August, Butch learned that his boys would take the place of Air Group Twenty-two on the *Independence* for carrier exercises. After a two-day battle problem with the rest of Bucky Lee's Air Group Six on the fabulous new *Essex,* the VF-6 pilots slept on board the *Independence* the night of 4 August while she was moored alongside Ford Island. The next morning came the real fun, when Butch brought VF-6 out to land on board that "very narrow" flight deck. That day and the next the *Independence* operated with the *Essex* again in a task group under Rear Admiral Sherman. They tested the idea of an all-fighter CVL that would handle combat air patrols over the ships while the F6Fs on the big carrier escorted strikes.[2]

Despite a great deal of flying and occasional fumbling by the *Independence*'s green crew, everything went well until dusk on 6 August. Eight CAP F6Fs led by George Bullard and Moose Merritt waited to land. The first five got down all right, but at 1948 the lack of wind forced the CVL to suspend recovery. That left Lt. (jg) Robert B. Locker and ensigns Alfred T. Kerr and Henry T. Landry still aloft. An untimely rain squall caused further delay, only compounded when the landing signal officer called for his illuminated wands and then found that they did not work. Neither did the *Independence*'s radio transmitter. By this time the sun had disappeared, and the three pilots were running low on fuel. Butch and the rest of VF-6 fretted and, as Johnny Altemus recorded in his diary, "got madder & madder at all this damn business." At 2005 Sherman finally decided to send the three F6Fs to the big island of Hawaii, "*hoping* they had enough gas." Altemus added, "And this is the ship to which we've been assigned!" Kerr made it on board the *Essex,* Locker reached Hilo, but Landry sustained serious injuries after a scary night flight that terminated in a crash in the mountains near Kamuela.[3]

On 9 August, Butch informed VF-6 that they were now reassigned indefinitely from Air Group Six to the *Independence*. The good news was that their prospects for action had increased greatly. Fresh carriers seemed to appear daily at Pearl Harbor: the new *Yorktown* (CV-10) and *Lexington* (CV-16); two lights, the *Princeton* (CVL-23) and *Belleau Wood* (CVL-24); and HMS *Victorious*. The bad news was having to leave VB-6 and VT-6 behind on Maui. On 11 August, Butch again brought the whole squadron, thirty-four F6Fs (including two borrowed from VF-22), out to the *Independence* for more exercises, this time along with the *Yorktown*. Again a mishap on the ship left a bad impression. On the morning of Friday, 13 August, the last scheduled day, Ens. John R. Ogg happened to roll his Hellcat into the port catwalk while landing. The ship could not pull the heavy Grumman out of its precarious roost and had to cancel further air operations. Butch and some of the other VF-6 pilots switched over to the *Yorktown* and later flew back to NAS Puunene, but the unlucky *Independence* had to slink back to Pearl with the Hellcat perched askew on deck. From that point the nickname *Evil I* began to catch on, to the dismay of her crew.

By mid-August AirPac had settled on twenty-four F6F Hellcat fighters and nine TBF Avenger torpedo bombers as the optimum plane complement for light carriers. That meant reshuffling fighter strength to place that many aircraft on each CVL. Thus, not only was VF-6 temporarily separated from its parent Air Group Six, but, worse, Butch's Boys would not even get to operate as a squadron from the same flattop. Two-thirds of VF-6 (Divisions I–VI), twenty-four F6Fs under Butch's direct command, became part of the *Independence*'s Air Group Twenty-two. Lt. Howard Crews would take the other dozen VF-6 Hellcats (Divisions VII, VIII, and IX) to join Air Group Twenty-three on board the *Princeton*. At the same time, VF-22 from the original *Independence* air complement reinforced Air Group Twenty-four on the *Belleau Wood*. Crews noted the "feverish preparations [in] getting our planes ready" and speculated,

"Looks like something is really cooking this time." He was right.[4]

On 22 August, Butch told VF-6 of the split and immediately prepared his twenty-four Hellcats to fly out to the *Independence,* which had sailed that morning from Pearl. Late that afternoon VF-6 assembled on the *Evil I* along with VC-22's nine TBFs. Butch reported to Jim Peters, the group commander who also led VC-22. A 1931 Annapolis graduate, the ruggedly handsome and blunt-speaking Peters had come up through patrol and observation squadrons before instructing fledgling aviators at Pensacola, Jacksonville, and Corpus Christi.[5]

Warmup at Marcus

On 23 August in the waters north of Kauai, Rear Adm. Charles A. "Baldy" Pownall organized Task Force Fifteen with his flagship *Yorktown* and the *Essex* and *Independence,* as well as the new fast battleship *Indiana* (BB-58), two light cruisers, eleven destroyers, and a fleet oiler. For the first time in the U.S. Navy, all three flattops operated together within the same screen of cruisers and destroyers. To their delight, Butch and VF-6 learned from Captain Fairlamb that they were headed into action. Pownall's carriers were the first to set out from Pearl for battle since the *Saratoga* sortied the previous November. Admiral Nimitz wished to shake down his new carriers by roughing up tiny Marcus Island (Minami-Tori-Shima), stuck out in the middle of nowhere 2,640 miles west of Pearl and just 1,000 miles east of Tokyo. Marcus was a small, triangular coral island with an airfield and little else. The last American visit had occurred on 4 March 1942, with a swift dawn strike by thirty-eight planes from the *Enterprise* air group. Now Pownall's three flattops planned a more impressive sojourn on Dog Day, 31 August (according to the West Longitude time preferred by the Pacific Fleet; local time was 1 September).[6]

Deliberately avoiding contact to ensure surprise, Pownall aimed TF-15 across the remote waters of the North Pacific, passing far to the north of both friendly Midway and enemy Wake islands. On 27 and 28 August in the vicinity of Milwaukee Banks, all ships refueled from the oiler *Guadalupe* (AO-32). Cloudy, squally weather during the next several days provided a welcome shield from possible Japanese eyes as the task force descended upon Marcus. On the thirtieth Pownall swung southwest for the final approach to the target.

The North Pacific

Pownall's operations order decreed dawn strikes against Marcus by the *Yorktown* and *Essex* air groups, followed by additional raids throughout the day as needed. To the dismay of Butch and his boys, the *Independence* was relegated to the role of "duty" carrier, providing combat air patrol and air-search missions. Pownall allowed for only one actual strike by Air Group Twenty-two against Marcus, a modest afternoon foray by nine TBFs and four F6Fs tagging along with one of the *Essex* attack waves. No one who knew Butch would ever doubt that he would be leading those escort fighters.

After midnight on 31 August, TF-15 sliced through the calm, almost glasslike, seas at 28 knots. Beginning at 0422, two hours before sunrise, and from about 130 miles northeast of Marcus, the *Yorktown* launched her first strike of sixteen fighters, eleven dive bombers, and eighteen TBFs from Air Group Five, led by Comdr. Jimmy Flatley, now commander of the air group. The *Essex* followed suit at 0545 with sixteen Hellcats and twenty-four Dauntlesses of Air Group Nine. On the *Independence,* general quarters had sounded at 0410, sending Butch and his pilots to the fighter ready room to get the latest navigational information and await the word to man planes. Aft on her unlit flight deck, plane handlers had spotted a dozen VF-6 Hellcats for combat air patrol and the nine VC-22 TBFs for the morning search. At 0605 the carriers intercepted jubilant radio messages from the *Yorktown* attackers who pounded unwary Marcus. VF-5 F6Fs flamed all seven twin-engine medium bombers parked on the runway. They were the familiar Mitsubishi G4M1 Type 1 land-attack planes (*rikkōs*), now code-named Betty by the Allies. That ended any threat of immediate aerial opposition. Antiaircraft fire accounted for one VF-5 F6F and also ripped through the VT-5 TBF flown by Lt. James "Pop" Condit, Butch's old friend from the memorable July 1941 trip to New York. Pop ditched the Avenger about halfway between Marcus and the task force and got his crew into their life raft.

As the sun raised a rosy glow in the cloudy eastern sky, Butch and the other twenty *Independence* pilots sat in their cockpits with engines idling and wings still folded. Captain Fairlamb swung the CVL into what little wind was available. A yellow-liveried plane director coaxed Butch's F6F out of its lead parking spot to where blue-shirted plane handlers could open and unfold the Hellcat's broad wings. Guided by the plane director, Butch taxied onto the business end of the H2 catapult set forward into the flight deck on the port side. Green-shirted catapult crewmen secured bridles and the tail retainer onto the big Grumman. At Primary Fly on the bridge, the air officer replaced the red flag with a white one: "Start launching." At 0620 the catapult officer raised his arm as Butch revved the powerful Pratt & Whitney engine. After Butch snapped a salute, the catapult officer dropped his arm. With a whoosh and a jolt that pushed Butch back into his seat, the hydraulic catapult quickly accelerated the heavy Hellcat to flying speed out over the bow. On yet another battle morning, Butch circled the task force waiting for the rest of the CAP before climbing to patrol altitude. The nine TBFs fanned out to the west to cover a semicircle out to two hundred miles.

On the way back to home plate from Marcus, most of the *Yorktown* first-wave TBFs and a few of the SBDs happened upon a Japanese vessel about fifty miles northeast of the island. She was the special fishing boat *No. 15 Jitai Maru.* Estimates as to her size varied greatly, but she appears to have been seventy-five to one hundred feet long, with a small bridge and a deckhouse astern. Both bows sported the large rising-sun insignia that only invited retaliation. With gusto the *Yorktown*ers lined up to make strafing runs against the hapless craft and left her smoking and leaking oil from numerous .50-caliber holes. Not long after they left, Lt. (jg) Billy Burke Laughren, flying one of the VC-22 TBFs on search, missed her with four 325-pound depth bombs. These were but the first attacks against the unbelievably tough *No. 15 Jitai Maru,* the start of a barrage that must have caused hell for her frightened crew but earned her the sobriquet "the unsinkable ship." Afterward, between 0730 and about 1400 no fewer than sixty-seven fighters and thirty-six dive bombers riddled her with bullets yet failed to put her down.[7]

Around 1030 Butch's dozen F6Fs landed back on the *Independence* after an uneventful CAP. In the meantime, George Bullard had taken his place with the other twelve VF-6 Hellcats. Jim Peters returned from the morning search with the nine VC-22 TBFs, plus a VT-5 orphan from the first wave unable to get on board the *Yorktown*. The pilot of that Avenger was Lt. Comdr. David E. Dressendorfer, one of Butch's classmates at Annapolis and Pensacola. The Air Department refueled all the aircraft and armed each of the nine TBFs, including Dressendorfer's, with four 500-pound bombs for the scheduled strike against Marcus. Because of all the chatter that Pownall was monitoring about the "unsinkable ship," said by some to be a small tanker, he directed that one of the VC-22 TBFs lug a torpedo instead of bombs. Peters gave Laughren the fish and another chance to finish off the *No. 15 Jitai Maru.*

With the intention of having her strike group latch onto the last *Essex* wave, the *Independence* catapulted the first plane at 1334. However, the catapult that had proven so vital, and that had worked so well up to now, picked this moment to misbehave. The *Essex* aircraft had already departed before Peters collected his eight TBFs—minus Dressendorfer, who had to drop out and return to the *Yorktown*—and Butch's four escort F6Fs. Lt. (jg) Alex Vraciu took his customary position on Butch's wing, and the second section comprised Lt. (jg) Sy Mendenhall and Ens. Willie Callan. Marcus bore 130 miles to the south-southwest.[8]

On the way out Peters took the strike up to ten thousand feet. About thirty miles shy of Marcus the *Independence* aviators spotted the stricken *No. 15 Jitai Maru* laboring heavily in the calm seas, but other business was pressing. Ahead on the horizon a pall of black smoke marked Marcus. Since the two early-morning raids, the *Yorktown* and *Essex* had dispatched an additional eight strikes, with sorties by 79 SBDs, 60 TBFs, and 101 F6Fs. Although the attackers had pummeled almost all resistance, the raids were not a cakewalk. Antiaircraft fire "though not heavy was at times very accurate" and accounted for two F6Fs and one TBF.[9]

At 1435 Peters and Butch moved their respective flights into attack positions. Sharply contrasted against the dark blue ocean, Marcus looked a mess, sprinkled with numerous fires, bomb craters, and the pyres of seven Bettys spread along the runway on the south edge of the island. The seven bomb-armed TBFs nosed over for glide-bombing runs, while Laughren, with the torpedo, stayed out of gun range. Butch led his four Hellcats into a low-level strafing pass from north to south over the battered island. They walked their bright red .50-caliber tracers into anything that looked important. Not much AA fire seemed evident. Despite the damage from previous strikes, Butch noticed that three large radio masts were still standing.

After one run, Butch made sure that the TBF attacks had gone well, then gathered Vraciu, Mendenhall, and Callan for the flight back to the task force. Out ahead, the *No. 15 Jitai Maru* drifted dead in the water, but with the rising-sun insignia still defiant on her bow. This time her number came up. Screaming in just above the waves, Butch led the Hellcats against the helpless vessel. Their bullets churned the sea alongside and straddled her with strikes. The TBFs showed up while the F6Fs were riddling the target. Laughren was itching to launch his fish, and Peters had saved a 500-pounder as well.

As Sy and Willie followed through with their second firing pass, an overeager Alex Vraciu abruptly reefed around for another attack out of order ahead of Butch (and later "caught hell" for it). Angered at seeing the enemy vessel still seemingly untouched, he was shooting at close range when the little ship suddenly exploded with a bright flash. A "cumulus-like anvil of white smoke" quickly rose high into the sky. The stern portion broke away and sank almost immediately, leaving the bow burning fiercely. Looking back just after he pulled away from the target, Sy watched as the vessel disintegrated and wondered whether a torpedo had done the deed. Later, to his surprise, he discovered that Laughren never fired his fish. Sy thought it was a good thing that one of the F6Fs had not been perched directly over the target when she corked off, a sentiment Alex strongly shared.

Actually, the culprit was Lt. (jg) Joseph R. Kristufek, a VT-5 pilot from the *Yorktown*. At 1350, in response to reports that Pop Condit's raft had been spotted northeast of Marcus, the *Yorktown* sent out a special search of eight TBFs, but only Kristufek's Avenger carried a payload, the usual four 500-pound bombs. Unnoticed by any of the *Independence* aviators, he happened onto the scene while Butch's division was busy working over the *No. 15 Jitai Maru*. Observing what he thought was an *Essex* Hellcat strafing a small enemy vessel, Kristufek rolled into a glide-bombing attack and evidently salvoed all four of his bombs together. They must have detonated at the same time upon or immediately adjacent to her stern. The ship broke in half with a satisfying blast. Kristufek photographed the floating bow section and went his merry way toward Marcus, leaving Butch and his boys somewhat baffled but understandably thinking that *they* had sunk a ship solely with their machine guns. Butch's flight landed back on board the *Independence* at 1635. VC-22 did not feel all that cordial toward their guest fighters, because they had really wanted a piece of that enemy ship as well.

During the afternoon TF-15 withdrew northeast, back the way it had come. No enemy snooper ever approached the ships, nor were any submarines sighted, but a nervous Pownall was glad to get away as soon as he could. Neither the *Yorktown*'s special search nor the submarine *Snook*, on rescue duty, ever sighted Pop Condit's raft. However, the loss of the *No. 15 Jitai Maru* proved fortunate for him and his two crewmen. The trawler *Shōei Maru*, sent out to look for the missing vessel, picked them up instead on 4 September. Although their imprisonment by the Japanese was especially brutal, all three Americans survived the war.[10]

The Marcus defenders reported five attack waves by an estimated 165 planes and claimed twelve shot down for the loss of thirty-seven men killed and seven aircraft destroyed. Actually, TF-15 flew 367 sorties and dropped 116 tons of bombs, including 2,000-pounders, for the loss of three aircraft. The raid appeared to have demolished most of the island's permanent installations, at least those visible to the naked eye. It had provided a nearly bloodless introduction of green carriers and aviators to battle. In that respect the "public relations cruise," as Sy Mendenhall dubbed it, had been a great success.

VF-6's combat debut on the *Independence* went reasonably well, given the fact that both the squadron and the ship's crew were still feeling their way. After Butch's death, Admiral Nimitz awarded him a Distinguished Flying Cross for leadership and heroic conduct on 31 August 1943. In the action report Captain Fairlamb praised VF-6 for operating in "exemplary fashion." The only problem, the report noted, were some "erratic" landings on the part of VF-6 pilots, believed to have been caused by having the F6Fs retain their belly tanks, which might have slightly changed the Hellcat's flight characteristics. Another possible reason given was fatigue due to long (four- to five-hour) CAPs. The pilots certainly disliked these marathon sessions, dubbed "anus patrols" by sore-bottomed aviators from another flattop. Actually, the problem was the landing signal officer, who was "dedicated" but not well qualified. He left the ship in October, and "everything improved." Pownall thought so much of VF-6's performance that he recommended that the CVLs carry only fighters, but his suggestion was not accepted.[11]

September Doings

On the morning of 7 September, Butch led his portion of VF-6 from the *Independence* to the familiar confines of NAS Puunene on Maui. There he learned that on 25 August, Sandy Crews's twelve F6Fs had flown out to the *Princeton*. Together with the *Lexington* and *Belleau Wood,* she had supported the unopposed occupation on 1 September of Baker Island. With regard to finding enemy aircraft, Sandy's detachment enjoyed much more luck than Butch's. That same day Lt. (jg) Dix Loesch, flying on CAP, scored VF-6's first kill by downing a huge four-engine Kawanishi H8K1 Type 2 flying boat (Emily). Lt. (jg) Thaddeus T. Coleman, Jr., bagged another Emily shadower two days later. So much for a supposedly quiet sector.

As things transpired, Butch's own contingent did not find Maui all that quiet. According to the VB-6 history, fighter pilots crowing about their first combat cruise, with cavalier disregard to the feelings of their less fortunate associates in the other two squadrons, resulted in some "wild evenings" in the Puunene Officers' Club. After a short rest, Butch resumed training with Air Group Six that included simulated attacks on Maui and an exercise at sea with the *Essex*. On 14 September VF-6 suffered another tragedy when Lt. (jg) Bob Locker and Ens. Herschel Pahl collided over Maui. Locker was killed and Pahl injured.

On 19 September the *Cowpens* (CVL-25) tied up at Pearl. She needed more fighters to fill out the air group, so as usual AirPac turned to VF-6. Now Butch's squadron was to be equally divided among three light carriers. He personally retained only a dozen F6Fs (Divisions I–III) with Jim Peters's Air Group Twenty-two on the *Independence,* now rejoined by Lt. Leland L. Johnson's VF-22, the original VF squadron. No one would have any trouble distinguishing between the Hellcats of the two units, for VF-22 had painted fake wheels on the lower fuselages of their F6Fs, fondly hoping to fool the Japanese into thinking they were F4Fs. George Bullard would take twelve VF-6 fighters (Divisions IV–VI) over to Air Group Twenty-five on the *Cowpens.* On 24 September the *Princeton* brought back Crews's VF-6 contingent (Divisions VII–IX) after a foray into the Gilbert Islands. In yet another round of musical chairs, his dozen F6Fs were to switch from the *Princeton* to the *Belleau Wood*'s Air Group Twenty-four. The move was a big blow to VF-6's morale. The squadron cohesion and esprit de corps that Butch had worked so hard to foster was sacrificed on the altar of expediency.[12]

Soon after returning, Sandy Crews had to be hospitalized with a stomach ailment, so Butch reorganized VF-6. Lt. Paul Rooney, a talented, well-respected 1939 Annapolis graduate, stepped up to the third spot as operations officer and assumed command of the *Belleau Wood* detachment. Sy Mendenhall took over Rooney's division (II) in the skipper's flight and Alex Vraciu the second section in Division I. Although still healing from his 6 August crash, Ens. Hank Landry became Butch's new wingman.

The new VF-6 organization went into effect on 29 September. That day the *Independence* and *Cowpens* sailed from Pearl Harbor as part of Rear Adm. Alfred E. Montgomery's Task Force Fourteen to participate in carrier exercises off Oahu. The *Independence* landed twenty-four F6Fs (Butch's twelve from VF-6 and Johnson's twelve from VF-22) and VC-22's nine TBF Avengers. Butch met the new CO, Capt. Rudolf L.

Johnson, the able former XO of the *Independence* who had recently relieved Fairlamb. Also on board was Rear Adm. Van H. Ragsdale, commanding Carrier Division Twenty-two. On the next day Montgomery formed the task force into one unit that included the *Essex, Yorktown,* and *Lexington* in addition to the two CVLs. The sight of all five flattops maneuvering together was indeed impressive. On 1 October the *Belleau Wood* departed Pearl to join the armada.

The three *Essex*-class and three *Independence*-class flattops massed 372 aircraft (183 F6Fs, 108 SBDs, and 81 TBFs). To Butch and the other participants it seemed a waste to assemble what was the biggest concentration of American carriers to date and not introduce it to the Japanese. They would not be disappointed. Montgomery informed TF-14 that it was going to raid Wake Island, two thousand miles west of Oahu and famed for its spirited defense prior to its capture in December 1941. Now the atoll sported an air base loaded with fighters and medium bombers. D (for Dog) Day would be 5 October (West Longitude time; local time was 6 October). Happy like the rest of VF-6 at the prospects of action, Johnny Altemus, now serving on the *Belleau Wood,* quipped in his diary, "The attack (again Dog Day!) (Migawd I've been through so many Dog Days—real and practice—I'm beginning to bark & wag my a——!)."[13]

A Visit to Wake

For TF-14 the approach to the target was uneventful. On 4 October, while running in at 25 knots, the ships avoided contact by Wake's search, so surprise the next morning seemed likely. That evening the aggressive Montgomery, known as "Red Neck" because of scars from injuries he had sustained as a young aviator, advised the task force that he would remain off Wake for a second day of attacks on 6 October. That proved to be a particularly astute decision.[14]

Montgomery's plan called for a dawn strike on Wake by forty-eight F6Fs and twenty-four TBFs drawn from the *Essex, Yorktown, Lexington,* and *Cowpens* to catch the Japanese planes on the ground and knock out the airfield. Follow-up attacks from these carriers would target gun positions and installations. In the meantime, he would detach his seven cruisers, escorted by seven destroyers, to race southward and early that afternoon shell the island simultaneously from north and south.

Montgomery assigned Ragsdale with the *Independence* and *Belleau Wood* to provide close air support for the two bombardment groups. The *Independence* would cover the ships pounding Wake from the south while the *Belleau Wood* did the honors for those to the north. The two CVLs were to launch a dawn search of twelve TBFs and thereafter fly combat air patrol and antisub missions over themselves and their cruiser charges. Although Capt. Alfred M. "Mel" Pride, the *Belleau Wood*'s CO, later asserted in a BuAer interview that Ragsdale's two light carriers had been "singularly privileged at Wake" to cover the cruisers, it is doubtful that Butch or the rest of the aviators felt so at the time. Again he flew from a "duty" rather than an "attack" carrier. It seemed like VF-6, or at least that portion with Butch, was destined to follow the big boys and only clean up their crumbs.[15]

In the predawn hours of 5 October the weather one hundred miles north of Wake turned out to be particularly forbidding: heavily overcast and rainy. In the darkness the four strike carriers started launching their seventy-two first-wave aircraft in order to put them over the target at 0545, a half-hour before sunrise. A follow-up strike began taking off almost immediately after the first wave departed. Tipped off either by radar or by a patrol boat lurking twenty miles north of Wake, the Japanese frantically scrambled all available fighters at 0540. That gave the first two waves much more opposition than they expected, including the long-anticipated first meeting of carrier-based Grumman F6F-3 Hellcats and the Mitsubishi Zero fighters, now code-named Zeke.

Twenty-three of twenty-seven A6M2 Zeros from the 252 Air Group made it aloft to contest the skies over still-darkened Wake. Part of the Twenty-second Air Flotilla, the group had been formed in Japan in September 1942. From November of that year through February 1943, the 252 fought bitter air battles in the Solomons before being transferred to the Central Pacific and split among several atoll air bases. That dawn they engaged what they estimated as one hundred–plus American fighters and bombers and claimed fourteen (including four unconfirmed) for the loss of fifteen Zeros. Three of the eight pilots who survived the hellish encounter were wounded.[16]

For their part, the Hellcat pilots of the first and second waves reported fighting thirty-three Zekes and claimed twenty-seven. Lucky to fly the first strike from the *Cowpens*, George Bullard nailed one Zeke in the dawn fracas. TF-14 analysts believed that none of their aircraft actually fell to enemy fighters, although fierce antiaircraft fire downed several planes. It was an auspicious debut for carrier Hellcats against Zekes, a result that would be played over and over again. Strafing and bombing planes tallied an additional eight Zekes and nineteen twin-engine bombers destroyed on the ground. No doubt they accounted for most of the 755 Air Group's twenty-five Type 1 (Betty) and older G3M3 Type 96 (Nell) *rikkōs* believed to be on the island. However, their boast of "no further air opposition from Wake-based planes" was not valid, as Butch would soon discover.

The *Independence* (Scarlet Base) launched her first CAP at 0615, about the same time Rear Adm. Ernest G. Small's Southern Bombardment Group—the heavy cruisers *Minneapolis* (CA-36), *New Orleans* (CA-32), and *San Francisco* (CA-38), plus three destroyers—left the main body bound for the waters south for Wake. Ragsdale's two flattops followed the cruisers but went no closer than thirty to fifty miles northeast of Wake. Butch's turn to fly came at 0915, when the *Independence* sent the following eight VF-6 F6Fs aloft to cover Small's approach to Wake:

Division I	Division II
Lt. Comdr. Edward H. O'Hare	Lt. Sy E. Mendenhall
Ens. Henry T. Landry	Ens. John P. Staniszewski
Lt. (jg) Alexander Vraciu	Lt. (jg) Bayard Webster
Ens. Allie W. Callan, Jr.	Lt. (jg) Robert L. Klingler

Butch's mission was to orbit over the heavy cruisers until relieved and then strafe Wake afterward if circumstances permitted. He operated under the control of Lt. (jg) Nelson H. Layman, the fighter director officer (FDO) on the flagship *Minneapolis*.[17]

For Small's ships and their air cover, the forenoon passed uneventfully. Off to starboard, the pillars of smoke from burning Wake gradually increased in size. The cruisers bypassed Wake to the east and headed for the prescribed bombardment area off the south coast. Suddenly at 1145, near the end of Butch's patrol, the *Minneapolis*'s radar detected a bogey twenty-nine miles due west, that is, south of Wake. To her Combat Information Center (CIC) personnel, the contact appeared to be several aircraft climbing as if they had just taken off from the atoll. That was correct. For reasons best known to itself, Wake's brain trust sent aloft at 1130 three Zeros from the 252 Air Group flown by young flight petty officers second class, all wingmen who had survived the morning debacle. Matsumoto Yasuo led the flight, with Kosaka Magoichi on his left wing and Tobita Kazuo on his right. Against overwhelming enemy air superiority, their sortie was a tragic exercise in futility.

Layman piped up on the radio and gave the steer to Butch's eight Hellcats at eighty-five hundred feet. Once Butch had flown south of Wake, Layman swung him southward. At 1205 and about fifteen miles west of the cruisers, Butch's keen eyes first spotted the quarry out ahead and about thirty-five hundred feet below. Three brownish green Zekes, deployed in a loose vee, were sauntering north in the opposite direction back toward Wake. Butch carefully maneuvered his flight for a swift bounce before the unsuspecting and outnumbered Japanese could take fright and scatter. Because his radio was out, Alex Vraciu, the second section's leader, kept an especially close eye on his leader. Suddenly from the way Butch began flying it became obvious that he had sighted something. Sure enough, three Zekes were headed toward them. Butch's stalking likewise alerted Sy Mendenhall (also with a bum radio), who led Division II.

Butch swung his division to starboard to set up a steep high-side run from above and to the right of the trio of Zekes. That placed Vraciu's section on the inside of the turn, and he knew from Butch's training just what to do. Butch and his wingman, Landry, would take the outside plane in the vee (Kosaka), leaving the nearest one (Tobita) for Vraciu and Callan.

Cool and concentrated as ever, Butch flew a textbook high-side gunnery pass against the most distant of the elegant-looking Japanese fighters. With a smooth turn toward the enemy at just the right moment, he dived to increase speed and reach the proper aiming point. From a full deflection angle almost perpendicular to the target, Butch opened fire with his six .50-caliber Brownings and held the proper shooting angle as his Hellcat curved around astern of Kosaka's Zeke. His bullets sliced through the cowling and into the engine, piercing cylinders and cutting oil and fuel lines, causing it to smoke. Very likely slugs raked the unprotected cockpit as well. Wounded or even already dead, Kosaka slumped forward, and his Mitsubishi gently nosed down toward a cloud layer.

Shifting his aim forward, Butch lunged at the leader, but Matsumoto, alerted by the squiggles of red tracers knifing through the formation, took violent evasive action. Butch momentarily jumped his tail, but the F6F was going 50 knots too fast to stay there, so Matsumoto evaded.

Fully aware of how to fight a much more nimble Zeke, Butch climbed to regain position above for another pass. However, his green wingman Hank Landry incautiously followed Kosaka's stricken fighter.

Vraciu was not sure that the Zekes had sighted the F6Fs until they actually fired. While Butch took out Kosaka, he ripped into Tobita's fighter from above and to the right. The Mitsubishi first shed black smoke from the cowling and then suddenly erupted in flames. Vraciu had to pull up abruptly to avoid hitting the burning airplane. Although thrilled with his first victory, he reacted correctly to the situation by climbing to rejoin Butch above the fight. Up over the battle scene, Vraciu could not find him and lost contact with Willie Callan as well. In the meantime, Callan fired at one of the Zekes, probably Kosaka's, already finished by Butch.

Following Callan down into the fight, Mendenhall spotted the three Zekes and ended up on the tail of one (Tobita, Vraciu's kill) that was burning "furiously." He saw another also on fire. The third Zeke (Matsumoto) executed a wingover directly in his face, then disappeared into a cloud. Mendenhall briefly flew wing on one of the already finished Japanese: Butch's victim, nosed down in a shallow dive, with the pilot crumpled in the cockpit and the engine streaming flames.

After making his pass, Callan was excited to see his erstwhile target drop toward the water. As he later said, he was now "ready to shoot anything that moved." Soon another enemy aircraft skulked below, so he started down after it. At the same time, Mendenhall recognized an F6F and tried to get it to join up but grew wary at its aggressive approach. It was Callan, his former wingman, who failed to return his friendly feelings. Mendenhall turned hard into the F6F to prevent it from pulling enough lead to hit its twisting opponent. Callan saw to his horror that he was fighting Sy's Hellcat. Mendenhall's rudder sported one bullet hole from the brief encounter. VF-6 had recently painted out the national insignia on the upper right and lower left wings by using dark blue paint on the lighter blue background. That left large dark circles in their places. To Callan the sun shining on Mendenhall's upper right wing caused the blotch to resemble the Japanese red rising-sun circle, or "meatball." He was not the only one to be fooled that day.

Now reconciled, Mendenhall and Callan climbed over the cloud where Sy had seen the last Zeke go, but it had disappeared. In fact, Matsumoto had discovered Landry's F6F neatly set up below and pounced. When tracers suddenly zipped past from directly above, Landry rolled out of the way and caused the Zeke to overshoot and recover out in front. Hank repaid the compliment with bullets of his own, and the Zeke rolled over on its back and flopped down, presumably a goner. At least so Landry believed, but Matsumoto survived.

Immediately after fighting the Zeke, Landry was again beset by tracers from above. This time he reefed into a hard turn and pulled up into his attacker to offer only a full deflection shot. Even so, some slugs caught him in the rear fuselage behind the cockpit. To Landry's great surprise, his assailant turned out to be Butch, no less shocked. To Butch, like Callan, the other airplane's wing insignia reflected light in a way that made it appear to be a meatball. Later, after both pilots returned to the *Independence,* Butch was very apologetic. He had seen the Zeke dive after Landry and chased it. He thought his target was this bandit pulling out after shooting down his wingman. After landing back on board, Butch quickly informed Jim Peters of the error in identification. For both mishaps, the *Independence* report blamed "poorly executed painting out of former insignia," which left darker-toned round blotches on the wing's gray-blue background that greatly resembled the enemy's circular insignia.[18]

Meanwhile, Callan continued climbing over the fight and found his leader, Vraciu. "In the corner of his eye" Alex discerned a tiny Zeke racing hard toward Wake. He and Callan pursued Matsumoto all the way to the island. They saw him set down on the runway, taxi off into the sand as soon as he could check his speed, and hastily abandon his aircraft. Swooping in, Vraciu set the fighter ablaze. While zigzagging low over Wake, he noticed a twin-engine bomber on the ground, so he and Callan came around for another pass and burned the Betty. With no sign of Butch and getting low on fuel and ammunition, Vraciu turned northeast toward home plate. At the same time, but from much farther back, Butch and Landry were also chasing Matsumoto. After seeing Vraciu burn the Zeke, they likewise shot up a piece of Wake's real estate and riddled another parked Betty.

Mendenhall had lost contact with all the other planes in the battle area. Soon another F6F joined up, either wingman Ens. John Staniszewski or possibly Lt. (jg) Max E. Frellsen of VF-22 from the third CAP. The two F6Fs flew to Wake, where amid black puffs from heavy AA they tried to take out gun positions by firing at the muzzle flashes. After a couple of strafing runs, Sy and his wingman circled the island, then headed back to the ship.

To Layman on the *Minneapolis* Butch reported, "Tally ho, shot down two, other one not sure." Not ready to give up, he and Landry returned alone on station over the cruisers. Around 1220 the *New Orleans*'s radar picked up a large bogey ninety-five miles southeast that her CIC tracked forty-four miles south-southeast before the bogey turned east again. The FDO sent Butch's section south to investigate. About twenty miles south of Wake he sighted the familiar bulbous profile of a Betty, the first he had seen aloft since the memorable twentieth of February 1942. Approaching from head-on, he rolled into a high-side run. This time only one of his six machine guns responded. Nevertheless, his flawless gunnery poured bullets into one engine and the wing root, crippling the Betty. For his own part, Landry let the bomber pass, then dived in from high side and also aimed at one of the engines. However, he held his run too long and got sucked in behind the target. There he traded shots with the tail gunner lobbing big 20-mm tracers before the F6F dropped out of the line of fire. Having regained altitude and proper attack position, Butch finished the Betty on his second pass. Over Landry's protests, he shared the kill with his wingman, but the Navy subsequently awarded all of the credit to Butch, for what was his seventh confirmed victory.

While Butch destroyed the lone Betty, the Southern Bombardment Group had commenced shelling Wake. Now low on gasoline and nearly out of ammunition, Butch took Landry back to the *Independence* and landed shortly after 1300. Called up to the bridge, he briefed Admiral Ragsdale and Captain Johnson about the situation over Wake. Someone handed him a steel helmet, which he put on backwards, and then he gave thumbs-up. Later, in the VF-6 ready room, Butch asked Vraciu in a friendly way what had happened to him and Callan during the fight. Alex related how after the initial flurry he had climbed above the cloud, to which Butch replied that he and Landry had gone below it. Callan rather sheepishly told Butch about the identification error, when he had pinked Sy Mendenhall's F6F in the tail. Butch simply replied that they would have to get the misleading insignia painted out, then he told Willie he had done the same thing to another F6F. Willie was off the hook, but Butch tweaked him for not allotting enough lead when shooting—which would not have done Sy any good!

In the meantime, Admiral Small's Southern Bombardment Group massaged Wake for two hours with nearly fifteen hundred rounds of 8-inch and seventeen hundred 5-inch shells. Only one enemy shore battery bravely replied, inflicting minor damage on the *Minneapolis* and *New Orleans,* but counterbattery fire soon silenced it. At 1312, after Butch departed the scene, two fighters shot down a Curtiss SOC Seagull floatplane from the *New Orleans* acting as a gunnery spotter. Lt. Alford M. Robertson and George W. McCarthy, aviation radioman first class, bailed out. Wounded by being strafed in midair, both survived to be rescued by the destroyer *Schroeder* (DD-501). Supposedly two Zekes accounted for the biplane, but Japanese records show that Wake had none aloft at this time. Instead it appears that two VF-22 F6Fs from the *Independence* shot down the SOC in another, much more serious, case of mistaken identity.

At 1354 a second lone Betty south of Wake fell to Lt. John R. Behr, Lt. (jg) James A. Bryce, Lt. (jg) Donald C. Stanley, and Lt. James H. McConnell of VF-22. It appears that the Betty that Butch got and the one destroyed by VF-22 were two Type 1 *rikkōs* from the 755 Air Group commanded by Warrant Officer Kawano Godai and Flight Chief Petty Officer Wakizaka Nobukichi. That morning they had departed Maloelap in the Marshalls and searched independently for the U.S. carrier force before risking an approach to Wake. They never reached the atoll.[19]

To reinforce beleaguered Wake, the Twenty-second Air Flotilla sent a strike group seven hundred miles north from Maloelap. Lt. Comdr. Ishihara Kaoru led seven Type 1 land-attack planes from the 755 Air Group, escorted by a like number of 252 Air Group Zeros under Lt. Tsukamoto Yūzō, a veteran of the Battle of the Coral Sea. Their first encounter with defending U.S. fighters took place around 1515, forty miles south of Wake. Four F6Fs led by Lt. (jg) Harvey G. Odenbrett from the VF-6 contingent on the *Belleau Wood* tore into a flight of Bettys and Zekes and shot down one Betty for the loss of Ens. Edward J. Philippe.

At 1505 Butch gathered the four F6Fs of VF-6's Division I and departed the *Independence* for combat air patrol. Fifteen minutes later Lt. Robert R. Marks, her FDO, sent him to check out a radar contact sixty-two miles south of the ship. For the next twenty minutes Butch searched through the clouds, peering into the setting sun and playing tag with the enemy, who evidently could see the Hellcats from time to time. At 1556 he finally spotted three Zekes above at eighteen thousand feet but could not overtake them as they fled westward.

Thinking he could not break through the ring of F6Fs around Wake, Ishihara ordered his flight to turn back. He wanted the escort fighters to land on Wake, but because the Zeros carried no radios, he could not communicate with them. Eight pursuing Hellcats from the *Belleau Wood* caught up with the Japanese at 1620 about one hundred miles south of Wake and claimed three Zekes and three Bettys. They actually shot down two land-attack planes and two Zeros. The surviving *rikkōs* kept going back south. Tsukamoto's four Zeros sneaked into Wake and gingerly landed around 1730 on the cratered runway. They discovered that the island was a mess. After dark another Zero and a Betty from this group ditched in the Marshalls.

Butch brought his division back to the *Independence* at 1815, just before sundown. In the meantime, she had joined the *Lexington* and *Cowpens*. Butch's flight time that long day amounted to 7.4 hours and Alex Vraciu's to 7.8 hours. To his surprise, Alex found that he had made the two thousandth landing on the *Independence* and received the traditional cake at dinner on 10 October.

In TF-14, enthusiasm abounded as to the results obtained that day against Wake. The wisdom of Montgomery's decision to stay another day and really wreak havoc on Wake became obvious. On 6 October, Butch turned out early in order to fly the *Independence*'s first combat air patrol after the dawn strike got off. The weather was even worse than it had been the previous morning. Against Wake, Jim Peters led eight VC-22 TBFs escorted by eight F6Fs, including four under Lt. Moose Merritt of VF-6. The *Independence* began catapulting the sixteen aircraft at 0620. After they departed it was Butch's turn with the remaining eight VF-6 F6Fs of his own and Sy Mendenhall's divisions. Sy had good reason to remember the launch, because the catapult failed and only pitched his F6F into the water out ahead of the ship. He clambered out of the sinking Hellcat and was rescued by the faithful *Schroeder*. Butch flew the balance of the patrol without incident, which pretty much described the *Independence*'s second day at Wake.

On 6 October the carriers launched three strikes on Wake that greatly added to the destruction achieved on the fifth. That evening TF-14 retired to the northeast. Montgomery was pleased with its efforts. On both days his aviators had dropped about 340 tons of bombs, while the bombarding ships had fired 520 tons of shells into Wake. They claimed extensive damage to the water supply facilities, power station, supply dumps, and buildings, as well as sixty-seven planes destroyed on the ground and in the air. The attackers lost eleven planes in combat (apparently ten to AA, one to Zekes) and thirteen more operationally. Nevertheless, as Montgomery realized, the neutralization of Wake was only brief. Japanese planes had flown there the night of 5–6 October, left at dawn on the sixth, and returned soon after the attacks ceased. Only an invasion of Wake would knock it out for good.

Butch likewise had good reason to be satisfied by VF-6's performance, split up among three CVLs as his boys were. The squadron received credit for four Zekes, one Betty, and one Nell destroyed in the air. They included Butch's sixth and seventh victories, which brought a gold star to the Distinguished Flying Cross awarded posthumously for Marcus. The only VF-6 combat loss was Ed Philippe with the *Belleau Wood* detachment. He failed to return after the fight the afternoon of 5 October. On the sixth, in addition to Sy Mendenhall's takeoff mishap from the *Independence*, Ens. Albert W. Nyquist suffered severe burns during a horrifying crash-landing on the *Belleau Wood*.

The Wake Island raid would be the last occasion Butch would lead VF-6 in battle. A new assignment was in the offing, which Butch characteristically did not reveal so as not to distract his men.

13

Air Group
Commander

"No paperwork CAG!"

On the morning of 11 October 1943, as the flattops that had raided Wake reentered Hawaiian waters, their air groups scattered among several naval air bases on Oahu and Maui. The three VF-6 contingents off the *Independence, Cowpens,* and *Belleau Wood* gratefully reassembled in the familiar dust of NAS Puunene on Maui. There the balance of Air Group Six—Bombing Six and Torpedo Six—had remained, discouraged over missing the big show at Wake and wondering how long they would be marooned without a flattop of their own. Itinerant VF-6 endured a different predicament, namely, would they ever fly and fight together from the same carrier, instead of the dinky CVLs? Not in the foreseeable future, it seemed. The squadron had made itself just too useful filling out the light carrier air groups, and AirPac had no well-trained replacements on hand. The three divisions (I, II, and III) of the skipper's own *Independence* contingent found orders awaiting them to switch immediately to NAS Hilo on the big island of Hawaii, there to catch up with the rest of the *Evil I*'s Air Group Twenty-two. As soon as facilities could accommodate them, the rest of VF-6 (six divisions with twenty-four F6Fs) were to shift to nearby NAS Kahului on Maui.

Butch O'Hare did not fly to Maui along with VF-6 but rode the *Independence* to Pearl Harbor. There at AirPac headquarters on Ford Island it was confirmed that he would immediately relieve Comdr. Bucky Lee as commander of Carrier Air Group Six (CAG-6), according to orders dated 17 September 1943. On 12 October the squadron learned of the upcoming change of command, but circumstances permitted no real farewell, particularly from Butch's old flight at Hilo. The news that the CO had left VF-6 hit the men hard. In his diary Johnny Altemus griped, "Everybody feels very badly about losing him—he was very popular with the pilots." Equally disgusting was the knowledge that the squadron would "still stay broken up" among three light carriers. Altemus commiserated with Butch, complaining that he was "Group Commander with no Air Group!" That was not entirely true. Air Group Six was there, but dispersed, and hoped that the impending return of the *Enterprise* meant redemption for them all.[1]

On 13 October, without much ceremony at Puunene, Butch proudly took over Air Group Six. Now, as CAG, he assumed the responsibilities and enjoyed the perquisites of the top carrier flying job the Navy had to offer. No longer just a leader of fighters, he now oversaw the training and eventual operational deployment of three diverse squadrons and a hundred pilots. Two of his squadron COs he had known since at least shortly after Air Group Six was formed: lieutenant commanders John L. Phillips, Jr., of VT-6 and Isaiah M. Hampton of VB-6. Taking his place as skipper of VF-6 was Lt. Comdr. Harry W. "Stinky" Harrison, a highly experienced reservist and most recently XO of VF-5 on the *Yorktown*. Butch's close friend Charlie McCord stayed with VF-6, while Lt. Wallace M. Parker became his new administrative officer.

The same day Butch took command, he rather gingerly borrowed from VT-6 a TBM-1 Avenger, the Grumman TBF-1 manufactured by the Eastern Aircraft Division of General Motors, and began familiarizing himself with the jumbo torpedo bomber. Since mid-1942, Avengers, minus payload and crammed with additional fuel, had been the nominally assigned aircraft for carrier air group commanders to fulfill their principal combat assignment as strike coordinator. The Grumman F4F-4 Wildcat, the only carrier fighter available until mid-1943, lacked the endurance and photo equipment for such a mission. Flying an Avenger meant a radical comedown for a fighter jock used to throwing all over the skies the fastest and most agile aircraft the fleet could offer.

For his personal CAG aircraft, Butch explored a happier alternative, pioneered by a couple of ex-VF squadron COs who had likewise fleeted up to CAG earlier that year. In the spring of 1943 Comdr. Jimmy Flatley, who formed Air Group Five for the new *Yorktown,* adopted as his personal mount an F6F christened 00. He found that for CAG duty the Hellcat surmounted all of the drawbacks inherent in the old Wildcat. Only for attacks under conditions of low visibility would a radar-equipped TBF be superior. Comdr. Jack Raby, Flatley's counterpart in the *Essex*'s Air Group Nine, followed his lead. While serving as strike coordinators in August on the Marcus raid, both CAGs flew F6Fs. In October Comdr. Leonard B. Southerland, CAG-16 on board the second *Lexington,* joined the ranks of the fighter-flying CAGs. He much preferred the Hellcat because of its superior ability to take vertical target photos. For the time being, CAGs who had come up through fighters flew Hellcats, while ex–dive bomber or torpedo pilots tended to fancy Avengers. Butch proved no exception. Later in October he happily drew Grumman F6F-3 Hellcat Bureau Number 66168 from the fleet pool to become his principal CAG plane, which he also numbered 00.

While Butch readied his air group for the next carrier deployment, he suffered what he intended as only a temporary separation from his beloved VF-6. On 21 October, Stinky Harrison's dozen VF-6 Hellcats left Pearl on board the *Independence.* Along with the *Essex* and *Bunker Hill* (CV-17), she was bound for the distant South Pacific to support the upcoming landings on Bougainville by fending off Japanese air power at Rabaul. At the same time, George Bullard and Paul Rooney were preparing their VF-6 detachments to return to the *Cowpens* and *Belleau Wood* for what would become a totally different combat assignment.

By 21 October, Butch knew that the *Enterprise* would return in early November to Pearl after her lengthy refit at Bremerton. She would bring with her Comdr. Roscoe L. Newman's Air Group Ten, whose squadrons had served on the *Big E* for over a year. ComAirPac preferred to give Air Group Ten additional training ashore on Maui, opening the door for Butch's Air Group Six to deploy to the *Enterprise.* However, he needed a loose VF squadron to complete the team, and he had to find it quickly.

The only suitable squadrons immediately available in the Hawaiian area were Fighting One and Fighting Two, both temporarily orphaned from their parent air groups. Lt. Comdr. Bernard M. Strean's VF-1 had spent more time in the islands and enjoyed far more opportunity to train. Had anybody asked them, "Smoke" Strean's outfit would have loved to join Butch on the *Enterprise,* but that was not the Navy's way. AirPac had another assignment in mind for them, one that required the additional experience they had accrued. They were slated as air garrison for an island atoll about to be captured by the Marines. To get there VF-1 would ride the escort carriers *Barnes* and *Nassau* to their bleak new base, where Butch would encounter them again.[2]

That left only VF-2. Formed on 1 June 1943 at Quonset Point, Rhode Island, as a component of Air Group Two, the new Fighting Two ("The Rippers") was a conventional VF squadron of officer pilots, nearly all of whom were rookies. That differed radically from VF-2's previous incarnation as the illustrious "Flying Chiefs," composed primarily of enlisted naval aviation pilots (NAPs). The CO, Lt. Comdr. William A. Dean, Jr., had briefly commanded VB-2 that spring when Butch formed Air Group Six. A 1934 Annapolis graduate, Dean had flown before the war with VF-5 on the old *Yorktown.* Tending to be quiet and introspective, he showed fine judgment and real tolerance for the inevitable mistakes of his inexperienced charges.[3]

VF-2's ranks included a welcome nucleus of VF-10 veterans who had fought at Guadalcanal: John C. Eckhardt, Leroy E. Harris, Roy M. Voris, and William K. Blair. Butch knew them from September and October 1942, when VF-10 had trained alongside VF-3 on Maui just before they left for the *Enterprise.* Another battlewise VF-2 pilot was Ens. Merriwell W. Vineyard, an American who had joined the Royal Canadian Air Force in 1941 and transitioned into fighters with the Royal Air Force. In May 1942 Vineyard flew off the first *Wasp* to Malta with his Spitfire crammed with bottles of Coca-Cola. He survived four months of fierce air fighting at the besieged Mediterranean island before resigning to join the U.S. Navy.

In early October 1943 VF-2 flew cross-country to NAS Alameda and embarked for the ride out to Pearl. On 18 October they settled in at NAS Barbers Point on Oahu, where they readied their thirty-six F6F-3s and waited for the call to action. That would apparently not be long in coming, for Pearl Harbor was crammed with warships obviously gathering for some new venture into enemy waters. On 25 October, Bill Dean returned from a conference at Ford Island with the happy news that they had avoided VF-1's fate and would be "going on board one of the big, first class carriers in about 10 days to play a part in the next big push."[4]

Beginning on 29 October, Butch took a closer look at VF-2, when Dean's crew joined VB-6 and VT-6 for tactical exercises during an overnight stay on the *Lexington*. He brought 00 out to the *Lex*, where along with her captain, Felix L. Stump, he watched as novice mistakes marred the carrier debut of VF-2. While landing, even Bill Dean suffered the embarrassment of smashing into the barrier. Ens. Thomas L. Morrissey, VF-2's able air combat intelligence officer and assiduous chronicler, honestly assessed their performance: "Hooks up, wheels up, poor air discipline, and several narrow escapes marked the carrier landings." Yet once back aloft, the squadron performed well working with Lt. Comdr. Allan F. Fleming's fighter direction team. Nevertheless, VF-2 ended up back at their shore base wondering if they had blown their audition and would miss the next combat operation.[5]

On Halloween, Butch profited from another opportunity to evaluate VF-2 when Air Group Six again flew out to the *Lexington* for a short training cruise. This time everything went smoothly, with smiles all around. Dean and his men learned to their great pleasure of VF-2's official attachment to Air Group Six. They quickly took the measure of their famous new CAG, described by Morrissey as "a quiet, easy-going person with a delightful personality—aside from being a topnotch flyer." The new CAG displayed no pretention but preferred to be called Butch "by young and old, seniors and juniors."[6]

In response to Butch's request for a VF-2 wingman during the training flights, Dean assigned him Ens. Warren Andrew Skon. Age twenty-four, formerly a student at the University of Minnesota, "Andy" Skon had earned his wings in April 1943. Quiet and thoughtful, steady and thoroughly competent, Skon fitted well with Butch's temperament and style of leadership. Once Butch had the chance to fly with him, Skon became his permanent wingman. To Skon's pleasure, he was "very much a flying CAG," who liked nothing better than to be aloft at the head of his air group.[7]

Now that Butch had assembled his team, he huddled with Phillips, Hampton, and Dean to implement tactics designed to support an amphibious landing. Acting as a stand-in for the absent *Enterprise,* the *Lexington* joined the light carriers *Belleau Wood* and *Monterey* (CVL-26) for exercises coordinated with troop landing maneuvers at Maalaea Bay on Maui. On 1 November after more combat air patrol flights, the

Lex dispatched the entire air group on a mock strike against Maui. VF-2 practiced strafing objectives in conjunction with simulated bombing by the SBDs and TBFs. The next day the squadrons flew to Maui while the *Lexington* proceeded back to Pearl. VF-2 returned to Barbers Point on 3 November.

Only a week remained before Air Group Six embarked on board the *Enterprise,* now expected on 6 November. After a short turnaround she would sail on the tenth, ostensibly on a training cruise, but the brass knew better. Butch gladly informed VF-2 that the task group commander considered the squadron proficient for strike and support missions as well as combat air patrol. Dean hoped to give his men more opportunity for field carrier landing practice and to schedule night training, which VF-2 lacked, but did not have the time. No one realized how deadly important night operations would soon be for Butch and his men.

The *Big E*

On 6 November, Roscoe Newman's Air Group Ten showed up at NAS Puunene, and that evening the *Enterprise* docked at Pearl. The next day Butch reported on board to meet his immediate superior, Comdr. Thomas Hamilton, the new air officer and someone quite familiar to him as the former Annapolis football coach. Butch also discovered to his pleasure that Lt. Comdr. Robert W. Jackson, an old friend and fellow VF-3 pilot prior to the war, still ran Air Plot. He hoped to facilitate the attachment of Air Group Six to the *Enterprise,* but as things transpired, he would not have much time.

The *Enterprise*'s crew immediately took to their celebrated new CAG and became fiercely proud of him. Despite his lofty status as one of America's best-known war heroes, Butch appeared completely natural and unpretentious. Ens. Claude L. Dickerson, a former warrant gunner with the aviation ordnance gang, remembered how just the sight of Butch often drew a crowd of admiring sailors, and how he spoke a few quiet words "to everyone coming and going" without regard to rank or position.[8]

Butch's presence on board coincided with a change of command on the *Enterprise.* On 7 November Capt. Matthias B. Gardner relieved Capt. Samuel P. Ginder as CO. A highly regarded former pilot, Matt Gardner had lately served as chief of staff to admirals John McCain and Aubrey Fitch, in charge of the jerry-built Aircraft, South Pacific Force, the land-based aviation command. There he played a vital role in the victory at Guadalcanal.

If Gardner was outstanding, the carrier task group commander who broke out his flag on the *Enterprise* was in a class by himself. Only forty-seven, Rear Adm. Arthur W. Radford—"Raddy" to his many friends—had attained flag rank in July 1943 without ever commanding a ship, an exceptional occurrence. A 1916 graduate of the Naval Academy, he completed flight training four years later. In 1930 he led VF-1B, the glamorous "High Hats," on the *Saratoga,* with a green Jimmy Thach as one of his complement. On a fast track to senior rank, Radford mastered a wide variety of assignments afloat and ashore in the 1930s. At the start of the war he served as director of Aviation Training and oversaw its massive expansion. In September 1943 as commander of Carrier Division Eleven, he led light carriers in the occupation of Baker Island and a raid on Tarawa. The next month, with his flag on the *Lexington,* he commanded one of the task groups against Wake and had stayed on board through the recent maneuvers. Radford was a brilliant officer, innovative, decisive, and sincere. Now on the *Enterprise* he would come to rely strongly on the CAG of his new flagship.[9]

As one of the Pacific Fleet's senior carrier commanders, Radford helped plan the next major operation: the first American amphibious assault on the Central Pacific route that led directly to Japan. Code-named Galvanic, the final plan outlined an advance by Vice Adm. Raymond A. Spruance's Central Pacific Force into the Gilbert Islands, a chain of sixteen atolls astride the equator just west of the International Date Line. The principal objectives were Tarawa, site of a Japanese airfield; Makin, about one hundred miles to the northeast; and Abemama, about seventy miles south of Tarawa. Makin appeared to be more weakly defended than Tarawa—only a token force garrisoned Abemama—but was closer to numerous Japanese air bases in the Marshalls, as well as being at the extreme range of Allied land-based air support. Success in the Gilberts would open the door to the Marshall Islands and ultimately the Marianas as well.

Spruance recognized three different enemy threats: land-based air, submarines, and even the Combined Fleet should it sortie from Truk. In response to the danger, his Fifth Fleet comprised the most powerful naval force yet amassed: six large, five light, and eight escort carriers that wielded nine hundred aircraft, as well as six new and seven old battleships. Each main objective merited a separate invasion force. Rear

Adm. Richmond Kelly Turner's Northern Attack Force (Task Force Fifty-two), with a reinforced regiment from the Army's Twenty-seventh Division, formed up at Pearl and aimed for Makin. Staging in from the South Pacific against much more formidable Tarawa was the Southern Attack Force (TF-53) with the Second Marine Division (Reinforced). Spruance set the date of the landings (yet another D-Day or "Dog Day") as 20 November (West Longitude time; local time was 21 November).

Rear Adm. Charles Pownall's Task Force Fifty, the Fast Carrier Force of the Pacific Fleet, operated as four separate task groups. Two were to depart Pearl together bound for Makin or the waters north of there. The first was Pownall's own Task Group 50.1 (the *Yorktown, Lexington,* and *Cowpens*), the Carrier Interceptor Group, which would raid Mili and Jaluit, the nearest enemy bases in the Marshalls, and in general run interference for both invasion forces to the south. Radford's Task Group 50.2, the Northern Carrier Group (the *Enterprise, Belleau Wood,* and *Monterey*), drew the assignment of close support for the Makin invasion. Coming up from the south after air strikes against Rabaul would be Rear Admiral Montgomery's Task Group 50.3, the Southern Carrier Group, with the *Essex, Bunker Hill,* and *Independence* in support of the Tarawa landings. Last was Task Group 50.4, the so-called Relief Carrier Group (the *Saratoga* and *Princeton*) under Rear Adm. Ted Sherman. On 18 November, two days prior to D-Day, Sherman would strike Nauru, southwest of the Gilberts, and thereafter move into reserve.[10]

Placed on alert on 8 November, Air Group Six furiously loaded its gear on board the *Enterprise* while the aviators waited with their planes at NAS Barbers Point and on Maui for the word to fly out to their new carrier. Plans for a shakedown cruise had been only a diversion, and everyone now prepared for swift departure. Given the hasty deployment and the lack of time to get acquainted with each other's methods—a "distinct handicap," according to the *Enterprise* brass—Hamilton's Air Department and Butch's flyers had to make many adjustments. With all the new replacements, the *Enterprise*'s crew came across as pretty green, but as always her fighting spirit was unsurpassed.[11]

Before dawn on 10 November, the two northern carrier groups and Turner's Northern Attack Force weighed anchor and passed through the narrow entrance of Pearl Harbor and out to sea. Butch had already gone on board the *Enterprise* to see to final arrangements. With some anticipation he found a good perch on the island to watch the arrival of his squadrons on the *Big E*.

By 1000 the piercing drone of seventy-one aircraft reverberated in the skies above the carrier. Another twenty planes were either already stowed on board in the hangar or were flying antisubmarine patrol. VF-2 brought out thirty-seven F6F-3 Hellcats. According to Tom Morrissey, their landings exhibited the "usual narrow shaves [that] made it intensely interesting—to onlookers!" Lt. (jg) John F. McCloskey received the dubious distinction of flying Hellcat 00, Butch's own pet CAG plane, and it may have made him a bit nervous. Finally, after two wave-offs from the landing signal officer, he set down without further ado and gratefully relinquished 00 to the plane handlers. According to Morrissey, his antics almost gave the CAG "apoplexy." Given Butch's customary demeanor, that is highly unlikely, but that did not prevent VF-2 from kidding McCloskey.[12]

That afternoon most of the air group flew tactical exercises. The only serious incident ensued after the Hellcat flown by Ens. Byron M. Johnson experienced mechanical troubles. After two tries, he thumped down hard, scraped the deck with a wing, and ended up in the port catwalk. To add to his woes, his belly tank ruptured, setting the Hellcat on fire in the kind of accident that had so severely burned Ens. Al Nyquist in October on the *Belleau Wood*. This time Lt. Walter L. Chewning, the *Enterprise*'s new catapult officer, courageously jumped onto the flaming aircraft and pulled Johnson out of the cockpit unharmed. Before the Airedales could clear the flight deck aft, another VF-2 F6F pilot, Ens. S. S. Osborne, had to ditch when the ship could not bring him on board, but the destroyer *Brown* (DD-546) safely recovered him. That evening Butch instructed VF-2 to jettison belly tanks prior to an emergency landing. With a misbehaving F6F, a pilot was to line up for a long, shallow approach in the groove before taking the cut and setting down on deck.

On 11 November, Butch announced to Air Group Six the overall plan for the Gilberts, then concentrated on Makin, the specific target that his planes would assault. From the air Makin Atoll resembled a giant necklace, roughly triangular in shape, some sixteen miles by eight miles in size, that enclosed a large lagoon of brilliant blue water. The narrow, low-lying islands connected by coral reefs made up the beads of the necklace. Only two passes allowed large ships into the lagoon. Butaritari, the principal island, constituted most of the southern rim of the atoll. Thirteen miles long but averaging only a quarter-mile in width, Butaritari was thickly covered with tall coconut palms. The Japanese had built defenses only within a mile-long section in the island's center, the site of the main settlement, where four piers poked into the lagoon. There the Japanese had constructed a small seaplane base.

First occupied by the Japanese in December 1941, Makin was no stranger to American troops. In August 1942, 221 Marine Raiders led by Lt. Col. Evans F. Carlson landed there in rubber boats launched from two submarines, swiftly overran a small garrison, and departed. Meant simply to divert attention from the invasion of Guadalcanal, the foray only demonstrated to the Japanese their utter weakness in the region. They soon remedied that deficiency by turning hitherto unoccupied Tarawa into a fortress guarded by nearly five thousand men.[13]

In accordance with general directives from Radford's staff, Air Group Six began detailed preparations for its air attacks. On 14 November the air combat intelligence officers (ACIOs) received, courtesy of Turner's amphibious force, detailed aerial target maps of the crucial western half of Butaritari, derived from photos taken by long-range bombers and through a sub's periscope. An elaborate grid system enabled pilots and spotters to identify exact locations and targets.

Intelligence estimated the enemy garrison at between six hundred and eight hundred men—a good guess, as the Makin detachment of the Imperial Navy's Third Special Base Force numbered seven hundred sailors under a former enlisted man, Lt. (jg) Ishikawa Seizō. Over half were aviation and labor troops, with limited combat value. Aerial photographs revealed gun positions but could not always demonstrate whether the weapons were indeed real or were dummies fabricated by the garrison. The island defenses were thought to comprise three 8-cm coastal guns (correct), three heavy 8-cm dual-purpose AA guns (correct), one medium AA gun and ten possibles (actually, none present), and twenty-four machine guns with eighty-nine more possible (in reality, a dozen 13-mm heavy machine guns, including two twin AA mounts and numerous smaller machine guns).

In coordination with the other two carriers, Air Group Six's attacks were set to commence on 19 November (D-1 Day) with preinvasion strikes against Makin. Assigned targets included the coastal defense guns, AA guns, observation towers, radio stations, and any other threatening installations. On D-Day itself Butch would oversee the aircraft that bombed and strafed Butaritari from 0545 to 0615. A brief shore bombardment by four old battleships, four cruisers, and six destroyers would follow. The troop landings would take place in two waves, the first at H-Hour (0830) on Red Beach on Butaritari's west coast. The sec-

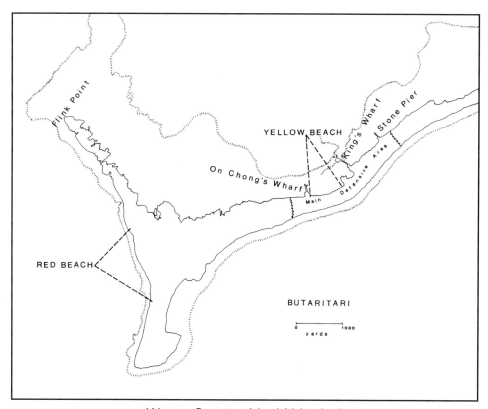

Western Butaritari Island, Makin Atoll

ond was to begin at W-Hour (1030) on Yellow Beach on the north or lagoon side of the island. Butch's *Enterprise* aircraft were to pound Yellow Beach until the landing craft drew to within one hundred yards of shore, then shift inland against any obstacles that might impede the advancing troops. Thereafter the group would fly air support as directed by strike coordinators, in addition to usual combat air and antisubmarine patrols.

While the Makin invasion forces slowly ate up the miles to the objective, Butch oversaw the integration of his air group into the *Big E*'s routine and reviewed planning for the initial strikes. He encouraged his rookies now headed into battle for the first time, as when he was overheard to tell a VF-2 pilot, "There isn't a Jap plane made that I can't shoot down. This F6F you're flying is better than anything they've got.

So—you can't lose! Go in there and knock 'em out of the sky."[14]

On 15 November five majestic fast battleships arrived from the South Pacific to join the two northerly carrier task groups. Three—the *Massachusetts* (BB-59), *North Carolina* (BB-55), and *Indiana* (BB-58)—took their places in TG-50.2, greatly enhancing AA protection for Radford's flattops. When Butch's busy schedule allowed him to roam topside, he witnessed a remarkable spectacle well described by Tom Morrissey: "We have been escorted by a most impressive force—the whole fleet seems to be converging on little Makin and Tarawa; and the sight of our battle wagons, leading a group of carriers, including the LEXINGTON, YORKTOWN, and our own 'Big E,' the COWPENS, MONTEREY, BELLEAU WOOD, and the numerous CVEs, with escorting destroyers far out on the horizon, all defies adequate description."[15] As of the sixteenth the combined task force passed into extreme attack range of Japanese bombers based in the Marshalls. The next morning the *Enterprise* began flying combat air patrols.

On 18 November (D-2) the crucial phase of the campaign opened with raids by the two southerly carrier task groups roaring up from the South Pacific. As a diversion, Sherman's TG-50.4 pounded Nauru, and Montgomery's TG-50.3 struck its objective, Tarawa. The presence of American carriers galvanized Japanese land-based air, divided among four bases in the Marshalls and Gilberts. With only ninety-one aircraft, Vice Adm. Kira Toshi-ichi's Twenty-second Air Flotilla was weaker by nearly half of the 175 planes CentPac expected. Kira's principal strike component was the familiar 755 Air Group with forty Mitsubishi G4M1 Type 1 (Betty) and Mitsubishi G3M3 Type 96 (Nell) land-attack planes. As will be seen, their modest numbers belied their very real threat to the American carriers.

After dark on the eighteenth Montgomery received a foretaste of the danger when a snooper harassed the task group. He felt certain that the intruder had summoned a night torpedo strike group and then had withdrawn at high speed to the south. His caution was appropriate, for thirteen Bettys sortied against the Tarawa raiders. In the darkness only three located TG-50.3 and erroneously claimed torpedoing one "medium-sized" carrier. In return, AA fire torched one Betty, and four others from the strike never returned to base. TG-50.3 emerged unhurt, for which Montgomery was especially grateful. On radar it appeared that two formations of enemy planes, each estimated at ten to fifteen, had flown past the task group.

Makin—First Day

After a trouble-free run to the target, now at 0300 on 19 November (D-1), Radford's TG-50.2 was poised sixty miles east of Makin. Reveille summoned Butch and the rest of the *Enterprise* pilots from their bunks to prepare for the scheduled dawn air strike. In the wardroom Butch joined in the traditional hearty prebattle breakfast of steak and eggs. Afterward the aviators assembled in their respective ready rooms and checked out the latest position reports and news on their targets. Out on the darkened flight decks, mechanics and plane captains bustled around the thirty-five aircraft that made up the first deck load: sixteen SBD-5s from Ike Hampton's Bombing Six and nineteen F6Fs (Butch's CAG section and Bill Dean with seventeen from VF-2).[16]

Soon the word came to man planes. Pilots and aircrewmen swarmed out onto the flight deck and made their way to their mounts. Butch clambered into 00's cockpit and stowed his chart board. Andy Skon seated himself in the next Hellcat on deck. With the announcement "Start engines," puffs of smoke shot out of the aircraft exhausts as the shotgun shell starters turned over their radial powerplants. The Airedales had spotted four SBDs first in line. At 0445 Tom Hamilton leaned out of his roost in Air Control overlooking the flight deck to signal the order to launch planes. Walt Chewning's catapults thrust the first pair of SBDs into the air, and his crew immediately positioned the next twosome. Among the many spectators, Morrissey watched the "blue tongues of flame spouting from the exhausts of the SBDs as they raced down the deck and disappeared into the night."[17]

After the four SBDs departed, the Fly I officer brought Butch's Hellcat up to the line, signaled him to rev the powerful engine, took Butch's salute, and dropped the flag. Propelled by the catapult, 00 hurtled down the flight deck and clawed its way aloft. Skon came next. As more planes took off, "formations took shape in a myriad of red and green 'Christmas' lights from the wing tips against a very black sky." The last aircraft from the strike left the *Enterprise*'s deck at 0513. Because of mechanical trouble, one SBD never made it off, and VF-2 suffered a tragic loss. Circling at six hundred feet during rendezvous, Ens. Robert Wayne Harrold in F-21 evidently suffered engine failure but could not make it all the way back to the carrier. At 0525 his Hellcat raised a splash to port of one of the battleships. Radford detached a destroyer to rescue Harrold,

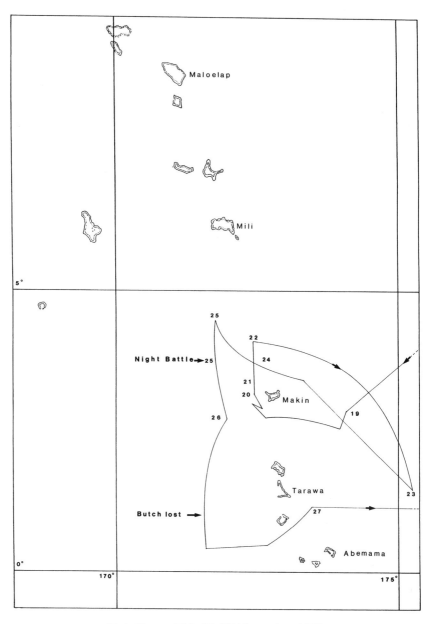

Task Group 50.2, 18–27 November 1943

but she found nothing. Neither did two separate searches dispatched that day by the *Enterprise*.[18]

Aided by a crescent moon, Butch completed the rendezvous of his strike group, now reduced to thirty-three aircraft. Makin lay fifty-five miles west. He took the eighteen F6Fs up to sixteen thousand feet while Hampton's heavily laden SBDs eased up to twelve thousand. Nearing Makin Atoll, Butch found the weather clear, but with a dark line of incoming squalls. At first light he could distinguish the thin ribbon of surf-washed islands making up the atoll's southern coast, with his actual objective the eastern prong of the wishbone configuration at the bottom of Butaritari.

As the breaking dawn silhouetted the atoll, Butch carefully positioned the fighters to swoop in as soon as he had sufficient light to distinguish specific targets. Finally at sunrise, 0612, he led the eighteen F6Fs into a steep dive toward Butaritari. Someone was awake on the seemingly slumbering island. Angry tracers swirled around at least some of the Hellcats as they plummeted below twelve thousand feet. Butch, Skon, and a section of VF-2 F6Fs that had latched on aimed for the radio station and two associated sixty-foot radio towers located in the center of the defended area, not far from King's Wharf and the principal nest of AA guns. At five thousand feet Butch triggered his six Brownings, sending squiggles of red tracers floating down toward the target. Only when the ground loomed in his sights did he relent, recover at three hundred feet, and scoot out over the lagoon. Skon and at least one other VF-2 pilot followed. Butch led them around against gun pits at the base of On Chong's Wharf, near where troops would land the next day. Diving in one long string, Dean's fourteen F6Fs strafed the heavy gun positions at the base of King's Wharf. Afterward Dean gathered his Hellcats and hastened back to the *Enterprise* to rearm, while Butch and Skon remained behind to observe the bombing.

Following the fighters, the fifteen dive bombers let down in a high-speed approach to nine thousand feet, and at 0614 Hampton pushed over. The SBDs split up by sections to go after suspected AA gun positions and released their thousand-pounders at two thousand feet. Four of the dozen bombs they dropped were later judged direct hits. Three pilots could not release their payloads, the first indication of a mechanical problem that would plague VB-6, and consequently Butch, for the next several days. The SBD crews noticed no return fire during their dives, so Butch's fighters had done their job of suppressing the enemy gunners. Only after VB-6 had reformed and made ready to depart did one of the 8-cm high-angle guns loose a few shells that burst well short of the aircraft.

While the SBDs completed their attacks, Butch and Skon strafed positions near Stone Pier on the eastern edge of the defended zone. They never saw the one Japanese aircraft lurking in the area, a Nakajima E8N1 Type 95 reconnaissance seaplane (Dave) that scurried aloft before dawn. As the SBD crews left the area, they noticed the biplane stooging around at four thousand feet. It evidently followed them back toward the task group. Butch and Andy stayed near the target to await the arrival of the second strike wave. After the rude awakening, Butaritari burned in several locations. Native canoes appeared in the lagoon, their occupants paddling furiously to get away from their now endangered homes.

Around 0640 the *Enterprise* dispatched the second wave of fourteen VT-6 TBFs, one VB-6 SBD photoplane, and six VF-2 F6Fs. Ten minutes later, when about twenty miles out from the ships, Lt. Tex Harris, leading the six escort fighters cruising at five thousand feet, happened to sight ahead the selfsame Dave approaching about two thousand feet below. The brave biplane swung in after the TBFs, but Harris's flight intervened and swiftly destroyed it for VF-2's first kill.

Around 0700 Lt. Comdr. John Phillips, leading the torpedo bombers, encountered the squall line near the atoll and dipped below the clouds. He formed his squadron into a column and pushed over in a glide-bombing attack. The Avenger pilots released their bulky 2,000-pound general-purpose bombs—fused for maximum fragmentation as "daisy cutters"—against buildings located between Stone Pier and King's Wharf. Massive explosions rocked the island and raised more smoke from gutted structures. Butch and Skon joined Harris's half-dozen Hellcats in shooting up likely targets in the same area plastered by the TBFs. After taking in the first two strikes against Makin, Butch led the second wave on the flight back to the ships.

By the time Butch got back on board, the busy *Enterprise* had launched the third strike of a dozen SBDs and six F6Fs against Makin. Flight deck crewmen motioned Skon over to his right wing, where a 13-mm round had ripped a hole in the underside and torn a .50-caliber ammunition can. He never even knew he had been hit. While the F6Fs were being refueled and rearmed, aviation metalsmiths and ordnancemen repaired the damage. Before Butch could go again, a short delay ensued when Lt. John E. McInerny's Tare-87 plowed into a 40-mm mount while landing. Fortunately no one was injured, but plane handlers tossed the battered Avenger over the side. Soon after, the *Enterprise* flight deck crew spotted the next wave for takeoff.

Beginning at 1052, the *Big E* launched Butch with a dozen Hellcats and eleven TBFs for the fourth round against Makin. The results were about the same as before. Starting around 1130, Butch, Skon, and six more F6F pilots worked over sites clustered around On Chong's Wharf, near the center of Yellow Beach, while the other four fighters shot up King's Wharf. Butch later commended two freelancing VF-2 pilots, ensigns Charles H. Carroll and Richard H. Combs, for igniting a couple of structures around On Chong's Wharf. The TBFs sprinkled 2,000-pound presents all along the lagoon side of the defense zone, where the Army would land the next day. Around 1320, while Butch and company circled the *Enterprise* awaiting a clear deck, the fifth and last D-1 Day strike against Makin left with thirteen SBDs and four F6Fs.

That afternoon Butch studied the strike assessments. During the day Air Group Six had flown 173 sorties, including 108 against Makin, for the loss of one F6F (Ensign Harrold missing) and one TBF (McInerny's) jettisoned. One VB-6 SBD had suffered minor damage, as had Skon's F6F. The *Belleau Wood* and *Monterey* had completed 167 sorties, including 97 against Makin, for the loss of two F6Fs. In addition to Tex Harris's kill, a section from the *Monterey*'s VF-30 had destroyed a Betty snooper that afternoon thirty miles out as the task group passed to the south of Makin.

Radford decided that the "bombing accuracy [against Makin] was not up to expectancy, but considerable damage to AA installations resulted." The Makin garrison probably would have agreed. Ishikawa's spotters counted no fewer than 266 carrier planes rampaging overhead in seven waves, and his gunners claimed a dozen shot down (four unconfirmed). Butch knew that his green air group would improve with more combat experience. After his own two forays following Butch over Makin, with daring low-level strafing runs that nearly scraped the coconut palms, Skon also took the measure of his CAG in combat: "Butch seemed in his glory. . . . No paperwork CAG Butch! The flying, risks, and in the air leading of his air group were his style of command."[19]

During the day the other carrier groups executed their missions. Pownall's TG-50.1 with the *Yorktown, Lexington,* and *Cowpens* loosed ten strikes against Mili and Jaluit in the Marshalls to prevent enemy bombers from using these advance airfields. During daylight Pownall kept twenty-four Hellcats on combat air patrol at all times, but strangely, no enemy planes showed up over the most exposed task group. Not so for Montgomery's TG-50.3 (*Essex, Bunker Hill,* and *Independence*), hitting Tarawa for the second consecutive day. His combat air patrol knocked down three Betty snoopers. That day the 755 Air Group lost sixteen bombers (six on the ground at Mili and most of the rest to bad weather, accidents, and unknown causes) and retained only about eighteen Bettys and Nells in flyable condition.

D-Day on Makin

After midnight on 20 November TG-50.2 approached within forty miles west of Makin. Prevailing southeasterly winds dictated that the task group run toward the island while conducting air operations. On the *Enterprise* reveille sounded at 0230, rousing Butch and his sleepy aviators to breakfast and flight quarters. Overnight the thirty-six vessels of Turner's Northern Attack Force crossed the last miles to smoldering Makin, lowered boats, and prepared to disembark the first of sixty-five hundred soldiers and Marines of Maj. Gen. Ralph C. Smith's landing force. The Fire Support Group, made up of the four old battleships *New Mexico* (BB-40), *Pennsylvania* (BB-38), *Idaho* (BB-42), and *Mississippi* (BB-41), four heavy cruisers, and six destroyers, maneuvered into position to begin the bombardment after dawn. To the south Rear Adm. Henry M. Mullinnix's Air Support Group, with the escort carriers *Liscome Bay* (CVE-56), *Coral Sea* (CVE-57), and *Corregidor* (CVE-58) likewise spotted their flight decks with aircraft for dawn flight operations to fly combat air and antisubmarine patrols.

Beginning at 0441, ninety minutes before sunrise, the *Enterprise* dispatched her first Makin strike of twelve F6Fs (Butch's 00 and eleven from VF-2), a like number of VB-6 SBDs, and eleven TBFs from VT-6, plus four more F6Fs for combat air patrol. Unlike the previous morning, this time the Air Group Six aviators encountered trouble from the very beginning. Rapidly changing wind direction forced Radford to suspend launching and repeatedly alter course. Not until 0531 did the last plane leave the *Enterprise*. To make things worse, a thin overcast at fifteen hundred feet made the night rendezvous quite tricky. The upshot was that Butch ended up only with Andy Skon's Hellcat, eleven Dauntlesses, and six Avengers. He aimed the group for Makin and started up to twelve thousand feet.[20]

Unbeknownst to Butch, the *Enterprise* had provided the pilots an erroneous start position a whole degree (sixty miles) north of her actual location. The ship followed Butch's departure by radar and sent him a course correction by VHF radio. In the confusion, an F6F, an SBD, and a TBF had latched onto one another and independently proceeded to Makin, where they joined Butch. En route the TBF had used its ASB-1 air-search radar to pinpoint the island, as did three other TBFs. Thus, of the original strike only three fighters, twelve dive bombers, and ten torpedo bombers reached the objective. The other ten (nine F6Fs and one TBF) mistakenly flew all the way to Tarawa, one hundred miles south of Makin.

As first light creased the eastern horizon, Butch saw the amphibious ships clustered off the western shore of Makin Atoll. At 0610, as scheduled, he led the three F6Fs barreling in steeply toward familiar topography, Yellow Beach on the lagoon side of the central defended zone on Butaritari, where an infantry battalion would land later that morning. The three pilots fired their eighteen Brownings into buildings and gun positions at the base of King's Wharf. Coming around, Butch aimed his section toward several small wrecked vessels aground on the reef off On Chong's Wharf. This time he dipped as low as seventy-five feet before pulling out. Tracers from a couple of machine guns challenged but failed to hit the strafers. Butch's third pass roughed up positions around On Chong's Wharf itself.

The pilots of Ike Hampton's Bombing Six carefully watched the antics of the three fighters. As Butch and company scooted out of the way, eleven SBDs started down from nine thousand feet looking for the best places around On Chong's Wharf to deliver their thousand-pounders. Six SBDs aimed for On Chong's Wharf and the little complex of buildings near its base, while five attacked the fortified area just west of there. Lt. (jg) James C. Hoisington in B-41 had to drop out shortly after releasing his bomb and ditched near Makin. He and his radioman ended up on Turner's flagship, the *Pennsylvania*.

After Bombing Six completed its runs, it was Torpedo Six's turn. At 0630 the squadron XO, Lt. Comdr. William G. Privette, brought the ten TBFs, each laden with one 2,000-pound bomb, around to the north of Makin. The massive payloads blasted holes from On Chong's Wharf eastward to the eastern edge of the defensive zone. Turner's amphibious observers later noted that one 2,000-pounder, striking a position, had "considerably scrambled the trench, Japs, and trees for some distance," with over forty Japanese dead found in and around the area. One prisoner later revealed that the dawn air strike had killed Ishikawa, the island commander. Despite the mix-up in getting to the target, Butch had good reason to be satisfied with the performance of Air Group Six.[21]

At 0640, as the *Enterprise* aircraft withdrew from Makin, the Fire Support Group loosed its first salvo. A torrent of 14-inch, 8-inch, and 5-inch shell bursts thundered into the western half of Butaritari. Very likely Butch, observing from offshore, tried to figure out which of the squat profiles of the three *New Mexico*–class battlewagons represented his old warship. He must have enjoyed the satisfaction of seeing the *New Mexico* fire her guns in anger for only the second time in her long career. Tragically, during the bombardment a turret fire on her sister, the *Mississippi*, killed forty-three sailors.

Between 0709 and 0743 the aircraft from the first Makin strike (and the Tarawa sightseers) landed back on board the *Enterprise*. Only Hoisington's SBD was missing. While Butch was debriefed and waited for 00 to be refueled and rearmed, the first landings took place at Butaritari. At 0830 (H-Hour) the First and Third Battalions of the 165th Infantry Regiment walked ashore virtually unopposed on Red Beach on the western edge of the island. A strike group from Rear Admiral Pownall's TG-50.1, led by Lt. Comdr. Charles L. Crommelin, CAG-5 on the *Yorktown*, flew in support. Lt. Comdr. John Phillips, CO of VT-6, circled overhead in his TBF as liaison between the strike planes and Turner's air coordinator. Despite the lack of opposition, terrain rendered difficult the process of getting men and equipment ashore on Butaritari. Troops advanced only slowly eastward toward the central defended zone.

Beginning at 0910, the *Enterprise* launched her second Makin strike, with Butch leading seventeen F6Fs and a dozen TBFs to support the W-Hour landings set to begin at 1030. As he arrived near Makin, a steady progression of boats plied to and fro between Red Beach and the transports anchored a mile west of Butaritari. Well to the north a small flotilla of LVT Alligators and landing craft in widely spaced waves churned past Flink Point into the lagoon proper. They carried a battalion of the 165th Infantry Regiment and an attached medium tank unit toward Yellow Beach on the north coast of the fortified zone. An eyewitness described the appearance of the island about this time:

Brilliant mid-morning sun poured down, intensifying the blue and green of the water and throwing Butaritari Island in shadow, but the renewed bombardment was raising banks of grayish smoke and dust over which swirled billows of thick, black smoke from fuel stores on the shore between the wharves and in the area behind King's Wharf. The light wind carried plumes of smoke over the tree tops for thousands of feet toward the west.

Butch positioned his fighters to strafe Yellow Beach when the first wave fired its rockets. At 1005 the destroyers *MacDonough* (DD-351) and *Phelps* (DD-360), cruising in the lagoon, started pounding Yellow Beach with their 5-inchers.[22]

In deep contrast to the situation at Tarawa, where the Second Marine Division confronted fierce opposition and was hanging on by its fingernails, the atmosphere at Makin had grown rather relaxed. This is reflected in the dialogue between Turner's air coordinator (code name Viceroy) and some of the pilots. At 1001 Viceroy queried John Phillips (Clipper 1) in the VT-6 liaison TBF, "If you see any nice females down there save me one." Phillips replied, "It looks like all the girls have skivvy shirts on," to which Viceroy sympathized, "Ah, that's too bad." At 1001 Viceroy urged, "Let's put on a good show for the big shots. They are all out there with their glasses and sunbonnets." That moved Butch to reply, "We have already put on a good show." Viceroy responded, "Ha, Ha, Ha. Give 'em hell keed." A voice cut in on the circuit, "Let's have a little less bull—— from the bull," to which Viceroy moaned, "Somebody has lost their sense of humor."[23]

About eleven hundred yards from Yellow Beach, each of the sixteen LVT Alligators in the first wave fired six rockets against the beach. That gave Butch the signal to come in. At 1025, with the first wave only six hundred yards offshore, the destroyers ceased fire in order to let the F6Fs strafe. At 1030 Butch led the seventeen F6Fs in steep dives against Yellow Beach, On Chong's Wharf, and the hulks west of On Chong's Wharf. When the LVTs drew to within one hundred yards of the shore, the fighters ceased fire and got clear. At 1041 the lead LVT touched King's Wharf, and little figures could be seen jumping out to engage the Japanese. The shallow reef forced subsequent waves to disembark their tanks and infantry 150 to 200 yards from land. Even so, fire directed at them proved relatively light.

At 1040, when Butch radioed that he had completed his attack, Bill

Privette maneuvered the dozen Avengers over the target. Each TBF, armed with twelve 100-pound bombs, executed four separate bombing runs to suppress enemy fire. Privette gathered his turkeys five miles west of Makin and reported compliance to Viceroy, who sent the flight back to the ship. The F6Fs, except for Butch and Skon, had already departed. They stayed awhile, watching the troops move inland. The situation looked to be well in hand. Butch returned to the *Enterprise* and landed shortly after noon.

The first ground-support air group, ten SBDs from VB-6, were already en route by the time Butch turned for home plate. Phillips in Clipper 1 had to break off when AA punctured the bomb bay tank and leaked gasoline into the aircraft. He jettisoned the tank over the target and retired low on fuel. The SBDs bombed the troublesome hulks off On Chong's Wharf, but the two subsequent support air groups returned with their payloads when Viceroy had no need for their help.

After 1330, lookouts on the *Enterprise* sighted Makin to the east, and soon the task group closed within a few miles of the "gutted island." While Butch coordinated activities from on board ship, Phillips survived more adventures on his second liaison flight when AA nearly severed his elevator control cables. His radio operator, John C. Sullivan, aviation radioman second class and a former telephone lineman, managed to splice the wires sufficiently to allow Phillips to attempt a landing back on board, accomplished safely at 1530.[24]

Radford assessed the day's air operations as "effective." The *Enterprise* had flown 131 sorties (including 74 on strikes and 35 air support) for the loss of one SBD. Comparable figures for the two accompanying light carriers were 108 sorties (11 strike and 8 air support) for the loss of one *Belleau Wood* fighter. To Butch, events on Makin appeared to be proceeding well, if slowly. So far the Makin operation seemed likely to be a snap, especially if Japanese aircraft and submarines continued to stay away.[25]

14

Butch's Black Panthers

"Implement the night combat plan"

At dusk on 20 November, Butch looked forward to shutting down Air Group Six operations on the *Enterprise* after a long and tiring but eminently successful "Dog Day" at Makin. The invasion was well under way with no obvious complications up to this point for Rear Admiral Radford's TG-50.2. Suddenly the fighter radio circuit in the *Enterprise* Combat Information Center erupted with distant alarms emanating from Rear Admiral Montgomery's TG-50.3 (the *Essex, Bunker Hill,* and *Independence*) operating near Tarawa a hundred miles south of Makin. Because of the warning, Butch's life would never be the same.

Fourteen torpedo-armed land-attack planes, nearly all that remained in the battered 755 Air Group, had delivered TG-50.3 a nasty surprise. Using the setting sun to silhouette the American ships, the *rikkōs* raced in at low level, their bellies nearly scraping the waves. Only at the last instant had a screening destroyer alerted the other ships. Despite defending Hellcats that swarmed over the attackers, one Betty shoved its fish into the starboard quarter of the *Independence,* Butch's old ship, with a third of VF-6 still on board. Seventeen bluejackets died in the blast that flooded the aft fire and engine rooms. Recovering from a temporary loss of propulsion, the *Evil I* limped south toward Funafuti, gratefully getting clear before the Japanese could reprise their spectacular success. She was out of the war for eight months. In what they jubilantly christened the First Gilbert Islands Air Battle, the Japanese claimed two carriers and one destroyer sunk, though at the cost of half the strike group and all the senior flight officers. The 755 Air Group had shot its bolt, but help was on the way from Japan.[1]

Thus, events quickly justified Radford's apprehensions regarding the threat of enemy air power in the Gilberts. For the first time a Japanese land-based bomber had actually torpedoed an American carrier. In October, Radford had participated in the great debate that raged at Pearl Harbor over the employment of the fast carriers during the upcoming Galvanic invasions. Singling out enemy land-based air as the greatest initial danger, Vice Adm. Jack Towers and his carrier admirals wanted to exploit the power and mobility of their flattops with massive preinvasion raids against air bases in the Marshalls, "eliminating enemy air and damaging airfields until they ceased to be a factor."[2]

Yet Vice Admiral Spruance and his truculent amphibious commander, Rear Admiral Turner, forestalled widespread carrier strikes against the Marshalls. Worried that the Combined Fleet might sortie from Truk to save the Gilbert Islands garrisons, Spruance insisted that all eleven fast carriers and their new battleship escorts remain close to the invasion forces to protect the amphibious ships from air attack and be on hand for a possible fleet action. Even worse for the carrier admirals, Spruance restricted their flattops to patrolling narrow defensive sectors off the Gilberts. To Radford such a static role rendered the carriers "little more than sitting ducks for the enemy's planes, submarines, and now fleet." However, despite vehement protests, Spruance would not change the plan, except to add a few carrier raids on Jaluit and Mili in the Outer Marshalls, but not against the much bigger air bases at Kwajalein and Maloelap.[3]

"Sitting Ducks"

Soon after TG-50.2 cleared Pearl on 10 November, Radford had summoned Matt Gardner, his new flag captain, and Butch, his young CAG, up to Flag Plot. There he explained the problems posed by Japanese land-based air. Would bombers attack the ships during the day or at night? Radford knew why they must come at night. He flourished dispatches from the South Pacific that revealed how on 11 November, strikes from the *Essex, Bunker Hill,* and *Independence* had shattered enemy naval strength at Rabaul. Subsequently their Hellcats and AA guns handily repulsed several daylight air attacks, with claims of eighty-eight planes destroyed. Given such massive casualties incurred in futile day strikes, Radford felt that the Japanese air commanders in the Marshalls must consider night torpedo strikes as their only chance of success against the well-defended American carriers.[4]

Unfortunately the Japanese medium bomber crews, Butch's old adversaries, had already well demonstrated their unique ability, despite the lack of airborne radar, to execute massed torpedo strikes at night. Their most spectacular success to date had occurred shortly after sunset on 29 January 1943 near Rennell Island south of Guadalcanal. Thirty-one *rikkōs* from the 701 and 705 Air Groups crippled the heavy cruiser *Chicago* (CA-29) with two torpedo hits. However, Lt. Comdr. Higai Jōji, the principal proponent of the massed night torpedo strike, died in the attack. The next day the 751 Air Group finished off the *Chicago* with a costly day torpedo strike. Now in November, even as the invasion forces converged on the Gilberts, small numbers of night raiders were scoring again in the South Pacific. Before dawn on 13 November, land-based bombers hunting U.S. carriers had torpedoed the light cruiser *Denver* (CL-58) off Bougainville, and she had to be towed to safer waters.[5]

Yet despite the obvious threat, the flattops wielded no night fighters at all for Galvanic. The only defenses they—or any other naval vessels, for that matter—could employ against night torpedo attacks were evasive maneuvers and antiaircraft fire. Such passivity greatly worried Radford: "To sit there, knowing what was about to develop, and calmly assume that our AA would take care of any attacking planes as they came in was precisely what the 'Nip' desired us to do. With sufficient torpedo planes at his disposal and being allowed to choose the moment and method of attack, it was only a question of time before the Task Group would be swarmed upon."[6] Alone among the Pacific Fleet's carrier admirals, Radford was determined not just to suffer until someone else provided night fighters. Instead, he would create his own night defenders right on the *Enterprise,* and in Butch he possessed a skilled, tough leader who could do it.

It is worth a digression here to sketch the tardy evolution of naval night-fighter doctrine and explain why no carrier night fighters were ready for Galvanic.[7]

The Royal Flying Corps created night fighters in 1915 to counter German zeppelin raids. Groping through the dark on what became known as "cat's eye" missions, British night fighters relied on the help of ground searchlights to find their elusive prey. In the next war both Britain and Germany had by late 1940 eschewed day attacks in favor of night bombing. Their night fighters at first relied upon traditional "cat's eye" tactics, but intense night-bombing offensives forced them to develop sophisticated defenses based upon ground and airborne intercept (AI) radars.

Long adept at night carrier operations, including radar-directed torpedo strikes, the Royal Navy decided in late 1941 to create carrier night fighters mainly to destroy German patrol bombers that shadowed convoys. By the end of 1942 No. 746 Squadron was working on night-fighter doctrine using two-seat radar-equipped Fairey Fulmar fighters. The intention was to replace them with the new Fairey Firefly. However, the airborne radar proved unsuitable for low-level intercepts, while other delays prevented carrier qualification of night fighters until the spring of 1944. That year small flights of Fulmars from No. 746 Squadron operated from three escort carriers as convoy protection on the Gibraltar and North Russia runs. The first RN carrier night-fighter squadron was not formed until January 1945 and never actually saw combat during World War II.

Since 1925, U.S. Navy aviators had also made night carrier landings, and the nerve-racking night qualifications were (and are) the bane of every carrier pilot. The flattops showed special lights, and landing signal officers wielded illuminated wands. However, by the fall of 1943 no one in the U.S. Navy as yet had actually developed a carrier night-strike or defense capability, although implementation on both scores was imminent.

In April 1942 the Navy created Project Argus (later called Afirm) at NAS Quonset Point to test its own aircraft and airborne radars to devise a suitable night-fighter doctrine. The project head, Lt. Comdr. William E. G. Taylor, a radar expert and former CO of the first RAF Eagle Squadron, naturally looked to the British for inspiration. In April 1943 Lt. Comdr. Gus Widhelm, an aggressive ex–dive bomber pilot and Butch's former flight instructor, formed the first U.S. Navy night-fighting squadron. VF(N)-75 operated Vought F4U-2 Corsairs, a special night variant of the gull-wing fighter that featured the model AIA, a primitive air intercept radar. On 1 August, Widhelm rushed all six available F4U-2s down to the

Solomons to help defend bases bedeviled by night intruders. They went into action beginning 2 October over Munda, New Georgia, but the first kill did not occur until 1 November. Widhelm's XO, Lt. Comdr. Richard E. "Chick" Harmer, remained behind at Quonset to await nine more F4U-2s. Lt. Comdr. Evan P. Aurand's VF(N)-76 worked up with the more highly regarded Grumman F6F-3E, the radar-equipped night-fighter version of the Hellcat.

Although the Navy's first night-fighter squadron had reached a combat theater, it flew only from land bases. Nothing as yet afforded the same capability at sea. On 9 September a worried Admiral Nimitz directed Towers at AirPac to look into assigning a Hellcat night-fighter squadron to each carrier division so that every big flattop would wield a division of four planes. Towers advised Nimitz that such night fighters trained only at Quonset and that proper equipment (aircraft and radar) would not be available even there until November. In late September, during a staff conference in San Francisco, Admiral King also expressed his deep concern over the need for night fighters on board the carriers. Towers repeated that the development of night-fighter doctrine and the actual deployment of night fighters on carriers would require considerably more time.[8]

Given his vital new mission of improvising a carrier night-fighter capability, Butch worked essentially in a vacuum, with little knowledge of how others had tackled the same problems. He had to develop everything from scratch without taking effort away from the principal mission: invading the Gilberts. At the same time and in stark contrast to Butch's plight, the Naval Air Training Command instituted a training syllabus for prospective carrier night-fighter pilots that called for a six-week course with ninety-nine hours of ground school and seventy-five hours aloft. It was estimated that a carrier night-fighter squadron required a minimum of four months to get ready for combat. On the other hand, Butch had only a few days and because of radio silence and other restrictions no opportunity to test ideas aloft, let alone practice them.[9]

While en route to the Gilberts, Radford, Gardner, and Butch decided that their first goal must be to defeat the troublesome enemy snoopers that often latched on at dusk, tracked the task group beyond sundown, and directed the night strikes to the target. Success there might actually prevent attacks. However, how could defending planes engage the elusive night shadowers?[10]

Actual night-fighting experience over Europe and elsewhere had demonstrated that airborne radar was absolutely essential for effective night intercepts, particularly against scattered, low-flying targets. Its absence restricted night operations largely to rare conditions of high visibility, such as a full moon on a clear night, or the use of searchlights—suicidal for ships trying to remain hidden from night attackers. However, the only *Enterprise* aircraft so equipped were Grumman TBF-1 and TBF-1C Avenger torpedo bombers in VT-6 and Douglas SBD-5 Dauntless dive bombers from VB-6 on board for familiarization. Instead of intercept radars, such as the AIA, they utilized the less precise ASB-1, a short-range airborne search radar—wavelength 60-cm, with a Yagi antenna installed under each wing—designed to find surface targets at sea. This radar featured the old A-scan or "blip type" scope with a jagged line read on a rectangular glass plate—much more difficult to use than the PPI (plan position indicator) scope with circular display and continuous sweep. The ASB radar operator conducted his search manually, one side (one antenna) at a time. Against single aircraft the ASB's range was low: ten miles perhaps for a very large flying boat, down to four or five miles for smaller planes.[11]

Because of their greater endurance and superior radar installation, Butch deemed the TBF-1Cs far more suitable than the SBDs for night intercept work. They could be fitted with special flame dampeners to hide the telltale engine exhaust flares so conspicuous at night. Yet the burly TBF-1Cs were much slower and more lightly armed than the F6F-3 Hellcat fighters, with only twin .50-caliber machine guns firing forward in addition to a single .50-caliber turret gun and a .30-caliber underside "stinger." Barely as fast as the Japanese bombers they would oppose, the Avengers nevertheless would have to do the job.[12]

Thus, Lt. Comdr. John Phillips, CO of VT-6, became a key participant in Butch's night-fighting experiment. A college-educated naval enlistee, "Phil" Phillips used the Navy Preparatory School to earn an "at large" appointment to the Naval Academy and graduated in 1933. After receiving his wings in January 1938, he flew two years with VT-6 on the *Enterprise,* then taught at Pensacola for nearly three more. In March 1943 he formed Torpedo Seven at NAS San Diego with a leavening of VT-6 veterans. That was fitting, for with the general air group redesignation in July 1943, VT-7 became the second VT-6. The soft-spoken, good-natured thirty-three-year-old Virginian was respected for clear thinking and innovation.[13]

Assigned to operate the ASB-1 radar in the CO's aircraft (Tare-97), Lt. (jg) Hazen B. Rand was a twenty-five-year-old electrical engineer from Avon, Massachusetts. He trained in radar theory and operation before joining VT-6 in July 1943 as squadron radar instructor and maintenance officer. Now Rand received a combat assignment of great importance. Bright and articulate Alvin B. Kernan, aviation ordnanceman first class, manned the turret gun. Looking even younger than his twenty years, he had served since October 1941 in the VT-6 ordnance gang on the *Enterprise* and the first *Hornet* (CV-8), but he had become an air gunner only that summer. Overcoming stiff competition within the fleet, Kernan had earned a slot in the naval pilot program and was to report for flight training after this cruise.[14]

Chosen to fly the second TBF was the VT-6 operations officer, Lt. John McInerny, a distinguished ex–fighter pilot (VF-8 at Midway) with almost eighteen months in VT-6, including combat at Guadalcanal. His borrowed radar operator, Lt. (jg) David L. Sargent, was Rand's counterpart expert in Bombing Six. Tough Marcell F. "Buck" Varner, aviation radioman second class—the oldest gunner in the squadron—rode in McInerny's turret.[15]

Support offered on board the *Enterprise* proved essential to the night-fighting plan. Butch consulted two highly experienced aviators, Air Officer Tom Hamilton and his subordinate, Comdr. Harry Sartoris, whose V-4 Division ran her Combat Information Center. There Butch learned the capabilities of the SM height-finding radar just installed during the *Big E*'s refit at Bremerton. As yet only the *Lexington* and *Bunker Hill* employed this new radar, particularly valuable for tracking low-level aircraft. CIC used it in conjunction with the SK long-range air-search radar. Together both radars would facilitate the night intercepts that Butch contemplated.[16]

As far as Butch was concerned, the most important member of the CIC team was the senior fighter director officer, Lt. (jg) George P. Givens. His vital task was to position the TBFs in the path of one or more of the shadowers. Turning twenty-seven that November, he was a deck officer reserve who had completed the Pacific Fleet's Fighter Director School before reporting to the *Enterprise* in April 1942. A veteran of Midway, the Eastern Solomons, and Santa Cruz, then-Ensign Givens rose to senior FDO in December 1942, despite his youth and junior rank, mainly because of VF-10 skipper Jim Flatley's vigorous recommendation and assertion, "I'm willing to risk my reputation on him."[17]

In the short time Butch had served on the *Big E,* he had already made an equally powerful impression on Givens. On 10 November, the day the ship sailed from Pearl Harbor, Givens handled a routine fighter direction problem between eight VF-2 F6Fs on CAP and a flight of incoming TBFs pretending to be attackers. He misread the Avengers for the fighters, sent the CAP the wrong way, and thus botched the exercise. Butch appeared in CIC, asked what had gone wrong, and listened to the FDO's explanation. To Givens's surprise, the new CAG did not "chew him out" in front of everyone. So typical of Butch, he quietly replied, "We expect better direction and information in the future." The next day Givens scored an almost perfect practice interception, and Butch came up to CIC to offer a "friendly nod" and a "well done." Like so many who served under Butch, Givens would have done anything for him.[18]

Butch initially decided to put the two Avenger night fighters on the flight deck catapults after the *Enterprise* had shut down flight operations for the day. Their crews would sleep in the VT-6 ready room and remain on alert to man planes. If enemy shadowers bothered the task group, both TBFs would take off and CIC would attempt to direct them to a visual sighting of the enemy exhaust flares. Should neither Avenger find any of the evasive snoopers, they were to act as radar pickets, with their ASBs augmenting radars on the ships. Perhaps then they could greet an incoming strike. Another possibility, also not yet fully explored, was for the TBFs to mimic the shadowers and confuse the strike planes by dropping flares and float lights well away from the task group. The jettisonable fuel tank installed in each TBF's bomb bay provided enough gasoline to remain aloft from dusk to dawn, if need be. That lessened the need for night recoveries, which would force the *Enterprise* to show lights that might alert subs.

Only if an actual attack showed up after midnight and visibility happened to be good did Butch contemplate also launching a pair of the virtually night-blind VF-2 Hellcats on a sort of "cat's eye" mission. They would also carry sufficient fuel to remain aloft until after sunrise. The F6F pilots would have to do their best without radar to try to pick out enemy planes from their engine exhaust flames. Luftwaffe single-engine fighters without radar flew similar night sorties (known as *Wilde Sau,* or "Wild Boar") in European skies, and to find the British bomber streams they benefited from not only ground searchlights but also flames from the burning cities.

To prevent their being fired on by the ships in error, Butch told the night fighters to stay away from the task group unless actually engaging enemy planes. Should any of the night CAP have to ditch, they were to set down beside the plane guard destroyer. On 18 November (D-2), Radford outlined Butch's night-fighter procedures for the rest of the task group. However, the admiral kept secret from everyone his ace in the hole: his ability to eavesdrop on Japanese aircraft radio traffic through Lt. (jg) William W. Burd's radio intelligence unit attached to his staff on the *Enterprise*.[19]

The evening of 20 November, Radford gave Butch approval to implement the night combat contingency plans so hurriedly devised the preceding week. Sleep did not long survive that midnight, and returning consciousness brought the CAG more bad news from CIC. Rear Admiral Pownall's TG-50.1, deployed out to the north, warned of approaching enemy aircraft bound for Makin and Tarawa. At 0310, flight quarters roused the pilots of Air Group Six. Shaking off their drowsiness, they dressed and rushed to their ready rooms to learn what was up. Beginning at 0315 four separate bogeys dotted the *Enterprise* radar screens. One in particular seemed to be hunting TG-50.2. Outside, a quarter moon shone brightly in the night sky, with the stars obscured only in spots by a few clouds. Gardner sounded general quarters and prepared the *Enterprise* for battle.

According to plan, Phillips and McInerny manned the two radar-equipped VT-6 TBFs poised on the catapults and awaited the word to go. Two VF-2 Hellcats flown by XO Lt. John Eckhardt and Ens. Everett C. Hargreaves went on standby. As events transpired, the night fighters were not needed, no doubt to the relief especially of the VF-2 pilots. Radford had adroitly turned the task group into a convenient overcast that blanked out the moonlight. The lone bogey never closed, and the others passed well clear of the ships. In fact, the enemy comprised four Bettys from Roi that had ventured south to bomb Tarawa and drop supplies to the garrison. On the way home at least one paused to reconnoiter the waters west of Makin and suffered for it.

At 0540, just prior to sunrise, the *Enterprise* loosed Bill Dean with six VF-2 F6Fs for the dawn CAP and spotted the flight deck with seventeen more Hellcats as reinforcements and five VB-6 SBDs for antisubmarine patrol. FDO Givens adroitly positioned the CO's division to ambush an intruder droning up from the south at six hundred feet. At 0615 Dean's wingman, Ens. Daniel A. Carmichael, flushed a Betty whose starboard engine and fuselage Dean set afire with one burst from his six guns. Within a few seconds the land-attack plane had plunged into the sea seventeen miles due south of the *Enterprise*. Spent shell casings that tumbled from Dean's wings gashed the leading edge of Carmichael's right wing—the only damage suffered by the two F6Fs.

During the day Air Group Six, along with aircraft from the light carriers *Belleau Wood* and *Monterey*, flew more ground-support strikes against Makin. VF-2 strafed a sunken hulk and suspected gun positions along the beach. Butch did not join his boys that day. Instead he concentrated on problem number one, night fighting. That evening Lt. Roy "Butch" Voris, VF-2 flight officer, and Lt. (jg) Richard J. Griffin waited on alert behind the two TBFs as VF-2's contribution should a night attack develop. Evidently in the haste of organizing the mission no one informed them that they would go only if danger materialized after midnight. Putting their heads together, Voris and Griffin decided that if the word came at 0200 or later, they would have the gas to circle until dawn. Otherwise it was a dip in the sea when fuel ran out and fond hopes that the plane guard destroyer would spot them. In any event, they did not have to try their luck that night.

The Second Plan

Early on the morning of 22 November, as TG-50.2 ran northwest of Makin, ship radars detected four Bettys passing well out to the west in transit on another nocturnal bombing mission against Tarawa. As on the previous night, the enemy remained many miles from Radford's ships. While waiting on alert in the VT-6 ready room along with the rest of the night-fighter crews, an impatient Hazen Rand remarked, "I wish I could be chasing those bastards with our plane radar!" Phillips asked, "Do you think you could do any good, Rand?" He said he could. Phillips relayed Rand's comments to Butch with the suggestion that the TBFs might play a more aggressive role and go after the distant Japanese bombers. Later that morning Butch met with Phillips and Rand in the CAG ready room to discuss Rand's idea to use the TBFs to hunt the night intruders bothering Tarawa.[20]

Butch added a whole new wrinkle to Rand's suggestion. Butch's idea was that should the threat come after midnight, when all planes carried enough fuel to stay up until dawn, a pair of Hellcats would accompany each TBF to increase greatly the firepower of the night fighters. Under suitable conditions the *Enterprise* would launch two sections, each consisting of one TBF-1C and two F6F-3s. Each section would rendezvous independently in vee formation with its TBF in the lead. Butch counted on the ability of his pilots to fly formation at night with minimal illumination. Givens would vector the teams toward the nearest or largest group of enemy planes and attempt to place them a mile or two astern and to one side of the enemy formation. From there the TBF radar operators would guide their teams to within sight of the bomber engine exhaust flames, at which point the TBF pilots would direct their fighters to break off, close into range, and fire. The whole thing sounded simple, but as with so much in warfare, the actual execution would be extremely dangerous.

Although Butch almost certainly was unaware of it, his plan somewhat resembled the Turbinlite program of hunter-killer teams that the RAF had tried in 1942 to compensate for their lack of radar-equipped night fighters. The basic concept involved using a Douglas Boston (A-20 Havoc) light bomber, fitted with both AI radar and a powerful Turbinlite searchlight in its nose, to guide a single-engine "satellite" fighter (usually a Hawker Hurricane) to within firing range of an enemy night bomber. Unfortunately the RAF found the Turbinlite flights completely ineffective (one kill in 1942) and discontinued the practice in January 1943. German night bombers, often flying dispersed at medium altitudes, used evasive maneuvers to escape the hunter-killer teams.

On 22 November, Butch organized two teams of night fighters:

No. 1 Team

TBF-1C	Lt. Comdr. John L. Phillips, Jr. (CO, VT-6), pilot
	Lt. (jg) Hazen B. Rand (VT-6), radar operator
	Alvin B. Kernan, AOM1 (VT-6), turret gunner
F6F-3	Lt. Comdr. Edward H. O'Hare (CAG-6)
F6F-3	Ens. Warren A. Skon (VF-2)

No. 2 Team

TBF-1C	Lt. John E. McInerny, Jr. (VT-6), pilot
	Lt. (jg) David L. Sargent (VB-6), radar operator
	Marcell F. Varner, ARM2 (VT-6), turret gunner
F6F-3	Lt. Comdr. William A. Dean, Jr. (CO, VF-2)
F6F-3	Lt. Roy M. Voris (VF-2)

Butch decided on the appropriate nickname of Black Panthers for his new night fighters.

Recently Voris reminisced that the idea of employing a TBF to guide two F6Fs into a night interception came as a "tremendous surprise" when Dean told him that the CAG wanted them both for a special night-fighting team. That afternoon Butch and his night-fighter pilots hiked up to Radford's flag bridge to brief the admiral and his staff. With space at a premium, Voris kneeled down on the deck. Later that day Butch announced to the whole air group that the Black Panthers were going to hunt the so-called Tokyo Express of bombers that nearly every morning prior to dawn had bypassed the task group en route to and from Tarawa.[21]

The audacious new plan did not thrill everyone. Lt. James H. Trousdale, Jr., a newly assigned FDO, later recorded that *Enterprise* CIC personnel seemed "astonished and perhaps doubtful of the outcome." Not all felt that way. Givens, for one, knew Butch better than the others: Butch "always had a smile of self assurance, but never appeared arrogant. He impressed me as having all the self-confidence in the world, that he would never run into a situation that he couldn't handle." Givens thought Butch would succeed if anyone could.[22]

That day, with the troops making good progress on Makin, Spruance relieved TG-50.2 of its responsibility for ground-support flights. That left only the normal CAPs and antisubmarine patrols. On the twenty-third, as TG-50.2 fueled about one hundred miles east of Tarawa, Makin was declared secure. To the south at Tarawa the Marines valiantly overcame great resistance and expected to conquer Betio that day.

Butch used the respite to finalize his plans and rest his Black Panthers. He suggested to Radford that the *Enterprise* launch both teams around 0300 the next morning to interdict the usual enemy bombing mission to Tarawa expected to pass about sixty miles west of the ships. The need for radio silence and other considerations never permitted the teams to practice the new intercept tactics aloft during the day.

After its drink of oil, TG-50.2 steamed northwest once again and by early morning on the twenty-fourth had returned on station east of Makin. The night turned out to be cloudy and punctuated with squalls. Shortly after midnight Burd advised Radford that enemy planes were indeed bound for Tarawa. His radio intelligence team had copied radio traffic from three Bettys that had departed Roi around 2230.

The admiral ordered both Black Panther units into battle. At that time the task group was about seventy-five miles east of Makin. Beginning at 0259 the *Enterprise* catapulted the four F6Fs and two TBFs, all carrying extra fuel tanks, for what her deck log called a "special search." The night catapult shot, as always, proved rather thrilling. Evidently the fighter pilots had no trouble joining on their respective TBFs, and the teams independently flew out to the southwest.[23]

In the meantime, one of the Japanese trio succeeded in bombing Tarawa around 0330. However, neither it nor its compatriots ever drew closer than to within ninety to one hundred miles of Radford's ships. That was beyond the distance Butch had planned to operate away from the task group. Dave Sargent in John McInerny's TBF briefly pegged one bogey on radar, but no intercept was possible. Later the Black Panthers intruded onto the radar screen of another carrier task group, whose curious FDO asked what they were up to. Butch replied that they were hunting bogeys and asked if he had any. The FDO said negative, adding that *his* CAP did not get aloft so early. Reluctantly, Butch relented. The two teams climbed over the overcast and started eastward toward the task group in order to orbit and wait for dawn. Most alarmingly, McInerny's engine cut out intermittently, compelling him to add throttle. His fuel consumption increased greatly. Even so, he could not stay with his team but dropped behind to conserve gas.[24]

At about 0516 a brilliant flash of light illuminated the clouds beneath the Black Panthers, who had no idea what it was. From fifty miles away they witnessed the catastrophe that tore asunder the escort carrier *Liscome Bay* and killed 644 of her crew of 959, including Admiral Mullinnix. A part of Turner's Northern Attack Force steaming about twenty miles southwest of Makin, she fell victim to torpedoes from the submarine *I-175* that touched off her thinly protected ammunition magazines.

At 0544 the *Enterprise* dispatched into gray, squally skies the first of a dawn CAP of a dozen VF-2 F6Fs and six VB-6 SBDs for antisubmarine patrol. Butch with five of the six Black Panthers circled overhead, patiently waiting for the ship to let them land. With an unreliable engine and dwindling fuel, McInerny could not afford the luxury of patience. By the time his TBF reached the *Enterprise,* he was more than eager to come on board, but her flight deck was not clear. With the fuel gauge fluttering on empty, McInerny's crew was far from certain whether they would keep their feet dry on this hop. Finally at 0736 the *Big E* brought McInerny on board with only five gallons of gas sloshing in the TBF's tanks. An hour later she landed Butch's other five Black Panthers, along with the dawn CAP and the antisub patrol. The night fighters had endured a long, frustrating, and fatiguing mission of nearly six hours. Yet they made history with the first night-fighter mission ever flown from a carrier.

After rendering their reports, Butch and the rest of the Black Panthers gratefully took to their bunks, but the situation did not quiet down. Beginning at 0900 on the twenty-fourth, the task group intercepted radio traffic from search planes aggressively seeking the American carriers. The Japanese were trying something new. Burd noted call signs of several planes moving in and out of search sectors. One transmitted grid coordinates that appeared to be within fifty miles of the task group. At 1250 and again at 1410, bogeys dotted the radar screens. The carriers scrambled fighters, but the enemy did not approach. On the *Belleau Wood,* John Altemus recorded the day as a "blizzard of General Quarters and Battle Stations." To cap it off, his carrier suffered a collapsed forward elevator that injured ten men.[25]

In fact, a new adversary had entered the lists, one that would take the fight directly to Radford's ships. The previous day eighteen Mitsubishi G4M1 Type 1 land-attack planes from the 752 Air Group (part of the Twenty-fourth Air Flotilla) had reached Roi. They were the first of thirty-seven *rikkōs* to stage in from Kisarazu near Tokyo via Tinian and Truk to the Marshalls. While known as the First Air Group this unit helped conquer the Philippines and Dutch East Indies, deployed briefly to Rabaul to reinforce the Fourth Air Group, and in April wound up in the Central Pacific. Redesignated 752 in November 1942, the group was recalled in December to the homeland to reequip with Type 1 *rikkōs,* and in 1943 it sent detachments to fight in the North Pacific and the Solomons.[26]

The *hikōtaichō,* or senior flight leader, of the 752 Air Group was Lt. Comdr. Nonaka Gorō, "one of the most unusual characters in the Japanese Navy." A regular officer (Eta Jima sixty-first class, 1933), he was perhaps the closest counterpart to Butch the Imperial Navy possessed with regard to his skill, leadership, and especially his deep concern for his men. In that severely hierarchical service where officers routinely inflicted vicious beatings on enlisted personnel, Nonaka was a rare Naval Academy graduate who was genuinely beloved and respected by his aviators, the vast majority of whom were petty officers and seamen. Imbued with the samurai tradition (his father was a general), he was also a profane, sincere, fun-loving leader who liked nothing better than to party with his flyers, who were fiercely loyal to him. One reason behind this devil-may-care attitude toward authority was his bitterness that his older brother Shirō, an Army captain, had been forced to commit suicide for being a ringleader of the February 1936 "Young Officers" revolt in Tokyo. Nonaka Gorō became a renowned troubleshooter sent wherever danger threatened. His superiors regarded him as perhaps their toughest and most experienced bomber commander, and according to one Japanese author, they suffered his indignities only because he was too good a fighter to court-martial.[27]

Now suddenly shoved into battle, Nonaka wrestled with the dilemma of getting his lumbering, highly vulnerable Type 1 *rikkōs* past hordes of defending fighters to deliver their torpedoes against the American carriers. Because of alert enemy radar even the search planes and those on contact or tracking (*shokusetsu*) duty experienced great difficulty surviving within fifty or sixty miles of the deadly flattops. For day search and contact work, Nonaka's answer was to fly at "ultra-low-altitude," just ten meters above the waves, in order to stay below enemy radar. The *rikkōs* were to start this procedure one hundred miles from the enemy's suspected location, but to rise occasionally to look over the area before dropping closer to the sea. Needless to say, this brand of flying demanded skill and proved especially hard on the nerves of the search crews.

Like Radford and Butch, Nonaka felt that the only way the *rikkōs* could be effective against enemy carriers was by night torpedo attack. On 20 November the 755 Air Group had struck at dusk, when dwindling sunlight outlined the ships. Exact timing was tricky, and even with its perfectly delivered assault, the 755 suffered crippling losses. Nonaka was prepared to attack at night without benefit of moonlight and cued only by parachute flares and float lights. He improvised special assault tactics that he dubbed "Whirlwind" (*Tatsumaki*) in honor of those invented by the revered sixteenth-century general Uesugi Kenshin. Guided by contact planes dropping float lights and flares, the strike group was to fan out just short of the enemy fleet. The first element to sight the ships would attack and draw AA gunfire, alerting the rest to the enemy's presence, whereupon all aircraft would swarm to the target. Nonaka knew that such tactics would be extremely difficult to coordinate in darkness and in the face of opposition.[28]

On the afternoon of the twenty-fourth, Nonaka took eleven 752 *rikkōs* on his first search-and-destroy mission seeking carriers lurking off Makin. Two contact planes from the 755 Air Group scouted ahead to locate the enemy and guide Nonaka to the target after dark. For TG-

50.2 the real show began toward dusk. Because of Burd's radio intercepts, Radford knew that something was cooking. By sundown he had the task group "all buttoned up," the dozen warships arrayed in "5-Victor," the main defensive formation of two concentric circles: the inner (radius one thousand yards) with three carriers and the outer (radius twenty-five hundred yards) with three fast battleships and six destroyers. The skies had faded to "pitch black, with sudden rain squalls, yet stars broke through from time to time."[29]

Around 2020 the *Enterprise*'s radar displayed several bogeys that looked to be "flying separately—rather aimlessly, but closing slowly." They were the contact planes, followed by Nonaka's group. Radford slowed the task group to barely above steerageway in order to leave no wake. He instructed his captains not to open fire until he ordered or unless enemy planes directly threatened their ships. Butch remained in constant touch with the *Enterprise* CIC, but the call from the admiral to launch the Black Panther TBFs did not come. Suddenly, at 2054, the *Enterprise* and other ships sounded the torpedo defense alarm. To the *Big E*'s crew assembled at their battle stations, squawk boxes announced two groups of bogeys, one at forty miles and the other at fifteen miles, closing fast. The enemy appeared to split up and circle the task group from opposite sides.[30]

At 2125 a "lone wolf" bomber, marked by blue exhaust flames and the droning of its two engines, materialized aft of the task group. It was one of the contact planes cruising below five hundred feet, and its teammate skulked nearby. Peering up from the *Belleau Wood*'s flight deck, Altemus saw the bomber pass "directly overhead from port quarter to starboard bow" and circle around back astern. The other intruder crossed a mile astern of the ships. One of the seekers dropped a flare about a mile off the port bow.[31]

To almost everyone's surprise, Radford declined to give the order for the ships to fire (or for the *Enterprise* to loose the Black Panthers, for that matter). Monitoring Burd's radio intelligence circuit, he knew that these Japanese had not flashed a sighting report. They were ignorant of his exact location, and he wanted them to remain that way. He also needed to keep his own men unaware of the secret radio intelligence. "I knew my ship commanders thought I was crazy to let that Jap get away," Radford wrote in his memoirs, "but I could not tell them the story at that time." Nonaka's two minions relented, but they would be back the next two evenings.[32]

Later that night Butch's two Black Panther teams went on alert as scheduled. The crews dozed in their respective ready rooms. After about 2200 no fresh bogeys appeared on the task group radar screens, although a few Bettys evidently tried again to bomb Makin and Tarawa. The enforced inactivity gave the night fighters a chance to analyze their tactics. With all of the hullabaloo on the twenty-fourth, no one got much sleep during the day. Thus, Butch recommended to Radford that the teams alternate their duty nights.

The Third Plan

It undoubtedly irritated Butch to have seen that snooper saunter right over the *Enterprise* without any interference, and it got him thinking again. Obviously the time of greatest danger of night attack occurred shortly after sundown, when the shadowers (or "shads," in FDO vernacular) were active. On Thursday morning, 25 November, Thanksgiving Day, Butch proposed to Radford a radical new way of aggressively employing the night fighters, made possible by the word that the airfield on newly conquered Betio Island in Tarawa Atoll was set to open for business. Butch recommended that one Black Panther team take off at sunset and go directly after the snoopers. That was even more risky than previous efforts. For one, the F6Fs could not carry enough fuel to remain aloft until the following dawn. That would force the Black Panthers either to land back on board that night—with the peril of illuminating the carriers to possible submarine attack—or to find their own way to Tarawa. Since the state of the airfield was questionable, Butch received permission to fly there that afternoon to look it over and take photographs.

Early on the twenty-fifth Radford started northwest of Makin. With Pownall's TG-50.1 relinquishing the hot seat to refuel and rest, TG-50.2 temporarily became the most northerly carrier group, closest to enemy air bases in the Marshalls. The three flattops maintained combat air patrols over the ships and also above Makin to prevent a reprise of the fighter-bomber raids the enemy had tried the previous two days against the atoll. During the day Radford moved south, bypassing Makin from the west.

In response to radar contacts, the *Enterprise* scrambled a dozen VF-2 Hellcats at 1135, but they found nothing. However, the Japanese certainly did. Using Nonaka's ultra-low-altitude search tactic for the first time, Warrant Officer Tanaka Kisaku, in command of one of the few surviving 755 Air Group Bettys, chanced to sight TG-50.2 around noon and, more remarkably, lived to tell of it. At 1215 he informed base of three carriers, one battleship, and three cruisers located forty-five miles north of Makin and steaming north at 20 knots. That report riveted Japanese attention to those perilous waters.

Butch departed the *Enterprise* at 1305 and flew southeast to Tarawa to check out the field on Betio and deliver a message from Radford. Worried about what the chewed-up airstrip might do to his own CAG Hellcat 00, he took a VF-2 F6F instead. Another VF-2 F6F went along as well, as did Phillips in a TBF so that he could bring the CAG back in case of plane trouble.[33] At 1500 the three circled Betio, marveled at the destruction, took photos, and carefully observed the airstrip—newly christened Hawkins Field after a fallen Marine hero, 1st Lt. William Deane Hawkins. Butch later related to VF-2 that beginning a mile or more from shore, the wretched island reeked of death.

The air garrison, forty-four F6Fs of Lt. Comdr. Strean's luckless VF-1, had just flown in from the escort carriers *Barnes* and *Nassau* and crowded around the devastated airstrip in the center of the tiny island. Butch's own landing was also touchy, avoiding obstacles and potholes that the newly arrived Seabees had not yet been able to fill. Once safely down, he delivered the admiral's message to the command post. It requested that Capt. Jackson R. Tate, commander of the Tarawa air base, provide twenty-four-hour fighter director liaison and emergency landing arrangements. Unfortunately something there must have gone awry, for during the next two days Radford received no confirmation from Tate.[34]

Before departing, Butch exchanged a few words with Strean, who had been Phillips's roommate at Annapolis. They talked briefly about night tactics and Strean's tests using ship searchlights to pinpoint attackers for night fighters. Strean discovered that the bright beams blinded his own pilots, and so he dismissed the experiment. He recalled Butch as having been "cordial but all business." After his short sojourn Butch gratefully departed Tarawa to join his companions overhead. Knowing that he too might have to land there at night, Phillips also took a good look at the devastated landscape. As the sun neared the western horizon, Butch set course northwest toward home plate about 150 miles away.[35]

Even before Butch's flight could get back, the Japanese had again marked Radford's ships. A second wave of searchers departed Roi at

1300 and found good hunting, ultimately three different groups of American ships north and east of Makin. Nonaka staged thirteen torpedo-armed 752 *rikkōs* from Roi to Maloelap, where they quickly topped off tanks and got away around 1430. Shortly after 1630, Warrant Officer Takano Takashi's Type 1 from the valiant 755 Air Group latched onto TG-50.2 and skillfully used the ultra-low-altitude tactic to maintain contact. At 1645 his radio message placed two "medium-sized" carriers, three battleships, and six screening ships about seventy-five miles northwest of Makin. Fortunately for Radford, Takano's navigation was off by about thirty miles, but the homing signals he transmitted gave Nonaka the correct heading to follow. On the *Enterprise,* Burd quickly relayed the bad news to the admiral, who kept the CAP searching until 1735. To the intense frustration of FDO George Givens, the F6Fs never picked up the wave-hugging snooper before impending darkness compelled their recall. In the meantime, Butch's flight landed around 1705, and the last of the dozen VF-2 CAP fighters came on board the *Enterprise* at 1741.

By 1817, sundown, TG-50.2 had again formed up warily in 5-Victor. The night was clear, with only moderate cloud cover, but the moon had yet to rise. Around 1840 the *North Carolina*'s radar discovered a bogey fifteen to twenty miles north that drew closer and shadowed the task group from off its starboard quarter. That was Takano, who climbed to a safer altitude once darkness compelled the enemy carrier fighters to land.[36]

That evening's attack developed so quickly that Radford would not commit his night fighters despite Butch's fervent request to take the Black Panthers aloft. The rugged conditions at Tarawa weighed heavily on the admiral's mind. Obviously the island was far from ready for the Black Panthers should they need to take refuge there that night.

Just after 1850 the snooper suddenly turned toward the ships. Fully aware this day that the Japanese knew where he was, Radford authorized all ships, except the carriers in the center, to open fire if the opportunity arose. At 1858 the shadower circled eight miles out from the formation. A minute later the *North Carolina*'s lookouts noticed a blinking light northeast over the horizon: Takano announcing his presence to Nonaka with an RO-type float light that ignited on the water and burned brightly with a yellowish orange flame.

Up on the *Big E*'s flag bridge, Radford used the TBS radio to transmit rapid course changes for the task group. He followed his basic tactic of keeping the attackers astern if at all possible. Actual radar contact with the low-flying strike occurred at 1904, when the *North Carolina* discovered a large bogey, perhaps a dozen planes, twenty-four miles northeast. The *Enterprise* sounded GQ, followed by torpedo defense. To the pilots crowded in their ready rooms, the "boots and saddles" trumpet calls meant "Here we go again." Butch smiled at the VF-2 pilots who showed up festooned "with Mae Wests, back packs, whistles, revolvers, and everything that would tend to make life on the South Pacific a luxurious experience."[37]

At 1911 Nonaka, anticipating contact, deployed the strike into three flights to open the Whirlwind assault, but this move was premature. Still well north of TG-50.2, they groped through foul weather. That proved to be a crucial setback, for despite Takano's help, none of Nonaka's pilots knew exactly where the enemy was. In the meantime, Takano flitted around the ships. Beginning at 1916 he dropped a line of float lights about five miles southeast of and parallel to the task group's heading in order to mark its course. Radford responded by swinging around to the southwest.

Following the separate Japanese flights on radar, the *Enterprise* CIC advised Radford that at 1920 two sections of attackers—actually, Nonaka's main body—had rejoined. However, Nonaka inadvertently withdrew from the area and never sighted the ships. His third element orbited about twenty-eight miles north of the task group. Radford turned sharply southeast, to keep them astern. Still trying to set up the strike, Takano released five Type 96 parachute flares ahead of the ships. The Americans admired the adroit performance that silhouetted the task group from astern, but they thought that these particular flares fell too far away and thus illuminated too small an area. Radford swung radically away to the northeast, leaving the flares far astern.

Cued by the flares, however, the third element of Nonaka's force, four Type 1 *rikkōs* under Lt. Natsume Heihachirō, raced south toward what appeared to be two carriers, three cruisers, and five destroyers. At the same time, Takano lunged from the southeast, trying to goose the ships into opening fire and revealing their position. At 1938 Radford cannily withheld permission to fire on the shad, even though it had drawn into range. He executed another radical turn away from the attackers.

A minute later the whole exercise became academic. The raiders had arrived. *Enterprise* lookouts noticed blinking lights, then several screening ships cut loose to protect themselves. Their gun flashes lit up the skies. At 1940 a Betty emerged almost silently out of the gloom ahead of the *North Carolina* and skimmed past at masthead height less than two hundred yards off her starboard side. It was Natsume's wingman, Flight Chief Petty Officer Kitade Masao, who did not have long to live. Two 20-mm guns smothered the land-attack plane with tracers. Just astern of the battleship, the Betty blossomed bright orange flames and plunged meteorlike into the sea two miles beyond. For the next hour its gasoline blazed on the waves.

At 1941 two more Bettys tried to come in from the starboard quarter, but a blizzard of 5-inch VT (variable-time) Mark 32 proximity-fuze shells from the battleships promptly burst in their midst. That appeared to discourage them from pressing their attacks near enough to release their fish. At 1947 one Betty charged from the northwest, but by swinging the task group around yet again, Radford presented only a poor attack angle. The last effort occurred a minute later, when an aircraft challenged the *North Carolina* and the destroyer *Brown*. At six thousand yards the battlewagon's massive starboard 5-inch battery quickly got on target, and the enemy relented. Soon TG-50.2 ceased fire after a most exciting hour of cat and mouse with the Japanese.

Radford felt fortunate that one or more of his ships had not swallowed a torpedo. To him it seemed that the enemy had retired "for no apparent reason." Burd opined that the enemy main body must not have seen the ships, for their radio operators did not "sound excited." Indeed they were not, for during most of the attack Nonaka's other nine *rikkōs* were floundering in thick clouds some seventy-five miles north of the battle area, too far away to unleash their Whirlwind. Even so, in what the Japanese dubbed the Second Gilbert Islands Air Battle, Natsume's three surviving crews claimed two carriers sunk at the cost of Kitade's aircraft! In turn, TG-50.2 suffered no damage whatsoever, while the *North Carolina* received credit for one bomber and another as a probable kill. At the same time, a couple of contact planes used flares and float lights to tease Turner's TF-52 near Makin, fooling the admiral into believing that he had driven off a major attack.[38]

As if the evening had not been not sufficiently thrilling, the destroyer *Radford* (DD-446) managed a neat bit of revenge. After his namesake made a sound contact at 2045, Radford detached her to investigate. With a series of excellent depth-charge runs, the *Radford* evidently destroyed the *I-19*, the sub that had sunk the *Wasp* (CV-7) on 15 September 1942 and gashed the *North Carolina*.

Only involuntary spectators to what transpired after sundown, the Black Panthers would much rather have been in the air. Butch discovered what it was like to experience an enemy air attack from a ship's deck rather than the cockpit of a fighter, and he did not care for it at all. Radford gave the no. 1 team the balance of the night off. He wanted them well rested and ready to meet the air assault he expected the next evening.

15

26 November
1943

*"They threw the book
at us tonight"*

In the early hours of Friday, 26 November, Rear Admiral Radford's Task Group 50.2 steamed southward from Makin toward Tarawa. Radford anticipated one more day and, especially, night in "hot waters" gravely threatened by air attack, but after that, big changes were in the offing. On the twenty-fifth Vice Admiral Spruance had announced a major reshuffling of all the carrier task groups, to take place over the next two days. On 27 November Radford himself was to transfer his flag from the *Enterprise* to the *Saratoga* and take over Rear Adm. Ted Sherman's TG-50.4, while the *Big E* and the *Belleau Wood* were to join Rear Admiral Montgomery's *Essex* to reform TG-50.3. No one knew what would become of Butch's experimental night missions after Radford left.[1]

For the *Enterprise*, morning operations proved routine, with the usual CAP and antisub patrols. Also becoming routine were the ubiquitous enemy snoopers. Late that morning Flight Chief Petty Officer Kamimura Shunzō's Type 1 *rikkō*, one of seven from the 752 Air Group on search from Roi, flashed word of one carrier, three battleships, and other vessels forty miles northwest of Tarawa. Then the radioman urgently tapped out the letters HI-HI-HI, meaning "enemy planes approaching." Thereafter Kamimura went missing without a trace. Evidently he sighted TG-50.2, but no U.S. aircraft did him in, at least intentionally. The best guess is that while trying evasive action at ultra-low level, the *rikkō* flew into the sea. It would not be the only mysterious disappearance that day.

"I'm Going Flying"

That morning Butch and the other Black Panthers slept in, then prepared for the evening's activities. The no. 1 team went on alert for launch at dusk, with the no. 2 team on standby. Butch appeared well rested and eager to go. According to his friend Lt. Comdr. Bob Jackson, the *Enterprise* air operations officer, he was "enthused" about his new night tactics and "seemed particularly anxious to be in the air that evening."[2]

That afternoon Butch invited the press to his private haunt, the no. 1 or CAG ready room. He was in rare form. Expounding on night attacks while leaning forward in his comfortable black leather recliner, he said, according to Associated Press correspondent Eugene Burns, something like this:

> Those Japs can't attack us by day and make it profitable any more. Our Hellcats and AA guns are too much for them. Two weeks ago, at Rabaul, one fighter squadron knocked down approximately fifty planes in one afternoon, with the loss of two of their own. The Japs have got the word. All right then. So what's the answer? They know it takes torpedoes hitting below the water line to sink our ships permanently. And the only time to sock their fish home is at night when they can avoid our fighters.
>
> And those Japs know that we must close with their land bases to protect our beach landings, as we are now doing at Tarawa and Makin. So they play cagey and lay low until we steam within easy range of their night-flying Mitsubishi bombers.
>
> Last night five torpedo wakes were counted in our formation, and then they used only twelve planes. We'll have to depend on more than AA's and luck to answer. The Good Book just won't open at the right chapter and verse every time. Once the Japs get set on this night business, it's going to be curtains for us, unless—.

Burns considered this the normally laconic Butch's "longest speech."[3]

At 1554 the *Enterprise* dispatched two VT-6 TBFs east to Tarawa to deliver messages to lay the groundwork for the expected Black Panther mission that evening. Radford asked Captain Tate to guard VHF radio channels and warned of the possible landing of the Black Panthers. He wanted the field to furnish boundary lights, if possible.

Even as Radford and Butch laid out their plans, the Japanese prepared their own. At 1430 four Type 1 *rikkōs* under flight chief petty officers Yamada Yoshinobu and Takahashi Shin-ichi of the 755 Air Group and Kawakita Mitsuo and Mitsuyama Shinji from the 752 Air Group departed Maloelap for contact duty to amplify sightings previously made. Lt. Comdr. Nonaka followed at 1515 with sixteen Type 1s armed with torpedoes. This day he divided his strike into smaller *chūtai* (divisions) of four planes in place of the usual nine or six and also increased the number of *shōtai* (sections) by making them each two instead of three planes. He hoped this more flexible flight organization would facilitate his Whirlwind night torpedo tactics.[4]

At 1605 Nonaka passed over Arno Atoll, south-southeast of Maloelap, where he became concerned about the horrible weather, ten-tenths cloud cover. At that time engine trouble forced Reserve Ens. Takuma Masao from the second *chūtai* to turn back, leaving fifteen attackers. Thirty minutes later, when Nonaka crossed over Mili, the weather was still poor but not enough to hide his strike group from radar and an alert watcher peering through the periscope of the submarine *Plunger* (SS-179) on station there for air rescue duty. At 1650 her skipper, Lt. Comdr. Raymond H. Bass, counted fourteen Bettys headed southeast. He moved his sub a bit farther out and at 1715 risked surfacing to send his report.[5]

The *Plunger*'s sighting occurred the exact instant the contact planes flown by Kawakita and Mitsuyama latched onto TG-50.2 west of Tarawa. Their excited radio messages—prefaced with TE-TE-TE, for "enemy sighted"—crackled in the earphones of Lieutenant (jg) Burd's radio intelligence unit on the *Enterprise*. Burd swiftly realized that these searchers were working with a strike group leader. Radford received the *Plunger*'s message, the first of Burd's intercepts, and a sighting report of an enemy plane from the destroyer *Boyd* (DD-544) all about the same time. Probably tipped off by the *Enterprise* CIC, Butch reacted swiftly. Radford later recalled, "On the bridge, as I decided what to do, Lieutenant Commander O'Hare approached me and requested that I send one of the Black Panther groups out." The admiral agreed.[6]

After getting permission to sortie, Butch called Lt. Comdr. Phil Phillips and Ens. Andy Skon up to Flag Plot high in the island. Skon remembered Butch's words:

> Phil, we are launching as dark sets in tonight. We'll go off first, then we'll join up on you, Phil, after you get airborne. CIC will get us joined up and will get you, Phil, close enough so your radar operator can fix you behind a Betty. You'll close all three of us close in behind the Betty with your radar, then say "lifting up and out," and we'll take him with our twelve guns.
>
> We'll probably not get back aboard, but will have to go find Tarawa for a landing. The strip was just taken yesterday, for Seabee repair. Won't have lights. Won't have a homer. We'll be lucky if we even find the damned place, and then don't fall in a pothole.

According to Skon, "That was vintage Butch, smiling and with his feet propped up on a second chair." Butch added, "Get a bite to eat now, you two, and your crew, Phil. We'll be late for supper. Be ready for the 'man planes' call to come any time around 1800."[7]

Before going down to the wardroom, Butch stopped in Air Plot and reported his status to Jackson as "half-way between a moment's notice and a scramble."[8]

With at least one snooper nosing around, Lt. (jg) George Givens, the *Enterprise* and TG-50.2 fighter director officer, was eager to polish it off before dark. At 1708 a bogey appeared on radar sixteen miles to the west-southwest. Because the *Big E*'s flight deck was tied up recovering the two TBFs back from Tarawa, Givens requested that the *Belleau Wood* dispatch a dusk CAP. At 1712 she obliged with four VF-24 F6Fs led by Lt. Robert P. Ross. Ten minutes later, after proceeding about twenty miles west, Ross spotted a Betty skulking some fifteen miles beyond. Realizing his danger, the Japanese plane commander belatedly dropped close to the waves and tried to outdistance the pursuing fighters, but at 1730 Ross's division caught up about forty miles out. Splitting up, the two pairs of F6Fs rolled into flat-side runs from opposite sides of the target. Ross's third pass ignited the Betty's port engine, causing the port wing to drop. The bomber exploded on the water. To the task group Givens delightedly announced, "Splash one Betty!" Ross had downed one of two 755 Air Group contact planes commanded by

Yamada and Takahashi. In the meantime, the other had succumbed at 1725 about twenty-five miles northwest of Makin, victim of an independent intercept by the FDO of TG-50.3 using Lt. James D. Billo's four VF-18 F6Fs from the *Bunker Hill*.[9]

At 1745, while Butch was enjoying dinner in the *Enterprise*'s wardroom, the squawk box interrupted with, "Night fighters, man your planes!" He fixed a sandwich from the rest of his steak and jumped up to go. To a steward who offered a dish of strawberry ice cream he responded, "No thanks. Keep it cold until I get back tonight." On the way out of the wardroom, Butch encountered Ens. Claude Dickerson, the "mustang" who served with the aviation ordnance gang, and asked, "What are you doing here?" Dickerson replied that he had completed disarming all but the ready aircraft, a precaution in case of torpedo attack, and had pulled his men up from below the third deck to "sweat out" the evening. In turn he queried the CAG as to his destination, to which Butch cheerfully answered, "I'm going flying."[10]

Butch hastened to the CAG ready room to grab his flight gear. United Press correspondent Charles P. Arnot saw him emerge from there: "Stocky Butch was pulling on his helmet over his close-cropped black hair. He had widened a bit in girth in recent months, but the extra poundage had not lessened his ability to fly a Hellcat. One of the pilots shouted, 'Go gettem, Butch.' O'Hare's reply was a grin. Then he dashed up a ladder to the flight deck."[11]

In Air Plot, Jackson encountered Butch again on his way up to the flag bridge for a last briefing from Radford. Butch smiled and said something about "having to see the man." Jackson observed his pleasure at getting another crack at the enemy, "a zest for adventure—another opportunity for a hunting trip, which . . . Butch loved." The admiral ordered him to intercept the expected enemy night-strike group and be prepared to land either back on board the *Enterprise* or at Tarawa.[12]

Down on the flight deck Butch clambered into 00, his personal Hellcat, and waved to Radford watching from the flag bridge. While helping the CAG adjust his straps and get situated, the plane captain, Omar Baxter Johnson, aviation machinist's mate first class, offered, "Luck, Mr. O'Hare." A smiling Butch replied, "Hell, we don't need luck with these cookies." Plane handlers positioned Butch's F6F on one of the forward catapults and Skon's on the other. Phillips, Lieutenant (jg) Rand, and gunner Al Kernan manned Tare-97 spotted behind the two fighters.[13]

At 1753, even as the Black Panthers made ready to go, the battleship

Indiana's radar registered a bogey twenty-seven miles northeast. Six minutes later a second intruder materialized twenty-three miles to the southeast. Both contacts also appeared on the *Enterprise*'s screens and precipitated a crucial change in plan. They were Kawakita's and Mitsuyama's contact *rikkōs,* which had skillfully used ultra-low-altitude flying to evade detection by the wide-ranging fighters while stalking the ships silhouetted by the setting sun. At 1800 the last of the day CAP, Ross's victorious VF-24 division, thumped down on the *Belleau Wood.* The stage was set for the Black Panthers.

At 1800, with the sun nearing the western horizon, Butch gave the catapult officer, Lt. Walt Chewning, a wink along with his salute (as Jackson later wrote to Rita, "An unusual procedure, yet so thoroughly typical of your husband"). His F6F rocketed down the deck, followed by Skon's. Behind them the catapult crew helped position the TBF for its shot. Once the launch was completed, Radford deployed TG-50.2 into the customary 5-Victor defensive formation.[14]

The original intent was for all three aircraft to join up immediately before setting out after the Japanese. However, before Phillips could even get the TBF aloft, Givens, the FDO, suddenly altered the plan. Despite the destruction of the first snooper, wily Japanese were still tracking the task group. Hoping that Butch could finish off the shadowers before dark and perhaps end the threat of attack once and for all, Givens vectored the two Hellcats eastward after one of the bogeys that bedeviled his radar screen. Should Butch not be successful, Givens still expected to rendezvous the F6Fs with the TBF prior to sunset.

The FDO's improvisation, however, certainly riled the admiral. Although Radford acknowledged CIC's "intense desire to get one of these snoopers," he felt that Givens "took advantage of the situation." On 4 December he wrote that sending the fighters out minus the TBF was "contrary to instructions," was done "without his knowledge," and "proved to be a serious error." Radford countermanded the FDO's orders as soon as he learned of them and worried—justifiably, as events showed—that the F6Fs and TBF would not succeed in getting joined before dark.[15]

On the way out Butch climbed only to eight hundred feet as he vainly sought the wave-hugging shadower. Soon after, Givens recalled the two F6Fs. About ten miles north of the ships, Phillips glimpsed Butch pointed northwest toward the outer perimeter where attackers often rendezvoused. However, he was slower than the F6Fs and could not keep up. Within a few minutes the bogey faded from the *Enterprise*'s radar screen, but no one thought the snoopers had given up. In fact, they had simply dropped as low as they dared. Their dark green camouflage blended in with the sea, rendering them invisible to Butch and Skon hunting above.

The sun set at 1819, and after the last light disappeared, the sky became quite dark, with no moon. Butch, Skon, and Phillips all flew in nearly total blackness, with no horizon or other discernible points of reference. They depended completely on their instruments, visible in muted glow. Phillips, for one, kept his cockpit lights off to maintain his night vision and flashed them only briefly to reactivate the luminescent paint on the dials. Beneath the Black Panthers the unseen sea was calm, barely stirred by the 5 knots of wind blowing from the south-southeast. Skon remembered "a dark, scuddy overcast whose bottoms were at about 1,500 feet." He kept formation on Butch by glancing at the blue section light on 00's turtleback and the bright engine exhaust flare—a task requiring intense concentration on his part, given his leader's rapid changes in course.[16]

For the next twenty minutes Givens kept Butch and Skon busy to the west and north hunting snoopers. The F6Fs repeatedly accelerated away from the TBF, with Phillips cutting inside Butch's turns in a futile attempt to catch up. The rendezvous would have to wait. The ships had established radar contact with three separate bogeys, one to the southeast and the others out to the northwest. At least one was a ghost and the other two the contact planes. By 1840 Butch and Skon were nearing the bogey detected thirty miles northwest of the task group.

Phillips had taken the same northwesterly vector into the deepening darkness. Down in the radioman's compartment Hazen Rand squinted into the green ASB radar scope. He set the range on the twenty-eight-mile scale and pointed the wing antennas directly forward. Soon he discerned a bogey seven miles ahead. Shifting to the seven-mile scale, he used the radar to home in on the target and called off the decreasing distances, hoping to get close enough to switch to the more precise two-mile scale. He coached Phillips to within forty-five hundred yards before the contact faded. Phillips never saw this bogey. Subsequently he circled and pursued several more radar contacts but never sighted any enemy planes.[17]

At 1850 one of the contact planes dropped a float light far out to the northwest and astern of the task group. It served as a base point to orient Nonaka. Skon recollected that the shadowing Bettys had "spread out around the task force, low on the water, at the fringe of the ship's radar for their low altitude, and momentarily blinking a white light now and then—apparently a prearranged signal technique among them." Upon later reflection he decided that some or even most of the flickering lights were actually float lights bobbing on the sea. At one point Givens informed Butch of bogeys all around him and hoped he would see their exhausts. Yet Butch had to reply, "No contact." In Skon's words the Bettys, "maneuvering and invisible in the now total darkness, could not be lined up on long enough even for a chance hit." After playing tag with Kawakita and Mitsuyama for nearly an hour, the F6Fs broke off to try to find the TBF.[18]

Prompted by the float light, Nonaka's strike group of fifteen Type 1 *rikkōs* established visual contact at 1900 with one friendly contact plane. That shadower pointed the way toward what was believed to be three American carriers, one battleship, four cruisers, and two destroyers hidden in the darkness just to the southeast. Nonaka deployed his aircraft much like a fisherman "spreading a net," so that one flight was bound to find the enemy and unleash the Whirlwind assault.

At the same time that Nonaka's *rikkōs* fanned out, the *Indiana's* radar registered two bogeys to the northwest, the first (one of the two shadowers) at five miles, the second (at least part of Nonaka's force) at eleven miles. The Black Panthers were patrolling farther out, about twenty to twenty-five miles northwest. Radford quickly executed an emergency left turn to swing the task group southeast away from the incoming Japanese. It would be the first of many such maneuvers to prevent the attackers from gaining favorable position ahead for their torpedo runs.

The First Attack on TG-50.2

At 1905 Nonaka's own flight spotted American ships looming in the distance. He radioed the order to "charge" (*totsugeki*, sent as TO-TO-TO) to alert the other aircraft. That also prompted Kawakita and Mitsuyama in the two contact planes to release the target course indicator float lights and illuminating parachute flares. On the *Enterprise,* Burd relayed the daunting intercept to the admiral, who immediately released all ships, except the carriers, to open fire at any targets within effective range. Within seconds several ships were blasting away with their potent 5-inch Mark 32 proximity-fuzed VT projectiles against the contacts their CICs had tracked on fire-control radars.

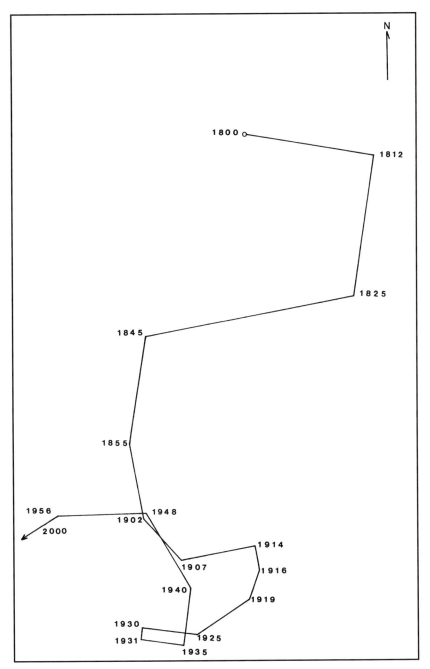

N

1800

1812

1825

1845

1855

1956   1948
     1902
2000

1914

1907   1916

1940   1919

1930
1931   1925

1935

Track Chart of Task Group 50.2, Evening of 26 November 1943

The first to shoot was the "*Showboat*"—the formidable *North Carolina*. At 1906 her entire port 5-inch battery of ten guns shattered the stillness with brilliant gun flashes and loud booms. Bursting shells ripped into what looked like a large flock of planes about five thousand yards north and closing her port quarter rapidly at low altitude. Under intense AA these aircraft quickly showed their tails. The *North Carolina*'s rude greeting caused this flight to back off and await a more advantageous opportunity to attack.[19]

At the same time that the *North Carolina* was foiling the first lunge, another batch to the northwest were menacing the task group from its starboard quarter. These raiders turned southeast about sixty-five hundred yards out to parallel the task group's course. Soon more steel than had been hurled against the first group barred their way, when the *Indiana*, the *Massachusetts*, part of the *North Carolina*'s starboard 5-inch battery, and at least one destroyer thundered away at them. The *Fletcher* (DD-445) claimed two Bettys shot down by her gunners and those from the *Indiana*, while the *North Carolina* thought she had finished a third. That happened not to be the case, for no flaming wreckage resulted. It is not certain whether these *rikkōs* fired any fish, although at 1912 the *Radford* warned of a torpedo wake that might have come from one of these Bettys.

The AA guns put on an incredible light and sound show. As John Altemus on the *Belleau Wood* remembered it, "The streaks of orange, red, and white tracers lit up the whole sky. The brilliant stars overhead paled into insignificance." Gene Burns thought the firing resounded like "all the steel mills in the world exploding." To him the battlewagons appeared to be "pitching up a hundred rainbows of hot lead." What Nonaka and his men made of the blinding gun flashes, fiery ribbons of tracers, and tempest of shell fragments is not recorded in available accounts.[20]

While the two lead groups confronted the target, the two contact planes, dubbed "Tojo the Lamplighters" by the ships, moved in to do their jobs. At 1907 one of them released four target course indicator float lights about eight miles south and ahead of the task group. Radford responded with an emergency turn 60 degrees left to steam northeast and again to forestall enemy planes from utilizing the dangerous attack angles ahead.

The second contact plane put in its appearance around 1912 some four to five miles to the west of the task group. This "Lamplighter" loosed the first of what would be a long, "brilliant stream" of twenty-four to thirty parachute flares that drifted eerily down. Radford described his ships as being "lighted up as if in daylight." To Burns the flares resembled "huge bridge lights over a deep stream." They cast strong shadows onto the *Enterprise*'s flight deck. Unexpectedly aided by the flares, however, the entire *North Carolina* starboard 5-inch battery pummeled a section of two or three Bettys sneaking in from the west. At 1915 one aircraft streamed bright flames and plunged into the water, where its gasoline blazed for at least fifteen minutes.[21]

Expecting torpedo planes to gather in the direction opposite from where the flares were being released, Radford swung right 90 degrees at 1914 to head directly south toward the flares and keep any attackers astern. Within the next five minutes he had turned right another 70 degrees, ending up on a southwesterly course aimed away from what had developed into the largest radar contact of bandits circling to attack.

In the meantime, between 1918 and 1924, about five planes, widely spaced from the southwest to the southeast, closed the formation rapidly at low altitude and mainly from ahead. Warnings of several torpedo wakes echoed over the TBS circuit. At 1918 one Betty crossed the *North Carolina*'s starboard bow at very close range, roared down the starboard side, and withdrew astern. Out to the west another relented and turned away. From 1920 to 1924 the *Indiana*'s port 5-inch and 40-mm guns blasted one enemy group four thousand yards to the east and claimed one, while the *North Carolina*'s port 5-inch group no. 2 roughed up one or two planes out to the southeast that retreated before being sighted.

In retrospect it appears that the Japanese first wave comprised about half of the fifteen *rikkōs*. One Betty fell to the torrent of AA fire. It seems that the other half of the strike orbited north of the battle area, looking for the opportunity to attack, but apparently Radford's adroit maneuvers confused them. In addition, these Bettys soon found more trouble in the form of the first night aerial opposition ever mounted from a carrier.

"Scratch One of the Bastards"

Years afterward Lt. Jim Trousdale described the tense atmosphere in the crowded *Enterprise* Combat Information Center during the night battle of 26 November. FDO George Givens and his assistants, of whom Trousdale was one, were "hunched around the plotting table in CIC, working out the interception, plotting in the two groups of approaching Japs and the small group of 'friendlies' going out to meet them." Givens had not reunited the Black Panthers, so Butch's section and Phillips's lone TBF were operating independently about twenty-five miles north of the task group. While the first wave assaulted the ships, Givens directed Phillips against what appeared to be the biggest group of bandits hanging back some distance away. Trousdale outlined the technique, noting how the FDO had to "swing the interceptors in behind and slightly below the enemy, but not too far behind, or it will turn into a tail-chase with the fighter never catching up." This maneuver needed to be done "just right, the first time." According to Trousdale, Givens succeeded in placing Phillips "just astern of the Japs, in perfect position." Unfortunately he could not do the same with Butch and Skon.[22]

Thus, the FDO adroitly put Phillips just behind a flight of Japanese waiting to go after the ships. On his ASB radar screen Rand discerned bogeys at three miles and skillfully guided Phillips to within about two thousand yards of them. Suddenly Phillips noticed the blue exhaust flares of enemy planes—as many as six twin-engine bombers in formation, he estimated, but more likely half that number at most. Radar also apparently disclosed another formation of "six" planes nearby "in a parallel row," but again that was probably double the actual Japanese strength.

Phillips joyfully announced on the radio, "I have them in sight, attacking." R. W. Gregory, Jr., seaman first class, one of the radar plotters, vividly remembers the excitement when this message resounded in CIC. Phillips stalked one of the bandits from directly astern. At 190 knots the TBF enjoyed a speed advantage of about 30 knots over the unwary Japanese. Peering through his Mark 30 torpedo director sight–cum–gun sight, he squeezed the trigger of his twin .50s when Rand gave the range as two hundred yards. Blasting away with streams of bright tracers, he kept on coming "right up the tail, 6-o'clock level behind" the Betty before breaking off at fifty yards and pulling out to the left. To Al Kernan in the turret, "the two .50-calibers in the wings felt like they were tearing the plane apart." The TBF's exhaust hidden by its flame dampener, the quarry had no idea that danger threatened until tracers appeared.[23]

As the Avenger recovered out to the side, Kernan saw "the surprised enemy opening up from his top turret, his blister gun, and his tail, the heaviest and most accurate fire coming from the 20-mm. [cannon] in the tail." The streams of tracers left Phillips fondly wishing for a bulletproof glass windscreen. It was already too late for the Betty. The TBF's incendiaries had ignited fuel in its left wing root. Kernan returned fire with his turret gun. Almost immediately the Japanese exploded in brilliant red flames. The overwhelmingly bright muzzle flashes and tracers (loaded one in three) from Kernan's .50-caliber machine gun temporarily blinded him and prevented him from seeing through his gun sight. Just to be able to aim, he subsequently unbuckled his safety belt and leaned way forward alongside the gun.[24]

The stricken Betty jettisoned its torpedo and lurched into the water a thousand yards beyond. The kill took place about twenty-five miles north-northeast of TG-50.2. Flaming gasoline spread over a large area—according to Kernan, a "red smear on the black water"—that burned until about 2030. Kernan noticed tracers from other Bettys evidently shooting at each other, so very likely the ambush had disrupted the flight's cohesion. At 1923 Phillips radioed in triumph, "Scratch one of the bastards." That elicited more cheers and back-slapping in the *Enterprise* CIC.[25]

Despite the Betty's imminent destruction, one of its gunners had retaliated with a Parthian shot. From three o'clock low, a 7.7-mm incendiary round tore through the aluminum-skinned bottom of the TBF. Passing just forward of the armor plate and into the radio compartment, the bullet holed Rand's left shoe and grazed his foot, but he failed to notice the wound immediately. He happened to be rather too busy, given that the fiery slug was "bouncing around in the compartment, setting fires in a couple locations, including a rack of flares." To smother the flames, he grabbed a blanket packed around the stinger gun, part of the survival gear carried for a possible Tarawa visit. Only a little later did Rand feel "something wet" and notice his left shoe "overflowing with blood."[26]

To the east of Phillips's location, Givens maneuvered Butch and Skon against another part of the Japanese strike group. The *Enterprise* squawk box informed anxious listeners on the ship, "Now O'Hare and Skon are closing on a bogey." Skon recalled that Butch and he "did fire several times at momentary fleeting shadows, and Butch thought he connected once, but there was no splash or fire." The VF-2 action report noted two Bettys as targets. Skon thought the enemy was now well alerted by the broad bands of tracers from the twelve Brownings wielded by the Hellcats—massive streams of red created by tracers loaded in a ratio of one to four. He was correct. A note in the 752 Air Group report stated that at 1925 "three or more enemy night fighters" intercepted the group but caused no damage.[27]

Japanese gunners repaid the compliment. About this time, listeners on the *Enterprise* heard Butch say rather dryly on the radio, "My God. There's a tracer coming through my wing. What a funny sensation." Jackson's letter to Rita placed this message seven minutes prior to Butch's last transmission, making it about 1923. After their own encounter, Butch and Skon noticed a "ball of flaming wreckage" several miles to the west and turned toward what was Phillips's first kill.[28]

Fateful Rendezvous

Butch asked the FDO, "Can you join us on Phil?" Givens replied, "Affirmative." In Skon's words, Butch wanted to try to "bring the original plan into play" by uniting the two Black Panther elements about twenty-five miles northwest of the ships. That was out near where the contact Betty had dropped the first yellowish orange float light about forty minutes before. Givens told Phillips to orbit at Angels 2 (two thousand feet) and directed Butch, "Vector 270 [degrees], Angels 2. Phil is 12 o'clock [directly ahead], ten miles." In fact, all the Black Panthers stayed lower than their assigned altitude, to keep under the low cloud base.[29]

While orbiting in a wide turn but before he could climb as instructed, Phillips unexpectedly picked out the exhaust flares of two Bettys flying at his same altitude (five hundred feet) about fifteen hundred yards ahead. Unlike his first opponents, this *shōtai* had very likely already fired its torpedoes against the task group. Now the pair were circling in a predetermined rendezvous area into which the Black Panthers had unwittingly trespassed. Phillips selected the bomber on the right, followed it through a slight right turn, and gained slowly, again with about a 30-knot speed advantage.

Givens advised Butch that Phillips was at eleven o'clock (almost directly ahead, but slightly to port) and four miles distant—almost near enough to see. Butch also glimpsed enemy planes. Consequently he warned Phillips, "Turn on your lights. I'm going to start shooting." Skon recalled Butch referring to the "turtleback light," Arnot thought he specifically mentioned the "toplight," while Burns recorded "cockpit light." All of these comments referred to the white dorsal recognition light on the TBF's headrest immediately behind the pilot. Butch added, "Phil, this is Butch. I think I got me a Jap."[30]

Although Phillips did not want to spook the Betty that he was stealthily pursuing, he also did not care for the idea of Butch possibly filling the TBF with lead. Consequently he snapped, "Roger. Wilco. Out." Then he blinked his recognition light. The Betty responded with evasive maneuvers, none particularly violent, so Phillips continued to close. From two hundred yards behind and slightly to starboard of the target, he opened with a healthy burst, perhaps forty to fifty rounds, from each of his two .50s, again with immediate positive results. Holed in the right wing root and cockpit, the Betty flamed spectacularly. Kernan added a squirt from his turret gun. The Japanese pilot attempted a controlled high-speed ditching and left a trail of burning fuel three hundred yards long on the water before the *rikkō* disintegrated and sank. Some crewmen apparently survived and got into a raft. Shortly after this fight, Kernan fired a few rounds at another Betty crossing under the TBF's tail but saw no obvious damage. Phillips resumed orbiting to port so Butch could effect the rendezvous.

At 1928 Phillips proudly radioed that he had downed another twin-engine bomber, so the *Enterprise* squawk box announced that Butch had got one bomber and Phillips his second. In the past five minutes Phillips had destroyed a pair of Type 1 *rikkōs*, a colossal feat for a slow torpedo plane. Butch and Skon also saw the flames marking the demise of the second bomber.

Immediately after the second fight, Kernan heard Rand call out over the intercom, "I'm hit." Through an understandable oversight, Rand had simultaneously transmitted his belated cry of pain over the TBF's radio transmitter, leading some on the *Enterprise* wrongly to ascribe it to Butch. Phillips instructed Kernan to help Rand, so he dropped from the turret into the radio compartment, checked Rand's wound, and asked the CO whether he should administer morphine. He was shocked to hear Phillips reply, "No, we will need the radar again." While there, Kernan fought the bucking TBF as he hoisted a fresh hundred-round magazine into his turret gun.[31]

With rendezvous imminent, Skon felt that CIC "did a fine job of getting Butch and Andy lined up well behind Phil and then slowly closing the gap." He thought then—and believes that Butch felt so, too—that Phillips was busy pursuing still a third Betty. The two F6Fs maneuvered with Butch "sightly on the outside of the shallow port turn; and Andy at Butch's 7 o'clock, tucked in close and slightly lower." Their intention was to assume a tight vee formation on the TBF that they expected would become visible out ahead, identified by its recognition light.

Skon recalled, "Butch quietly spoke up on the radio, 'Which side do you want, Andy?' This was the typically thoughtful, considerate Butch." As Skon was "already hanging slightly low and on the inside of the port turn," he replied, "I'll take port." Butch responded with a "Roger" (his last recorded transmission). Skon assumed the 8:30 position on Butch, able to keep his F6F "dimly in sight." He remembered the Hellcat's turtleback showing its blue section light and also relied on the bright bluish flare from Butch's engine exhaust stacks to keep station.[32]

According to the VT-6 action report (discussed below), Phillips supposedly switched on the TBF's running lights (red light on port wing tip, green on starboard wing tip, and white taillight) and kept them on during the join-up. However, this seems to be an error. At most Phillips showed his white upper recognition light and perhaps also the ventral red recognition light. Skon never actually saw the TBF and could not say what lights were on. Staying below the cloud base, Phillips flew in a gentle left turn at between 1,000 and 1,200 feet of altitude. The two F6Fs approached at about the same height, subject to the individual variation of their aircraft altimeters.[33]

While awaiting rendezvous, an obviously delighted Phillips exulted on the radio, "This is duck soup, Butch, if you ride in on their slipstream and then just pick them off one at a time." A moment later he asked, "Butch, this is Phil. Did you see my second one drop?" In just a few seconds, though, triumph would turn into tragedy.[34]

Now back in the turret, Kernan saw a white light abruptly emerge out the darkness to port and approach the TBF from the south. He requested permission to fire, but before Phillips could reply, Kernan immediately identified the aircraft as one of the Black Panthers, followed by the other. He recalled that the two F6Fs "slid suddenly in, coming down across our tail from above and aft." With the lead Hellcat displaying its bright white dorsal recognition light, Kernan saw its pilot clearly, but his imagination might have subsequently filled out the detail in the undoubtedly powerful portrait that appears in his memoirs: "Canopy back, goggles up, yellow Mae West, khaki shirt, and helmet, seated aggressively forward, riding the plane hard, looking like the tough Medal of Honor recipient, American Ace he was, Butch O'Hare's face was sharply illuminated by his canopy light for one brief last moment."[35]

The F6F closing on the TBF's starboard wing switched off its lights when about four hundred feet distant. At almost the same time, Kernan noticed a third plane unexpectedly materializing above and behind the other two and crossing over to starboard. For a second he wondered who this could be, because he had both of his teammates in clear view. Kernan alerted the skipper to the presence of the intruder. Simultaneously over radio and intercom Phillips evidently said something like, "Butch, there's a Jap joining up on you, coming in high. I'm instructing Kernan to shoot at him." Kernan remembers the message as "Butch, this is Phil. There's a Jap on your tail. Kernan, open fire." In his wartime diary Givens recorded a totally different version of Phillips's warning: "——dammit! There's more than three of us here. Cut loose Tony [*sic*], cut loose, cut loose!" Whatever Phillips said, Skon never copied the transmission.[36]

According to the VT-6 report, Kernan shot at the trespasser when it was about two hundred yards away, whereas Butch's F6F was considerably closer to the TBF. The Japanese returned fire, but not at the Avenger. In his memoir, however, Kernan stated that the Betty fired first, and that he responded. The VT-6 report gave Kernan's burst as about thirty rounds, but now he recollects shooting much longer, nearly emptying his hundred-round ammo can.

From the radioman's seat in the TBF's belly, Rand watched through the small starboard window, behaving, as he later joked, like a "rubbernecking tourist." Having temporarily secured the radar during the join-up—the ASB-1's antennas did not point astern—his duty now became "to observe visually when Butch ordered our planes to turn on their identification lights to assist a rendezvous." He glimpsed the intruder poised "above and almost directly behind Butch" and saw its tracers, evidently from the 7.7-mm machine gun in the nose, "flash down to the back of" the F6F, while Kernan's tracers were "arching *over* Butch's Hellcat at the Betty."[37]

Kernan watched as the Betty "broke away across our group to disappear in the darkness behind Skon." The F6F flying to starboard then crossed over to the other side. As the Hellcat dropped out of view, it seemed to release something that floated down almost vertically at a speed too slow for anything but a parachute. Something "whitish-gray" appeared below, perhaps a parachute or, much more likely, the splash of the plane plunging into the sea.[38]

At the same time, Skon, on the TBF's port side, had kept close attention to "Butch's shadow of a plane" flying to starboard. Without warning, "a two second stream of fire lit up, beginning at my 12:30 slightly up and slicing down at about a 15 degree down angle to my 3 o'clock, starboard beam, where it disappeared from view." Skon added, "It was

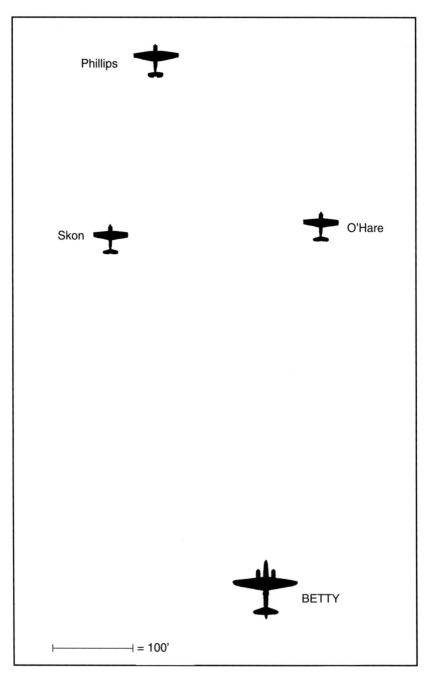

The Ambush of Butch O'Hare

a clearly visible, short burst, a bare two seconds or less." He never discerned the actual source of the tracers he had glimpsed so briefly: "My scan, as we were obviously closing in on our TBF, but with relative altitudes not known precisely, was threefold: (1) on Butch's plane at 2:30, slightly up; (2) at 12 o'clock to try to pick up Phil's TBF; and (3) quickly across my cockpit instruments to stay oriented. The stream of fire thus disappeared from view." With Skon's peripheral vision hindered by his goggles, he had "not a chance to swivel my head in two seconds." He reasoned later that the gunfire might have come from a Betty ahead and outside the turning TBF. "I could still catch Lt.Comdr. O'Hare's position from the turtleback light, and the tracers seemed to pass between us." Actually he had witnessed Kernan shooting at the Betty, which itself was out of Skon's view to his right.[39]

During the brief skirmish, Skon never established visual contact with the TBF, whose exhaust was masked by a flame dampener. In contrast, the TBF crew had easily picked out the F6Fs by whatever lights Butch might have been showing, and also by their blue exhaust flares, said to be visible from 750–1,000 yards from ahead and to the sides. The VT-6 action report declared that all *three* U.S. Navy aircraft had turned on their running lights. However, both Skon and Roy Voris (from the no. 2 Black Panther team) strongly disagree with that statement, Skon from his own direct observation and Voris on the basis of his experience with night-fighter tactics. Voris remembered using primarily recognition lights and *never* the running lights, which would have made the aircraft far too conspicuous. Kernan now is not certain whether Butch had his running lights on, but he distinctly recalls the white recognition light just behind Butch's cockpit.[40]

It appears that anticipating rendezvous, both Butch and Phillips had flipped on their dorsal white recognition lights. When the VT-6 air combat intelligence officer—himself not an aviator—drew up the report, he evidently misapplied the term *running lights* for *recognition lights*. If so, in the press of events no one either noticed the error or thought it important to correct it.

The point of all this is not what lights the aircraft were or were not showing, but that Kernan and Rand had clearly distinguished friend from foe. They were not confused as to who was who. The entire sequence—first one, then the second F6F in sight, followed at once by the intruder—happened within just a few seconds. The resulting gun battle likewise ended swiftly.

When last seen, Butch had slid out of formation to port underneath Skon's plane, pushing slightly ahead at about 160 knots. Skon quickly called him on the radio but heard no answer. At first he was unsure whether his leader was making a firing run or skidding out of control. Something, though, had to be very wrong, for Butch would never have maneuvered under him so abruptly without warning. He sensed that Butch was not in control of his plane as it steepened its falloff into what became a slanting dive deep to port. He instantly followed, but Butch's F6F increased the angle of its dive. Dropping perilously below three hundred feet, Skon lost sight of its turtleback light and pulled up sharply. He felt he had just missed plowing into the dark sea.[41]

Phillips himself never saw what happened, other than a flash of white—either a plane splashing into the water or a parachute opening. He likewise tried raising the CAG by radio: "Butch, this is Phil. Over. Butch, this is Phil. Over." No reply. According to listeners on the ships, Skon supposedly responded in words to this effect: "Mr. Phillips, this is Skon. I saw Mr. O'Hare's lights go out and, at the same instant, he seemed to veer off and slant down into the darkness." Phillips informed the *Enterprise* CIC, "Butch may be down." He flipped on his emergency IFF signal, so the ship's radar could get an exact bearing and distance. The *Enterprise* deck log recorded at 1934 that Butch was reported to have landed in the water bearing 324 degrees, distance twenty-six miles from the ship. CIC advised over the squawk box, "O'Hare is in the water! We have an exact fix on his position!"[42]

As Skon regained altitude, he heard Givens relay Butch's position. With no way of finding his leader, he sought out the TBF, "though not without difficulty." Seeing another aircraft close in, Phillips asked, "Skon, this is Phil. Are you on my wing?" He replied, "Affirmative." The two aircraft then orbited. Looking for any sign of Butch, Skon saw only one lonely "dull yellow light," the old Japanese base point float light, which had nearly burned out. For five solid minutes Givens tried to get Butch to answer, but nothing came back through the ether.[43]

The Second Attack on TG-50.2

After getting past the Black Panthers, the second wave of six or seven *rikkōs* approached TG-50.2 mostly from the north and west to play their part in the Whirlwind. Attacking at about the same time Butch went down, they came the closest yet to putting a fish into one of Radford's ships.

At 1928 the *North Carolina*'s lookouts noted the flames from Phillips's first kill on the northeastern horizon, but the task group could not afford to celebrate. A minute later the battlewagon blitzed several planes sneaking in from nine thousand yards to the northwest, and they turned away. At the same time, the drone of a lone plane was heard approaching from the north. Skimming along at only one hundred feet, the audacious Betty passed directly over the massive warship and escaped.

With torpedo planes again swarming in, Radford initiated a series of three 90-degree emergency turns at 1930 that within five minutes brought the task group around to almost due north. The next onslaught originated from the southwest. The *Indiana* and other screening ships on the starboard side opened a massive barrage against several bombers that paralleled the ships from four thousand yards out, then withdrew to the northwest.

Two minutes later another Betty emerged from the northeast out of the darkness only three hundred yards from the *North Carolina*'s starboard quarter. This time all of the 40-mm and 20-mm automatic weapons that could bear plastered the bold interloper, but they could not prevent it from traversing at masthead height the blazing battlewagon's stern. Leaving that inferno astern, the Betty abruptly changed course toward the center of the formation and ran into another torrent of AA fire. Stretched out prone on the *Belleau Wood*'s flight deck, Altemus saw what happened next:

> All of a sudden a twin-engined plane came roaring out of the dark from the p[o]rt side, banked sharply & passed over the flight deck astern. He must have been less than 300 feet as we all could see him plainly—going like a bat out of hell. The ship immediately went into a hard left turn to port—while everybody (and I *do* mean me) held their breath waiting for the torpedo to ram home. It missed us by not more than 10 feet!—clearly seen by the lookouts on our bow.

Wide-eyed spectators in the *Belleau Wood*'s starboard gun galleries looked inward toward the hull as the white torpedo wake zipped on past.[44]

At 1935 the *North Carolina* fired what would be the last salvo of the battle against a group of aircraft discovered about seven thousand yards to the north. They quickly retired. TG-50.2 breathed a collective sigh of relief at 1945 when radar showed all of the assailants drawing away northward. As if all the gun flashes and near-misses had not been not sufficient, Burd confirmed to Radford that this had been a "much bigger attack than any seen so far," and that the radar screens had been "covered with boogies [sic]." The Japanese left behind the pyre of one plane and several nearly extinguished yellowish float lights sputtering on the sea.[45]

Picking up the Pieces

While circling the area a few minutes after the battle, Phillips happened to sight ahead what he thought was another aircraft. He warned, "I see a bogey at twelve o'clock. Stay back! I see our friend!" Evidently for a moment he thought he had found Butch. Back on board the *Enterprise*, CIC announced, "Lt.Comdr. Phillips reports he has spotted O'Hare and he is safe. His position has been reported." Of course, this was an error.[46]

At 1955 Nonaka gathered eight *rikkōs* that had shown up at the group rendezvous and started north for battered Mili, the nearest available airstrip. Four others made it on their own farther north to Maloelap. Of the dozen aircraft of the 752 Air Group that reached safety, three land-attack planes returned despite being badly shot up, and three had sustained light damage. Three other Type 1s were missing: from the first *chūtai* Lt. (jg) Miyagawa Masayasu, a young Eta Jima graduate, and both of the wingmen in the fourth *chūtai* (flight chief petty officers Horinouchi Kaneo and Yasukochi Tsuchigorō). AA fire had torched one *rikkō,* and later Phillips shot down the other two. Kawakita and Mitsuyama, who flew the two 752 Air Group contact *rikkōs,* left the battle area at 2000. They justly received great praise for their superb work. The other pair of contact planes, Yamada and Takahashi from the 755 Air Group, never returned, having fallen to the CAP before sunset.

Nonaka's strike crews claimed the instant sinking of one large carrier and another big carrier or battleship, confirmed by the contact crews. In addition, they thought they had left a third carrier and two cruisers in dire condition. The high command later assessed the results of the Third Gilbert Islands Air Battle as two carriers and two cruisers sunk, and perhaps one battleship or one cruiser on fire. At this rate, it seemed, the U.S. Navy could not last long. In fact, none of the American ships suffered any battle damage, except a destroyer grazed by "friendly" AA. The Japanese certainly noticed the presence of enemy carrier night fighters, encountered here for the first time. Yet they did not seem such a big deal, for no Japanese actually saw any *rikkōs* go down as a result of their efforts, nor did the *rikkō* crews claim any enemy aircraft.

Radford informed the task group at 2005 that the Japanese had retired and advised that of "our own friendly Black Panthers . . . two out of the three are left as one went down. They followed the Nippers in and aided in breaking up the groups." A follow-up message reported that the night fighters had accounted for three Bettys, but "Lt.Cdr. Butch O'Hare is down." At 2029 Radford brought TG-50.2 southeast into the wind to conduct air operations. Following the *Enterprise*'s example, all ships turned on their red masthead truck lights. At 2050, with the flight deck dark except for the "dim 'dustpan lights' and the Landing Signal Officer's two lighted wands," Skon profited from the expert guidance of the senior LSO, Lt. Horace I. "Hod" Proulx, and dropped in smartly for his premier night carrier landing. He had done an excellent job staying with Butch throughout that chaotic night. The bullhorn summoned him to the flag bridge to see the admiral. In contrast, Phillips, highly experienced at night flying, encountered a great deal of trouble getting on board. A light coating of oil on his windshield obscured the LSO's signals until the TBF loomed just over the ramp. His first approach was high and elicited a wave-off. The next time, he gratefully took Proulx's cut and at 2100 flopped down hard on deck.[47]

Corpsmen tended to Rand, Kernan stretched his cramped legs, and Phillips hastened up to the flag bridge to join the admiral and Skon. There Radford expressed to both pilots his heartfelt appreciation for what the Black Panthers had done to break up the torpedo attack. In his memoirs he expressed regret at not having had the power to make immediate awards: "What an impression it would have made on all hands had I been able to pin Navy Crosses on these heroes as they disembarked from their planes on the deck." He added, "I was convinced that our first carrier-borne night fighter attack had saved the task group from serious casualties."[48]

As for Butch, Radford did what he could under the circumstances. At 2250 he broke radio silence to provide the position (1°26' north latitude, 171°56' east longitude) where the Hellcat had gone into the water and requested that Tarawa initiate a rescue search after dawn with Dumbos (rescue flying boats) to find him. He received an immediate acknowledgment. Tarawa certainly knew that something was up from the bright AA gun flashes clearly visible on the western horizon. Matt Gardner arranged for VT-6 TBFs to conduct a special search for Butch the next morning. Worried about the enemy submarines that were certain to have been drawn by all the gunfire that evening, Radford had too few destroyers to send any back in the darkness to look for Butch. At 2300 he had to detach the *Boyd* to investigate a suspected sub contact. After some inconclusive depth-charge attacks, she rejoined TG-50.2 the next morning.

Around 0400 on the twenty-seventh, Radford announced to Pownall and the other task force commanders the results of the first carrier night-fighter interception and offered his initial impressions: "They threw the book at us tonight—30 to 40 planes who put on a beautiful show. Do not believe we have an outfit who could touch them at this sort of thing." He added, "Believe our night fighters really saved the day. They mixed with the largest group, shot down 2, and apparently caused great consternation. Had this group been able to coordinate their attacks with other groups it would have been practically impossible to avoid all of them." Radford estimated that the Japanese had lost eight to ten Bettys to AA and night fighters. He reiterated his request for a dawn search for the downed fighter pilot—whom he did not name—and concluded, "Believe this first time night interceptions made from carrier and judging from the events of past 2 evenings we had *better* hurry with proper equipment."[49]

Butch's Black Panthers had stepped in to prevent a possible catastrophe to Task Group 50.2. In a letter written on 7 December 1943, Gardner described the *Enterprise* night-fighter mission as "an experiment, 'in extremis,' the group being neither trained nor equipped for that type of work." He concluded, "*It did demonstrate, however, the feasibility and effectiveness of carrier night fighters as a counter to Jap night air attack*" (emphasis in original). The Black Panthers did far more than that. Their heroism offered an example for the whole Navy.[50]

16

What Happened to Butch?

"Bullets from friend or foe"

When Lt. Comdr. Edward H. O'Hare failed to return from the night-fighter mission of 26 November 1943, shock and dismay filled the *Enterprise*. What a tragedy to lose him of all people, a Medal of Honor recipient and one of the most popular men on the ship. Everyone wanted to know: What happened to Butch? The first to ask that of the surviving Black Panthers was Rear Admiral Radford, who met with Lieutenant Commander Phillips and Ensign Skon as soon as they landed on the *Enterprise*. However, neither pilot actually saw what had befallen the group commander, and they could only speculate. The initial suspicion was "friendly fire." Phillips described to Radford how his turret gunner, Alvin Kernan, had shot at an aircraft crossing behind the TBF. He suggested that this could have been Butch's F6F. At the same time, according to Radford, Skon could not offer much, because he had had his hands full trying to maintain formation on Butch and never saw exactly what had forced him to drop away so unexpectedly.[1]

While the pilots briefed the admiral, Lieutenant (jg) Rand, the radar operator, had his wounded foot treated in sick bay, but Al Kernan experienced another kind of ordeal. In one of journalism's less glorious moments, AP correspondent Gene Burns cornered Kernan before he could even escape from the head. Pressing the young gunner for his account of the action, Burns hinted that Kernan may have had some responsibility for Butch's loss. Disgusted by the imputation, the exhausted Kernan refused to talk any longer to him.[2]

Late that night the two air combat intelligence officers, Lt. Ridley M. Sandidge of VT-6 and Ens. Tom Morrissey of VF-2, debriefed Phillips, Skon, and Kernan, but apparently not the wounded Rand, who seems to have had very little input into the VT-6 report, although contemporary newspaper stories later quoted him. In the wee hours of the twenty-seventh the ACIOs composed the action reports. Later that day, when Skon was waiting to go aloft, someone just handed him a statement to sign, and that was that. He had time for only a brief glance at it, and not until fifty years later did he enjoy the opportunity to study that document and decide that he would have altered or rewritten portions of the account imputed to him. The statement made it appear that Skon had observed Phillips's TBF at the rendezvous and witnessed the TBF gunner actually fire, whereas he himself never actually saw the Avenger or where those tracers originated. Rather than simply Skon's own recollections, the statement in fact incorporated assumptions made by the ACIOs based on their debriefings of the other participants.[3]

Yet no one on the *Enterprise* could have devoted more time to investigating that one mission, given the many other priorities and the imminence of combat. Trained to abstract key lessons for future study and not to write history, the analysts did not try to provide a critical reconstruction of events. However, their two action reports are the principal, often the only, sources utilized in the numerous published accounts of the air battle that cost Butch his life. In contrast, Hazen Rand's crucial testimony never got to be widely known.[4]

Subsequent to his postbattle meeting with the admiral, Phillips talked with his crewmen Rand and Kernan, who provided details of the fight that he had not personally witnessed. Rand dismissed the speculation that Butch had fallen to friendly fire, later stating, "[It] has always seemed to me that Kernan would have had to [have] shot off the tail of our torpedo bomber to have shot Butch." Consequently, on the morning of the twenty-seventh Phillips advised Radford that now he "was not so sure" whether his gunner had had anything to do with Butch's loss. In 1951 Radford informed historian Samuel Eliot Morison in confidence that he had deliberately excluded any reference in his report to the possibility that Kernan had been responsible for Butch's death, "because there was considerable doubt." In his memoirs the admiral simply ascribed Butch's death to "stray bullets that may have come from friend or foe."[5]

Kernan and others have theorized that on the evening of 26 November a lone Betty trailed the two F6Fs to the rendezvous with Phillips— an interpretation strongly supported by the evidence. It now appears that this intruder had already completed its torpedo attack against TG-50.2 and was seeking its mates in the rendezvous area north of the target. Drawn at first by the engine exhaust flares of the two Hellcats, the Betty's crew were startled by the recognition lights on the American planes, for the 752 Air Group report noted that the enemy night fighters ("three or more") had turned on their "formation" lights. That only occurred during the actual Black Panther rendezvous.[6]

Rand and Kernan clearly saw the Betty direct tracers against the F6F flying to starboard behind their TBF. That Hellcat then accelerated ahead off to port and out of sight. For his own part, Skon had observed a short burst of tracers suddenly emanate from the blackness ahead and pass between Butch and himself, but he saw neither the TBF in front (the one that had fired) nor the Betty behind all of them. He thought it odd that Butch would suddenly pull away and attack without alerting him by radio, especially because both pilots well knew how futile night intercepts were without benefit of the TBF's radar. Reflecting on the way the CAG F6F flew, its engine still running and the plane well trimmed, Skon later decided that Butch himself must have been hit instantly.[7]

Skon's surmise would seem to be correct. Butch fell to his old familiar adversary, a Betty. Most likely he died from, or was immediately disabled by, a lucky shot from the forward observer crouched in the *rikkō*'s narrow glassed-in nose. That crewman had swiveled his antiquated-looking Type 92 7.7-mm machine gun (Lewis design, with a hundred-round drum on the top) to point low to his right toward the nearest enemy plane and triggered just a few short bursts. Not seeing the target flame as a result of their brief fire, the Betty's crew probably shrugged off the fleeting encounter and submitted no claim for an aircraft destroyed. However, the nose gunner's 7.7-mm slugs very likely penetrated Butch's cockpit from above on the port side and ahead of the F6F's armor plate.

The F6F-3's design apparently had a flaw as to the shape and placement of the armor plate behind the cockpit that manifested itself when the pilot wore certain equipment. Lt. Comdr. Hawley "Monk" Russell, CO of VF-33 and the first to take Hellcats into action in the South Pacific, discovered this defect. In a report dated 30 September 1943 he warned that four of his pilots had "received bullets or shells in the cockpit from four to eight o'clock astern," and two had suffered serious wounds. It seems that when the pilots wore their parachute survival backpacks, they sat too far forward in the F6F's seat. Under certain circumstances that posture negated the protection of the silhouette-shaped armor back plate. Russell recommended that the size of the pack be reduced, that the size of the armor plate be increased, and that light side armor be installed to protect the shoulders and arms. Of course, it cannot be said for certain whether this consideration contributed to Butch's death, but it likely was a key factor.[8]

Beginning the night of 26 November on the *Enterprise* and lasting to this day, general opinion among aviation officers in the fleet has tended to follow the hasty first impressions formed immediately after the action: that the improvised rendezvous precipitated an accidental shootdown by the TBF gunner, who misidentified Butch's F6F as an enemy plane. This is reflected in the Naval Institute oral histories of two especially well-informed and respected officers. Rear Adm. Tom Hamilton, the *Enterprise* air officer, stated, "It's believed there was poor communication in a torpedo plane and the gunner of the torpedo plane opened up on Butch as he tried to rejoin." From what he learned when he brought Torpedo Ten (the Navy's first carrier night-strike squadron) on board the *Enterprise* in December 1943, Vice Adm. William I. Martin likewise concluded that Butch had been shot down "probably by the tail gunner in the torpedo plane, who thought he was firing at an enemy plane."[9]

The most influential and oft-cited published account of the night action also pointed to the TBF gunner as the likeliest culprit in Butch's loss. Comdr. Edward P. Stafford's beautifully written 1962 history *The Big E* relied primarily on the ship and squadron action reports and recollections of some former *Enterprise* personnel—not including, however, any of the living participants. Rather inexplicably, Stafford also played down the intensity of the night torpedo attacks on TG-50.2 and consequently the true importance of Butch's hastily improvised night-fighter defense. Through Stafford and other accounts based largely on the action reports, Butch has wrongly become known as one of America's most famous "friendly fire" casualties.[10]

Conversely, Radford's confidential judgment of the mission blamed the initial separation of the F6Fs from the TBF as the source of most of the trouble. In 1951 he stated, "If the young Fighter Director in the ENTERPRISE had not interfered with the planned operation, I believe that all three planes would have returned." This is as unfair to George Givens as the commonly held supposition of friendly fire has been to Alvin Kernan. Prior to Butch's last mission, Givens had spent eight nerve-racking days in the cramped *Enterprise* CIC serving as the TG-50.2 fighter director officer. Tremendous responsibility rested on his shoulders, and he had to make split-second decisions of great importance. The enemy's ultra-low-altitude search tactics initiated on 25 November especially frustrated him. If in this instance Givens erred in judgment, it was on the side of aggressiveness. Radford does not seem to have realized that once the Black Panthers joined the battle, the F6Fs would, as a matter of course, have separated from the TBF to chase Bettys. To intercept fresh bogeys the night fighters would have had to regroup by means of a rendezvous (such as the one that actually took place), always with the risk of Japanese interference.[11]

The just verdict is that the death of Butch O'Hare was a freak occurrence on a highly dangerous mission that employed experimental tactics. He was the first of seven carrier-based night-fighter pilots lost in combat, during which time the carrier night fighters flew 164 sorties, engaged the enemy on 95 occasions, and scored 103 victories.[12]

The Search for Butch

The word that Butch was missing quickly filtered out to the rest of the task group. Those who knew him personally, particularly the VF-6 pilots, showed great confidence in his skill and resourcefulness. John Altemus on the *Belleau Wood* represented all when he scribbled in his diary in the last hours of 26 November, "I'll bet anything that Butch squirms out of this okay."[13]

John Phillips assumed temporary command of Air Group Six on the *Enterprise,* while his XO, Lt. Comdr. Bill Privette, took over VT-6. At dawn on 27 November, Privette led a special search of three TBFs equipped with survival gear to drop to Butch should he be sighted.

Aided by knowing the exact position where he had gone into the water, VT-6 painstakingly checked out the battle area west of Tarawa. The sullen seas revealed only "oil slicks and jetsam from enemy planes and a blue-gray overturned Japanese life raft," but no sign of Butch.[14]

That afternoon Radford complied with the scheduled change of command by riding the *Brown* over to the *Saratoga* to reform TG-50.2 while the *Enterprise* formally joined Rear Adm. Montgomery's TG-50.3, which included the *Essex* and the *Belleau Wood*. Each task group moved to its next assignment. The *Enterprise* report stated that a destroyer was sent to look for Butch, but this is wrong. Very likely Captain Gardner confused the detaching of the *Boyd* to attack a suspected sub with a rescue mission for Butch.[15]

Sources also state that Rear Adm. John H. Hoover, commander, Aircraft, Central Pacific Force (ComAirCentPac), sent flying boats (Dumbos) to locate Butch. This does not appear to have occurred until the twenty-ninth, as Radford himself discovered after monitoring the message traffic. That day he prodded Spruance and Hoover as to whether flying boats indeed were available at Tarawa, and whether the search for the downed fighter pilot he had requested early on 27 November had ever been sent. Radford concluded, "Consider it essential morale purposes that pilots feel every possible effort being made to rescue if forced down."[16]

In fact, the flying boats that Radford thought were already operating from Tarawa did not arrive there until 2 December. Prior to that time Hoover's searches emanated from distant Funafuti and elsewhere in the Ellice Islands southeast of the Gilberts. On the twenty-eighth the waters west of Tarawa netted only a Japanese raft, whose occupants rashly fired at the patrol bomber that had swooped low to look it over. That day a Consolidated PBY-5 Catalina flying boat, flown by Lt. Harry M. Cocowitch of Patrol Squadron Seventy-two (VP-72), left Funafuti for Nanomea, another Ellice atoll. On the morning of the twenty-ninth Cocowitch proceeded west of Tarawa looking for Radford's downed fighter pilot. That would have been Butch—indeed, still alive only if he had survived the air battle and the abrupt night ditching, secured his raft, and lasted the past sixty hours.[17]

En route to Tarawa, Cocowitch received additional orders from Funafuti: "Life raft painted red with white bands X Occupants Japanese X Eliminate." First he sought the troublesome enemy raft but could not find it where expected. Later he happened upon the red rubber boat, where he began the search for the missing fighter pilot. That was about seventy miles downwind from Butch's last reported position. Cocowitch looked over the raft carefully and noticed four or five men hiding beneath it. ComAirCentPac thought the rafters were Tarawa defenders trying to escape the atoll. Instead they were very likely crew members from the second Betty shot down by John Phillips on 26 November. Cocowitch's crew obeyed orders and strafed the raft until it sank, then followed through on the search for the missing American pilot. The PBY carefully covered a band ten miles wide and seventy miles long to the point where Butch went into the water. "Although some general debris was seen, there were no indications of pilot, plane or raft."[18]

No further special searches were flown for Butch, although Radford's passionate complaint certainly got things moving much more quickly to find a *Bunker Hill* pilot who had also gone missing. In Butch's case the evidence is overwhelming that he died either from the Betty's bullets or a few moments later when his aircraft struck the sea and sank.

"Extraordinary Heroism"

Admirals Nimitz and Spruance visited Tarawa on 27 November, but it is not known when they learned that Butch was missing. That day Lt. (jg) Alex Vraciu and three other VF-6 pilots arrived there from Funafuti with Hellcats from the damaged *Independence*, but they heard the bitter news only the next day when they transferred to the *Essex*. After 29 November, hope for Butch's rescue waned. On 13 December, Nimitz directed that the new airfield on Abemama (Apamama) Atoll be called O'Hare Field in honor of Butch, who thus joined Marine Lt. William Deane Hawkins (awarded a posthumous Medal of Honor) and Rear Adm. Henry Mullinnix (lost on the *Liscome Bay*), the other heroes for whom airfields in the newly conquered Gilberts had been named. Capt. Wilson P. Cogswell officially opened O'Hare Field on 17 December 1943, and the facility supported the land-based air offensive against the Marshall Islands. The base was decommissioned on 16 October 1944, the war effort having shifted west, but strangely enough, another, more permanent, airport would come to bear Butch's name.[19]

Radford thought so much of Butch and the Black Panthers that he took the extraordinary step of recommending him for a second Medal of Honor. Captain Gardner of the *Enterprise* put forward the actual citation in a letter dated 13 December 1943:

Lieutenant Commander O'Hare personally organized and voluntarily led the first night fighter section of aircraft to operate from a carrier, at night against enemy aircraft, although he well knew the hazard involved. On the night of 26 November, 1943, when the Task Group containing his parent vessel was under threat of imminent attack by Japanese aircraft, off Tarawa, Gilbert Islands, he took off with his night fighter section, which with unswerving devotion to duty and extraordinary skill, intercepted the largest group of enemy aircraft, thereby effectively breaking up that phase of the attack and destroying two Japanese planes. His capable and determined leadership and his extraordinary heroism, which was beyond the call of duty, were responsible in large measure for saving an important Task Group from serious damage. From this action Lieutenant Commander O'Hare failed to return.[20]

Upon review, the Board of Awards of the Pacific Fleet changed the Medal of Honor recommendation for Butch to the second highest decoration for gallantry, a posthumous Navy Cross officially granted in March 1944. One wonders if the rumors of friendly fire as the cause of Butch's death adversely affected their deliberation. Radford strongly disagreed with the decision to downgrade the award: "I have always been sorry my recommendation was not approved, for I felt his was a clear case of heroism 'above and beyond the call of duty.'"[21]

Butch is believed to be the first World War II holder of the Medal of Honor to die in combat after receiving his award. Another was Col. Neel E. Kearby, a fighter pilot with the Fifth Air Force who earned the Medal of Honor for shooting down six Japanese fighters on 11 October 1943 over Wewak, New Guinea. He fell on 5 March 1944. Marine Gunnery Sergeant John Basilone, presented the Medal of Honor for valor on 24–25 October 1942 at Guadalcanal, was killed in action on 19 February 1945 at Iwo Jima. Butch was apparently the only World War II Medal of Honor recipient recommended for a subsequent award, but no one had actually received a second Medal of Honor since before World War I.[22]

John Phillips, Warren Skon, Hazen Rand, and Alvin Kernan likewise were awarded Navy Crosses for their gallant conduct on the evening of 26 November 1943—one of the few actions in American history in which all of the battle participants received high decorations.[23]

The Black Panther Legacy

Word soon spread among the other carrier task groups of the tactics used by Butch's Black Panthers to counter the ubiquitous snoopers and menacing night attackers. Rear Adm. Baldy Pownall applauded the *Enterprise*'s night-fighting effort and recommended "special commendations to those instrumental in its development and to those who participated in this initial venture." He noted the demand for night-fighter teams to be "almost unanimous."[24]

Following the *Enterprise*'s lead, most of the other big carriers in TF-50 had by the end of November formed their own night-fighter sections, each with one radar-equipped TBF and two F6Fs. They became known unofficially as "BAT teams." For example, Capt. Joseph J. "Jocko" Clark on the *Yorktown* immediately called for volunteers from Air Group Five and organized two teams. Having pulled back temporarily to safer waters, they took the opportunity beginning 30 November to practice late afternoons and evenings while directed by the *Yorktown* CIC.[25]

The evening of 4 December, following day strikes on Kwajalein, TF-50 was severely beset by Bettys from the 752 Air Group and the newly arrived 751. The *Lexington* took a torpedo in the stern, and only after gallant efforts at damage control did she reach tamer waters. Pownall did not allow the carriers to commit their BAT teams, "as under the conditions it was doubtful if safe recovery of the teams could be obtained." Although Pownall was concerned about the lack of a friendly land base, like Tarawa, where the night fighters could take refuge if need be, certainly the mysterious loss of Butch on a similar mission also weighed on his mind.[26]

Most of the carrier air groups returned on 9 December to Hawaii. Air Group Six left the *Enterprise* for NAS Barbers Point on Oahu. Four days later VF-2 returned to Air Group Two and was replaced by a reunited VF-6. Ironically, Air Group Six never again operated from the *Enterprise*. Because of more night-flying training, Air Group Ten resumed its accustomed place on the *Big E*. However, in January 1944 Lieutenant Commander Phillips and his aviators found a new home on the *Essex*-class carrier *Intrepid* (CV-11), just arrived from the States.

Experience during Operation Galvanic completely supported Radford's efforts to promote night fighters. On 29 November Vice Adm. Towers informed Commander in Chief, Pacific Fleet, of the immediate need for teams of four night fighters on each big carrier—not exactly news to Admiral Nimitz. The question became how quickly these radar-equipped Corsairs and Hellcats could deploy to the fleet. AirPac expected that by 15 December the nine F4U-2s of Lieutenant Commander Harmer's half of VF(N)-75—redesignated VF(N)-101 on 1 January 1944—would be ready, to be joined by 15 January by Lieutenant Commander Aurand's VF(N)-76 with twelve F6F-3Es. They had to be on schedule, for the fast carriers, reorganized as Task Force Fifty-eight under Rear Adm. Marc A. Mitscher, would sail in mid-January for Operation Flintlock, the invasion of the Marshalls.[27]

On 16 December, Radford, the new AirPac chief of staff, ordered Air Groups One, Two, Five, Six, Eight, Nine, Twelve, and Sixteen to form at least two night-fighter teams with TBFs and F6Fs and transfer them temporarily to NAS Puunene on Maui. There John Phillips, newly appointed as commander, Night Aircraft Training Unit, Pacific Fleet, tested doctrine and supervised their training. They served as a stopgap to ensure a carrier night-fighter force for Flintlock should the deployment of the F4U-2s and F6F-3Es be delayed. One Air Group Six night-fighter pilot was Alex Vraciu, who volunteered because of his high regard for Butch. Like his beloved CO, he flew wing on Phillips.[28]

The night-fighter teams worked with Lt. (jg) Alexander Wilding, Jr., a *Yorktown* FDO who went ashore to operate from the Argus radar units on Maui. The idea was to use a TBF as the bogey and send a three-plane BAT team to find it. Hearkening to the circumstances that led to Butch's loss, Radford stressed that the teams "must remain in close formation, that is, in sight contact at all times." If the fighters got separated from the TBF, they were to proceed immediately to a preestablished rendezvous and wait for it there. "This procedure is to insure that only enemy planes are attacked." However, Phillips did not actually employ the fighters so inflexibly. The BAT teams preferred to detach one F6F to make the intercept, keeping the other with the TBF. Radford had also directed that special efforts be made in perfecting the night-rendezvous technique—the crucial danger of this tactic. On the night of 7 January, for example, Lt. (jg) Milton W. Norling, a VF-2 veteran, was killed when his Hellcat climbed into the belly of a VT-2 TBF while trying to rendezvous at eighteen hundred feet. The F6F exploded in flames and dropped into the water.[29]

On 7 January, Radford summarized Phillips's recommendations for the fleet. Echoing the feelings of *Enterprise* FDO George Givens, he stressed that "every effort should be made toward the early destruction of [the snooper]." The "mere presence of interceptor aircraft," coupled with a few shoot-downs and Japanese planes burning on the water, would disrupt the "preconceived enemy plan." The next day Towers assigned "air group night-combat teams" to every large carrier for the invasion of the Marshalls.

Although raring to fight, the BAT teams of TBFs and F6Fs never got into combat because sufficient numbers of radar-equipped Corsairs and Hellcats became available. As of 16 January four-plane night-fighter detachments from VF(N)-101 and VF(N)-76 went on board the *Enterprise, Intrepid, Bunker Hill, Yorktown,* and *Essex.* These night-fighter pilots made no attempt to fly formation or operate together at all. Guided by his own radar, each fought as a lone wolf, carefully separated from the others so that everyone could be reasonably certain that any nearby plane was a foe and that no friendly aircraft would be mistaken for the enemy.[30]

In late January and early February 1944, during the landings on Kwajalein and other atolls in the Marshalls, Japanese night air attacks proved nonexistent. That happy result occurred because prior to the invasions, Mitscher's mighty TF-58 rampaged throughout the Marshalls, a privilege not accorded Pownall and TF-50 in November 1943. In one day, 29 January, Mitscher's aviators destroyed Japanese air power in the region. Subsequently, as Morison boasted of the Marshalls invasions, "not one United States naval vessel was attacked by an enemy plane during the entire operation."[31]

On 16 February 1944 Air Group Six on the *Intrepid* joined the rest of Mitscher's flattops in an epic assault against the long-feared Japanese fleet base at Truk. The raid proved a tremendous success, but at a grievous cost to the group. While flying a Hellcat, John Phillips, the group commander, failed to return from overseeing strikes against ships trying to escape Truk. Evidently the defending Zekes ambushed him and his VF-6 wingman, Ens. John Ogg. On another mission Lt. George Bullard, XO of VF-6, was shot down by cruiser AA and taken prisoner. Despite brutal captivity, he survived the war.

After dark Mitscher rather disregarded both the threat of Japanese night torpedo assault and what the Black Panthers had achieved from the *Big E.* Content to depend on AA fire and evasive maneuvering to deter night attackers, he launched only one of his fancy new night fighters, not enough to protect the fleet. Shortly after midnight on 17 February a technical glitch in that F6F-3E's radar allowed one night attacker to slip through. The unlucky *Intrepid* paid the price. A torpedo in her starboard quarter jammed the rudder hard to port and knocked her out of the war until September. At this point she assumed the moniker *Evil I,* a nickname taken over from the *Independence* (now the *Mighty I*). Air Group Six was disbanded after returning to Pearl Harbor and reformed only in April 1944.

After Truk, American carrier night fighters ruled the skies over their flattops, but Butch O'Hare's Black Panthers had showed the way. When night fighters were not present or not used properly, the carriers suffered. The Black Panthers made the difference in November 1943 against the gravest threat to arise against the Pacific Fleet's flattops between the great carrier battles of 1942 and the advent of the suicide kamikazes in October 1944.

CHAPTER

17

Remembrance

*"Butch was admired
by everyone"*

In Phoenix, Selma O'Hare had been making the rounds for Thanksgiving dinner, sharing the traditional feast at several houses for several days. As she was returning with Marilyn by car from one of the dinners, an announcer on the car radio read the news and reported several Japanese planes shot down off the Gilberts with the loss of only one American plane.

"That's Edward," Selma said in a very definite tone.

"Oh, Mother, that's ridiculous." Marilyn responded adamantly.

As though frozen in her seat, staring straight ahead, Selma replied, "It's Edward."

All the family knew that Butch was in danger; any flight, whether in war or peace, carried a certain degree of risk. In his letters Butch was upbeat for the most part, but he seemed to convey an unspoken premonition. The family would not know until 1953 that in early November 1943 he had spoken of his premonition to Frank Hoogs on Maui. Just before going on board the *Enterprise,* Butch sat up late one night with

Frank sharing a bottle of Scotch. "Frank, I won't be coming back this time."

"Ah, Butch, no Jap can shoot you down."

"I don't know about that, Frank; all I know is that this time I'm not coming back and I need you to do me a favor. After the war I want you to visit with my sister Patsy and I want you to go and see 'Buttons.' You will know what to say; just promise me you will do that for me."

In 1953 Frank kept his promise to Butch. In 1976, several years after Frank's death, Patsy traveled to Maui to visit Ethel Hoogs. Together they toured the old abandoned airfield at Puunene and hunted for the remains of bunkers and other sites around the field where Butch had lived for most of his last two years.

In the United States—and, according to the time being used there by the Fifth Fleet, in the Gilberts as well—it was already the twenty-sixth day of November when Butch died. When official word did arrive on 9 December, it was only a message that Butch was missing; there was some hope. Patsy and Marilyn held on to that slender thread, but Selma knew that Butch was gone, and she waited for no further confirmation. She immediately departed for Coronado to be with Rita and her granddaughter. By 10 December, Rita had also accepted the harsh reality that Butch was not coming back.

The news that Butch was missing spread quickly once the family was notified and press accounts were released by the Navy. Papers throughout the country featured stories with headlines such as "Famed Flier Missing" and "O'Hare Shot down in the Pacific."

Messages poured in to the family from the Navy, relatives, friends, and strangers. There were letters from Admiral Nimitz himself and Harold Miller, now a captain serving in England. Capt. Matt Gardner of the *Enterprise* wrote on 11 December to assure Rita, "We left no stone unturned to find him."[1] Lt. Comdr. Bob Jackson wrote her from the *Enterprise* to say, "Your grief is mine also. The Admiral himself [Radford] said that 'he never saw one individual so universally well liked.'" Lt. Comdr. John Phillips—who himself had only two more months to live—wrote to Rita on 15 December, "His loss will be mourned by the entire country, the Navy and particularly by all the men in his air group. Butch was admired by everyone from the admirals to the messboys for his skill, courage and daring as a fighter pilot. He was loved by all he came in contact with for his fairness, his consideration and his desire to help younger and less experienced men."

Of all the messages forwarded to Rita expressing sympathy, love, and concern, none was more personal than the one from her brother-in-law Dr. Paul Palmer, himself still at the front in the Solomon Islands. Acknowledging Butch's loss as "the first real tragedy in my life," he continued:

> I have been praying so very hard for our dear Lord to see to it that Butch turns up safe and sound and returns to his loved ones. If He deems otherwise and Butch is gone, I'm sure with all of us in back of him, Butch is in Heaven. You know, Rita, it has been only a short time since Butch was baptized and with such a fresh start, his stay in Purgatory could not be very long even without our prayers. . . . Heaven has been described as a place that is so wonderful that those who are there are happy beyond anything we can comprehend. Our greatest joys and happiness on this earth mean nothing in comparison with the perpetual and continuous joy of those in Heaven. If Butch is gone, then how perfectly happy he is . . . and shortly we will all be together again.

In St. Louis a Solemn Pontifical Mass of Requiem was offered for Butch in the St. Louis Cathedral on the morning of Monday, 20 December 1943. Present were many who had organized and participated in his triumphant 1942 parade. The service closed with these words:

> As a symbol of our fighting men and as an officer and gentleman who knew what his job was to do, and did it well, this morning we proudly salute Lt. Commander O'Hare with the traditional Navy greeting "Well Done." In the prayer of his church that remembers him in a life beyond the heroic life that he led here, we fervently pray that God may have mercy upon his soul and grant him peace and everlasting happiness.

Other close friends of Butch honored his passing in their own ways. The Hoogs family invited "Butch's Boys," the VF-6 pilots, back from the Gilberts, to Christmas dinner at their home on Maui. There they raised a toast to their dear friend. Lt. (jg) George Rodgers of VF-6 expressed their feelings in several poems he wrote on the *Cowpens* after learning that Butch was missing. One favorite is this:

> *Yours is peace for an endless time,*
> *   And yours is the berth you sought,*
> *These hearts of ours are pained, yet proud*
> *   In the glory of how you fought.*

No more will the gay-colored flags at mast
  Call you and your men to land,
For the "cast" you answered in silence at night
  Was sent by a Mightier Hand.

Perhaps where you went the sea breeze blew
  With a fullness in its blast,
As you approached the deck of the heavenly ship
  With a "roger" to the last.

And He on His bridge returned your salute;
  The report of your battle won,
Then echoed the hearts of all of us
  With a "very well done, my son!"

Though gone from this world, Butch continued to serve his country. In January 1944 a new poster was devised to help dramatize the Fourth War Loan Drive. It depicted a white flight path from a dark sky bearing the name O'Hare, a column of water rising from the ocean representing his downed plane, and the statement, "He can't buy a bond—is your excuse as good?" Just before his death the Butch O'Hare Trophy had been awarded to Ralston-Purina for the highest per capita bond purchases among St. Louis firms employing five hundred persons or more in the Third War Loan Drive.

Within a matter of days after Butch was lost, the first of many official tributes was paid to him when the field at Abemama was named in his honor. In the Navy press release that announced the naming of the Abemama airfield, Rear Admiral Radford was quoted as saying that he would recommend Butch for a second Medal of Honor, but as has been shown, the recommendation was knocked down to a Navy Cross that was presented to Rita in June 1944. She had already received the posthumous Distinguished Flying Cross with gold star for a second award. A Purple Heart, the least desired medal in the pyramid of honor, was awarded later at the end of the period—a year and a day—established by law to officially declare dead a serviceman missing in action.

One way the Navy honors its fallen heroes is to name destroyers and destroyer escorts after them. On 22 June 1945 Selma, Patsy, and other family, including Patsy's four-year-old daughter, proudly attended the launching of the *Gearing*-class destroyer USS *O'Hare* (DD-889) at Consolidated Steel Corporation in Orange, Texas. As official sponsor, Selma broke a bottle of champagne across the bow as the new ship slid into the water port side first. Commissioned on 29 November 1945, soon after World War II ended, the *O'Hare* was converted in 1953 to a radar picket destroyer (DDR-889) and underwent modernization in 1963. In 1972–73 she served off Vietnam, often providing naval gunfire support. Almost thirty years to the day after Selma launched the *O'Hare,* the warship was transferred to the Spanish Navy and rechristened SNS *Mendez Nuñez* (D 63).[2]

On 9 December 1945 Orson Welles broadcast a special program from San Francisco interviewing the nearest relatives of three war heroes for whom new theaters at Naval Station Treasure Island were to be dedicated. One was named for Butch, his mother participating from ABC affiliate KXOK in St. Louis. The other two honored were Marine Gunnery Sergeant John Basilone, the Guadalcanal Medal of Honor recipient killed at Iwo Jima, and Doris Miller, a black mess attendant awarded the Navy Cross for courage under fire during the attack on Pearl Harbor. Miller went down with the *Liscome Bay* two days before Butch was lost.

Perhaps the greatest single tribute to Butch was the naming of what was to become one of the world's greatest airports, Chicago O'Hare International. Although Selma had effectively deterred earlier efforts to name entities for her son, she had no say in the effort to name the airport for Butch. Originally farmland, the site functioned during World War II as an aircraft assembly plant with associated airstrip. Acquired after the war by the city of Chicago for construction of a new airport, it was known as Orchard Place Airport until being dedicated in Butch's memory on Sunday, 18 September 1949.

On 19 April 1947 Col. Robert R. McCormick, editor and publisher of the *Chicago Tribune,* delivered a radio address on the "Chicago Theater of the Air" program broadcast over the Mutual Broadcasting System. It was on that occasion that he first advocated naming the new airport for Butch. The timing of the address was significant in that official confirmation from Treasury Department sources was just surfacing in regard to EJ O'Hare's role as an undercover informant. Alban Weber, who distinguished himself as a destroyer-escort commander during World War II before being elected a Chicago alderman (Fiftieth Ward), had voted for the O'Hare airport name proposal. On 27 April 1993 he confirmed that although Butch's achievements carried the greatest weight in the decision, consideration of EJ's role had also influenced McCormick's advocacy of the proposal.[3] Too, it was through EJ that Chicago had a tie to Butch, a St. Louis native.

Picking up on McCormick's suggestion, the Naval Airmen of America, a veterans' organization, soon petitioned the Chicago City Council to name the airport for Butch. It took over two years for the City Council to act, but Alderman John J. Hoellen's proposal passed three months before the dedication.

Landing on Saturday, 17 September, in a Navy transport plane at Naval Air Station Glenview, Selma O'Hare said to the press, "I am a very proud woman that this honor is being paid to my son. But in a sense, it isn't just to his memory. It is for all the boys who gave their lives in the war. I know Edward would feel that way." At formal ceremonies the next day she unveiled a large bronze plaque depicting Butch about to climb out of the cockpit of an F4F Wildcat. Below was his Medal of Honor citation, and at the bottom in smaller letters the plaque read:

THIS PLAQUE IS PRESENTED TO THE CITY OF CHICAGO
AT THE DEDICATION OF O'HARE FIELD, SEPTEMBER 18, 1949
AS AN EVERLASTING TRIBUTE TO THE MEMORY OF
LIEUTENANT COMMANDER EDWARD H. O'HARE, U.S. NAVY
BY THE NAVAL AIRMEN OF AMERICA

By any standard, the dedication of O'Hare Field was spectacular. One hundred and seventy-five planes participated, and two hundred thousand people were present to watch the Blue Angels perform in their new F9F Panther jets, a climbing contest between an F8F Bearcat—the Navy's fastest propeller plane—and an F2H Banshee jet, simulated air attacks on the field, a mass flyover, and other aerial demonstrations. Present for the ceremonies were Governor Adlai E. Stevenson, Maj. Martin H. Kennedy, Colonel McCormick, Adm. J. J. "Jocko" Clark, and a host of other military and civilian dignitaries. Selma, Patsy, and Marilyn were particularly pleased to have Rear Adm. Austin Doyle, who had entertained Butch and Rita in Washington, D.C., seven years earlier, as their official host along with George Benson, who represented the Naval Airmen of America.

Another dedication ceremony was held 29 October 1955, when the airport was officially opened to commercial air traffic. And on 23 March 1963 O'Hare International Airport, by then greatly expanded, was rededicated. President John F. Kennedy joined the O'Hare family and Mayor Richard J. Daly for the occasion, with the president laying a wreath in memory of Butch.

On Sunday morning, 18 February 1951, Selma O'Hare attended her last formal tribute to Butch. In company with Marilyn, she assisted with the unveiling of a bronze plaque honoring Butch and with the dedication of the O'Hare Room in Bancroft Hall at the U.S. Naval Academy. Vice Adm. Harry W. Hill, superintendent of the academy, introduced retired admiral John Towers, who conducted the dedication ceremony for the memorial plaque. Of all the tributes to him, Butch would have enjoyed this one the most. If those who have passed to the next life can indeed view the proceedings of those who have not, Butch no doubt fixed himself a ham sandwich (on rye with mustard), opened a "white soda," choked up at the sight of his mother and sister still feeling the pain of his absence, saluted Admiral Towers, and then had a good laugh as room 3219 was declared the O'Hare Room. In 1995 a bronze plaque describing the essence of his military life still rests to the left of the door; on the right is an oft-reproduced photo of him; and above the door of 3219 is a small bronze plaque proudly declaring it the O'Hare Room. But Butch never lived there!

Anyone who ever read his letters would know how much Butch cared for his old alma mater. As it was for most other service academy graduates, the Army-Navy football game was a red-letter day on his calendar, and even though his active-duty demeanor was such that he often appeared to his men to be more a reserve officer than an academy graduate, when the pressure was on he called upon the pride and attributes instilled in him while at the academy. Still, on that day in 1951 he would have been amused that 3219 was declared his room instead of 4001, 1132, 1306, 1413, 3043, 1129, or 1215. Since 1951, though, room 3219 has taken on a life of its own. Midshipmen have been and will continue to be inspired by the man himself rather than the place where he slept. Too modest to admit it, Butch would nonetheless have been proud of the plaques and room 3219. For certain, his daughter and sisters are.

In October 1959 the O'Hare family was advised of yet another honor being planned for Butch. While Butch most likely would have enjoyed the plaque dedication at the academy more than his other posthumous honors, he would have treasured most the October 1959 announcement. In a letter to Patsy, T. Claude Ryan, president of Ryan Aeronautical Company, wrote that his company was planning to donate a perpetual trophy for the high-scoring individual in the Fighter All-Weather competitions at the Naval Air Weapons Meets: "In agreement with Vice Admiral R. B. Pirie, Deputy Chief of Naval Operations (Air), we are pleased to name this trophy in honor of your distinguished brother, Lieutenant Commander E. H. (Butch) O'Hare. It is only fitting that he should be so honored, for the best of the Naval and Marine aviators will compete for this trophy each year." The memorial trophy itself was a fourteen-inch sterling silver tray mounted on dark blue velvet in a silver-framed shadow box. Each annual winner would receive a small replica plate identical to the main trophy. The first award was presented on 4 December 1959.

To those in the service, the annual Naval Air Weapons Meet was known by a particular nickname that the Navy Fighter Weapons School at NAS Miramar subsequently adopted. It became familiar to the general public after the release of a popular 1980s movie called *Top Gun.* With the memorial trophy being awarded yearly in Butch's name, credence and documentation accrue to him as the original Top Gun. The first naval aviator to earn fame in World War II for courage and outstanding expertise in combat, Butch would have shared with Ryan and the Navy the same few words he had spoken to President Roosevelt on 21 April 1942: "That is very nice—thank you very much."

In the summer of 1973 Butch was enshrined with other Missouri Medal of Honor recipients at the state capitol in Jefferson City. In addition, a large portrait was hung in Soldier's Memorial in St. Louis. On 3 October 1982 Kathleen represented her father for his induction into the *Yorktown* Carrier Aviation Hall of Fame on board the museum carrier in Charleston Harbor, South Carolina. At the time of this dedication, no one knew that Butch had flown on board the *Yorktown* before the Marcus Island raid. On 13 August 1943 he had emerged from his Hellcat and walked close by the island that from 1982 has displayed his two-foot by four-foot bronze plaque. Inducted on that same day were old friends Jimmy Thach, who wore four stars before retirement; Jimmy Flatley, retired as vice admiral; and Adm. Arthur "Raddy" Radford, who rose to chairman of the Joint Chiefs of Staff. Also inducted that day were Lt. Comdr. John C. Waldron and Rear Adm. C. Wade McClusky, both of Midway fame; Capt. David McCampbell, who ended World War II as the Navy's top ace, with thirty-four kills; and Adm. Marc Mitscher. Serving as induction speaker for Butch was another friend from his VF-3 days, Adm. Noel Gayler, former commander in chief, Pacific.

The year 1992, the fiftieth anniversary of Butch's historic fight in defense of the old *Lexington,* was especially memorable for the O'Hare family. Mayor Richard M. Daly proclaimed 20 February 1992 to be Lt.

Comdr. Edward "Butch" O'Hare Day and personally hosted a special ceremony for thirty members of the O'Hare family at the gigantic O'Hare International Airport. Present for the festivities were veterans from Butch's old VF-6, including Alex Vraciu, Sy Mendenhall, Willie Callan, and Hank Landry. Chicago Alderman Edward Burke (Fourteenth Ward) took the lead in offering tribute to Butch and organized the program in such a manner as to ensure that "Butch and his boys" remained the focus—a rarity in politics. The family moved on to Pensacola, where on 8 May, Butch was inducted into the Naval Aviation Hall of Honor at the National Museum of Naval Aviation. Inducted on the same day was another old friend, Adm. Austin Doyle. In 1990 the O'Hare family had presented to museum director Capt. Robert L. Rasmussen, USN (Ret.), Butch's naval sword and the watch he had been given by the city of St. Louis after the parade in 1942.

In late October and early November 1993 the family visited South Carolina for more ceremonies on board the *Yorktown*. The O'Hares were guests at the dedication of the National Congressional Medal of Honor Exhibit as part of the Patriots Point Naval & Maritime Museum. The exhibit on board the *Yorktown* honors all 3,404 recipients of the nation's highest award for valor, with Butch being commemorated on the World War II console. The following morning the family was present as officials from Grumman Aircraft Corporation and Patriots Point Museum dedicated an original F4F Wildcat to Butch's memory. Meticulously restored by Grumman employees, the Wildcat is painted in what F-15's colors had been on 20 February 1942.

At all the ceremonies, pilots and nonaviator squadron mates have made their way to Kathleen, Patsy, Marilyn, and other members of the family to say hello and to share at least one fond memory of Butch. One of Alex Vraciu's favorite reminiscences is how Butch's teachings saved his life on more than one occasion. Sy Mendenhall never fails to remember his great compassion for his men. Willie Callan will never forget his competitive spirit. USS *Independence* (CVL-22) veteran Herman Backlund, concerned that many in the city of Chicago had no idea for whom the airport was named, wrote a small book on the subject. In that same spirit, one former pilot of Air Group Six proved a point to an acquaintance when he turned to another seventy-year-old veteran and said, "What would you do if I told you this man said Butch O'Hare was no good either as a person or as a pilot?" Rising, the veteran said, "I'll punch him in the nose!" After a few tense seconds, he became convinced that the challenge had been intended only to prove the point that Butch's men still loved him as much in 1992 as they had fifty years earlier. Indeed, it was his example and spirit that gave them direction.

All of the tributes have been greatly appreciated by the O'Hare family, even those generations born after Butch was gone. Although any of the O'Hares can handle most social situations, they are nonetheless as laconic as Butch when it comes to making "thank you" speeches at ceremonies honoring him. One of the more memorable acknowledgments came from Mrs. Ed Lowry, Patsy's eldest daughter, when she quietly approached a flag officer at the Naval Academy during the class of 1937 reunion and thanked him for showing so much consideration to her mother. She told him that his attention to her mother had been the best possible manner to show his respect, admiration, and affection for Butch.

Tributes have also come from unexpected sources. Visiting China in 1982 soon after the death of her husband, Patsy Palmer tripped and fell inside her hotel, severely injuring herself. Airlines were often reluctant to transport injured people, and Pan Am representatives cautioned Patsy that the pilot might not want to accept responsibility for her. At the airport Patsy, lying flat on a stretcher, told the captain, "If you will take me home, I'll cause you no [legal] trouble." At that point he asked her name, and when he heard "Patricia O'Hare Palmer," he replied, "If not for your brother, we wouldn't be here. . . . I was a Navy pilot and I became one primarily from being inspired by Butch's legacy. I'll make room for you if I have to throw luggage off the plane."

EJ O'Hare often stated the principles of courage and confidence that guided his life, and his example played a significant role in the development of his son's character and the course his life took. Living in a period of American history when life was as much an exercise in survival as a pursuit of happiness, neither EJ nor Butch knew the privilege of growing old. Their principles proved to be dangerous ones that led them to their fateful rendezvous.

Although Edward H. O'Hare experienced a rendezvous with death on 26 November 1943, a kinder fate destined him for a continuing rendezvous with students of American naval history. Although he did not seek the notoriety attendant upon his fame, he nonetheless is remembered for carrying it as regally as any king. And few kings were ever so widely respected and genuinely liked as Butch O'Hare.

Epilogue

It has been said that no one is really dead as long as those who knew him still live. In that sense both EJ and Butch O'Hare still live, their lives bringing joy to those who knew them. So for the time being, the story goes on.

EJ O'Hare would have been pleased that Frank Wilson acknowledged his salient role in helping put Al Capone in prison. Even though Wilson's revelations in 1947 clearly demonstrated that EJ had served the interests of the Treasury Department, and though later disclosures demonstrated his continuing assistance to the FBI and other law enforcement agencies, not everyone knew the "rest of the story." As a consequence, even into the 1990s stories about Butch that mention his father still retreat to the days in 1939 when the Treasury Department could not step forward to acknowledge EJ's long and valuable work as an undercover informant and declare him one of the "good guys."

If EJ could visit this world for a day, he would find the site of his death in Chicago not greatly changed since 1939. Of course, the trolley cars are gone, the road has been widened, and most of the telephone poles are gone. Looking up and down Ogden Avenue, he would agree that Capone's people chose well the location of the shooting, for the several blocks on either side had too many people and would have made a clean escape more difficult. Several miles to the south he would be pleased to see the new buildings and grandstands at Sportsman's Park and Hawthorne Race Course. If in season, he would take in a few races—still horses, no dogs. Looking north from the place of his death, EJ would be pleasantly surprised to see the taller, more impressive skyline of his adopted city. Driving up north through the western suburbs, he would be proud of the road signs directing traffic to O'Hare International Airport. Drawing nearer, he would be amazed to see so many buildings and businesses named O'Hare. At the airport he would be overwhelmed to see the growth of his favorite mode of travel, and to find the memorial plaque and small display honoring Butch. He would agree that the airport was the best place for the large plaque. However, he would think a more prominent location therein was needed.

If time permitted on EJ's one-day visit back to this world, he would be pleased to see that the old house in St. Louis on Holly Hills still looked nearly new, and he would be sad to see that the old home at Eighteenth and Sidney had been torn down to make room for Interstate 55. At the cemetery in St. Louis, he would be simultaneously happy and sad to see Selma's grave next to his.

Selma had soldiered on after Butch's death, representing him on numerous patriotic occasions and remaining active in the Gold Star Mothers Association until her death. Although terminally ill in 1958, Selma was determined to live until the anniversary of her son's death. On 27 November of that year, knowing she had reached her goal, she crossed the bridge from this life to join her son on the other side.

Patsy O'Hare Palmer still resides in Phoenix, her husband—and Butch's great duck-hunting friend—gone since 25 August 1981. In many respects Dr. Palmer was a casualty of World War II, changed physically and emotionally by the constant stress of operating on wounded and dying men, knowing that the loss of each one who slipped away would hurt someone else as badly as he had been hurt by the loss of Butch. Patsy and Paul had six children: Patricia, Paul junior, Victoria, Abigail, Edward, and Michael. Patsy acknowledges that she might have had more had not the fifth child been a boy; she was determined to have a son she could name Butch. Today, Edward O'Hare "Butch" Palmer— who displays some physical resemblances to his uncle and is just as nice—frequently packs his uncle Butch's over-and-under shotgun into his car and heads off to hunt ducks. But it is not as much fun now as it was before 27 October 1994, when his brother, Dr. Paul Vincent Palmer, Jr., died after having been accidentally shot in the arm while hunting in Oregon.

Marilyn O'Hare Platt resides just outside St. Louis in Kirkwood, Missouri, in a large antebellum home with two daughters living in the same block and another only a few blocks away. Marilyn raised five children (Judy, Marilyn, Philip, Athalia, and Tacy), all of whom speak of

Butch as though they had known him personally. Their telephone lines light up when new tributes to their uncle are announced or some new information about his life is unearthed. Marilyn's first husband, Phil Tovrea, who became an ace in World War II flying P-38 Lightnings, died on 18 January 1981. Marilyn's second husband, Richard Platt—whom she married after the divorce from Phil—died on 21 December 1992.

Near the end of World War II, "Nick" Nicholson hosted a small party at the Hotel Del Coronado for academy "great friends" Mort Lytle and Charles Putman. Also invited to represent Butch was his widow, Rita. Later, on 26 May 1945, Rita and Mort Lytle married. They had not known each other before Nick's party, although Rita had heard of Mort through Butch. At their first meeting, Mort was saddened by the sight of his best friend's widow and baby seemingly lost in a tragic world. Since May 1945, however, he has put light back into Rita's life. Adopting Kathleen, he has loved her as his own, and their relationship could not be better. It would appear that Butch has been as successful in befriending angels as he was people on earth, for he could have asked for nothing better than to have had his great friend Mort provide love and care for Rita and "Buttons." Ironically, as one closes the 1937 *Lucky Bag,* the Naval Academy yearbook, the photograph of Butch on page 141 closes directly onto the one of Mort on page 140.

Kathleen (Kathi) "Buttons" O'Hare Lytle grew up in California and Virginia. In 1963 she married Robert Nye, a corporate pilot and flight engineer. All five of their children are boys (Robert junior, Stephen, Christopher, Patrick, and Kenneth). In their large kitchen–dining room hangs a small shadowbox displaying Butch's Medal of Honor, Navy Cross, Distinguished Flying Cross (with gold star), Purple Heart, and campaign medals. The original baby-blue ribbon for the Medal of Honor shows the effects of age, and all the medals are sometimes askew in the frame from guests constantly taking them down for a better look. Earlier the boys had enjoyed an unequaled display for show-and-tell at school.

Most of Butch's fellow pilots are gone: Flatley in 1958, Bullard in 1966, Thach in 1981. Nearly all his boyhood friends have also passed on. Yet academy "great friends" Mort, Nick, and Putt enjoy good health into 1995; pilots Alex Vraciu, Sy Mendenhall, Willie Callan, Hank Landry, and Andy Skon are also well and active. Alex—who finished the war with nineteen kills and was inducted into the *Yorktown* Carrier Aviation Hall of Fame in August 1995, once again joining on his skipper's wing—retired as a commander. Sy retired at the same rank and returned to his first love: farming and raising cattle. Willie wore the four stripes of captain and often visits Sy, like him now living in Arkansas. Andy, who scored seven victories in World War II, also retired as a captain. Whitey Feightner, likewise an ace (nine kills), retired as rear admiral. He never regrets not having learned to ride horses or shoot ducks like Butch, and still chases a golf ball around the fairways and greens.

In late 1995 all of Butch's wartime friends followed with interest the installation of a new exhibit at the National Museum of Naval Aviation. Three walls from the home on the Von Tempsky estate on Maui were removed and shipped to Pensacola. On them are the signatures of hundreds of pilots, the wall panels serving as a giant guest book for the many dinner guests of the Von Tempskys. Many famous names appear, but none more renowned than Butch, who wrote on 21 June 1942, "May it always be here (the wall I mean)."

It will. And it will be a place where Butch can continue to inspire naval aviators, his example of leadership and combat valor speaking to the ages.

Butch's Citations

Medal of Honor

For conspicuous gallantry and intrepidity in aerial combat, at grave risk of his life above and beyond the call of duty, as Section Leader and Pilot of Fighting Squadron THREE, on 20 February 1942. Having lost the assistance of his teammates, Lieutenant O'Hare interposed his plane between his ship and an advancing enemy formation of nine attacking twin-engined heavy bombers. Without hesitation, alone and unaided, he repeatedly attacked this enemy formation, at close range in the face of intense combined machine-gun and cannon fire. Despite this concentrated opposition, Lieutenant O'Hare, by his gallant and courageous action, his extremely skillful marksmanship in making the most of every shot of his limited ammunition, shot down five enemy bombers and severely damaged a sixth before they reached the bomb release point. As a result of his gallant action—one of the most daring, if not the most daring single action in the history of combat aviation—he undoubtedly saved his carrier from serious damage.

Navy Cross

For extraordinary heroism while serving as Air Group Commander aboard the U.S.S. ENTERPRISE, member of a Task Group, in the vicinity of the Gilbert Islands on November 26, 1943. When warnings were received of the approach of a large force of enemy torpedo bombers, Lieutenant Commander O'Hare unhesitatingly volunteered to lead the first fighter section of aircraft to take off from a carrier at night and intercept the Japanese attackers. Although limited in the special training necessary for so dangerous an undertaking and fully aware of the hazards involved, he fearlessly led his three-plane group into combat against the largest formation of hostile aircraft and assisted in shooting down two enemy planes and dispersing the remainder. Lieutenant Commander O'Hare's brilliant leadership and courageous initiative in the face of grave peril undoubtedly prevented the infliction of serious damage upon an important Task Group and were in keeping with the highest traditions of the United States Naval Service.

Distinguished Flying Cross

For heroism and extraordinary achievement while participating in aerial flight as Commander of a Fighting Squadron during action against enemy Japanese forces stationed on Marcus Island, August 31, 1943. In the face of tremendous antiaircraft fire, Lieutenant Commander O'Hare repeatedly led his squadron in persistent and vigorous strafing raids against hostile establishments on the island. Pressing home his own individual attacks with grim determination and courageous disregard for his own personal safety, he contributed materially to the superb combat efficiency which enabled his squadron to destroy all grounded aircraft and to demolish a high percentage of defensive installations. His superb organizing ability and inspiring leadership were in keeping with the highest traditions of the United States Naval Service.

Gold Star in Lieu of the Second Distinguished Flying Cross

For heroism and extraordinary achievement in aerial combat as Commander of Fighting Squadron SIX during operations against enemy Japanese forces at Wake Island on October 5, 1943. Sighting three hostile fighters south of the island, Lieutenant Commander O'Hare overtook the planes and singlehandedly destroyed one while his unit accounted for the other two, pursuing the stricken planes down the runway on Wake Island where, in the face of terrific Japanese antiaircraft fire, two twin-engined bombers and a fourth fighter were destroyed on the ground. Continuing his daring tactics, Lieutenant Commander O'Hare intercepted a third hostile bomber, closing for the attack and leaving the enemy a crippled and vulnerable target for final destruction by another plane of his unit. His inspiring leadership and gallant fighting spirit under the most perilous conditions reflect great credit upon Lieutenant Commander O'Hare, his command and the United States Naval Service.

Notes

The life of Butch O'Hare was recounted in numerous newspaper and magazine articles published in the late winter and spring of 1942 just after his Medal of Honor sortie, and again in Lloyd Wendt's four-part 1949 *Chicago Sunday Tribune* series. Although the newspaper and magazine articles provide a chronological background and serve as a good starting point, not one consulted by the authors was free from errors of fact or interpretation. All personal information concerning Butch and his father derived from such secondary sources has been corrected herein by surviving family members, especially Butch's sisters, Mrs. Patricia O'Hare Palmer and Mrs. Marilyn O'Hare Platt, as well as by O'Hare family papers. Unless otherwise noted, Mrs. Palmer and Mrs. Platt are the primary sources for the personal experiences of their father and brother.

Abbreviations
NA National Archives
NHC Naval Historical Center
RG record group

Prologue
1. Throughout the text (as opposed to bibliographic citations), all Japanese names are presented in Japanese order: surname first, then given name.

Chapter 1: Mother and Father March Butch to Western Military Academy
1. *St. Louis Dispatch,* 23 Apr. 1942.
2. Ibid.
3. *Chicago Sunday Tribune,* 20 Oct. 1949, 6.
4. Robert St. Peters to SE, 19 Apr. 1994.
5. *St. Louis Star-Times,* 5 Mar. 1942; Col. R. L. Jackson to Mr. and Mrs. O'Hare, 9 Dec. 1931.

6. *St. Louis Post Dispatch,* 27 May 1954, 3-F.
7. O'Hare family papers.
8. Ibid.

Chapter 2: Life off Campus, 1927–1933

1. Ens. E. H. O'Hare, USN, Aviation Training Records, in National Museum of Naval Aviation, Pensacola.
2. O'Hare family papers.

Chapter 3: EJ Goes under Cover for the Treasury Department

1. The mindset of the 1920s and 1930s cannot be fully understood by most Americans living today. Few contemporary Americans can imagine life without certain taken-for-granted safeguards: the protection of a strong national defense; a social security system to assist in retirement; Medicare; and a welfare system that is supposed to prevent the societal polarization that can lead to internal upheaval. In the 1920s and 1930s, national defense was questionable both in quality and quantity; social security did not appear until 1935 and was then thought by many to be a dangerous form of socialism rather than social progress; health care was paid from one's own pocket; care for the elderly was the responsibility of children or other family; and a few existing resources of private welfare were usually accepted only with great embarrassment and loss of personal pride. In order to be safe, to eat, to maintain health, to care for the infirm and elderly, one had to look to oneself; the resources of big government— often decried by a contemporary society that has never had to live without it— were not there. EJ O'Hare lived and made his life decisions in that era—when he was the primary provider for himself, his wife, her mother and brother, three children, and several other relatives.
2. Frederick Lewis Allen, *Only Yesterday* (New York: Harper and Brothers, 1931), 245–69.
3. Frank J. Wilson (as told to Howard Whitman), "How We Trapped Capone," *Collier's,* 26 Apr. 1947, 15.
4. Frank J. Wilson and Beth Day, *Special Agent: A Quarter Century with the Treasury Department and the Secret Service* (New York: Holt, Rinehart, and Winston, 1965), 32.
5. See Paul Aurandt, *Paul Harvey's "The Rest of the Story"* (New York: Doubleday, 1977), 189–93, the section "Redeeming the Family Honor" concerning O'Hare, which is replete with errors of fact and interpretation; also Max Lucado, *"And the Angels Were Silent"* (Portland, Ore.: Privately printed, 1992), 45–51.
6. Wilson and Day, *Special Agent,* 55. Butch's class rank from U.S. Naval Academy Alumni Association, Register of Alumni.
7. Wilson and Day, *Special Agent,* 32; O'Hare family papers.
8. O'Hare family papers.
9. Ibid.

10. Ibid.
11. Ibid.
12. Northern Trust Co. to Selma O'Hare, 12 Oct. 1940.

Chapter 4: The Naval Academy, Class of 1937

1. Butch to Selma O'Hare, 4 Oct. 1932.
2. Butch to Selma, 31 Oct. 1932.
3. Ibid.; Butch to Selma, 17 Dec. 1932.
4. Butch to Selma, 6 Dec. 1932, 9 Dec. 1932.
5. Butch to Patsy O'Hare, 5 Jan. 1933; Butch to Selma, 12 Feb. 1933; Arthur W. Bryan to Col. R. L. Jackson, 13 Mar. 1933.
6. O'Hare family papers; Butch to Selma, 12 Feb. 1933, 22 July 1933.
7. Butch to Selma, 2 Aug. 1933.
8. Capt. Charles Francis Putman, USN (Ret.), interview with SE, Nov. 1994; Butch to Patsy, 29 Sept. 1933.
9. Butch to Patsy, 29 Sept. 1933.
10. Butch to Selma, 20 Jan. 1934, 31 Oct. 1933, 2 Aug. 1933, 6 Nov. 1933.
11. Butch to Selma, 20 Nov. 1933, 13 Dec. 1933, 10 Jan. 1934, 18 Jan. 1934, 20 Jan. 1934.
12. Butch to Selma, 26 Feb. 1934, 13 Dec. 1933.
13. Butch to Selma, 12 Apr. 1934, 15 Mar. 1934, 1 June 1934, 8 Oct. 1934.
14. Butch to Selma, 7 Jan. 1935.
15. Butch to Selma, 10 Dec. 1936.
16. Capt. Richard Nicholson, USN (Ret.), interview with SE, Nov. 1994.
17. Butch to Selma, 20 May 1935, 26 Oct. 1936, 17 Mar. 1936.
18. Butch to Selma, 30 Mar. 1937.
19. Butch to Selma, 22 Jan. 1933.
20. Butch to Selma, 12 July 1934, 26 June 1936, 18 Jan. 1934, 12 Apr. 1934.
21. Butch to Selma, 12 July 1934.
22. Ibid.; E. H. O'Hare USN Personnel Records.
23. Butch to Selma, 1 July 1935, 17 June 1935, 10 July 1935, 29 July 1935.
24. Butch to Selma, 20 July 1936.
25. Butch to Sophia Lauth, postcard dated 5 July 1936; Butch to Selma, 20 July 1936, 29 June 1936.
26. Butch to Selma, 27 Nov. 1932, 18 Feb. 1935, 11 Nov. 1935, 21 Mar. 1937; Nicholson interview with SE, May 1995.
27. Butch to Patsy, 5 Jan. 1933; Butch to Selma, 8 Nov. 1932.
28. Butch to Selma, 15 Mar. 1934, 17 July 1935, 24 June 1935; Butch to Patsy, 17 Apr. 1934; Butch to Selma, 21 Mar. 1937, 7 Jan. 1936, 7 Oct. 1935.
29. Putman interview with SE, Nov. 1994; Nicholson interview with SE, Nov. 1994.
30. Butch to Selma, 16 Aug. 1933; Nicholson interview with SE, May 1995.
31. Butch to Selma, 24 Feb. 1934, 2 Aug. 1933, 18 Feb. 1935, 3 Feb. 1936, 15 Feb. 1937.
32. Butch to Selma, 2 Aug. 1933, 28 Oct. 1935, 25 Feb. 1935, 11 Mar. 1935.

33. Butch to Selma, 8 Nov. 1934, 3 Dec. 1934, 19 Nov. 1934.
34. Butch to Selma, 4 Nov. 1935, 28 Oct. 1935; O'Hare family papers.
35. Butch to Selma, 22 July 1933, 2 Aug. 1933, 27 Jan. 1935, 31 Jan. 1937.
36. Butch to Selma, 29 July 1935, 17 Dec. 1933.
37. Butch to Selma, 17 June 1935, 4 Nov. 1935, 15 Mar. 1934, 15 Feb. 1937, 8 Mar. 1937.
38. Butch to Selma, 10 July 1935, 17 June 1935, 24 June 1935, 24 June 1935, 1 July 1935, 17 July 1935, 7 Oct. 1935, 11 Nov. 1935. "Jack Benny and his groceries of 1936": Benny's program would have a series of jokes one week on groceries, the next week on cars, and so on.
39. Butch to Selma, 9 Dec. 1935, 11 Mar. 1935, 14 Oct. 1935, 14 Jan. 1935, 28 Jan. 1935.
40. Nicholson interview with SE, May 1995; Butch to Selma, 10 Feb. 1936, 4 May 1936.
41. Butch to Selma, 9 Mar. 1936.
42. Butch to Selma, 28 Apr. 1937, 29 Mar. 1934, 23 Feb. 1937, 15 Mar. 1937, 19 Apr. 1937.
43. O'Hare family papers; Butch to Selma, 2 Mar. 1936.
44. Class rankings derived from U.S. Naval Academy Alumni Association, *Register of Alumni.*
45. Ibid., consulted for statistics.

Chapter 5. To Float and to Fly

1. Butch to Selma O'Hare, 1 Mar. 1937, 21 Mar. 1937.
2. Butch to Selma, 23 Apr. 1935, 29 July 1935, 30 May 1935.
3. For a historical sketch of the *New Mexico,* see U.S. Navy, Naval History Division, *Dictionary of American Naval Fighting Ships,* vol. 5 (Washington, D.C.: GPO, 1970), 65; for her modernization, see Norman Friedman, *U.S. Battleships: An Illustrated Design History* (Annapolis: Naval Institute Press, 1985), chap. 10.
4. Butch to Selma, 30 Sept. 1937. References to Butch's duties appear in "U.S.S. *New Mexico* Roster of Officers," 1 July 1937, 1 Jan. 1938, 1 Sept. 1938, and 1 Oct. 1938, in USS *New Mexico* Historical File, Ships' History, NHC.
5. Butch to Selma, 27 July 1937.
6. Ibid.; Butch to Selma, 19 Nov. 1934.
7. Butch to Selma, 27 July 1937, 4 Aug. 1937, 22 Aug. 1937.
8. Butch to Selma, 30 Sept. 1937, 8 Oct. 1937.
9. Butch to Selma, 30 May 1938, 27 July 1937, 22 Aug. 1937, undated (spring 1938).
10. Butch to Selma, 28 Nov. 1938, 22 Oct. 1938, 31 Oct. 1938.
11. Butch to Selma, 8 Oct. 1938, 28 Nov. 1938.
12. Butch to Marilyn O'Hare, 16 Feb. 1939.
13. Butch to Marilyn, 12 Apr. 1937.
14. Letter of commendation in E. H. O'Hare USN Personnel File.
15. All details pertaining to Butch's performance in flight training come from his file at NAS Pensacola, now held by the National Museum of Naval Aviation, Pensacola.

Chapter 6. The Sky Turned Black

1. Ens. E. H. O'Hare, USN, flight log book, Nov. 1939.
2. The details of EJ's assassination were derived from family remembrance, multiple newspaper accounts (the St. Louis papers contain numerous errors), and Chicago police reports.
3. Text of letter dated 6 Oct. 1937 and found in EJ's home soon after his death. It was reproduced, spelling mistakes and all, in the *Chicago Daily Tribune*, 14 Nov. 1939.
4. Soon after his separation EJ began a relationship with Ursula "Sue" Granata, an attractive woman then in her early twenties. The sister of two men heavily involved in state and national politics, Sue remained with EJ until his death. In November 1939, Chicago newspapers ran photos and identified her as EJ's fiancée. Laurence Bergreen's *Capone: The Man and the Era* (New York: Simon and Schuster, 1994), 588, describes her as EJ's "mistress." Patsy O'Hare Palmer remembers, "Sue was a lot of fun, a great shopper and she was good to father." Neither Patsy nor her sister Marilyn believes that EJ would have ever married Sue or any other woman.
5. Stories in the *St. Louis Globe Democrat* and *St. Louis Post Dispatch,* Mar. 1962.
6. Conversation between Toni Cavaretta and Marilyn O'Hare Platt, ca. 1955.
7. Dorothy Hyland, an attractive woman with considerable willpower—she once refused to give up the center line to an oncoming car and plowed into it, only to find that the other driver was her daughter—also contested her romantic breakup with EJ. EJ reported to his daughters that once, after she met him at the St. Louis airport, she tried to shoot him.
8. Butch's log lists the plane as an 03U-1, a close cousin of the SU-1, and the pilot listing reads "Premo," but the discrepancies can be attributed to Butch's state of mind at that tragic time.
9. *St. Louis Post Dispatch,* 11 Nov. 1939.

Chapter 7. Wings, Love, and War

1. Ens. E. H. O'Hare, USN, Aviation Training Records, in National Museum of Naval Aviation, Pensacola, for this and all subsequent quotations relating to Butch at Pensacola.
2. Adm. Willard J. Smith, USCG (Ret.), Oral History, U.S. Naval Institute, 111.
3. Biography completed by graduating students at NAS Pensacola, 26 Jan. 1940, in Lt. Comdr. E. H. O'Hare, USN, Officer Biographical File, NHC.
4. Adm. John S. Thach, USN (Ret.), Oral History, U.S. Naval Institute, 139. Small portions of Admiral Thach's oral history have been excerpted in E. T. Wooldridge, ed., *Carrier Warfare in the Pacific: An Oral History Collection* (Washington, D.C.: Smithsonian Institution Press, 1993), but all quotations here are from the original oral history.
5. Capt. O. B. Stanley, USN (Ret.), telephone interview with JBL, 17 Aug. 1994.
6. Details of flights from Lt. Comdr. E. H. O'Hare, USN, flight log books, 1939–43, in O'Hare family papers.

320 Notes to Pages 93–108

7. Quotation from Lt. Frederick Mears, *Carrier Combat* (New York: Doubleday, 1944), 24. On the *Saratoga* and *Lexington,* see Robert C. Stern, *The* Lexington *Class Carriers* (Annapolis: Naval Institute Press, 1993).

8. Thach oral history, 141–44.

9. Lt. Comdr. W. W. Harvey, USN, Officer Biographical File, NHC; Thach oral history, 139.

10. Stanley telephone interview with JBL, 17 Aug. 1994; Adm. Noel A. M. Gayler, USN (Ret.), Oral History, U.S. Naval Institute, 129–31.

11. Comdr. Don Lovelace, Jr., USN (Ret.), telephone interview with SE, Mar. 1994; Nicholson interview with SE, Nov. 1994.

12. Gayler oral history, 138–39; Stanley telephone interview with JBL, 17 Aug. 1994.

13. On the filming of *Dive Bomber,* see Bruce W. Orriss, *When Hollywood Ruled the Skies: The Aviation Film Classics of World War II* (Hawthorne, Calif.: Aero Associates, 1984), 25–30.

14. Clyde E. Baur to SE, 3 Mar. 1994; Thach oral history, 157–58; ComAirBatFor mailgram 162300 of May 1941 ("test all F2A-2 to 30,000 feet"), in VF2A-2 airplane jackets, box 7, Commander, Aircraft, Battle Force, RG-313, NA.

15. Commander in Chief, Pacific Fleet, to Chief of Naval Operations, 5 June 1941, noting that only eight F2A-2s were flyable on shore and none on carrier, also noting the F2A-2's "structural weaknesses," in ComAirBatFor, A8, box 18, RG-313, NA; Thach oral history, 159.

16. John B. Lundstrom, *The First Team: Pacific Naval Air Combat from Pearl Harbor to Midway* (Annapolis: Naval Institute Press, 1990), 478.

17. Rear Adm. James W. Condit, USN (Ret.), telephone interview with SE, 30 Oct. 1993.

18. Joseph Elliott Albert Wedder, MM File, Bureau of Aeronautics, RG-72, NA; VF4F-3/L11-1 aircraft trouble report, Bureau of Aeronautics, General Correspondence, box 4932, RG-72, NA.

19. Commander, Aircraft, Battle Force, to Chief, Bureau of Aeronautics, 22 Oct. 1941, in ComAirBatFor, A8, box 18, RG-313, NA.

20. Lt. Comdr. John S. Thach, 1941–42 notebook, in J. S. Thach Papers, National Museum of Naval Aviation, Pensacola.

21. Thach oral history, 146–57. For a full discussion of the Thach Weave, with diagrams, see Lundstrom, *First Team: Pacific Naval Air Combat,* 477–85.

22. Lt. Comdr. John S. Thach, USN, "The Red Rain of Battle: The Story of Fighter Squadron Three," pt. 1, *Collier's,* 5 Dec. 1942, 14.

23. Lt. Comdr. Donald A. Lovelace, personal diary, 8 Dec. 1941, courtesy of Comdr. Donald Lovelace, Jr., USN (Ret.).

Chapter 8. Four Minutes over the *Lady Lex*

1. Quotation in chapter subtitle from Thach 1941–42 notebook.

2. Capt. O. B. Stanley, USN (Ret.), 1941–42 personal narrative, 2, copy courtesy of Captain Stanley.

3. Ibid., 3; Thach oral history, 173–74; Gayler oral history, 153.

4. Clyde Baur to SE, 3 Mar. 1994.

5. The best account of the battle for and attempted relief of Wake Island is Robert J. Cressman, *A Magnificent Fight: The Battle for Wake Island* (Annapolis: Naval Institute Press, 1995); see also Lundstrom, *First Team: Pacific Naval Air Combat*, 32–44.

6. Lovelace diary, 18 Dec. 1941.

7. Thach oral history, 175–77; Thach 1941–42 notebook; "The War Record of Fighting Six, December 7, 1941 to June 21, 1942," in NHC.

8. Gayler oral history, 140–41; Stanley 1941–42 personal narrative, 4.

9. Stanley 1941–42 personal narrative, 5.

10. Thach oral history, 177–80.

11. The basic sources on the TF-11 cruise are Commander, Task Force Eleven, to Commander in Chief, Pacific Fleet, ser. 0123 (26 Mar. 1942), "Cruise of Task Force ELEVEN from January 31 to March 26, 1942"; and Vice Adm. Wilson Brown, unpublished memoir, "From Sail to Carrier Task Force," in Wilson Brown Papers, Nimitz Library, U.S. Naval Academy. See also Lundstrom, *First Team: Pacific Naval Air Combat*, 83–109.

12. Lt. Comdr. John S. Thach, USN, Bureau of Aeronautics interview, 26 Aug. 1942, 2; Stanley 1941–42 personal narrative, 7.

13. Brown memoir, 12.

14. Lovelace diary, 8 Feb. 1942.

15. Thach oral history, 181–82.

16. Lovelace diary, 19 Feb. 1942.

17. Brown memoir, 10, 8.

18. Ibid., 10–11.

19. The basic U.S. sources on the 20 February air battle are Commander, Task Force Eleven, to Commander in Chief, Pacific Fleet, ser. 076 (24 Feb. 1942), "Report of Action of Task Force ELEVEN with JAPANESE Aircraft on February 20, 1942"; and Commanding Officer, USS *Lexington,* to Commander, Task Force Eleven, ser. 004 (23 Feb. 1942), "Report on Air Attack on LEXINGTON on February 20, 1942." The present volume's account of the 20 February air battle corrects certain errors in Lundstrom, *First Team: Pacific Naval Air Combat*, 88–107, that relate to the organization of VF-3 and the formation of the Japanese bombers in the second wave.

20. Thach oral history, 183.

21. Ibid., 188; Thach, "Red Rain," pt. 1, pp. 15, 36.

22. The principal Japanese sources on the 20 February air battle are Japan, Self Defense Force, War History Office, *Senshi Sōsho* (War History Series), vol. 49, *Nantōhomen Kaigun Sakusen, 1* (Southeast Area Naval Operations, 1: To the Beginning of Operations to Recapture Guadalcanal) (Tokyo: Asagumo Shimbunsha, 1971), 88–92; Fourth Air Group, *kōdōchōsho* (combat log), 20 Feb. 1942; and articles in *Japan Times and Advertiser,* 9 and 14 Mar. 1942, which include narratives from unidentified pilots whose identities can be deduced from other sources.

23. The origins of the Fourth Air Group are detailed in Japan, Self Defense Force, War History Office, *Senshi Sōsho*, 49:83, 86–87, and Fumio Iwaya, *Chūkō* (Medium Attack Plane) (Tokyo: Genshobō, 1976), 262–63.

24. Robert C. Mikesh, *Japanese Aircraft Code Names and Designations* (Atglen, Pa.: Schiffer Publishing, 1993), 11. On the Betty in general, see R. J. Francillon, *Japanese Aircraft of the Pacific War* (London: Putnam, 1970), 378–87. The Imperial Navy also referred to the land-attack planes as *chūkōgekiki,* or "medium attack planes," abbreviated *chūkō.*

25. Stanley 1941–42 personal narrative, 10.

26. Vice Adm. H. S. Duckworth to JBL, 9 Jan. 1974.

27. Gayler oral history, 158.

28. Brown memoir, 18.

29. Ibid., 18–19; Stanley 1941–42 personal narrative, 11.

30. Butch O'Hare radio broadcast, 30 Mar. 1942, transcript in O'Hare family papers. Butch evidently never wrote a report of his combat on 20 February, but like all the VF-3 pilots, he gave his report orally; the recording of this report was later lost. Therefore his own experiences must be deduced from the several interviews he gave after the battle.

31. Thach oral history, 196.

32. Stanley Johnston, *Queen of the Flattops* (New York: Dutton, 1942), 95.

33. The story about catching the Japanese by surprise was related by Butch in 1943 to George Givens; George Givens to Rear Adm. Carl R. Doerflinger, 7 Oct. 1987, in George Givens Papers, courtesy of Mrs. Mary Givens.

34. *Japan Times and Advertiser,* 14 Mar. 1942.

35. Butch O'Hare radio broadcast, 30 Mar. 1942; *Japan Times and Advertiser,* 14 Mar. 1942. In *Queen of the Flattops,* 95, Stanley Johnston quotes Butch as saying that engines dropped out of these aircraft, but this detail appears nowhere else in any of Butch's accounts, and the author may have embellished the story. As will be shown, only one bomber that Butch attacked actually lost an engine.

36. Butch O'Hare radio broadcast, 30 Mar. 1942.

37. *Japan Times and Advertiser,* 9 Mar. 1942.

38. Quotations from Wayne Thomis, "The Real Story of Hero O'Hare," *Washington Times-Herald,* 9 June 1942, using material from United Press dispatches and the *Chicago Tribune.*

39. Stanley 1941–42 personal narrative, 11; Lovelace diary, 20 Feb. 1942.

40. Brown memoir, 17–18; *Boston Daily Globe,* 9 Mar. 1942, with dispatch of United Press correspondent Francis McCarthy, who was on one of the heavy cruisers.

41. *Japan Times and Advertiser,* 14 and 9 Mar. 1942.

42. Ibid., 9 Mar. 1942.

43. Ibid.

44. Butch O'Hare radio broadcast, 30 Mar. 1942; John Field, "How O'Hare Downed Five Jap Planes in One Day," *Life,* 13 Apr. 1942, 18.

45. Thach oral history, 283; Lloyd Wendt, "Five Jap Planes Measure the Heroism of Butch O'Hare," *Chicago Sunday Tribune Graphic Magazine,* 25 Sept. 1949, 11.

46. Clyde Baur, telephone interview with JBL, Mar. 1995.

47. Thach oral history, 283–84.

48. Thach, "Red Rain," pt. 1, p. 37.

49. Thach oral history, 198–99. On the *daitai* markings I (JBL) am indebted to James F. Lansdale, who corrects the error in *First Team: Pacific Naval Air Combat,* 104–5, referring to "command stripes."

50. Thach, "Red Rain," pt. 1, p. 37.

51. CO, USS *Lexington,* ser. 004, 6; Stanley telephone interview with JBL, 17 Aug. 1994.

52. J. S. Thach to Lloyd Wendt, 30 Nov. 1948, in Thach Papers, National Museum of Naval Aviation, Pensacola; Wendt, "Five Jap Planes," 17.

53. Message 232146 of Feb. 1942, CTF-11 to CinCPac, ComANZAC, info CominCh, in CinCPac Secret & Confidential Message File, RG-38, NA.

54. Stanley 1941–42 personal narrative, 12.

55. Message 270642 of Feb. 1942, CTF-11 to CinCPac, in CinCPac Secret & Confidential Message File, RG-38, NA; Thach oral history, 180–81.

56. Stanley 1941–42 personal narrative, 12; Lovelace diary, 4 Mar. 1942.

57. Brown memoir, 21. The basic source on the Lae-Salamaua raid is Commander, Task Force Eleven, to Commander in Chief, U.S. Fleet, 25 Mar. 1942, "Report of Attack on Enemy Forces in Salamaua-Lae Area, March 10, 1942" (which includes reports of Commander, Task Group 11.5, USS *Lexington* and USS *Yorktown*). See also Lundstrom, *First Team: Pacific Naval Air Combat,* 124–32.

58. Thach oral history, 203–4.

59. Ibid., 205–6.

60. Stanley 1941–42 personal narrative, 15.

61. Lovelace diary, 26 Mar. 1942.

Chapter 9. The Uncomfortable Hero

1. *St. Louis Star-Times,* 5 Mar. 1942.

2. Associated Press story in *Seattle Post Intelligencer,* [?] Mar. 1942.

3. *St. Louis Post Dispatch,* 9 Mar. 1942.

4. Abstract of letter in Lt. Comdr. E. H. O'Hare, USN, "OO" File, RG-72, NA; messages (all of Apr. 1942) 062008, CominCh to CinCPac, 072016, ComCarDivOne to CinCPac, and 081909, CinCPac to CominCh, in CinCPac Secret & Confidential Message File, RG-38, NA.

5. O'Hare family papers.

6. Dennis E. McClendon and Wallace F. Richards, *The Legend of Colin Kelly, America's First Hero of WWII* (Missoula, Mont.: Pictorial Histories Publishing, 1994). This biography offers the standard, but wrong, interpretation of Kelly's target as the heavy cruiser *Ashigara,* but it was in fact the *Natori.* See the *Natori*'s action report in Chief of Naval Operations, OP29 Naval History, "Japanese World War II Naval Records Seized in Post-war Japan," microfilm JT1, NHC.

7. Letter dated 8 Apr. 1942 [from Secretary of the Navy Frank Knox] recommending Medal of Honor, cited on Lt. Comdr. Edward H. O'Hare Citation Card, U.S. Navy Board of Decorations, Citation Card File, Ships' History, NHC, where is added, "In view of the outstanding nature of the service rendered by Lt. O'Hare, its immediate undoubted value to the U.S.S. LEXINGTON, and its glorious example to all the personnel of the air services of the United States, it is further recommended that Lt. O'Hare be advanced one grade in rank."

8. Final wording of citation from U.S. Navy Department, *Medal of Honor, 1861–1949: The Navy* (Washington, D.C.: GPO, 1949), 232. The preliminary citation on Lieutenant Commander O'Hare's Citation Card differs slightly.

9. United Press story, 24 Apr. 1942.

10. Mrs. A. K. Doyle via Hill Goodspeed, July 1994.

11. Abstract of letter in Lt. Comdr. E. H. O'Hare, USN, "OO" File, RG-72, NA.

12. *St. Louis Star-Times,* 20 Apr. 1942; Associated Press story, 21 Apr. 1942.

13. *St. Louis Daily Globe Democrat,* 26 Apr. 1942.

14. *St. Louis Star-Times,* 25 Apr. 1942.

15. *St. Louis Globe Democrat,* 26 Apr. 1942; *St. Louis Star-Times* (Saturday afternoon), 25 Apr. 1942.

16. Letter in Lt. Comdr. E. H. O'Hare, USN, "OO" File, RG-72, NA.

Chapter 10. The King of Maui

1. Lt. (jg) Howard Clark and ensigns Richard Rowell, Dale Peterson, and Newton H. Mason.

2. Lt. Comdr. John S. Thach, "The Red Rain of Battle: The Story of Fighter Squadron Three," pt. 2, *Collier's,* 12 Dec. 1942, 46. For squadron activities, see VF-3 war diary, 30 June 1942–31 Dec. 1942, in NHC.

3. For the history of the Maui airfields, see NAS Puunene war diary, 1942–43, in NHC; Capt. John E. Lacouture, USN (Ret.), "Maui Aviation," *Wings of Gold,* spring 1989, 45–47.

4. Lundstrom, *First Team: Pacific Naval Air Combat,* 482–85.

5. VF-3 war diary, Oct.–Nov. 1942, in NHC; O'Hare flight log book. On the Corsair, see Barrett Tillman, *Corsair: The F4U in World War II and Korea* (Annapolis: Naval Institute Press, 1979).

6. Lt. (jg) John P. Altemus, diary, 20 Oct. 1942, courtesy of Randy Altemus.

7. Capt. A. W. Callan, USN (Ret.), telephone interview with SE, 14 Apr. 1994.

8. Comdr. S. E. Mendenhall, USN (Ret.), telephone interview with SE, 3 Feb. 1994.

9. Callan telephone interview with SE, 14 Apr. 1994.

10. Mendenhall telephone interview with SE, 3 Feb. 1994; Rear Adm. E. L. Feightner, USN (Ret.), telephone interview with SE, 23 Apr. 1994.

11. Clyde Baur to SE, 3 Mar. 1994.

12. Altemus diary, 24 Oct. 1942; Comdr. S. E. Mendenhall, telephone interview with JBL, 1 Nov. 1995.

13. ACRM W. Decker, USN (Ret.), telephone interview with SE, 6 May 1994.

14. Feightner telephone interview with SE, 23 Apr. 1994.

15. Ibid.

16. Capt. John E. Lacouture, USN (Ret.), to SE, 3 Mar. 1994; Lacouture, "Maui Aviation," 47; Ron Youngblood, "The Von Tempsky Wall," *Maui News,* 16 Oct. 1994, via Alan A. DeCoite; Stanley Johnston, *The Grim Reapers* (New York: Dutton, 1943), 102.

17. Comdr. A. Vraciu, USN (Ret.), telephone interview with SE, 20 Jan. 1994; Mendenhall telephone interview with SE, 3 Feb. 1994.

18. Butch to Selma O'Hare, 13 Nov. 1942; Butch to Marilyn O'Hare, 28 Nov. 1942, 9 Oct. 1943.

19. Butch to Selma, 3 Sept. 1942, 13 Nov. 1942; Butch to Marilyn, 9 Oct. 1943.

20. The phrase in the subhead is from Capt. Howard W. Crews, USN (Ret.), personal diary, 16 Feb. 1943, courtesy of Carolyn Crews-Whitby; see also the entries for 23–31 Jan. 1943; Rear Adm. George C. Bullard, USN, Officer Biographical File, NHC.

21. Mendenhall telephone interview with SE, 3 Feb. 1994.

22. Baur to SE, 3 Mar. 1994.

23. Crews diary, 16 Feb. 1943.

24. Ibid., 17 Feb. 1943; Altemus diary, Mar. 1943.

Chapter 11. Home and Back

1. Details in "History of Torpedo Squadron 6," 17 Dec. 1944, with text of airmailgram message 151810 of Mar. 1943, ComAirGroupSix to CominCh; see also Commander, Fighting Squadron Six, to Chief of Naval Operations, "History of Fighting Squadron Six," 31 Dec. 1944. Both in NHC.

2. Barrett Tillman, *Hellcat: The F6F in World War II* (Annapolis: Naval Institute Press, 1979).

3. Crews diary; Altemus diary. For the *Nassau*'s operations, see William T. Y'Blood, *The Little Giants: U.S. Escort Carriers against Japan* (Annapolis: Naval Institute Press, 1987), 30–33.

4. Capt. Herschel A. Pahl, USN (Ret.), *Point Option: Carrier Warfare in the Pacific through the Eyes of a Junior Fighter Pilot* (Privately printed, 1988), 44, 46.

5. Callan telephone interview with SE, 14 Apr. 1994.

6. Vraciu telephone interview with SE, 20 Jan. 1994.

7. Joe D. Robbins to SE, undated (1994).

8. Pahl, *Point Option,* 49.

9. Altemus diary, 27 June 1943.

10. Crews diary, 21–30 June 1943; Pahl, *Point Option,* 50.

11. Pahl, *Point Option,* 50–51.

12. Capt. George F. Rodgers, USN, "O'Hare: A Name with a Proud Past," *Chicago Sunday Tribune,* 24 Mar. 1963, 6; Sgt. Merle Miller, "What's Butch O'Hare Doing These Days?" *Yank,* undated clipping in O'Hare family papers.

13. Altemus diary, 29 June 1943, 8 July 1943; Crews diary, 1–3 July 1943.

14. Altemus diary, 9 July 1943.
15. USS *Enterprise* fly sheet for operations, 12 July 1943, in Altemus diary; details of exercise in "Bombing Squadron Six History 15 March 1943–15 December 1944," in NHC.
16. Actual orders for the change are in CominCh confidential dispatch 081321 of July 1943. For the dispute over Felix, see CO, VF-6, to Chief of Naval Operations, 3 Nov. 1944, and CAG-3 to BuAer, 31 Oct. 1945, both in VF-31 File, Aviation History Branch, NHC; see also Thomas F. Gates, "Track of the Tomcatters: A History of VF-31," 4 pts., *The Hook,* fall 1984, winter 1984, spring 1985, summer 1985.
17. Altemus diary, 26 July 1943.
18. Ibid., 1 Aug. 1943.

Chapter 12. Marcus and Wake

1. For CVLs, see Norman Friedman, *U.S. Aircraft Carriers: An Illustrated Design History* (Annapolis: Naval Institute Press, 1983), 177–91; Lt. Comdr. Ashley Halsey, Jr., USNR, "The CVL's Success Story," *U.S. Naval Institute Proceedings,* Apr. 1946, 522–31 (quotation from 528). For the USS *Independence,* see USS *Independence* war diary and "War History 'Mighty I,' May 1941–2 Sept. 1945," both in NHC.
2. Altemus diary, 5 Aug. 1943.
3. Ibid., 7 and 8 Aug. 1943.
4. Crews diary, 18–24 Aug. 1943.
5. Rear Adm. James M. Peters, Officer Biographical File, NHC.
6. The basic sources on the Marcus Island raid are Commander, Task Force Fifteen, to Commander in Chief, Pacific Fleet, "Attack on Marcus Island—31 August 1943," 22 Sept. 1943; Commanding Officer, USS *Essex,* to Commander in Chief, Pacific Fleet, ser. 10001 (3 Sept. 1943), "Action Report—Marcus Island Raid" (with squadron and ACA-1 reports); Commanding Officer, USS *Yorktown,* to Commander in Chief, Pacific Fleet, ser. 1042 (6 Sept. 1943), "Air Attack on Marcus Island on 31 August 1943" (with squadron and ACA-1 reports); and Commanding Officer, USS *Independence,* to Commander in Chief, Pacific Fleet, ser. 006 (7 Sept. 1943), "Action Report Attack on Marcus Island 31 August 1943" (includes ACA-1 reports); also the detailed account in Clark G. Reynolds, *The Fighting Lady: The New* Yorktown *in the Pacific War* (Missoula, Mont.: Pictorial Histories Publishing, 1986), 32–45. For the Japanese side, see Japan, Self Defense Force, War History Office, *Senshi Sōsho* (War History Series), vol. 62, *Chūbu Taiheiyō Homen Kaigun Sakusen, 2* (Central Pacific Area Naval Operations, 2: From June 1942 On) (Tokyo: Asagumo Shimbunsha, 1973), 389–90.
7. Reynolds, *Fighting Lady,* 43.
8. Sources on the VF-6 Marcus mission are VF-6 ACA-1 action report, 31 Aug. 1943 (included in CO, USS *Independence,* ser. 006); also Comdr. Alex Vraciu to JBL, 18 July 1994; Comdr. S. E. Mendenhall to JBL, 21 Jan. 1995; and telephone

interviews by SE with Vraciu (20 Jan. 1994), Mendenhall (3 Feb. 1994), and Callan (14 Apr. 1994).

9. Commander in Chief, Pacific Fleet, "Monthly Analysis of the Situation in the Pacific Ocean Areas," Aug. 1943, 12.

10. Reynolds, *Fighting Lady*, 43–45; Japan, Self Defense Force, War History Office, *Senshi Sōsho*, 62:390.

11. CO, USS *Independence*, ser. 006; Reynolds, *Fighting Lady*, 52; Mendenhall telephone interview with SE, 3 Feb. 1994; CTF-15 to CinCPac, 22 Sept. 1943.

12. USS *Independence* war history, NHC.

13. Altemus diary, 30 Sept. 1943.

14. The basic U.S. sources on the Wake raid are Commander, Task Force Fourteen, to Commander in Chief, Pacific Fleet, ser. 00288 (n.d.), "Attack on Wake Atoll, 5 and 6 October 1943, Action Report on," in Commander in Chief, Pacific Fleet, to Commander in Chief, U.S. Fleet, ser. 001865 (28 June 1944), "Attack on Wake Atoll, 5–6 October 1943," with copies of all ship and squadron action reports attached. See also "'Transcript of Recording of Critique on WAKE of 5–6 October 1943.' Held at Submarine Base 14 October 1943."

15. Rear Adm. A. M. Pride, USN, OpNav interview, OPNAV-16-V-#50 (20 June 1944), 3.

16. The basic sources on the defense of Wake are Japan, Self Defense Force, War History Office, *Senshi Sōsho*, 62:410–14, and 252 Air Group, *kōdōchōsho* (combat log), 6 Oct. 1943. On the 252 Air Group, see Ikuhiko Hata and Yasuho Izawa, *Japanese Naval Aces and Fighter Units in World War II* (Annapolis: Naval Institute Press, 1989), 113–16.

17. The basic sources for the light carrier and cruiser operations at Wake are Commanding Officer, USS *Independence*, to Commander in Chief, Pacific Fleet, ser. 008 (10 Oct. 1943), "Action Report Attack on Wake Island, October 5 and 6, 1943," whose enclosures include Commanding Officer, VF-6, "Forwarding of ACA-1 Reports for Wake Island, Strike of 5–6 October 1943" (ACA-1 reports for Lt. Comdr. E. H. O'Hare, Lt. S. E. Mendenhall, Lt. [jg] A. Vraciu, Ens. A. W. Callan, and Ens. H. T. Landry); Commanding Officer, USS *Belleau Wood*, to Commander in Chief, Pacific Fleet, ser. 0010 (11 Oct. 1943), "Attack on Wake Island October 5 and 6, 1943" (with squadron and ACA-1 reports); and Commander, Task Group 14.2, to Commander in Chief, Pacific Fleet, 12 Oct. 1943, "Action Report Shore Bombardment of Wake Island on 5 October 1943, Z plus 12 Time" (including reports of individual cruisers and destroyers). Also telephone interviews by SE with Vraciu (20 Jan. 1994), Mendenhall (3 Feb. 1994), and Callan (14 Apr. 1994); Vraciu to JBL, 18 July 1994; Mendenhall to JBL, 21 Jan. 1995, 7 Dec. 1995; and Mr. Henry T. Landry, telephone interview with JBL, 22 Jan. 1995.

18. CO, USS *Independence*, ser. 008; Comdr. J. M. Peters's statement in Wake Island critique (cited in n. 14 above).

19. Information on 755 Air Group from Dr. Izawa Yasuho to JBL, 2 June 1994.

Chapter 13. Air Group Commander

1. Altemus diary, 12–14 Oct. 1943.
2. "History of Fighting Squadron One," in NHC.
3. For VF-2, see the superb wartime history by the air combat intelligence officer based on his diary and other documents: Lt. Thomas L. Morrissey, USNR, *The Odyssey of Fighting Two* (Privately printed, 1945).
4. Ibid., 30.
5. Ibid., 31.
6. Ibid.; Capt. W. A. Skon, USN (Ret.), to JBL, 15 Apr. 1994.
7. Skon to JBL, 15 Apr. 1994.
8. Claude Dickerson, interview with SE, Dec. 1994.
9. Adm. Arthur W. Radford, USN (Ret.), Officer Biographical File, NHC.
10. Rear Adm. Samuel E. Morison, *History of United States Naval Operations of World War II,* vol. 7, *Aleutians, Gilberts, and Marshalls, June 1942–April 1944* (Boston: Little, Brown, 1951), 114–20.
11. The basic official reports on TG-50.2 and the *Enterprise* in the Gilberts are Commander, Carrier Division Eleven (Task Group 50.2), ser. 00133 (5 Dec. 1943), "Preliminary Report of Gilberts Operation"; and Commanding Officer, USS *Enterprise,* to Commander in Chief, Pacific Fleet, ser. 0177 (15 Dec. 1943), "Operations as a Unit of Task Group 50.2 from 10 November to 27 November 1943—Report of." Both in NHC.
12. Morrissey, *Odyssey of Fighting Two,* 36.
13. Sources on the defense of the Gilberts include Japan, Self Defense Force, War History Office, *Senshi Sōsho,* 62:441–504; U.S. War Department, Historical Division, *The Capture of Makin (20 November–24 November 1943)* (Washington, D.C.: War Department, 1946); and Philip A. Crowl and Edmund G. Love, *Seizure of the Gilberts and Marshalls* (in the series *U.S. Army in World War II: The War in the Pacific*) (Washington, D.C.: GPO, 1955).
14. George P. Givens to Capt. Richard Nicholson, 23 Jan. 1988, in Givens Papers, courtesy of Mrs. Mary Givens.
15. Morrissey, *Odyssey of Fighting Two,* 38.
16. The basic official sources for Air Group Six's operations off Makin and Tarawa, 19–27 November 1943 are Commander, Air Group Six, to Commanding Officer, Task Force 50.2 (30 Nov. 1943), "Aircraft Action Report—Forwarding of" (an enclosure to CO, USS *Enterprise,* ser. 0177, that includes ACA-1 reports of VB-6, VF-2, and VT-6); and USS *Enterprise* war diary, 19–27 Nov. 1943. Both in NHC.
17. Morrissey, *Odyssey of Fighting Two,* 40.
18. Ibid.
19. ComCarDiv 11, ser. 00133, enclosure D, 2; Skon to JBL, 15 Apr. 1994.
20. Butch's flight log book (filled out after his death) records only 0.5 hour for this flight, but Captain Skon confirms that this is an error; Skon to JBL, 6 Jan. 1995, with copies from his own log book.
21. War Department, *Capture of Makin,* 35.

22. Ibid., 54–55.
23. Dialogue in VT-6 ACA-1 report no. 8, enclosure A, "Log of Liaison Plane Kept by Lt. W. H. Fitzpatrick, A-V(S) USN." For a personal account by a participant, see Alvin Kernan, *Crossing the Line: A Bluejacket's World War II Odyssey* (Annapolis: Naval Institute Press, 1994), 102–3.
24. VT-6 ACA-1 report no. 8; Kernan, *Crossing the Line,* 103–6.
25. ComCarDiv 11, ser. 00133.

Chapter 14. Butch's Black Panthers

1. USS *Independence* war history, NHC; Japan, Self Defense Force, War History Office, *Senshi Sōsho,* 62:475–77.
2. Stephen Jurika, Jr., ed., *From Pearl Harbor to Vietnam: The Memoirs of Admiral Arthur W. Radford* (Stanford: Hoover Institution Press, 1980), 15–16; hereafter cited as *Radford Memoirs.*
3. Clark G. Reynolds, *Admiral John H. Towers: The Struggle for Naval Air Supremacy* (Annapolis: Naval Institute Press, 1991), 442–43; *Radford Memoirs,* 16–17.
4. Jack Alexander, "They Sparked the Carrier Revolution," *Saturday Evening Post,* 16 Sept. 1944, 50.
5. U.S. Pacific Fleet, South Pacific Force, Intelligence Section, air battle notes from the South Pacific, no. 29 (18 Dec. 1943), "Japanese Night Torpedo Plane Attacks," in NHC; Iwaya, *Chūkō,* 337–41.
6. Commander, Carrier Division Eleven, to Commander, Air Force, Pacific Fleet, "Carrier Night Fighter Operations," undated copy in Adm. A. W. Radford Papers, NHC, courtesy of Dr. Jeffrey Barlow. This report, ca. 1 Dec. 1943, is Radford's first written comment about carrier night fighters in the Gilberts.
7. Barrett Tillman, "Night Hookers, Part 1, 1942–1945: A History of Carrier Night Operations," *The Hook,* spring 1988, 41–52; Comdr. James Seton Gray, Jr., USN, "Development of Naval Night Fighters in World War II," *U.S. Naval Institute Proceedings,* July 1948, 847–51; Vice Adm. William I. Martin, USN (Ret.), Vice Adm. Turner F. Caldwell, USN (Ret.), and Comdr. Edwin R. Jenks, USN (Ret.), "Black Chickens and Bat Teams," *Naval Aviation News,* Mar. 1972, 37–41. A new analysis of night-fighter operations emphasizing Europe is Ken Delve, *Nightfighter: The Battle for the Night Skies* (London: Arms and Armour Press, 1995).
8. Reynolds, *Towers,* 437.
9. Chief of Naval Operations to Commander, Air Force, Pacific Fleet, ser. 011431 (18 Nov. 1943), "Night Fighter Program—Radar Control and Interception— Equipment for," copy in Vice Adm. J. H. Flatley Papers, courtesy of the Flatley family.
10. In addition to Radford's first report (cited in n. 6 above), the basic official sources for the Radford-O'Hare night-fighter tactics are Commander, Carrier Division Eleven, to Commander, Air Force, Pacific Fleet, ser. 00134 (4 Dec. 1943), "Carrier Night Fighter Operations," and Commanding Officer, USS *Enterprise,* to Com-

mander, Air Force, Pacific Fleet, ser. 0020 (7 Dec. 1943), "Carrier Night Fighters," both in ComNavAirPac, A16-3, box 221, RG-313, NA; also Rear Adm. Samuel P. Ginder, USN, to Commander in Chief, Pacific Fleet, ser. 00132 (4 Dec. 1943), "Japanese Torpedo Plane Attacks against Task Group 50.2 on November 25 and 26, 1943," and Commander, Air Force, Pacific Fleet, to Commander in Chief, Pacific Fleet, ser. 0033 (9 Jan. 1944), "Analysis of Enemy Night Torpedo Attacks—Central Pacific—18 November–5 December 1943," both in NHC.

11. Office of the Chief of Naval Operations, Aviation Training Division, "Operation of Airborne Radar," Sept. 1944, courtesy of Phil Edwards, National Air and Space Museum.

12. Hazen B. Rand to JBL, 18 May 1994; Barrett Tillman, *Avenger at War* (New York: Scribner's, 1980).

13. On Phillips, see Officer Biographical File, NHC; Kernan, *Crossing the Line,* 95, 98.

14. Hazen Rand to JBL, Apr. 1994; Kernan, *Crossing the Line,* 98, 101.

15. Marcell F. Varner to JBL, 20 Apr. 1994.

16. On the *Enterprise* CIC and radars, correspondence and telephone interviews by JBL with R. W. Gregory, Jr., radar operator (5 Apr. 1994), and Victor Bottari, Jr., a CIC officer (11 Jan. 1995).

17. Lt. Comdr. J. H. Flatley to CO, USS *Enterprise,* memo dated 5 Dec. 1942, in Flatley Papers, courtesy of the Flatley family. For the fighter director controversy during Santa Cruz that led to Givens's promotion, see John Lundstrom, *The First Team and the Guadalcanal Campaign: Naval Fighter Combat from August to November 1942* (Annapolis: Naval Institute Press, 1994), 457–59.

18. George Givens to Rear Adm. Carl R. Doerflinger, 7 Oct. 1987, in Givens Papers, courtesy of Mrs. Mary Givens.

19. Message 181830 of Nov. 1943, CTG-50.2 to TG-50.2, copy with ComCarDiv 11 undated report in Radford Papers, NHC, courtesy of Dr. Jeffrey Barlow. On Burd, see Lt. (jg) W. W. Burd report, Radio Intelligence Unit Reports, SRH-317, RG-457, NA. In *Radford Memoirs,* 17, the RI officer is erroneously identified as Lt. W. L. Kluss, but Kluss served with Radford in 1945.

20. Hazen Rand to JBL, Apr. 1994, including the draft of an unpublished article from ca. 1979 written by his son Christopher B. Rand and entitled "Who Killed Butch O'Hare?" It also contains his father's recollections.

21. Capt. R. M. Voris, USN (Ret.), telephone interview with JBL, 22 Mar. 1994.

22. Lt. Comdr. James H. Trousdale, Jr., USNR, "The Birth of the Navy's Night Fighters," *U.S. Naval Institute Proceedings,* June 1952, 621; Givens to Doerflinger, 7 Oct. 1987.

23. USS *Enterprise* deck log, 24 Nov. 1943, RG-24, NA. In his flight log Marcell Varner wrote, "Butch O'Hare almost crashed us in dark (flying wing)" (copy enclosed with Varner to JBL, 20 Apr. 1994), but this must have been a pilot from the no. 2 team, because Butch flew with the no. 1 team. In a letter to JBL dated 17 July 1994 Captain Voris wrote, "I do specifically recall that after launch and as I climbed through and broke out of a cloud layer I encountered and immediately identified John McInerny's TBF. I was surprised that the rendezvous occurred so unexpectedly easy."

24. Comdr. Frank W. Wead, USNR, "Missing in Action," *Skyways,* Oct. 1944, 60.

25. Burd report, SRH-317, 214; Altemus diary, 24 Nov. 1943.

26. For deployment of the Twenty-fourth Air Flotilla to the Gilberts, see Japan, Self Defense Force, War History Office, *Senshi Sōsho,* 62:483–85. On the 752 Air Group, see Itō Fukusaburō, "Dai 752 Kaigun Kōkūtai to Nonaka Gorō Shōsa" (Lt. Comdr. Nonaka Gorō with the 752 Naval Air Group), in Chūkōkai (Medium Attack Bomber Association), *Kaigun Chūkō Shidanshu* (Historical Anthology of the Navy Medium Attack Bomber) (Tokyo: Chūkōkai, 1980), 413–29. Itō was Nonaka's second in command during the Gilberts campaign.

27. Hatsuho Naito, *Thunder Gods: The Kamikaze Pilots Tell Their Story* (Tokyo: Kodansha International, 1989), 53 and passim. In October 1944 Nonaka became *hikōtaichō* of the 721 Air Group (*Jinrai,* or "Heavenly Thunder"), whose Bettys lugged the manned rocket-powered *Oka* ("Cherry Blossom") bombs into battle. The high command hoped that the new weapon would result in massive destruction of Allied ships and turn the tide of the war. Profoundly disturbed by the concept of organized kamikaze suicide attacks, Nonaka felt that the *Okas* (dubbed Baka or "idiot" bombs by the U.S. Navy) would be ineffectual and a tragic waste of life. Even so, he worked hard to keep unit morale up while never failing to tell his commanders that the whole idea was a fiasco. On 21 March 1945 Nonaka died leading the first *Oka* mission south of Kyūshū, when Hellcats shot down all eighteen Bettys short of the target.

28. Itō's article in *Kaigun Chūkō Shidanshu,* 424–25.

29. Altemus diary, 25 Nov. 1943.

30. *Radford Memoirs,* 17.

31. Altemus diary, 25 Nov. 1943.

32. *Radford Memoirs,* 18.

33. Skon did not fly this mission, and it is not known who accompanied Butch and Phillips.

34. VF-1 war diary, 25 Nov. 1943, in NHC. Eugene Burns's 27 Nov. 1943 Associated Press dispatch (published 11 Dec. 1943) wrongly gave Butch credit for being the first carrier pilot to land at Tarawa. The first was Lt. William W. Kelly of VF-18 on the *Bunker Hill,* who landed at about 1000 on 24 November; see Robert Olds, *Helldiver Squadron* (New York: Dodd, Mead, 1945), 115–16. On Tate, see Commander, Central Pacific Force, to Commander in Chief, Pacific Fleet, ser. 0234 (29 Dec. 1943), endorsement to Commander, Task Group 50.3, ser. 00317 (11 Dec. 1943), in NHC.

35. Vice Adm. B. M. Strean, USN (Ret.), interview with SE, Nov. 1994.

36. The basic official sources for the 25 November 1943 night attack are Commanding Officer, USS *North Carolina,* to Commander in Chief, Pacific Fleet, ser. 008 (6 Dec. 1943), "Action of 25 November 1943," courtesy of Kim Robinson Sincox, curator of USS *North Carolina;* and 752 Air Group, *kōdōchōsho* (combat log), 26 Nov. 1943 (Z-9), in War History Office, Tokyo, courtesy of Dr. Izawa Yasuho.

37. Morrissey, *Odyssey of Fighting Two,* 49.

38. *Radford Memoirs,* 18; Burd report, SRH-317, 215; Japan, Self Defense Force, War History Office, *Senshi Sōsho,* 62:490–91.

Chapter 15. 26 November 1943

1. Message 260238/260248 of Nov. 1943, ComCentPac to all CTF, in CinCPac Secret & Confidential Message File, RG-38, NA.

2. Lt. Comdr. R. W. Jackson to Rita O'Hare, Dec. 1943, copy in O'Hare family papers.

3. Eugene Burns, "Butch O'Hare's Last Flight," *Saturday Evening Post,* 11 Mar. 1944, 19. For another version of the speech, see Lloyd Wendt, "The Last Flight of Heroic Butch O'Hare," *Chicago Sunday Tribune Graphic Magazine,* 9 Oct. 1949, 20.

4. On the Third Gilbert Islands Air Battle, see Japan, Self Defense Force, War History Office, *Senshi Sōsho,* 62:491–92, and 752 Air Group, *kōdōchōsho* (combat log), 27 Nov. 1943 (Z-9). The four *chūtai* commanders were Lt. Itō Fukusaburō, Lt. Natsume Heihachirō, Lt. Nomura Takashi, and Lt. Saitō Sōichi. Lt. Comdr. Nonaka rode in Itō's aircraft.

5. USS *Plunger,* "Report of Ninth War Patrol," 18 Dec. 1943, in NHC; message 270450 of Nov. 1943, *Plunger* to ComSubPac, in CinCPac Secret & Confidential Message File, RG-38, NA.

6. Burd report, SRH-317, 216–17; *Radford Memoirs,* 18.

7. Skon to JBL, 15 Apr. 1994.

8. Jackson to Rita O'Hare, Dec. 1943.

9. USS *Belleau Wood,* VF-24 ACA-1 report no. 1 (27 Nov. 1943), and USS *Bunker Hill,* ser. 0023 (15 Dec. 1943), VF-18 ACA-1 report no. 23 (27 Nov. 1943), both in NHC.

10. Burns, "Last Flight," 19; Dickerson interview with SE, Dec. 1994.

11. Charles P. Arnot, United Press International, "Famed Flier Down," *Honolulu Advertiser,* 11 Dec. 1943.

12. Jackson to Rita O'Hare, Dec. 1943.

13. Burns, "Last Flight," 19; Johnson's identity from Richard M. Woods, a fellow *Enterprise* plane captain, via *Enterprise* historian James T. Rindt.

14. Jackson to Rita O'Hare, Dec. 1943. The basic official sources on the 26 November night-fighter mission, in addition to the TG-50.2 and *Enterprise* reports (cited in n. 11 of chap. 13 and nn. 6 and 10 of chap. 14), are VF-2 ACA-1 report no. 11 (27 Nov. 1943), with annex A, statement of Ens. Warren A. Skon, A-V(N), USNR, and VT-6 ACA-1 report no. 7 (27 Nov. 1943).

15. Adm. Arthur W. Radford to Capt. Samuel E. Morison, confidential letter dated 23 Feb. 1951, in Radford Papers, NHC, courtesy of Dr. Jeffrey Barlow; Com-CarDiv 11, ser. 00134, 2. In his 9 October 1949 *Chicago Sunday Tribune* article, Lloyd Wendt asserted that the air officer (Comdr. Tom Hamilton) had briefed Butch immediately before he manned his fighter. At that time Butch supposedly learned that the FDO would immediately vector him and Skon after the snooper and try to rendezvous with the TBF later. Wendt also stated that Butch told this to Skon and Phillips prior to launch. However, this is not confirmed in any other source. Neither Skon nor Phillips seems to have known of any change in plan prior to launch.

16. Kernan, *Crossing the Line,* 111–12; Skon to JBL, 15 Apr. 1994.

17. Hazen Rand to JBL, Apr. 1994, 18 May 1994; Christopher B. Rand, unpublished article, "Who Killed Butch O'Hare?" 8. Technical details on the ASB are from CNO, "Operation of Airborne Radar," Sept. 1994 (cited in n. 11 of chap. 14).

18. VF-2 ACA-1 report no. 11; Skon to JBL, 15 Apr. 1994, 27 Apr. 1994.

19. On the battleship AA action, see Commander, Task Unit 50.2.3 (Rear Adm. Glenn B. Davis, ComBatDiv 8), ser. 0025 (23 Dec. 1943), "Action Report, Night of 26 November 1943," including reports of the USS *Massachusetts,* ser. 0014 (11 Dec. 1943), and USS *Indiana,* ser. 001 (11 Dec. 1943), plus the excellent report, Commanding Officer, USS *North Carolina,* to Commander in Chief, Pacific Fleet, ser. 009 (17 Dec. 1943), "Action of 26 November 1943"; all in NHC (copy to JBL of *North Carolina* report courtesy of Kim Robinson Sincox, curator, USS *North Carolina).*

20. Altemus diary, 26 Nov. 1943; Burns, "Last Flight," 69, 71. Rear Adm. Samuel P. Ginder, an observer on the *Enterprise,* boasted, "Truly that 5-V disposition formed a ring of steel around the Carriers and gave the torpedo planes a wholesome respect for our withering gunfire"; Ginder to CinCPac, ser. 00132, 3.

21. *Radford Memoirs,* 18; Burns, "Last Flight," 71.

22. Trousdale, "Birth of the Navy's Night Fighters," 622.

23. VT-6 ACA-1 report no. 7; Gregory telephone interview with JBL, 5 Apr. 1994; Kernan, *Crossing the Line,* 112.

24. Kernan, *Crossing the Line,* 112–13.

25. Ibid., 112; George Givens, 1987 narrative, in Givens Papers, courtesy of Mrs. Mary Givens.

26. Hazen Rand to JBL, Apr. 1994; Rand, "Who Killed Butch O'Hare?" 9.

27. Skon to JBL, 18 Apr. 1994, 6 Jan. 1995; VF-2 ACA-1 report no. 11; Morrissey, *Odyssey of Fighting Two,* 51; 752 Air Group, *kōdōchōsho* (combat log).

28. Jackson to Rita O'Hare, Dec. 1943.

29. Givens 1987 narrative; Skon to JBL, 15 Apr. 1987. In a letter to JBL dated 28 Jan. 1995, Captain Skon noted that in November 1943 "the radio communication equipment and its capabilities for netting and information exchange among aircraft and ships was still a crude albeit rapidly growing field of technology. . . . Both the means to operate the equipment and its installation in aircraft cockpits left much to be desired in the way of human engineering, from the pilots' viewpoint." He stressed that on the night flight of 26 November, just before Butch's death, "the central point of information exchange was Commander Phillips in his TBF. As the delayed rendezvous of Butch and Skon with Phil's TBF played out, Phil was busy talking to his CIC Controller [George Givens] on *Enterprise,* exchanging air-to-air radio information with Butch, talking on his TBF intercom with his radar operator [Hazen Rand], and trying to keep his turret gunner [Al Kernan] also apprised. This was a daunting combination, with aircraft communication equipment of that day." The TBF crew heard Phillips's radio transmissions, but not what Phillips himself received in return (Dr. Alvin Kernan, telephone interview with JBL, 4 Oct. 1995). It seems that Rand's "I'm hit" message

mistakenly went out on the radio transmitter as well as the intercom. To a certain extent this validates Captain Skon's contention that "it is not certain who was hearing what information amongst Phillips, his two aircrewmen, Butch and Skon, and the ship's CIC controller."

30. Skon to JBL, 15 Apr. 1994; Arnot, "Famed Flier Down"; Burns, "Last Flight," 71. VT-6 ACA-1 report no. 7 mentions the "recognition light."

31. Kernan, *Crossing the Line,* 113–14; Rear Adm. Thomas J. Hamilton, USN (Ret.), Oral History, U.S. Naval Institute, 78.

32. Skon to JBL, 15 Apr. 1994, 17 May 1994, 23 June 1994, 6 Jan. 1995.

33. VT-6 ACA-1 report no. 7; Skon to JBL, 6 Jan. 1995. Captain Skon added: "Neither the ship's radar nor the planes' altimeters could assure at that point whether Butch and [I] were on the TBF level, or a little below or above. Pressure altitude was set into the altimeter manually by each pilot, just before takeoff from the carrier's deck, itself some 60 feet or so above the water. At best, with in-flight pressure altitude changes, the altimeter could be relied upon during a long flight to some plus or minus 50 feet, and varying per aircraft."

34. Burns, "Last Flight," 71.

35. Kernan, *Crossing the Line,* 115.

36. Ibid.; Burns, "Last Flight," 71; George Givens diary, in Givens Papers, courtesy of Mrs. Mary Givens.

37. Hazen Rand to JBL, 18 May 1994. Eugene Burns's Associated Press dispatch dated 27 Nov. 1943 (published 11 Dec. 1943) quoted Rand thus: "I saw a fourth plane's guns blinking red and he was shooting at Butch while our gunner, Kernan, was shooting at the Jap."

38. Kernan, *Crossing the Line,* 115–16.

39. Skon to JBL, 15 Apr. 1994, 17 May 1994, 23 June 1994, 6 Jan. 1995; Skon statement in VF-2 ACA-1 report no. 11.

40. Skon to JBL, 17 May 1994; VT-6 ACA-1 report no. 7; Voris telephone interview with JBL, 22 Mar. 1994, and letter dated 17 July 1994; Alvin Kernan, personal communication with JBL.

41. Skon to JBL, 15 Apr. 1994, 6 Jan. 1995; Skon statement in VF-2 ACA-1 report no. 11.

42. USS *Enterprise* deck log, 26 Nov. 1943, RG-24, NA; Morrissey, *Odyssey of Fighting Two,* 52; Burns, "Last Flight," 71.

43. Skon statement in VF-2 ACA-1 report no. 1; Skon to JBL, 15 Apr. 1994; Givens 1987 narrative.

44. Altemus diary, 26 Nov. 1943; Rear Adm. A. M. Pride, USN, OpNav interview, OPNAV-16-V-#50 (20 June 1944), 3; Commanding Officer, USS *Belleau Wood,* to Commander in Chief, Pacific Fleet, ser. 0015 (3 Dec. 1943), "Action against Makin Island November 19 through 26, 1943, Report of."

45. Burd report, SRH-317, 217.

46. Givens 1987 narrative; Morrissey, *Odyssey of Fighting Two,* 52.

47. CO, USS *North Carolina,* ser. 009; CO, USS *Indiana,* ser. 001; Skon to JBL, 15 Apr. 1994.

48. *Radford Memoirs,* 19.
49. Message 271657 of Nov. 1943, CTG-50.2 to CTF-50, in CinCPac Secret & Confidential Message File, RG-38, NA.
50. CO, USS *Enterprise,* ser. 0020, 2.

Chapter 16. What Happened to Butch?
1. Adm. Arthur W. Radford to Capt. Samuel E. Morison, confidential letter dated 23 Feb. 1951, in Radford Papers, NHC, courtesy of Dr. Jeffrey Barlow.
2. Kernan, *Crossing the Line,* 117–18, and personal communication.
3. Skon to JBL, 17 May 1994. The statement is annex A of VF-2 ACA-1 report no. 11.
4. VF-2 ACA-1 report no. 1; VT-6 ACA-1 report no. 7.
5. Hazen Rand to JBL, 18 May 1994; Radford to Morison, 23 Feb. 1951; *Radford Memoirs,* 19.
6. 752 Air Group, *kōdōchōsho* (combat log), 27 Nov. 1943.
7. Skon to JBL, 15 Apr. 1994.
8. U.S. Pacific Fleet, South Pacific Force, "The F6F-3 in the South Pacific," 30 Sept. 1943, 4, in NHC.
9. Hamilton oral history, 78; Vice Adm. William I. Martin, in Wooldridge, ed., *Carrier Warfare in the Pacific,* 152.
10. Comdr. Edward P. Stafford, USN, *The Big E: The Story of the U.S.S.* Enterprise (New York: Random House, 1962), 260–65. Incidentally, no other source has confirmed Stafford's assertion that Butch was suffering from a severe "head cold." A recent article based on Stafford is John G. Leyden, "Butch O'Hare: 'Friendly Fire' Victim?" *Aviation History,* Nov. 1995, 50–56. That Butch was a friendly-fire casualty is assumed in Eleanor D. Gaulker and Christopher G. Blood, "Friendly Fire Incidents during World War II Naval Operations," *Naval War College Review,* winter 1995, 116, but the offender here is Butch's "wingman."
11. Radford to Morison, 23 Feb. 1951.
12. Chief of Naval Operations, Office of Naval Intelligence, Air Branch, "Naval Aviation Combat Statistics World War II," 17 June 1946, 121–22.
13. Altemus diary, 26 Nov. 1943.
14. Eugene Burns, Associated Press dispatch dated 27 Nov. 1943 (published 11 Dec. 1943).
15. CO, USS *Enterprise,* ser. 0177.
16. Message 291902 of Nov. 1943, CTG-50.2 to ComCentPac, CTF-57, CO Tarawa, in CinCPac Secret & Confidential Message File, RG-38, NA.
17. Messages 281757 of Nov. 1943, CTF-57 to all CTF, and 291353 of Nov. 1943, CTF-57 to all CTF, in ibid.
18. Lt. Harry M. Cocowitch, Dumbo mission report, in VP-72 war diary, NHC.
19. Commander, Aircraft, Apamama, war diary, 30 Oct.–31 Dec. 1943, in NHC; message 140227 of Dec. 1943, CinCPac to ComCentPac, in CinCPac Secret & Confidential Message File, RG-38, NA.

20. Citation in U.S. Navy Board of Decorations, Citation Card File, Ships' History, NHC.
21. *Radford Memoirs,* 19.
22. During World War I five Marines serving with the U.S. Army's Second Division received both Army and Navy Medals of Honor for the same acts of gallantry.
23. Individual citations in U.S. Navy Board of Decorations, Citation Card File, Ships' History, NHC.
24. Commander, Task Force Fifty, to Commander, Air Force, Pacific Fleet, ser. 0080 (23 Dec. 1943), "Carrier Night Fighters," first endorsement to ComCarDiv 11, ser. 0134.
25. Lt. Alexander Wilding, Jr., personal diary, 30 Nov. 1943, courtesy of Dr. Clark G. Reynolds.
26. Commander, Carrier Division Three, to Commander in Chief, Pacific Fleet, ser. 0073 (23 Dec. 1943), third endorsement to Ginder to CinCPac, ser. 00132.
27. Message 300026 of Nov. 1943, ComAirPac to CinCPac, in CinCPac Secret & Confidential Message File, RG-38, NA.
28. Commander, Air Force, Pacific Fleet, confidential ser. 02330 (16 Dec. 1943), copy in Flatley Papers, courtesy of the Flatley family; Vraciu telephone interview with JBL, 15 Oct. 1995.
29. Wilding diary, 20 Dec. 1943–7 Jan. 1944; Morrissey, *Odyssey of Fighting Two,* 67.
30. Commander, Air Force, Pacific Fleet, to Distribution List, ser. 0025 (7 Jan. 1944), "Night Interception of Enemy Aircraft," in Flatley Papers, courtesy of the Flatley family.
31. Morison, *Aleutians, Gilberts, and Marshalls,* 221.

Chapter 17. Remembrance

1. All letters quoted herein are from the O'Hare family papers.
2. USS *O'Hare* Ships' Sponsor File, Ships' History, NHC. Rita O'Hare was first approached as sponsor, but she could not be present, so she recommended Selma instead; Rita O'Hare to Secretary of the Navy, 30 Mar. 1945.
3. Alban Weber, interview with SE, 27 Apr. 1993.

Sources

Published

Books

Allen, Frederick Lewis. *Only Yesterday.* New York: Harper and Brothers, 1931.

Aurandt, Paul. *Paul Harvey's "The Rest of the Story."* New York: Doubleday, 1977.

Backlund, Herman. *Setting the Record Straight about O'Hare the Hero.* Key Largo: Sunshine Printing, 1993.

Bauer, Dan. *Great American Fighter Aces.* Osceola, Wisc.: Motorbooks International, 1992.

Bergreen, Laurence. *Capone: The Man and the Era.* New York: Simon and Schuster, 1994.

Blee, Capt. Ben W., USN (Ret.). *Battleship* North Carolina *(BB-55).* Wilmington, N.C.: USS *North Carolina* Battleship Commission, 1982.

Brown, Capt. Eric, RN. *Wings of the Navy.* London: Jane's, 1980.

Cannon, Charles B. *The O'Hare Story.* New York: Vantage Press, 1980.

Chūkōkai (Medium Attack Bomber Association). *Kaigun Chūkō Shidanshu* (Historical Anthology of the Navy Medium Attack Bomber). Tokyo: Chūkōkai, 1980.

Clark, Adm. J. J., with Clark G. Reynolds. *Carrier Admiral.* New York: John Day, 1967.

Cowdery, Ray. *Capone's Chicago.* Lakeville, Minn.: Northstar Commemoratives, 1987.

Cressman, Robert J. *A Magnificent Fight: The Battle for Wake Island.* Annapolis: Naval Institute Press, 1995.

Crowl, Philip A., and Edmund G. Love. *Seizure of the Gilberts and Marshalls.* In the series *U.S. Army in World War II: The War in the Pacific.* Washington, D.C.: GPO, 1955.

Delve, Ken. *Nightfighter: The Battle for the Night Skies.* London: Arms and Armour Press, 1995.

Ewing, Steve. *USS* Enterprise *(CV-6): The Most Decorated Ship of World War II.* Missoula, Mont.: Pictorial Histories Publishing, 1989.

Fraley, Oscar, and Paul Robsky. *The Last of the Untouchables*. New York: Pocket Books, 1988.

Francillon, R. J. *Japanese Aircraft of the Pacific War*. London: Putnam, 1970.

Frank, Richard B. *Guadalcanal*. New York: Random House, 1990.

Friedman, Norman. *U.S. Aircraft Carriers: An Illustrated Design History*. Annapolis: Naval Institute Press, 1983.

———. *U.S. Battleships: An Illustrated Design History*. Annapolis: Naval Institute Press, 1985.

Gerler, Lt. William R., USNR, ed. *World War II History of Carrier Air Group Six Prepared by the Officers and Men of the Last Cruise*. N.p., ca. 1945.

Godwin, John. *Alcatraz, 1868–1963*. Garden City, N.Y.: Doubleday, 1963.

Gunston, Bill. *Grumman: Sixty Years of Excellence*. New York: Orion, 1988.

Halper, Albert, ed. *The Chicago Crime Book*. Cleveland: World Publishing, 1967.

Hata, Ikuhiko, and Yasuho Izawa. *Japanese Naval Aces and Fighter Units in World War II*. Annapolis: Naval Institute Press, 1989.

Hollatz, Tom. *Gangster Holidays: The Lore and Legends of the Bad Guys*. St. Cloud, Minn.: North Star Press, 1989.

Irey, Elmer L., and William Slocum. *The Tax Dodgers: The Inside Story of the T-Men's War with America's Political and Underworld Hoodlums*. New York: Greenberg, 1948.

Iwaya, Fumio. *Chūkō* (Medium Attack Plane). Tokyo: Genshobō, 1976.

Izawa, Yasuho. *Rikkō to Ginga* (*Rikkō* and *Ginga*). Tokyo: Shinsenshi Shirizu, 1995.

Japan, Self Defense Force, War History Office. *Senshi Sōsho* (War History Series). Vol. 49, *Nantōhomen Kaigun Sakusen, 1* (Southeast Area Naval Operations, 1: To the Beginning of Operations to Recapture Guadalcanal). Tokyo: Asagumo Shimbunsha, 1971.

———. *Senshi Sōsho* (War History Series). Vol. 62, *Chūbu Taiheiyō Homen Kaigun Sakusen, 2* (Central Pacific Area Naval Operations, 2: From June 1942 On). Tokyo: Asagumo Shimbunsha, 1973.

Jensen, Lt. Oliver, USNR. *Carrier War*. New York: Simon and Schuster, 1945.

Johnston, Stanley. *The Grim Reapers*. New York: Dutton, 1943.

———. *Queen of the Flattops*. New York: Dutton, 1942.

Jurika, Stephen, Jr., ed. *From Pearl Harbor to Vietnam: The Memoirs of Admiral Arthur W. Radford*. Stanford: Hoover Institution Press, 1980.

Kaikōkai (Naval Aviation Association). *Kaigun Kūchū Kimmusha (Shikan) Meibō* (Register of Naval Aviation Duty Officers). Tokyo: Kaikōkai, 1954.

Kenney, George C. *General Kenney Reports*. New York: Duell, Sloan, and Pearce, 1949.

Kernan, Alvin. *Crossing the Line: A Bluejacket's World War II Odyssey*. Annapolis: Naval Institute Press, 1994.

Kobler, John. *Capone: The Life and World of Al Capone*. New York: G. P. Putnam's Sons, 1971.

Lambert, John W. *The Pineapple Air Force: Pearl Harbor to Tokyo*. St. Paul: Phalanx Publishing, 1990.

Larkins, William T. *U.S. Naval Aircraft, 1921–1941. U.S. Marine Corps Aircraft, 1914–1959.* New York: Orion Books, 1988.

Lundstrom, John B. *The First South Pacific Campaign: Pacific Fleet Strategy, December 1941–June 1942.* Annapolis: Naval Institute Press, 1976.

———. *The First Team and the Guadalcanal Campaign: Naval Fighter Combat from August to November 1942.* Annapolis: Naval Institute Press, 1994.

———. *The First Team: Pacific Naval Air Combat from Pearl Harbor to Midway.* Annapolis: Naval Institute Press, 1990.

McClendon, Dennis E., and Wallace F. Richards. *The Legend of Colin Kelly, America's First Hero of WWII.* Missoula, Mont.: Pictorial Histories Publishing, 1994.

McPhaul, John J. *Deadlines and Monkeyshines: The Fabled World of Chicago Journalism.* Englewood Cliffs, N.J.: Prentice-Hall, 1962.

———. *Johnny Torrio: First of the Gang Lords.* New Rochelle, N.Y.: Arlington House, 1970.

Mears, Lt. Frederick. *Carrier Combat.* New York: Doubleday, Doran, 1944.

Mikesh, Robert C. *Japanese Aircraft Code Names and Designations.* Atglen, Pa.: Schiffer Publishing, 1993.

Mingos, Howard. *American Heroes of the War in the Air.* New York: Lanciar, 1943.

Morison, Rear Adm. Samuel E. *History of United States Naval Operations of World War II.* Vol. 3, *The Rising Sun in the Pacific, 1931–April 1942.* Boston: Little, Brown, 1948.

———. *History of United States Naval Operations of World War II.* Vol. 7, *Aleutians, Gilberts, and Marshalls, June 1942–April 1944.* Boston: Little, Brown, 1951.

Morrissey, Lt. Thomas L., USNR. *Odyssey of Fighting Two.* Privately printed, 1945.

Murray, George. *The Legacy of Al Capone: Portraits and Annals of Chicago's Public Enemies.* New York: G. P. Putnam's Sons, 1975.

Naito, Hatsuho. *Thunder Gods: The Kamikaze Pilots Tell Their Story.* Tokyo: Kodansha International, 1989.

Ness, Eliot, and Oscar Fraley. *The Untouchables.* New York: Popular Library, 1960.

Olds, Robert. *Helldiver Squadron.* New York: Dodd, Mead, 1945.

Olynyk, Frank J. *USN Credits for the Destruction of Enemy Aircraft in Air-to-Air Combat, World War 2.* Aurora, Ohio: Privately printed, 1982.

Orriss, Bruce W. *When Hollywood Ruled the Skies: The Aviation Film Classics of World War II.* Hawthorne, Calif.: Aero Associates, 1984.

Pahl, Capt. Herschel A., USN (Ret.). *Point Option: Carrier Warfare in the Pacific through the Eyes of a Junior Fighter Pilot.* Privately printed, 1988.

Pasley, Fred D. *Al Capone: The Biography of a Self-Made Man.* Garden City, N.Y.: Garden City Publishing, 1930.

Reynolds, Clark G. *Admiral John H. Towers: The Struggle for Naval Air Supremacy.* Annapolis: Naval Institute Press, 1991.

———. *Famous American Admirals.* New York: Van Nostrand Reinhold, 1978.

———. *The Fast Carriers: The Forging of an Air Navy.* New York: McGraw-Hill, 1968.

———. *The Fighting Lady: The New* Yorktown *in the Pacific War.* Missoula, Mont.: Pictorial Histories Publishing, 1986.

Schoenburg, Robert J. *Mr. Capone.* New York: Morrow, 1992.

Sherman, Frederick C. *Combat Command.* New York: Dutton, 1950.

Spector, Ronald H. *Listening to the Enemy: Key Documents on the Role of Communications Intelligence in the War with Japan.* Wilmington, Del.: Scholarly Resources, 1988.

Spiering, Frank. *The Man Who Got Capone.* Indianapolis: Bobbs- Merrill, 1976.

Stafford, Comdr. Edward P., USN. *The Big E: The Story of the U.S.S.* Enterprise. New York: Random House, 1962.

Stern, Robert C. *The* Lexington *Class Carriers.* Annapolis: Naval Institute Press, 1993.

Swanborough, Gordon, and Peter M. Bowers. *United States Navy Aircraft since 1911.* New York: Funk and Wagnalls, 1968.

Tibbets, Paul W., Jr. *The Tibbets Story.* New York: Stein and Day, 1978.

Tillman, Barrett. *Avenger at War.* New York: Scribner's, 1980.

———. *Corsair: The F4U in World War II and Korea.* Annapolis: Naval Institute Press, 1979.

———. *Hellcat: The F6F in World War II.* Annapolis: Naval Institute Press, 1979.

———. *The Wildcat in World War II.* Annapolis: Nautical and Aviation Publishing, 1983.

Ugaki, Matome. *Fading Victory: The Diary of Admiral Matome Ugaki, 1941–1945.* Pittsburgh: University of Pittsburgh Press, 1991.

U.S. Naval Academy. *The Lucky Bag.* Annual of the Regiment of Midshipmen. Annapolis: U.S. Naval Academy, 1934–37.

U.S. Navy, Bureau of Navigation. *Navy Directory of the U.S. Navy and U.S. Marine Corps Officers.* Washington, D.C.: GPO, 1937–42.

———. *Register of Commissioned and Warrant Officers of the U.S. Navy.* Washington, D.C.: GPO, 1937–43.

U.S. Navy, Naval Historical Center. *Dictionary of American Naval Fighting Ships.* 2d ed. Washington, D.C.: GPO, 1991–.

U.S. Navy, Naval History Division. *Dictionary of American Naval Fighting Ships.* 8 vols. Washington, D.C.: GPO, 1959–81.

U.S. Navy Department. *Medal of Honor, 1861–1949: The Navy.* Washington, D.C.: GPO, 1949.

U.S. War Department, Historical Division. *The Capture of Makin (20 November–24 November 1943).* Washington, D.C.: War Department, 1946.

Waldrop, Frank C. *McCormick of Chicago.* Englewood Cliffs, N.J.: Prentice-Hall, 1966.

Wilson, Frank J., and Beth Day. *Special Agent: A Quarter Century with the Treasury Department and the Secret Service.* New York: Holt, Rinehart, and Winston, 1965.

Wooldridge, E. T., ed. *Carrier Warfare in the Pacific: An Oral History Collection.* Washington, D.C.: Smithsonian Institution Press, 1993.

Y'Blood, William T. *The Little Giants: U.S. Escort Carriers against Japan.* Annapolis: Naval Institute Press, 1987.

Articles

"Air Group Six." *Naval Aviation News,* Oct. 1949, 20–21.

Alexander, Jack. "They Sparked the Carrier Revolution." *Saturday Evening Post,* 16 Sept. 1944, 9ff.

Arnot, Charles P. "Famed Flier Down." *Honolulu Advertiser,* 11 Dec. 1943.

Bauer, Daniel. "The Forgotten Hero." *Air Classics,* Dec. 1988, 35ff.

Burns, Eugene. Associated Press dispatch, 27 Nov. 1943, released 11 Dec. 1943.

———. "Butch O'Hare's Last Flight." *Saturday Evening Post,* 11 Mar. 1944, 19ff.

Field, John. "How O'Hare Downed Five Jap Planes in One Day." *Life,* 13 Apr. 1942, 12–18.

Gates, Thomas F. "Track of the Tomcatters: A History of VF-31." 4 pts. *The Hook,* fall 1984, winter 1984, spring 1985, summer 1985.

Gaulker, Eleanor, and Christopher G. Blood. "Friendly Fire Incidents during World War II Naval Operations." *Naval War College Review,* winter 1995, 115–22.

Gray, Comdr. James Seton, Jr., USN. "Development of Naval Night Fighters in World War II." *U.S. Naval Institute Proceedings,* July 1948, 847–51.

Halsey, Lt. Comdr. Ashley, Jr., USNR. "The CVL's Success Story." *U.S. Naval Institute Proceedings,* Apr. 1946, 522–31.

"Hero in a Hustle." *New Horizons,* Apr. 1942, 27.

"Hero's Week." *Time,* 4 May 1942.

Lacouture, Capt. John E., USN (Ret.). "Maui Aviation." *Wings of Gold,* spring 1989, 45–47.

Leyden, John G. "Butch O'Hare: 'Friendly Fire' Victim?" *Aviation History,* Nov. 1995, 50–56.

Martin, Vice Adm. William I., USN (Ret.); Vice Adm. Turner F. Caldwell, USN (Ret.); and Comdr. Edwin R. Jenks, USN (Ret.). "Black Chickens and Bat Teams." *Naval Aviation News,* Mar. 1972, 37–41.

Rodgers, Capt. George F., USN. "O'Hare: A Name with a Proud Past." *Chicago Sunday Tribune,* 24 Mar. 1963, 6.

Stillwell, Paul. "John Smith Thach, Adm., USN, 1906–1981." *Navy Times,* 25 May 1981, 21.

Thach, Lt. Comdr. John S. "The Red Rain of Battle: The Story of Fighter Squadron Three." *Collier's,* 5 Dec. 1942, 14ff., and 12 Dec. 1942, 16ff.

Tillman, Barrett. "Night Hookers, Part 1, 1942–1945: A History of Carrier Night Operations." *The Hook,* spring 1988, 41–52.

Trousdale, Lt. Comdr. James H., Jr., USNR. "The Birth of the Navy's Night Fighters." *U.S. Naval Institute Proceedings,* June 1952, 621–23.

Wead, Comdr. Frank W., USNR. "Missing in Action." *Skyways,* Oct. 1944, 59–61.

Wendt, Lloyd. "The Background of Butch O'Hare." *Chicago Sunday Tribune Graphic Magazine,* 2 Oct. 1949, 6ff.

———. "Five Jap Planes Measure the Heroism of Butch O'Hare." *Chicago Sunday Tribune Graphic Magazine,* 25 Sept. 1949, 10ff.

———. "The Heroism of Butch O'Hare." *Chicago Sunday Tribune Graphic Magazine,* 18 Sept. 1949, 4ff.

————. "The Last Flight of Heroic Butch O'Hare." *Chicago Sunday Tribune Graphic Magazine,* 9 Oct. 1949, 16ff.

Wilson, Frank J. (as told to Howard Whitman). "How We Trapped Capone." *Collier's,* 26 Apr. 1947, 14ff.

Newspapers

In addition to the specific articles listed above, the following newspapers were also consulted:

Boston Daily Globe
Chicago Daily Tribune
Chicago Herald American
Chicago Sun
Chicago Sunday Tribune Graphic Magazine
Christian Science Monitor
Cleveland Press
Edwardsville (Illinois) Intelligencer
Honolulu Advertiser
Japan Times and Advertiser
Los Angeles Times
New York Sun
New York Times
Pensacola News Journal
Philadelphia Evening Bulletin
Rochester Times-Union
St. Louis Globe Democrat
St. Louis Post-Dispatch
St. Louis Register
St. Louis South Side Journal
St. Louis Star-Times
San Diego Tribune-Sun
Seattle Post Intelligencer
Washington Evening Star
Washington Sunday Star
Washington Times-Herald
Western Military Academy Shrapnel

Unpublished

Official Records

The authors consulted records in the following official repositories:

National Archives, Washington, D.C.
National Museum of Naval Aviation, Pensacola

National Personnel Records Center, St. Louis, Mo.

Naval Historical Center, Washington, D.C.

Nimitz Library, U.S. Naval Academy, Annapolis

U.S. Naval Institute Oral Histories

Gayler, Adm. Noel A. M., USN (Ret.)

Hamilton, Rear Adm. Thomas J., USN (Ret.)

Martin, Vice Adm. William I., USN (Ret.)

Smith, Adm. Willard J., USCG (Ret.)

Thach, Adm. John S., USN (Ret.)

Diaries and Personal Narratives

Altemus, Lt. Comdr. John P., USNR (Ret.). Diary, 1942–43. Courtesy of Randy Altemus.

Brown, Vice Adm. Wilson. Unpublished memoir, "From Sail to Carrier Task Force." Wilson Brown Papers. Nimitz Library, U.S. Naval Academy.

Crews, Capt. Howard W., USN. Personal diary, 1942–43. Courtesy of Carolyn Crews-Whitby.

Donelon, John O., midshipman first class. "Edward Henry O'Hare: A Research Paper Submitted to the Head of the Department of English, History, and Government," 4 Mar. 1963. Copy in O'Hare family papers.

Flatley, Vice Adm. J. H. Papers. Courtesy of the Flatley family.

Givens, Lt. Comdr. George P., USNR (Ret.). Personal papers. Courtesy of Mrs. Mary Givens.

Lovelace, Lt. Comdr. Donald A. Personal diary, 7 Dec. 1941–2 Apr. 1942. Courtesy of Comdr. Donald Lovelace, Jr., USN (Ret.).

Radford, Adm. Arthur W. Papers. Naval Historical Center. Courtesy of Dr. Jeffrey Barlow.

Rand, Christopher. Unpublished article, "Who Killed Butch O'Hare?" Courtesy of Hazen B. Rand.

Stanley, Capt. O. B., Jr. 1941–42 personal narrative. Copy courtesy of Captain Stanley.

Thach, Lt. Comdr. John S. 1941–42 notebook. J. S. Thach Papers. National Museum of Naval Aviation, Pensacola.

Wilding, Lt. Alexander, Jr. Personal diary, 1943–44. Courtesy of Dr. Clark G. Reynolds.

Interviews and Correspondence

Backlund, Herman, USS *Independence*

Baur, ACMM Clyde E., USN (Ret.), VF-3/6

Bottari, Victor, Jr., USS *Enterprise*

Callan, Capt. Allie W., USN (Ret.), VF-3/6

Condit, Rear Adm. James W., USN (Ret.), VT-5

Decker, ACRM Wilton, USN (Ret.), VF-3/6

Dickerson, Claude L., USS *Enterprise*

Duckworth, Vice Adm. Herbert S., USN (Ret.), USS *Lexington*
Feightner, Rear Adm. Edward L., USN (Ret.), VF-3
Gayler, Adm. Noel A. M., USN (Ret.), VF-3
Givens, Mrs. Mary
Gregory, R. W., Jr., USS *Enterprise*
Jackson, Mrs. Catherine
Kernan, Dr. Alvin B., VT-6
Lacouture, Capt. John E., USN (Ret.)
Landry, Henry T., VF-3/6
Leonard, Rear Adm. William N., USN (Ret.), VF-11
Lovelace, Donald A., Jr.
Mendenhall, Comdr. Sy E., USN (Ret.), VF-3/6
Morrissey, Thomas L., VF-2
Nicholson, Capt. Richard, USN (Ret.)
Odenbrett, Capt. Harvey G., USN (Ret.), VF-3/6
Pahl, Capt. Herschel A., USN (Ret.), VF-3/6
Putman, Capt. Charles F., USN (Ret.)
Rand, Lt. Comdr. Hazen B., USNR (Ret.), VT-6
Robbins, Joe D., VF-3/6
St. Peters, Robert E.
Skon, Capt. Warren A., USN (Ret.), VF-2
Stanley, Capt. O. B., Jr., USN (Ret.), VF-3
Strean, Vice Adm. Bernard M., USN (Ret.), VF-1
Sutherland, James, USS *Lexington*
Thach, Adm. John S., USN (Ret.), VF-3
Varner, Marcell F., VT-6
Voris, Capt. Roy M., USN (Ret.), VF-2
Vraciu, Comdr. Alexander, USN (Ret.), VF-3/6

Index

About the Authors

Steve Ewing is senior curator at Patriots Point Naval and Maritime Museum in Charleston, South Carolina, and the author of six naval titles.

John B. Lundstrom is curator of American and military history at the Milwaukee Public Museum and author of *The First Team: Pacific Naval Air Combat from Pearl Harbor to Midway* and *The First Team and the Guadalcanal Campaign: Naval Fighter Combat from August to November 1942.*

The **Naval Institute Press** is the book-publishing arm of the U.S. Naval Institute, a private, nonprofit, membership society for sea service professionals and others who share an interest in naval and maritime affairs. Established in 1873 at the U.S. Naval Academy in Annapolis, Maryland, where its offices remain today, the Naval Institute has members worldwide.

Members of the Naval Institute support the education programs of the society and receive the influential monthly magazine *Proceedings* and discounts on fine nautical prints and on ship and aircraft photos. They also have access to the transcripts of the Institute's Oral History Program and get discounted admission to any of the Institute-sponsored seminars offered around the country.

The Naval Institute also publishes *Naval History* magazine. This colorful bimonthly is filled with entertaining and thought-provoking articles, first-person reminiscences, and dramatic art and photography. Members receive a discount on *Naval History* subscriptions.

The Naval Institute's book-publishing program, begun in 1898 with basic guides to naval practices, has broadened its scope in recent years to include books of more general interest. Now the Naval Institute Press publishes about 100 titles each year, ranging from how-to books on boating and navigation to battle histories, biographies, ship and aircraft guides, and novels. Institute members receive discounts of 20 to 50 percent on the Press's nearly 600 books in print.

Full-time students are eligible for special half-price membership rates. Life memberships are also available.

For a free catalog describing Naval Institute Press books currently available, and for further information about subscribing to *Naval History* magazine or about joining the U.S. Naval Institute, please write to:

Membership Department
U.S. Naval Institute
118 Maryland Avenue
Annapolis, MD 21402-5035
Telephone: (800) 233-8764
Fax: (410) 269-7940
Web address: www.usni.org